EXAMKRACKERS MCAT®

101 PASSAGES:
PSYCHOLOGY & SOCIOLOGY

OSOTE
PUBLISHING

Major Contributors:

Kaitlyn Barkley, M.D.
Andrew Elson
Austin Mattox
Jennifer Birk Goldschmidt, M.S.

Contributors:

Kristin Bater
Laura Burkbauer
Daniel Campbell
Erin Glennon
Jessica Grenvik
Jemma Howlett
Sunmee Huh
Michael Klug
Bryan Luu
David Rhode
Cindy Zhang

Art Director:

Erin Daniel

Designer:

Dana Kelley

ISBN 13: 978-1-893858-95-4

To purchase additional copies of this book or other books of the 101 Passage series, call 1-888-572-2536.

Examkrackers.com
Osote.com

PHOTOCOPYING & DISTRIBUTION POLICY

Read this First

Practice is essential to success on the MCAT®. MCAT® practice is the best way to develop the key skills you will need to get a high score.

The 101 passages and associated questions in this book were carefully designed to simulate exactly the content, length, style, tone, difficulty and format of real AAMC MCAT® passages, questions, and answer choices. Each chapter in this book has two tests of exact MCAT® section length. Both passage-based questions and stand-alone questions are just like the questions you will see on MCAT® day and are included in a 3:1 ratio, just like the real MCAT®.

The Examkrackers 101 Passages series covers every single topic and subtopic tested by the MCAT®. Topics that require more drilling and topics that are especially difficult are covered by multiple questions. Each chapter in *101 Passages: Psychology & Sociology* tests the content covered by the corresponding chapter in Examkrackers *Psychology & Sociology* manual. To maximize your MCAT® preparation, take the tests in each chapter following your review of that chapter in the manual. To stay in touch with how the science you review is tested on the MCAT®, coordinate your content review with simulated MCAT® practice, chapter by chapter.

The MCAT® is all about how flexible and adaptable you are with the basics. Real MCAT® passages and questions will often present you with new and unfamiliar situations. It is only through simulated MCAT® practice that you will learn to see what simple science is relevant and then recall and apply the basics with confidence. Through practice and focus on the questions you get wrong, you will develop essential skills that bring a high score on MCAT® day.

In this section you will find information on:

- Using the warm-up passage to assess your skills
- MCAT® Timing
- MCAT® Simulation
- How to use this book to increase your MCAT® score
- Scoring your practice tests
- Complete MCAT® preparation with Examkrackers

How to Begin: Assessing Your Skills

This book begins with one "warm-up" passage. Use it to familiarize yourself with the look, feel, and format of MCAT® social science passages and questions. Give yourself about eight minutes to take the warm-up test. While working through the passage and the associated questions, observe yourself and notice your own approach. Immediately after taking the warm-up test, look at the following checklist of strategies and skills. Based on the passage and questions in the warm-up, evaluate which skills come naturally to you and which skills you will work to build as you continue through this book.

- Energy
- Focus
- Confidence
- Timing
- Narrating the passage
- Identifying and answering research questions
- Applying simple science in new situations
- Clear, simple, and connected organization of the content in your mind
- Simplifying the questions and answers
- Eliminating weak answer choices

Choose two or three skills to focus on throughout Test 1 and continue to build new skills as you proceed through the book. Return to this page and check off strategies and skills as you master them.

MCAT® Timing

Examkrackers 101 books are great tools with which to master MCAT® timing before MCAT® day. The tests can be taken untimed or timed. As you initially practice brand-new skills, go slowly in order to master them. Take timed tests to prepare for timing on MCAT® day. The practice tests in this book are exactly like the real MCAT®: 10 passages and 59 questions in 95 minutes. Timing on MCAT® day is a skill that you will build through timed practice.

Take a 5 second break before reading each passage. Look at the clock only once, at the halfway point (the 29th question). If you are before the 47-minute mark, slow down. If you are after the 47-minute mark, speed up. Developing an intuitive sense for good MCAT® timing and pace is an essential skill. Eventually, you will come to know whether you are on pace as you go without looking at a clock. You will know when you are getting sandbagged in order to speed up and when you are rushing so that you can slow down.

After you take a test, assess your timing skills. If you did not finish the test before the allotted time, determine where you are spending time that you could save. If you finished with time to spare, determine how you could spend more time toward a higher score on your next practice test.

Plan a schedule in advance. Choose a distribution for these tests throughout your study period. For example, if you are studying over a ten-week period, take one test from this book every week on the same day. Do not save all the tests for the weeks immediately prior to the MCAT®, as MCAT® skills require time and practice to develop. It is important to stay in touch with the MCAT® and MCAT® practice throughout your study period. Between tests, give yourself adequate time to review the test you take each week. Consciously plan what you will do differently on the next test in order to increase your MCAT® score.

MCAT® SIMULATION

When you are ready to take your first simulated, full-length test, choose an environment that is not familiar or comfortable, e.g. a public library, not your couch at home. Ensure that you will maximize focus and minimize distraction for one sitting of at least 95 minutes. If needed, you may use disposable earplugs, just as on MCAT® day. During the test, do not look at or answer the telephone, do not sit and stare out the window, and do not get up for any reason, such as to get a drink or to go to the bathroom. Treat each practice test like the real thing.

It is always a good idea to mark up the multiple choice questions *on the test itself* as you go through them. If 'A' can't be correct, then mark it off and go to 'B'. If 'B' is *possible*, circle it, and go to 'C', and so on. That way you are eliminating and narrowing choices that are *not possible* or are *less likely*. Using the process of elimination is a very helpful technique on the MCAT®. The computer-based test allows the use of strikethrough and highlight functions right on the screen to help with narrowing down choices. It is not very practical or helpful to write your answers or considerations on a piece of notebook paper as this does not simulate MCAT® day.

How to Use This Book to Increase Your MCAT® Score:

REVIEW

Test and question review is the single most important thing you will do to change your MCAT® score.

Always leave time for review of each test. Your score will change through careful review of each practice test you take, not through repetitive practice. You will need ninety-five minutes to take the test and at least ninety minutes to review it.

Every question you get wrong is a gift, an opportunity to increase your score. Always think about how questions you get wrong are valuable – they are the pearls that will lead you directly to a high MCAT® score.

Immediately after completing each test, take notes on what happened during the test. Then, take a short break for an hour or less. Next sit down and check your answers. At the end of each test, you will be directed to the page in the back of the book where you can find the answers, and answer explanations, for that test. Every page of the tests has a tab and footer telling you what test you're working on. Every page of the answers and explanations has a tab and footer telling you which test is being covered. Always be sure these match when checking your answers. No need to flip through pages and pages of explanations looking for the right test.

Make a list of question numbers you marked and/or got wrong. Do not yet read the answer explanations.

Compare your score to the last practice test you took. Your raw score is the number you answered correctly out of 59. Did your raw score increase since the last test? If yes, what did you do differently? Make a note to keep doing what worked. If no, what was different today? Make a commitment to change strategies that did not work.

Make time to retake the questions you answered incorrectly before looking at the answer explanations. This allows you to build the most important MCAT® muscles of all: problem solving and independent thinking. Once you see the answer explanation, you lose the opportunity to learn how to solve the MCAT® question yourself. This may sometimes require multiple attempts or reinforcement of science, but the purpose of practice is for you to learn how to *solve* the questions. Reading the explanation of how to get to the right answer should come only after you have tried your hardest to find your own way there.

Once you have made a second attempt, read the answer explanation for each question you got wrong in order to learn to think in ways that will get you a high score. Examkrackers answer explanations are uniquely process-oriented, meaning that they reveal the way to think like the MCAT®. The answer explanations show you the reasoning process that leads to the elimination of each weak answer and the selection of the best answer. Our answer explanations will help you identify new strategies that work and will help you learn to think in ways that bring a high score.

It can also help to review those questions you got right in order to reinforce the skills, confidence and concepts that allowed you to solve those problems.

SMART PRACTICE

There are two kinds of practice: practice that is repetitive and practice that is smart. Practice that is repetitive, in which you do the same thing over and over again, will reinforce skills that you already have and will also reinforce any habits you may have that are not working.

1. Before each test, plan on what skills you want to add, build, reinforce or replace with this practice test. Use the list provided above as well as any skills you have added. Make specific "When... Then..." commitments (see below).

2. Be conscious or self-aware during each test, in order to evaluate what you are doing while you are doing it. Take notes during the test on what you are thinking or feeling, what skills you are struggling with, what is happening that you notice, etc.

3. Smart practice finally means evaluating immediately *after* each test how the commitments helped. If your score increased, what did you do differently that accounts for the increase—commit to continuing with this new skill. If your score decreased, what in your approach or environment was different— commit to replacing what is not working.

4. Repeat this process throughout the study period.

MAKING COMMITMENTS

Immediately after each test, make specific commitments for what you plan next – what will you keep doing more of and what still needs to change?

Commitments work best if new, good habits are linked to old, bad habits. I can make a commitment not to speed on the highway tomorrow, but inevitably I will find myself speeding yet again. Change comes when I decide that

When I speed, **then** I will immediately slow down to 54 mph.
Similarly:
When I fall into negative thinking while taking the test,
Then I will take a five-second break and refocus on the question in front of me.
Or
When I have trouble understanding what I am reading,
Then I will take a five-second break and resume reading, narrating with the basics that I know

When you commit to avoiding the mistakes that led you to incorrect answers in one test, you will see improvement in your raw score on the next test.

Look toward the next date you will take a practice test. Document your commitments and keep them ready at hand to review before you begin your next practice test.

Scoring Your Practice Tests

The goal is to see your scores on Examkrackers practice materials improve over time.

The best way to utilize your raw score is to be sure it increases with each practice test you take, whether as skill-building or simulation. The best way to do this is to make specific commitments to replace what isn't working with effective MCAT® skills.

Note: Even if Examkrackers derived a scaled score from thousands of our students, it would not accurately predict your AAMC MCAT® score. Unlike the AAMC MCAT® which includes easy questions, Examkrackers practice questions simulating the MCAT® are largely of the medium and difficult level, in order to improve your MCAT® skills and to help you learn how to think like the MCAT®. Our students are at different stages of preparation for the MCAT® and do not represent the MCAT® day student population. Any scaled score other than that directly from the AAMC does not correlate to AAMC MCAT® scores. Only a scaled score from the AAMC can accurately predict your AAMC MCAT® score.

Your goal should be to get more items right and fewer wrong with each Examkrackers practice test you take. A higher score with each practice test reflects that you are using the questions you get wrong and those you get right to learn and practice new skills that will increase your score.

Complete Your MCAT® Preparation

Note: *101 Passages: Psychology & Sociology* contains only psychology and sociology passages and questions to maximize your social sciences practice. The AAMC MCAT® integrates psychology, sociology and biology. For integrated MCAT® simulation, use our full-length, online *EK-Tests®*. Visit www.examkrackers.com for details.

To complete your preparation for the Psychological, Social, and Biological Foundations of Behavior MCAT® section, use this book along with the Examkrackers *Biology 2: Systems*, and *Reasoning Skills* manuals, and *MCAT® 101 Passages Biology 2: Systems*. Together these tools provide in-depth instruction in the skills needed to get a high score on the Psychological, Social, and Biological Foundations of Behavior MCAT® section.

To prepare fully for the four sections of the MCAT®, Examkrackers *Complete Study Package* includes six manuals packed with content review, MCAT® strategy, and guided practice. The corresponding *MCAT® 101 Passages* series allows you to practice the methods and build the skills taught in Examkrackers study manuals. Take an online or in person Examkrackers Comprehensive MCAT® Course (information available at our website, below).

Examkrackers Live MCAT® Hotline is a service available ten hours per week so your questions can be addressed directly and interactively by expert, high scoring MCAT® instructors.

EK-Tests® are the best full length simulated MCAT® product available on the market. Each electronic test matches the MCAT® in sources, style, format, question types, length, skills and content tested. Tools to maximize review and score improvement are built-in.

Regularly visit the Examkrackers Forums where students' questions are answered and any errata are posted.

Go to www.examkrackers.com or call 1.888.KRACKEM to learn more about Examkrackers materials, support and live MCAT® preparation, both online and in-person.

Toward your success!

TABLE OF CONTENTS

WARM-UP

0

Passage: 1
Time: 8 minutes

DIRECTIONS: Use this warm-up passage and questions to become familiar with MCAT® questions and to assess your skills before beginning Practice Test 1A.

Read the passage, then select the best answer to each associated question. If you are unsure of an answer, rule out incorrect choices and select from the remaining options. Indicate your selection beside the option you choose.

Passage 1 (Questions 1-5)

Social networking sites (SNS) are used for social and professional interaction with others. SNS often have groups for people who are united by sharing the same medical diagnosis. For example, groups for patients with irritable bowel disease (IBD) allow patients to share advice on medications, foods to avoid, and homeopathic remedies for symptoms. A newly diagnosed patient can be immediately surrounded by a support group of other patients that have been managing the illness. This support is clearly beneficial both psychologically and physically.

Previous studies have focused on the motivational factors of people to use SNS. The identified factors include social consciousness, acquiring social presence, avoiding loneliness, leisure and entertainment, acquiring the feeling of connectedness, extending one's social circle, and voicing one's opinion. Studies on SNS and user behavior have been conducted in the context of intensity of use, privacy concerns, disclosure rates, personality traits, cultural norms, self-presentation, gender differences, age differences, and self-esteem.

The term "user behavior" is used ambiguously with different interpretations, which makes it difficult to identify studies on user behavior in relation to SNS. A mapping study, which is a type of systematic literature review, was employed to identify potential studies from digital databases through a developed protocol. Thematic analysis was carried out for the classification of user behavior. Researchers found seven characteristics associated with behavior that have direct influence on SNS use. They include social investigation, social affiliation, frequency of use, information control, self orientation, reciprocity, and social boldness. There were also nine factors that have an indirect effect including ease of use, gratification, personality traits, self esteem, social influence, regret, emotion, boredom, and self-control.

This passage was adapted from "Investigation of user behavior on social networking sites." Waheed H, Anjum M, Rehman M, Khawaja A. *PLoS ONE*. 2017. 12(2) doi:10.1371/journal.pone.0169693 for use under the terms of the Creative Commons CC BY 4.0 license (http://creativecommons.org/licenses/by/4.0/legalcode).

Question 1

Ongoing global immigration and emigration have led to an increase in popularity of SNS support groups for individuals experiencing culture shock. Which of the following people would NOT benefit from this type of group?

- O **A.** A college freshman who moved to a big city from a small town.
- O **B.** A war veteran who is struggling with anxiety.
- O **C.** An American citizen returning to the United States after six months spent in China for a business venture.
- O **D.** A man who wakes up from a 10-year coma.

Question 2

When it comes to the mass media portrayal of social media, which of the follow sociological principles is most applicable?

- O **A.** Mass media transmits but does not diffuse ideas.
- O **B.** Mass media diffuses but does not transmit ideas.
- O **C.** Mass media diffuses and transmits ideas.
- O **D.** Mass media neither diffuses nor transmits ideas.

Question 3

SNS are a major force in cultural globalization. Which of the following factors also promotes globalization?

- O **A.** Gentrification
- O **B.** Online videogames
- O **C.** International terrorism
- O **D.** Economic interdependence

Question 4

How could a researcher design a study to assess the interplay between sex and gender in SNS user behavior?

- O **A.** Participants should report their assigned gender and chosen sex before answering a questionnaire on SNS user behavior.
- O **B.** Participants should report their assigned sex and chosen gender before answering a questionnaire on SNS user behavior.
- O **C.** Participants should report their assigned gender and chosen sex before researchers collect real time information on SNS user behavior.
- O **D.** Participants should report their assigned sex and chosen gender before researchers collect real time information on SNS user behavior.

Question 5

In what way might SNS groups contribute to social stratification?

- O **A.** Low-income individuals are unable to participate in SNS groups.
- O **B.** Working-class individuals do not have enough time to participate in SNS groups.
- O **C.** Private groups require an invitation to join.
- O **D.** Groups often allow individuals from different backgrounds to connect.

STOP. If you finish before time is called, check your work. You may go back to any question in this test.

ANSWERS & EXPLANATIONS for the Warm-Up Passages can be found on p. 163.

LECTURE 1

The Biopsychosocial Model, Society and Culture

TEST 1A

Time: 95 minutes
Questions 1–59

DIRECTIONS: Most of the questions in this test section are grouped with a passage. Read the passage, then select the best answer to each question. Some questions are independent of any passage and of one another. Select the best answer to each of these questions. If you are unsure of an answer, rule out incorrect choices and select from the remaining options. Indicate your selection beside the option you choose.

Passage 1 (Questions 1-4)

It is well recognized that educational achievement has consequences for health. It is therefore important that children complete the level of education that matches their potential. Researchers observed that discrepancies exist between children's educational potential predicted by the Cito Test (a cognitive assessment) at age 11 and their attained schooling level by age 14. To study the sources of these discrepancies, researchers collected data from 1510 generalized population participants at age 11 and again at age 14. They measured indicators of physical health, psychosocial health, lifestyle, life events and whether the student attended a higher or lower level of secondary education than predicted by the Cito Test. An assessment by the student's teacher on their abilities and potential was also obtained. At age 14, 14.5% of the children attended a higher level of education than predicted, and 13.6% a lower level. Odds ratios (OR) were used to compare the relative odds of the occurrence of the outcome of interest (attained level) given exposure to the variable of interest (child characteristic). The ORs for some of the characteristics are shown in Table 1.

Table 1 Child Characteristics and Attained School Level

	Characteristics	OR
Lower educational level than indicated by Cito Test	Teacher's assessment	7.6
	Male sex	1.9
	Education of parents – low	1.4
	Diagnosed attention disorder	2.5
	Asthma	0.5
	Drug use	5.0
	Parents divorced	1.6
Higher educational level than indicated by Cito Test	Teacher's assessment	24.5
	Male sex	0.8
	Education of parents – low	1.1
	Diagnosed learning disability	1.7
	Bedtimes on schooldays earlier than 10 PM	1.6

OR=1 Exposure does not affect odds of outcome

OR>1 Exposure associated with higher odds of outcome

OR<1 Exposure associated with lower odds of outcome

This passage was adapted from "Health-Related Factors Associated with Discrepancies between Children's Potential and Attained Secondary School Level: A Longitudinal Study." van der Heide I, Gehring U, Koppelman GH, Wijga AH. *PLoS ONE*. 2016. 11(12). doi:10.1371/journal.pone.0168110 for use under the terms of the Creative Commons CC BY 4.0 license (https://creativecommons.org/licenses/by/4.0/legalcode).

Question 1

The research described is best classified as what type of study design?

- **A.** A longitudinal study that makes comparisons within the demographic category of age.
- **B.** A cross-sectional study that examines aging and the life course.
- **C.** A case report that analyzes differences between age cohorts.
- **D.** A meta-analysis that examines the social significance of aging.

Question 2

What conclusion can be drawn about teacher expectancy based on the study's findings?

- **A.** The expectations set upon the teacher by those perceived to be their superiors in the educational bureaucracy influence students' final academic outcomes.
- **B.** If a child is at a higher or lower educational level at age 14 than indicated by the Cito Test score, their teacher's assessment was a very strong determinant of this discrepancy.
- **C.** Based on the Cito Test score, the children gain differing expectations for the roles and abilities of their teachers, which contributes to the eventual discrepancy between predicted and achieved educational level.
- **D.** Teachers play a crucial role in formalized educational structures, like schools, as they set expectations for social norms and behaviors students will need to operate in society.

Question 3

Interactions between the students and other people in their lives (parents, teachers, peers) affect educational outcome. Which of the theoretical approaches below is best suited to describe this aspect of social structure?

- **A.** Microsociology
- **B.** Conflict theory
- **C.** Social constructionism
- **D.** Rational choice theory

Question 4

Which of these processes do NOT help to explain the study results?

○ **A.** Discrimination by teachers against certain students based on their results on the Cito Test.

○ **B.** Out-group loyalty to certain students skews the teacher's initial assessment to favor students who come from a dissimilar background to the teacher.

○ **C.** In-group loyalty to students that come from a similar background as the teacher contributes to a biased teacher's assessment.

○ **D.** Prejudice by students against students that come from a dissimilar background as the majority contributes to a hostile schooling environment.

Passage 2 (Questions 5-8)

Why are some fields more diverse than others? Although many factors are undoubtedly at play, a recent proposal suggests that the fields in which women and African Americans are underrepresented (e.g., physics, philosophy) are those fields whose members believe that a spark of brilliance is required for success. The belief in the importance of untutored genius may be detrimental to the involvement of women and African Americans because of broad cultural stereotypes that portray the intellectual abilities of these groups in a negative light. Consistent with this Field-specific Ability Beliefs (FAB) hypothesis, a recent survey of academics across 30 disciplines found that fields with a stronger focus on brilliance were also less diverse.

These beliefs fall along a continuum, with one end emphasizing the role of effort, strategies, and other such controllable factors (a growth mindset) and the other end focusing instead on raw, unchangeable talent as a source of success (a fixed mindset). One's position on this continuum influences the goals and behaviors adopted in achievement settings. For instance, people with fixed (vs. growth) mindsets react more negatively to, and are generally warier of, mistakes because these could signal a lack of talent. By inducing a focus on looking effortlessly competent, fixed mindsets often prompt people to disengage from activities or contexts that might challenge them; as a result, fixed mindsets undermine persistence in domains or careers that are demanding (such as those in academia).

Environments that are geared toward identifying and grooming the next generation of intellectual superstars may systematically discourage members of social groups who, due to societal stereotypes, have—or expect others to have—less confidence in their intellectual abilities. For example, boys and girls receive different socialization about math and science, both in the classroom and at home, and African American children are more likely to attend high-poverty, low-performing schools.

This passage was adapted from "The Frequency of "Brilliant" and "Genius" in Teaching Evaluations Predicts the Representation of Women and African Americans across Fields." Storage D, Home Z, and Leslie S-J. *PLoS ONE*. 2016. doi:10.1371/journal. pone.0150194 for use under the terms of the Creative Commons CC BY 4.0 license (http://creativecommons.org/licenses/by/4.0/legalcode).

Question 5

The findings that gave rise to the FAB hypothesis are most likely to support which of following additional theories?

○ **A.** Social constructionism

○ **B.** Symbolic interactionism

○ **C.** Functionalism

○ **D.** Feminist theory

Question 6

In order to increase the number of physicists that are African American, exchange theory would suggest that:

- ○ **A.** universities be given a bonus payment from the state educational fund for each African American physicist that reaches tenure.
- ○ **B.** the number of tenured Caucasian physicists at state universities be reduced.
- ○ **C.** African American physicists advocate more prominently for permanent positions.
- ○ **D.** an increased rate of one-on-one interactions between university administration and African American physicists.

Question 7

Paragraph one of the passage suggests that broad social stereotypes exist that portray the intellect of women and African Americans in a negative light. These beliefs have been perpetuated through:

- ○ **A.** material culture.
- ○ **B.** non-material culture.
- ○ **C.** sanctions.
- ○ **D.** folkways.

Question 8

Which of the following characteristics is LEAST important in determining the number of underrepresented minorities in careers that are regarded as requiring "a spark of brilliance?"

- ○ **A.** Gender
- ○ **B.** Ethnicity
- ○ **C.** Gender identity
- ○ **D.** Age

Questions 9 - 12 do not refer to a passage and are independent of each other.

Question 9

Which of the following sociological perspective could BEST be used to analyze the interactions between a married couple undergoing a divorce and custody battle, and account for the repercussions on themselves and their children, ages three, seven and twelve?

- ○ **A.** Functionalism and social constructionism
- ○ **B.** Functionalism and conflict theory
- ○ **C.** Symbolic interactionism and social constructionism
- ○ **D.** Symbolic interactionism and conflict theory

Question 10

A developing country is going through a period of political instability in which its leaders change often by non-democratic means. How might a proponent of conflict theory explain the motivations and repercussions of these changes in political leadership?

- ○ **A.** The political upheaval was based on ideological differences and personal conflicts between individuals vying for power that cannot see eye-to-eye.
- ○ **B.** Each of the leaders was fighting for the interests of a particular group, and seize of power resulted in increased access to resources for the group in question.
- ○ **C.** Each political figure had his or her own idea of how to best create a stable and enduring society.
- ○ **D.** The political coups exclusively served the needs of the individual in control, and exploited the rest of the population.

Question 11

A researcher is interested in studying the effects of urbanization on healthcare. This research question falls into what category?

- ○ **A.** Microsociology
- ○ **B.** Social psychology
- ○ **C.** Macrosociology
- ○ **D.** Public sociology

Question 12

A study aims to examine and record the existence of a wide spectrum of human decision making behavior (ranging from emotional to calculated reasoning) by observing humans contemplating making a large purchase. Participants are business school students who have just attended a lecture on weighing costs and benefits. This is likely to:

- ○ **A.** introduce systematic error, offering falsely low support for exchange theory.
- ○ **B.** introduce random error, offering falsely high support for exchange theory.
- ○ **C.** introduce systematic error, offering falsely high support for rational choice theory.
- ○ **D.** introduce random error, offering falsely low support for rational choice theory.

Passage 3 (Questions 13-17)

Colorectal cancer (CRC) is one of the leading causes of death by cancer in the United States (US). Recently there has been great progress against CRC with overall US CRC mortality rates declining significantly. Unfortunately, mortality rates of CRC in New Mexico (NM) have not experienced as sharp of a decrease as the rest of the US. New Mexico also shows a unique pattern of incidence and mortality rates. The National Cancer Institute estimated that the CRC incidence and mortality rates for non-Hispanic Whites (NHW) were higher than for Hispanics nationwide, but that Hispanics have greater CRC mortality rates than NHWs in New Mexico.

It is thought that mortality rates for CRC have decreased over the years, primarily due to increased CRC screenings. However, there remains a concern that disparities in screening practices have contributed to NM's modest declines in CRC mortality. To study this further, a convenience sample of 247 participants who attended a CRC educational booth at one of 17 community events conducted in the NM border region was acquired. Each participant took a survey that assessed CRC knowledge. The three knowledge subcategories included general CRC knowledge, CRC screening knowledge and CRC risk factor knowledge. The results are shown in Table 1.

Table 1 Knowledge Differences Across Ethnic and Age Groups

	Race		Age	
	Non-Hispanic White	Hispanic	<50 years old	>50 years old
Total CRC knowledge	9.07	5.77	6.45	8.39
General CRC knowledge	1.44	1.00	1.05	1.39
CRC screening knowledge	4.17	2.43	2.83	3.77
CRC risk factor knowledge	3.47	2.34	2.57	3.24

Additional statistical analyses were performed to investigate the relationship between ethnicity, age, and physician interactions. Hispanics reported significantly fewer past physician-patient interactions regarding CRC compared to NHWs. Individuals younger than 50 reported fewer past physician-patient interactions regarding CRC than the older group, but the interaction was not significant.

This passage was adapted from "Assessing Colorectal Cancer Screening Behaviors and Knowledge among At-Risk Hispanics in Southern New Mexico." Sanchez J, Palacios R, Thompson B, Martinez V, O'Connell M A. *Journal of Cancer Therapy.* 2013. 4(6B) doi: 10.4236/jct.2013.46A2003 for use under the terms of the Creative Commons CC BY 3.0 license (http://creativecommons.org/licenses/by/3.0/legalcode).

Question 13

In conjunction with the findings in the passage, which of the following would provide evidence for the notion of healthcare disparities amongst different ethnic groups in the United States?

- **A.** The average income of the Hispanic population is roughly equal to the non-Hispanic white middle class.
- **B.** The lack of screening opportunities is the result of a decreased amount of Hispanic physicians available to perform the necessary tests.
- **C.** A larger proportion of Hispanic individuals are uninsured when compared to non-Hispanic individuals.
- **D.** Many of the Hispanic individuals in southern New Mexico are denied treatment at hospitals because they are not U.S. citizens.

Question 14

Suppose it was found that the sample obtained was unevenly distributed with regard to age, and a larger proportion of the non-Hispanic individuals were of the older age group. How would this affect the results of the study?

- **A.** The authors conclusions about the major cause of increased CRC mortality would be weakened
- **B.** The effect of age on general knowledge would need to be included in the conclusion, but the data still strongly supports the role of ethnicity on CRC knowledge
- **C.** It would show that Hispanic individuals are equally as educated on CRC as non-Hispanic individuals, but the results of the study were confounded by improper sampling.
- **D.** The results would be unaffected since the difference in knowledge between age groups is not statistically significant.

Question 15

A researcher repeats the study described in the passage. Which of the following changes would LEAST improve the confidence in the conclusions drawn?

- **A.** Utilizing the same survey but administering it to patients at a CRC-screening facility instead of a community health fair
- **B.** Using a more specific sampling procedure that only samples individuals who make a certain amount of income.
- **C.** Recruiting three times as many participants for the study
- **D.** Performing a t-test to compare the proximity to an urban area's effect on CRC knowledge

Question 16

Suppose a new study found that individuals with family members suffering from CRC were likely to have more general knowledge and more likely to undergo CRC screening. Which of the following does not represent a form of kinship through which this advantage could be gained?

- **A.** A brother and sister born to parents who divorce when the children are in elementary school
- **B.** A newly married couple with unique cultural backgrounds
- **C.** Two individuals who are adopted from separate orphanages by the same parents
- **D.** Two neighbors that agree to build a pool between their houses and share the expense

Question 17

Which of the following conclusions is best supported by the data in the passage?

- **A.** Disparities in healthcare delivery are due to major differences in medical knowledge between different social groups.
- **B.** The pattern of CRC mortality in New Mexico can possibly be altered via improved health education programs.
- **C.** Hispanics living in New Mexico have a higher incidence of CRC most likely due to participation in certain cultural-specific risk factors.
- **D.** The likelihood of mortality from CRC is higher in Hispanics because they are prone to a more aggressive form of CRC.

Next ▶

Passage 4 (Questions 18-22)

It is an obligation of healthcare providers to ensure an equal level of high-quality care for all patients who present to the healthcare system. Equal access to health facilities among all patients is necessary to eliminate healthcare disparities. Differences in health outcomes between income levels and areas of residence have been documented, with the existing literature pointing out that low-income or rural dwelling patients are more likely to receive sub-optimal care and worse outcomes. However, the existing literature regarding how urban or rural dwelling patients with different income levels select healthcare providers is insufficient.

In Study 1, a group of functional theorists analyzed insurance claim data of patients who received coronary arterial bypass graft (CABG) surgery. Healthcare providers' performance and patients' travelling distance to hospitals were used to define the patterns of healthcare provider selection. 30-day mortality after hospitalization for CABG surgery was used to define the quality of healthcare outcomes. 30-day mortality was determined by linking inpatient admission records with withdrawal certificate records.

The results showed that urban dwelling and higher income patients were prone to receive care from better-performance providers. The travelling distances of urban dwelling patients was 15 km shorter, especially when they received better-performance provider's care.

In Study 2, the same data was analyzed again. This time, researchers focused on the healthcare decision making of the patients, including number of visits to a healthcare provider and time between visits. The results showed that patients from rural areas were much less likely to seek healthcare treatment.

This passage was adapted from "Do the Preferences of Healthcare Provider Selection Vary among Rural and Urban Patients with Different Income and Cause Different Outcome?" Yu T, Chung K, Wei C, Hou Y. *PLoS ONE*. 2016. 1(4) doi:10.1371/journal.pone.0152776 for use under the terms of the Creative Commons CC BY 4.0 license (https://creativecommons.org/licenses/by/4.0/legalcode).

Question 18

Which of the following statements offers the best explanation for the results of Study 2?

○ **A.** Rural areas have undergone less modernization than urban areas.

○ **B.** Individuals who reside in rural areas live healthier lifestyles than do individuals from urban areas.

○ **C.** People from rural areas have developed a separate subculture which involves different healthcare beliefs compared to those held by people from urban areas.

○ **D.** Individuals from rural areas lack the social capital to be seen by healthcare providers.

Question 19

Which of the following sociological concepts can result in urban decline?

○ **A.** Gentrification

○ **B.** Suburbanization

○ **C.** Health disparities

○ **D.** Civil unrest

Question 20

Which conclusion is NOT consistent with the results of the passage?

○ **A.** The government should intervene in order to curb urbanization and reduce healthcare disparities.

○ **B.** Preferences of healthcare provider selection vary among rural and urban patients with different income levels.

○ **C.** Health authorities should propose appropriate solutions to eliminate healthcare disparities.

○ **D.** There is evidence of spatial inequality between urban and rural areas.

Question 21

Medicare functions to provide health insurance for Americans aged 65 and older. Medicare is part of which social institution?

○ **A.** Aging and the life course

○ **B.** Government and economy

○ **C.** Health disparity

○ **D.** Social significance of aging

Question 22

With which of the following additional beliefs regarding healthcare would the researchers from the passage most likely agree?

○ **A.** The healthcare system functions by allowing groups to compete for healthcare resources.

○ **B.** Healthcare professionals provide care to patients because it is in their own best interest.

○ **C.** Urban hospitals are better able to train new physicians than are rural hospitals.

○ **D.** The actions of healthcare providers prevent lost time due to illness. This allows society to maintain stability.

Passage 5 (Questions 23-26)

Medicalization is the process by which previously non-medical problems are defined and treated using a medical framework. In the process of medicalization, clusters of symptoms that were once disconnected become newly categorized as disorders. Medicalization is generally expansive in the sense that it creates new disorders faster than old ones are discarded. Some scholars fear a growing contamination of self-rated health by the widespread medicalization of seemingly superficial conditions or by potential overdiagnosis more generally. Expectations for health have generally increased over time, meaning individuals set a lower bar for reporting "poor" health. Furthermore, it is increasingly difficult to reach a cultural consensus regarding what is or is not disease, potentially allowing assessments of poor health to include a variety of symptoms only weakly related to disease and mortality. This process creates ambiguity surrounding the meaning of "excellent" health. While mortality and disability have declined over time, self-rated health has changed very little or gotten worse. One influence is simply increasing exposure to health-related information—patients are demanding more information from their physicians than they did in the past, and physicians are more inclined to use screening.

A longitudinal survey of 5000 American adults was performed to gauge the interaction between the perception of health and mortality. Respondents were asked the following two questions: (a) "Would you say your own health, in general, is excellent, good, fair, or poor?" and (b) "In the past year, have you used the internet to seek information about a health concern?" In 2010, 65% of American adults searched for health information online, compared to 25% in 2000. The results of the study are shown in Figures 1 and 2.

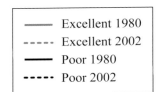

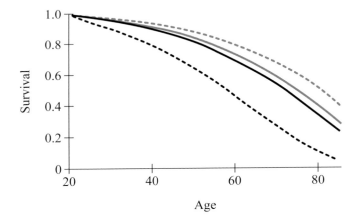

Figure 1 Survivorship curve of self rated health between 1980 and 2008

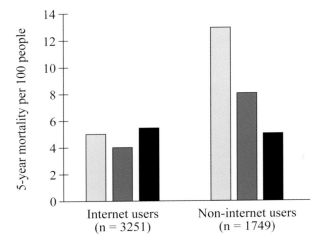

Figure 2 Mortality and self rated health in internet users

This passage was adapted from "The Increasing Predictive Validity of Self-Rated Health." Schnittker J., Bacak V. *PLoS ONE*. 2014. 9(1) doi: 10.1371/journal. pone.0084933 for use under the terms of the Creative Commons CC BY 4.0 license (https://creativecommons.org/licenses/by/4.0/legalcode).

Question 23

The internet was available to the public in 1996. Which of the following sociological effects would best relate this information to the results of the study?

○ **A.** Symbolic culture

○ **B.** Culture shock

○ **C.** Assimilation

○ **D.** Culture lag

Question 24

Which of the following could significantly decrease the study's correlation between self-rated health and mortality?

○ **A.** A popular entertainer stars in a campaign to promote exercise in youth.

○ **B.** Physicians stop reporting benign conditions found during screening to patients.

○ **C.** A new television segment on the nightly news makes people aware of the damaging effects of trans fats of cardiac health.

○ **D.** A health fad causes individuals to consume homeopathic supplements.

Question 25

Which of the following would most affect the external validity of the study?

○ **A.** Some individuals did not fill out question 2 of the survey.

○ **B.** The survey misspelled a word.

○ **C.** Older individuals prefer to use print media.

○ **D.** More health information on the internet is available in English than in Spanish.

Question 26

Which of the following best summarizes the results of this study?

○ **A.** High socioeconomic status increases access to health information.

○ **B.** Medicalization occurs at higher rates in those who use the internet.

○ **C.** The internet causes individuals to make better health decisions.

○ **D.** Internet usage has increased in the population over the course of the past decade.

Questions 27 - 30 do not refer to a passage and are independent of each other.

Question 27

Which of the following would NOT facilitate assimilation of an immigrant into a new culture?

○ **A.** Past exposure to the culture

○ **B.** Rapid culture shock

○ **C.** Comfort with pop culture

○ **D.** Proficiency in new language

Question 28

Which of the following is a testable hypothesis concerning material culture?

○ **A.** Humans did not successfully develop vaccines prior to the 20th century.

○ **B.** There were factions in ancient Rome that dissented against polytheism.

○ **C.** Polyandry has not been an acceptable practice outside of a small village in China.

○ **D.** The ancient Greeks developed rudimentary anesthetics for use in surgeries.

Question 29

Which of the following is the best explanation as to how inbreeding became a taboo in most cultures?

○ **A.** The behavior progressed from a folkway to a more to a taboo.

○ **B.** Humans are biologically programmed to avoid inbreeding.

○ **C.** Offspring produced through inbreeding experience decreased fitness.

○ **D.** Inbreeding was denounced as wrong by an influential religious group.

Question 30

Which of the following best describes why the hippies of the 1960s are characterized as a counterculture movement?

○ **A.** A smaller population developed a unique sense of style, music and living that integrated with the national culture.

○ **B.** The movement promoted peaceful coexistence among many of the different cultures residing in the United States.

○ **C.** Young people rejected the beliefs of their parents and the mainstream media when they spoke out against the Vietnam War and advocated for free love.

○ **D.** Because of the profound influence of the sexual revolution and civil rights activism during this time, the 1960s became a turning point in American popular culture.

Passage 6 (Questions 31-34)

Despite cultural, political and economic differences across different countries, more and more countries are moving toward more democratic regimes, with higher levels of civil liberties. At the same time, rising levels of education and standards of living in many parts of the world have given more and more people higher existential security. Parallel to these phenomena, the World Values Survey has found that cultures and therefore cultural values are changing too.

What is the relation between these phenomena that have transformed various societies? In the 1950s, empirical evidence showed a positive relationship between socioeconomic development and political democratization. More recent work demonstrated that democracy does not grow linearly with GDP per capita, but instead rapid and sudden democratization occurs once GDP per capita has surpassed a certain threshold.

On the contrary, countries starting with a certain level of democracy experience democratic decline. Democracy and GDP are just two of a large number of factors—including education health and cultural values—involved in the process of development. It is known that together these and other socioeconomic factors provide favorable conditions for democratization, but it remains unclear what the relation between them and democratic change precisely is.

One prominent modernization theory, the Human Development Sequence, proposes that cultural values mediate the effect that economic development has on democratization. Economic development provides the opportunities and means for a self-expressive and emancipated life and the desire to shape one's own life provides a motivation to change the rules by which people are governed, therefore demanding more democracy. Starting with democracy, improved education and a certain standard of living lead to an improved political climate. One micro-level explanation for this relationship is that education makes people more critical and autonomous and educated people are likely to demand political changes once they have reached a certain standard of living and financial security that relieves them from daily existential worries and allows for long-term planning of society.

This passage is adapted from "The Dynamics of Democracy, Development and Cultural Values." Spaiser V, Ranganathan S, Mann R, and Sumpter D. *PLoS ONE*. 2014. 10(1) doi:10.1371/journal.pone.0097856 for use under the terms of the Creative Commons CC BY 4.0 license (http://creativecommons.org/licenses/by/4.0/legalcode).

Question 31

Further research has shown that an increased number of women in the workplace also corresponds with higher existential security. This finding supports which of the following theories?

○ **A.** Functionalism

○ **B.** Conflict theory

○ **C.** Exchange-Rational choice

○ **D.** Feminist

Question 32

Why might increased educational levels by a population lead to increased existential security, as suggested by the passage?

○ **A.** As a population becomes more educated, violent crime decreases.

○ **B.** Increased education is evenly distributed across all members of a population.

○ **C.** Higher paying jobs often require more formal education than lower paying jobs.

○ **D.** As a population becomes more educated, the incidence of childhood illness decreases.

Question 33

As the amount of democracy increases within a particular society, which of the following would be expected to also increase?

  I. Rate of divorce

  II. Number of single-parent households

  III. Number of same-sex marriages

○ **A.** I only

○ **B.** II only

○ **C.** I and III only

○ **D.** I, II, and III

Question 34

Economically-developed countries are likely to encourage retirement planning in which of the following age cohorts?

○ **A.** 4-9 years old

○ **B.** 11-19 years old

○ **C.** 30-39 years old

○ **D.** 80-89 years old

Next ▶

Passage 7 (Questions 35-38)

Religions usually contain systems of ideas and rules about how life should be lived. The rules are not restricted to the family but cover how to behave in the community. These social norms prevent individuals from misconduct within the society.

Researchers designed a study to explore the relationship between several personal religion-related variables and social behavior, using three paradigmatic economic games: the dictator (DG), ultimatum (UG), and trust (TG) games. A large carefully chosen sample of the urban adult population (N = 766) was used. From participants' decisions in these games, researchers obtained measures of altruism, bargaining behavior and sense of fairness/equality, trust, and positive reciprocity.

Three dimensions of religiosity were examined: religious denomination; intensity of religiosity, measured by active participation at church services; and conversion to a different denomination than the one raised in.

The results showed that individuals with "no religion" made decisions closer to rational selfish behavior in the DG and the UG compared to those who affiliate with a "standard" religious denomination. Additionally, among Catholics, intensity of religiosity is the key variable that affects social behavior insofar as religiously-active individuals are generally more pro-social than non-active ones. Lastly, the religion one was raised in seems to have no effect on pro-sociality, beyond the effect of the current measures of religiosity. Importantly, behavior in the TG is not predicted by any of the religion-related variables analyzed. While the results partially support the notion of religious pro-sociality, on the other hand, they also highlight the importance of closely examining the multidimensional nature of both religiosity and pro-social behavior.

This passage was adapted from "Religious Pro-Sociality? Experimental Evidence from a Sample of 766 Spaniards." Branas-Garza P, Espin A, Neuman S. *PLoS ONE*. 2014. 9(8) doi:10.1371/journal.pone.0104685 for use under the terms of Creative Commons CC BY 4.0 license (http://creativecommons.org/licenses/by/4.0/leagalcode).

Question 35

Which of the following parameters of religiosity examined by the authors would NOT be present in a participant whom is spiritual but not overtly religious?

    I. Denomination

    II. Intensity

    III. Participant in formal organization

- ○ **A.** I only
- ○ **B.** III only
- ○ **C.** I and III only
- ○ **D.** I, II and III

Question 36

Which of the following religious organizations is considered the least extreme?

- ○ **A.** Church
- ○ **B.** Cult
- ○ **C.** Faction
- ○ **D.** Sect

Question 37

Which of the following would be expected in the DG?

- ○ **A.** One participant decides how to share money between two people.
- ○ **B.** Two participants decide how to share money between each other.
- ○ **C.** Two participants decide how to share money in a group.
- ○ **D.** All participants decide how to share money in a group.

Question 38

How would the results presented in the passage change if the study were conducted on a more secular populace?

- ○ **A.** There would be social choices on the DG and UG with trust on the TG.
- ○ **B.** There would be selfish choices on the DG and UG with trust on the TG.
- ○ **C.** There would be social choices on the DG and UG with no change on the TG.
- ○ **D.** There would be selfish choices on the DG and UG with no change on the TG.

Passage 8 (Questions 39-42)

Childhood family structure has been shown to play an important role in shaping a child's life course development. Family structure is an indication of the type and quality of parental investment received by a child. A key tenet of modern evolutionary theory's principle of inclusive fitness is that parents are favored by natural selection to allocate investment in their offspring.

Using data collected by the Institute for Sex Research, researchers designed a study to investigate the relationship between family structure and an array of traits related to sexual maturity, reproduction, and risk taking. Respondents were interviewed for several hours about very detailed aspects of their sexual behavior. Comprehensive information on demographic, socioeconomic, childhood family structure, education, and health were also collected.

Results showed that, for both sexes, living with a single mother or mother and stepfather during childhood was often associated with faster progression to life history events and greater propensity for risk-taking behaviors. However, living with a single father or father and stepmother was typically not significantly different than having both natural parents for these outcomes. The results withstood adjustment for socioeconomic status, age, ethnicity, age at puberty, and sibling configuration.

While these results support the hypothesis that early family environment influences subsequent reproductive strategy, the different responses to the presence or absence of different parental figures in the household rearing environment suggest that particular family constructions exert independent influences on childhood outcomes.

This passage was adapted from "A Not-So-Grim Tale: How Childhood Family Structure Influences Reproductive and Risk-Taking Outcomes in a Historical U.S. Population." Sheppard P, Garcia R, Sear R. *PLoS Med*, 2014. 9(3); doi:10.1371/journal. pone.0089539 for use under the terms of the Creative Commons CC BY 4.0 license (https://creativecommons.org/licenses/by/4.0/legalcode).

Question 39

What was the independent variable in this investigation?

- ○ **A.** Form of kinship
- ○ **B.** Traits related to sexual maturity, reproduction, and risk taking
- ○ **C.** Family form
- ○ **D.** This investigation does not contain an independent variable

Question 40

The study found that children living with a stepparent encountered higher levels of child abuse. Based on the passage, which statement provides the best explanation of this finding?

- ○ **A.** Children are less likely to listen to stepparents as opposed to biological ones.
- ○ **B.** Stepparents do not share any genes with the children they are caring for.
- ○ **C.** Households containing a stepparent a have lower average SES.
- ○ **D.** There are religious differences between those who stay married and those who remarry after divorce.

Question 41

Children who receive high levels of parental investment spend longer periods of time in education or career development. Which of the following sociological concepts is most related to this finding?

- ○ **A.** Educational stratification
- ○ **B.** Teacher expectancy
- ○ **C.** Cultural capital
- ○ **D.** Social exclusion

Question 42

Which of the following is NOT a potential confounder for this study?

- ○ **A.** The effects of death and divorce may have different consequences for children.
- ○ **B.** There may be cultural differences between women and men who remain single or remarry after widowhood or divorce.
- ○ **C.** Researchers did not use a random sampling technique when selecting participants.
- ○ **D.** Introducing a stepparent into the household may also reduce the investment from the biological parent in existing children.

Questions 43 - 46 do not refer to a passage and are independent of each other.

Question 43

A teacher assigns second-grade students to groups based on their reading ability. This is an example of:

○ **A.** the hidden curriculum.

○ **B.** teacher expectancy.

○ **C.** educational segregation.

○ **D.** meritocracy.

Question 44

Which of the following individuals has a high amount of power but a low amount of authority?

○ **A.** A robber pointing a gun at his victim

○ **B.** A parking attendant writing a ticket

○ **C.** A physician writing a prescription

○ **D.** The surgeon general speaking on public health

Question 45

Which of the following scenarios is LEAST relevant to division of labor in society?

○ **A.** A restaurant has different personnel specialize in different tasks, such as waiting tables, preparing food, and washing dishes.

○ **B.** One friend washes the dishes while the other dries them.

○ **C.** One country produces only wine while the other produces only cloth and each country imports the other's product.

○ **D.** One friend washes half of the dishes while the other washes the other half.

Question 46

The development of large disparities between children who do and do not reach their educational potential could lead to which of the following economic consequences?

○ **A.** Increased privatization of commercial activity

○ **B.** Decreased wealth disparity like that found in a socialist economy

○ **C.** Larger division of labor

○ **D.** Increased number of manual labor job positions

Passage 9 (Questions 47-52)

In 2011, Christchurch, New Zealand experienced a devastating earthquake which resulted in the death of 118 people. The earthquake occurred between waves of a cohort longitudinal study, which allowed investigators to examine the impact the disaster had on the population. Researchers became interested in the influence the disaster had on the faith of the population, which was measured in terms of religiosity. The investigators discovered a sharp contrast in individuals living within the disaster region and those living outside of the region in terms of their reported religiosity. Figure 1 is a map of the results. This finding offered the first macro-level demonstration that secular people tend to turn to religion in times of natural crisis.

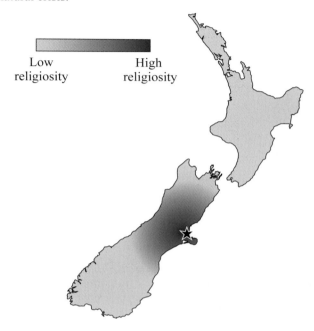

Figure 1 Visual display of Christchurch religiosity post disaster

Researchers also investigated the influence of religiosity on subjective personal health. It was found that loss of faith tended to be associated with subjective health decline for individuals within the disaster region. Subjective personal health in this investigation was defined as how an individual perceived their own health status. An individual with a sharp decline in their subjective health status may report themselves feeling ill more often. In order to measure the potential impact of the drop in subjective health amongst victims, researchers measured the mortality rate of the victim population for a year after the disaster. Data on migration and emigration rates within the year of the earthquake was also collected by sociologists working on the investigation.

This passage was adapted from "Faith after an Earthquake: A Longitudinal Study of Religion and Perceived Health before and after the 2011 Christchurch New Zealand Earthquake." Sibley C, Bulbulia J. *PLoS ONE*. 2012. 7(12) doi 10.1371/journal. pone.0049648 for use under the terms of the Creative Commons CC BY 3.0 license (http://creativecommons.org/licenses/by/3.0/legalcode).

Question 47

Based on passage information, victims within the disaster region likely experienced which of the following?

○ **A.** An increase in religiosity

○ **B.** A decrease in religiosity

○ **C.** No change in their degree of religiosity

○ **D.** There is not enough data within the passage to answer this question.

Question 48

The finding that faith tends to increase amongst disaster victims would contradict the proliferation of:

○ **A.** modernization within the population.

○ **B.** secularization within the population.

○ **C.** fundamentalism within the population.

○ **D.** mortality within the population.

Question 49

The researchers likely utilized which of the following measurements of mortality?

○ **A.** The crude mortality rate

○ **B.** An age specific mortality rate

○ **C.** The total mortality rate

○ **D.** The infant mortality rate

Question 50

Which of the following study designs would be useful in measuring the mortality rate of the disaster area population?

○ **A.** A cohort study

○ **B.** A cross-sectional study

○ **C.** A case-control study

○ **D.** An experimental study

Question 51

Suppose it was found in the wake of the disaster that neighborhoods of low socioeconomic status were impacted the most by the disaster. A finding that rescue groups provided less relief to these areas would be an example of which of the following?

○ **A.** Environmental injustice

○ **B.** Global inequality

○ **C.** Spatial inequality

○ **D.** Prejudice

Question 52

A sociologist writing about the disaster would agree with which of the following descriptions of the disaster and its impact on migration rates?

○ **A.** The earthquake is a push factor and migration to the area would increase.

○ **B.** The earthquake is a pull factor and migration to the area would increase.

○ **C.** The earthquake is a push factor and migration to the area would decrease.

○ **D.** The earthquake is a pull factor and migration to the area would decrease.

Passage 10 (Questions 53-56)

The United States population is made up of an increasing number of elderly individuals. Older individuals are commonly affected by multiple risks and morbidities, leading to functional impairment, nursing home admissions, or premature death, with enormous social and economic costs to society. These adverse outcomes might at least in part be avoidable.

Health risk assessment (HRA), a method successfully used in working-age populations, is a promising method for cost-effective health promotion and preventive care in older individuals. HRA is based on self-reports to guide risk factor interventions, with subsequent individualized feedback to participants on their health status and on how to promote health, maintain function, or prevent disease.

A study evaluated the effects of an approach to HRA and counselling in older individuals on health behaviors, preventive care, and long-term survival. The researchers derived a sample of 2,284 community-dwelling individuals aged 65 years or older registered with one of 19 primary care physician (PCP) practices in a mixed rural and urban area. Baseline data was obtained from a brief pre-randomization questionnaire. 874 participants were then randomly allocated to the intervention and 1,410 to usual care. The intervention consisted of HRA based on self-administered questionnaires and individualized computer-generated feedback reports, combined with nurse and PCP counselling over a 2-year period.

After 2 years, surviving participants were sent a short validated questionnaire to measure six health-related behaviors, (physical activity, fruit/vegetable/fiber intake, fat intake, seat belt use, tobacco consumption, alcohol use) and the and use of six preventive care services (blood pressure measurement, cholesterol measurement, glucose measurement, influenza vaccination, pneumococcal vaccination, fecal occult blood testing). When compared to baseline data obtained from the pre-randomization questionnaire, results showed an increased adherence to the six recommended health behaviors and an increased use of preventative care services in the group that received the intervention.

After 8 years, the mortality rate of both groups was assessed. The mortality rate was 3.16 per 100 person-years in the intervention group, as compared to 3.97 in the control group.

Question 53

What finding would most invalidate the results of the study?

- **A.** A higher initial level of vegetable intake in the control group compared to the experimental group
- **B.** A disproportionate number of incidental deaths in the control group compared to the experimental group
- **C.** The primary care physicians only participated because they believed the costs outweighed the benefits
- **D.** The presence of a hidden curriculum in the HRA

Question 54

Which answer best represents the views of a conflict theorist regarding this study?

- **A.** Since healthcare resources are limited, elderly patients limit the access of healthcare to other groups.
- **B.** Different social groups, such as nurses and doctors, all work together in order to care for elderly patient populations.
- **C.** Elderly individuals will only seek medical treatment when they are internally conflicted regarding their state of well-being.
- **D.** For practice implementation, a key factor for success is ensuring personal reinforcement of HRA-based recommendations by specially trained counsellors who take into account individuals' personal preferences.

Question 55

Based on the results of this study, it is reasonable to conclude that:

- **A.** in the future, more doctors will dedicate themselves to caring for elderly patients since HRA was shown to improve the health outcomes of elderly patients.
- **B.** multimodal interventions and coordination of care are effective when treating elderly patients because they help patients take agency for their own health.
- **C.** multimodal interventions and coordination of care are effective when treating elderly patients since HRA was shown to improve the health outcomes.
- **D.** elderly individuals consume a disproportionate amount of healthcare resources because they are more likely to be affected by multiple risks and morbidities.

Question 56

Which population pyramid represents the United States population as described in the passage?

○ **A.**

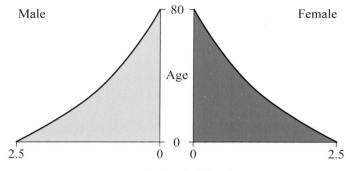

○ **B.**

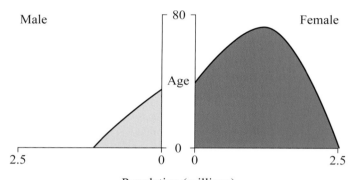

○ **C.**

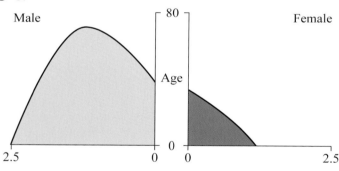

○ **D.**

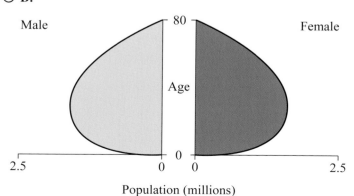

Questions 57 - 59 do not refer to a passage and are independent of each other.

Question 57

A study was conducted in a public school that measured teachers' expectations of students' capacity for academic achievement at the beginning of the school year, and the students' test scores at the end of the school year. Which flaw in internal validity would limit the ability to draw conclusions from this study?

○ **A.** The students in the study are not demographically representative of greater society, making it impossible to generalize the study's results on teacher expectancy to the rest of the population.

○ **B.** It was determined the students who performed poorly on tests belonged to an ethnic group against which a teacher held bias, and these students lived in a neighborhood that was heavily damaged by a hurricane during the school year.

○ **C.** The students were randomly assigned to groups that were told the teachers' opinion of them, and groups that were not told this information.

○ **D.** Teachers were asked about their perception of students' academic abilities before the students were administered any kind of testing.

Question 58

John and Mary have been dating and living together for over three years. John recently asked Mary to marry him, and they plan on having children once they get married. Which of the following describe John and Mary before and after they get married and have children?

○ **A.** Before, they form a social group; after, they form a social institution.

○ **B.** They form a social group and a social institution both before and after.

○ **C.** Before, they form neither a social group nor a social institution; after, they form a social institution.

○ **D.** Before, they form a social group; after, they form both a social group and a social institution.

Question 59

In terms of societal structure, a religion is best defined as:

○ **A.** a tendency to place a belief system first in life which frames how followers make sense of their own experiences.

○ **B.** a group behaviors, beliefs, and interactions that broke away from a traditional establishment that frames how members make sense of their own experiences.

○ **C.** a group with views or practices that place it outside of traditional society that frames how members make sense of their own experiences.

○ **D.** a group that holds an organized structure of behaviors, belief, and interactions that frames how members make sense of their own experiences.

STOP. If you finish before time is called, check your work. You may go back to any question in this test.

ANSWERS & EXPLANATIONS for Test 1A can be found on p. 166.

The Biopsychosocial Model, Society and Culture

TEST 1B

Time: 95 minutes
Questions 1–59

DIRECTIONS: Most of the questions in this test section are grouped with a passage. Read the passage, then select the best answer to each question. Some questions are independent of any passage and of one another. Select the best answer to each of these questions. If you are unsure of an answer, rule out incorrect choices and select from the remaining options. Indicate your selection beside the option you choose.

Passage 1 (Questions 1-4)

Epidemiological research has consistently shown that the prevalence of depression is approximately twice as high among women as among men. Because of this, researchers hypothesized that this discrepancy may be explained by variation in the recognition of mental illness due to differences in gender identity. Participants scoring high in femininity would be more likely to recognize depressive symptoms as manifestations of illness compared to participants scoring low in femininity; participants scoring high in masculinity would be less likely to recognize depressive symptoms as manifestations of illness compared to participants scoring low in masculinity. To test this hypothesis, 150 university students completed a questionnaire survey. The questionnaires involving a fictional Major Depressive Episode (MDE) case and a fictional Panic Disorder case were distributed separately. The results derived from the 72 students who evaluated the MDE case were analyzed.

Each participant was asked to judge (a) if he/she thought the male/female case subject was "somatically ill" and (b) if he/she thought the male/ female case subject was "psychologically ill". If the participant believed the case subject to be somatically or psychologically ill (or both), further inquiry was made as to the degree of severity of the somatic or psychological illness using a 4-point scale. Participants were also administered the Ito Sex Role Scale to evaluate where they fall in terms of gender identity. Researchers expected that the interpretation of the MDE case as indicating illness would be related to femininity. The results showed that participants who recognized case vignette subjects as ill scored higher in the gender role subscale of femininity. These findings suggest that recognition of MDE as an illness (regardless of its somatic or psychological symptomatology) is more likely to occur in individuals whose gender ideal or identity is high in femininity and empathy. Femininity and empathy thus form the framework of a self-schema that recognizes depressive symptoms as more "acceptable".

This passage was adapted from "Gender Differences in Recognising Depression in a Case Vignette in a University Student Population: Interaction of Participant and Vignette Subject Gender with Depressive Symptomatology." Andou J, Kitamura T. *Open Journal of Psychiatry*. 2013. 3(4) doi: 10.4236/ojpsych.2013.34041 for use under the terms of the Creative Commons CC BY 3.0 license (http://creativecommons. org/licenses/by/3.0/legalcode).

Question 1

Suppose the same experiment was performed, but some participants were given an introduction on the physiological causes of symptoms resembling those of depression. Based on the results of the experiment in the passage and knowledge of the biomedical approach to treating illness, which of the following outcomes would be expected?

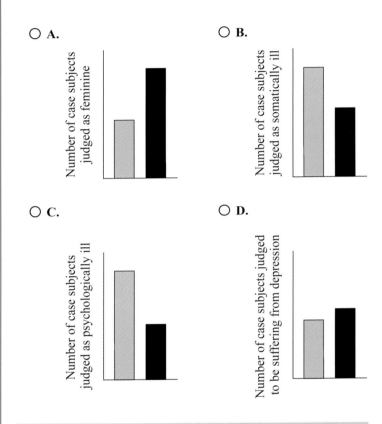

Question 2

The Ito Sex Role Scale was used to measure participants' identification with certain qualities traditionally considered to be either male or female. What would ensure that the participants' score on the Ito Sex Role Scale accurately represented measures of gender identity?

- **A.** The Ito Sex Role Scale was based on biologically observable markers of assigned gender.
- **B.** The Ito Sex Role Scale was created to represent ideals of gender roles that mirror what the participants observe in their society.
- **C.** The study's sample size was sufficiently large.
- **D.** The Ito Sex Role Scale was based on material culture rather than symbolic culture.

Next ▶

Question 3

Which of the following is the most likely reason that the researchers chose not to include the Panic Disorder arm of the study in their evaluation?

- ○ **A.** The panic disorder participant group only included 2 female participants.
- ○ **B.** The panic disorder cases served as a control group.
- ○ **C.** The attributes of panic disorder are not thought of as pathological in the participants' home culture.
- ○ **D.** Panic disorder does not produce any physically discernible symptoms at all.

Question 4

If the following figure were a part of the study, it would support which of the following findings?

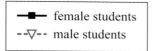

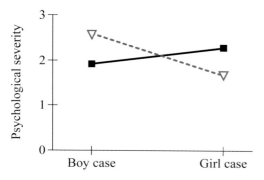

- ○ **A.** There were more male participants than female participants.
- ○ **B.** The boy case was presented chronologically earlier than the girl case.
- ○ **C.** Participants were more likely to rate psychological severity as high when they identified with the gender of the case subject.
- ○ **D.** Knowledge of traditional gender roles causes bias when rating severity of psychological incidents.

Passage 2 (Questions 5-10)

Refugee children arrive in the US from countries with a high burden of undernutrition, infectious disease, and poverty. Undernutrition increases a child's risk of morbidity and mortality associated with infectious disease, and poor cognitive and developmental outcomes. Undernutrition is not, however, the only form of malnutrition affecting children worldwide. Children, like adults, are experiencing an increasing prevalence of overnutrition (overweight and obesity). The extent that the dual burden of undernutrition and overnutrition affects refugee children before resettlement in the US is not well described.

Researchers investigated the prevalence of wasting, stunting, overweightness, and obesity among refugee children ages 0–10 years (the majority of which were from Somalia, Burma, and Iraq) at their overseas medical screening examination prior to definite resettlement in Washington State (WA). They compared the nutritional status of refugee children with that of low-income children in WA, whose nutritional states were assessed in the CDC's Pediatric Nutrition Surveillance System (PedNSS). The results are shown in Figure 1.

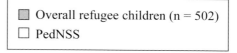

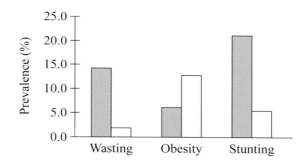

Figure 1 Prevalence of nutritional status categories among refugee children and the WA PedNSS

Additionally, researchers found evidence of the heterogeneity of the nutrition profile by country of origin among refugee children with significantly higher rates of obesity among the Iraqi children, wasting and stunting among the Somali children, and stunting among the Burmese children.

This passage was adapted from "Comparison of the Nutritional Status of Overseas Refugee Children with Low Income Children in Washington State." Dawson-Hahn EE, Pak-Gorstein S, Hoopes AJ, Matheson J. *PLoS ONE*. 2016. 11 (1) doi:10.1371/journal.pone.0147854 for use under the terms of the Creative Commons CC BY 4.0 license (https://creativecommons.org/licenses/by/4.0/legalcode).

Question 5

Which modification to the study would most likely result in refugee children presenting with a similar nutrition profile as those in WA?

○ **A.** Only analyzing data of refugee children from countries with a hyper-globalist perspective

○ **B.** Only analyzing data of refugee children from countries that carry a transformationalist perspective on globalization

○ **C.** Only analyzing data of refugee children from countries that have a high economic interdependence with the US

○ **D.** Only analyzing data of refugee children from countries with weak international communications infrastructure

Question 6

How could the researchers change the study design to determine what factors lead to a nutrition profile that is homogenous when refugees are compared to US residents?

○ **A.** To assess the effect of assimilation on nutritional profile, change the present cross-sectional design to a longitudinal design.

○ **B.** To assess the effect of assimilation on nutritional profile, change the present longitudinal design to a cross-sectional design.

○ **C.** To assess the effect of multiculturalism on nutritional profile, change the present cross-sectional design to a longitudinal design.

○ **D.** To assess the effect of multiculturalism on nutritional profile, change the present longitudinal design to a cross-sectional design.

Question 7

How does the concept of relative deprivation explain the influx of refugees from other countries?

○ **A.** The rate of emigration increases as greater numbers of first or second degree relatives relocate.

○ **B.** As family members immigrate, greater numbers of refugees are prompted to follow their relatives to the country where their family has been resettled in order to avoid social isolation due to relative deprivation.

○ **C.** The inability to meet minimal objective standards for food, shelter, clothing, or health care leads to a feeling of deprivation which prompts an exodus from one's home country.

○ **D.** The feeling of inequality due to relative deprivation can lead to creation of social movements.

Question 8

Researchers noticed anecdotally that several leaders came forward throughout the resettlement process and developed strategies for this social movement. This emergence takes place during which phase of social movement organization?

○ **A.** Emergence

○ **B.** Coalescence

○ **C.** Bureaucratization

○ **D.** Decline

Question 9

What statement is true regarding the two subject groups whose data is shown in Figure 1?

○ **A.** Immigrants within the PedNSS subject group are most likely from Mexico, Caribbean nations, and India, and experience overnutrition to a greater extent than the refugee children.

○ **B.** Immigrants within the PedNSS subject group are most likely from Mexico, Caribbean nations, and India, and experience undernutrition to a greater extent than the refugee children.

○ **C.** Immigrants within the PedNSS subject group are most likely from China, the United Kingdom, and Canada, and experience overnutrition to a greater extent than the refugee children.

○ **D.** Immigrants within the PedNSS subject group are most likely from China, the United Kingdom, and Canada, and experience undernutrition to a greater extent than the refugee children.

Question 10

Once resettled, what pattern of settlement best describes what the refugee population will experience in the coming decades?

○ **A.** Industrialization followed by urbanization

○ **B.** Urbanization followed by suburbanization

○ **C.** Suburbanization followed by urban decline

○ **D.** Urban renewal followed by gentrification

Questions 11 - 14 do not refer to a passage and are independent of each other.

Question 11

Which of the following is NOT a true statement regarding gender?

○ **A.** Gender identity is different than biological sex

○ **B.** Gender identity is the internal sense of gender an individual experiences

○ **C.** Gender identity is always binary

○ **D.** Acceptance of gender presentation largely varies based on culture

Question 12

A researcher devises a study examining the effects of technology on education and classroom management. She provides laptops and appropriate software for two third grade classes and follows their academic performance as well as that of two control third grade classes in the same school through twelfth grade. The results of the study will be used to design lessons utilizing technology for following students. Which of the following poses the most significant barrier to this goal?

○ **A.** The lack of randomization of participants

○ **B.** The drop-out rate of students in the selected school

○ **C.** The intergenerational gap in access to and use of technology

○ **D.** The sample size of the study

Question 13

With regard to social movements, mass demonstrations against administrative practices and physical confrontations are examples of:

○ **A.** relative deprivation.

○ **B.** strategy.

○ **C.** tactics.

○ **D.** a proactive social movement.

Question 14

A sub-Saharan African country has historically been poor in natural resources and agricultural abilities and, as a result, its population suffers from poverty, low education levels, and limited access to healthcare. However, its government acquires the resources to open affordable and accessible hospitals. In what way is this likely to affect this country's population pyramid?

○ **A.** The pyramid will likely widen towards the base in coming years.

○ **B.** The pyramid will likely narrow towards the top in coming years.

○ **C.** The pyramid will likely widen towards the top in coming years.

○ **D.** The pyramid will likely narrow towards the base in coming years.

Passage 3 (Questions 15-18)

In the first decade of the HIV epidemic, disparities in HIV incidence became clear in the United States—racial and ethnic minorities and men who have sex with men in large, coastal cities were hardest hit, and the incidence rate in men was nearly fifteen times the rate in women. By 2010, the characteristics of the HIV-infected population had shifted dramatically: women composed 21% of HIV cases in the United States and the incidence rate for men was only 3 times the rate in women. While recent studies have described the current demographic characteristics of HIV-infected people in different parts of the United States, there are none that directly present the characteristics of regions defined by high HIV prevalence among women compared with men. Researchers designed a study to identify and describe these regions. In order to do this, data from AIDSVu was analyzed. AIDSVu comprises HIV surveillance data from state and local health departments that was organized by the US Centers for Disease Control and Prevention. Select findings from the study are represented in Figure 1.

■ lower deciles

Figure 1 HIV prevalence by county

A second study was performed in which the data from AIDSVu was correlated to socioeconomic status. It was found that counties with higher levels of HIV-infected people also have a higher percentage of people living in poverty.

This passage was adapted from "Women and HIV in the United States." Breskin A, Adimora A, Westreich D. *PLoS ONE*. 2017. 12(2); doi:10.1371/journal.pone.0172367 for use under the terms of the Creative Commons CC BY 4.0 license (https://creativecommons.org/licenses/by/4.0/legalcode).

Question 15

The differences in gender norms regarding sexual behavior are an example of:

O **A.** conflict theory.

O **B.** the social construction of gender.

O **C.** gender identity.

O **D.** gender segregation.

Question 16

The results of the study show evidence of which of the following sociological concepts?

O **A.** Environmental justice

O **B.** Patterns of social mobility

O **C.** Global inequalities

O **D.** Migration

Question 17

Which of the following is true regarding sexual orientation?

O **A.** It is not dependent on the sex or gender of the person.

O **B.** There is no difference between who a person is attracted to and who they have sex with.

O **C.** It is binary.

O **D.** It is determined at birth.

Question 18

All of the following were demographics mentioned in the passage EXCEPT?

O **A.** Sexual orientation

O **B.** Race and ethnicity

O **C.** Socioeconomic status

O **D.** Immigration status

Passage 4 (Questions 19-22)

Previous studies have documented lower breast cancer survival among women with lower socioeconomic status (SES) in the United States. Socioeconomic disparity in breast cancer survival can be explained by stage at diagnosis, treatment, race and rural/urban residence.

To study the effects of these factors and SES on breast cancer survival, 112,543 women from a wide range of urban and rural areas nationwide diagnosed with breast cancer during 1998-2002 were followed through the end of 2005. The study showed that women living in the lowest SES areas had the lowest percentage of early stage cancer (40%) compared to women living in the highest SES areas (51%). Women living in the lowest SES also had the highest percentage of advanced stages of cancer. The proportion of minority women living in the lowest SES areas was nearly four times higher than that of the highest SES areas. The proportions of women from the two lowest SES areas who received the first course treatment were lower than that of the highest SES areas (<40% versus 57%).

Researchers then used six models to assess the association between SES and cause-specific survival. To do this, researchers estimated the hazard ratio (HR), which represents the risk of dying from breast cancer. Researchers first estimated the hazard ratio (HR) based on SES only. This is the base model (model 0). The hazard ratio was then calculated for additional models by making sequential adjustments for: 1) age at diagnosis; 2) stage at diagnosis; 3) first course treatment; 4) race; and 5) rural/urban residence (Table 1).

Table 1   Hazard Ratio (HR) of Breast Cancer Mortality by Socioeconomic Status (SES)

SES group	Model 0 SES only	Model 1 Model 0 + age at diagnosis	Model 2 Model 1 + stage	Model 3 Model 2 + treatment	Model 4 Model 3 + race	Model 5 Model 4 + rural/urban
Highest	1.00	1.00	1.00	1.00	1.00	1.00
Upper middle	1.05	1.01	1.00	1.00	0.99	0.99
Lower middle	1.23	1.09	1.08	1.07	1.06	1.04
Lowest	1.31	1.19	1.10	1.08	1.03	1.03
p-value for SES	<0.0001	<0.0001	<0.0001	0.003	0.07	0.20

Question 19

How can environmental justice and socioeconomic status be related to the data presented in Table 1?

- **A.** An increase in environmental justice could eliminate survival disparities associated with lower SES.
- **B.** Factors such as stage at diagnosis, treatment, race, and rural/urban residence have no effect on survival disparities associated with lower SES.
- **C.** A decrease in environmental justice could eliminate survival disparities associated with lower SES.
- **D.** Hazard ratios eliminate the significance of environmental justice and socioeconomic status in this study.

Question 20

Findings from this study best support which conclusion about cancer screening and spatial inequality?

- **A.** Minority patients are less likely than higher SES groups to participate in cancer screening even if screening options are available.
- **B.** Increasing breast cancer screening in minority patients could reduce socioeconomic disparity in breast cancer survival.
- **C.** Increasing breast cancer screening in lower SES neighborhoods could reduce socioeconomic disparity in breast cancer survival.
- **D.** Breast cancer screening in lower SES neighborhoods is costly and unlikely to affect survival rates.

Question 21

The equalization of hazard ratio in model 5 of Table 1 is most related to adjustment for:

○ **A.** demographic parameters.

○ **B.** socioeconomic status.

○ **C.** race.

○ **D.** patient age.

Question 22

In this study, the large sample population of 112,543 women from a wide range of demographic backgrounds makes the findings:

○ **A.** variable.

○ **B.** generalizable.

○ **C.** inconclusive.

○ **D.** valid.

Passage 5 (Questions 23-26)

In the United States, health research concerned with health inequalities between continental population groups has been dominated by studies concerned with "racial" disparities in health. However, ethnicity is more rooted in shared ancestry, language, and culture and may be more appropriate for research about disparities in health.

Arab Americans (AA) are ethnic minorities in the United States who trace their ancestral, linguistic, or cultural heritage to one of 22 Arab countries. Research shows that AAs may have higher risk of cardiovascular disease, cancer incidence, and smoking than Whites. Moreover, immigration, acculturation, and discrimination may be important determinants of health and disease among AAs.

In a study of all deaths among AAs and non-Arab and non-Hispanic Whites between 1990–2007, researchers found that both AA males and females had lower life expectancy than non-Arab and non-Hispanic Whites by 2 and 1.4 years, respectively. All-cause mortality was higher among AAs of both sexes than among non-Arab and non-Hispanic Whites. Age-specific mortality was higher among AAs than among non-Arab and non-Hispanic Whites among all age groups except males aged 25–44 years and females aged 5–44 years.

Among males, AAs were better educated, were more likely to be married, and reported higher household incomes than their non-Arab and non-Hispanic White counterparts. Among females, AAs reported higher household incomes and were better educated than non-Arab and non-Hispanic White females.

Despite better education and higher incomes, AAs can expect to live about 2 years shorter than their non-Arab and non-Hispanic White counterparts. Given these findings, public health departments in areas with significant numbers of AA minorities might consider interventions that target chronic disease risk factors among AAs and curb the spread of infectious diseases among this ethnic group.

This passage was adapted from "Ethnic Inequalities in Mortality: The Case of Arab-Americans." El-Sayed AM, Tracy M, Scarborough P, Galea S. *PLoS ONE*. 2011. 6(12) doi: 10.1371/journal.pone.0029185 for use under the terms of the Creative Commons CC BY 3.0 license (http://creativecommons.org/licenses/by/3.0/legalcode).

Question 23

An Arab American pursues a career that leads to great financial success, and his children inherit his wealth when they come of age. Which of the following concepts does NOT apply to this situation?

○ **A.** Vertical mobility

○ **B.** Social reproduction

○ **C.** Upward mobility

○ **D.** Intergenerational mobility

Question 24

Which conclusion is best supported based on the age-specific mortality data in this study?

- **A.** There is a higher infectious disease and chronic disease mortality burden among Arab Americans compared to non-Arab and non-Hispanic Whites.
- **B.** There is a lower infectious disease and chronic disease mortality burden among Arab Americans compared to non-Arab and non-Hispanic Whites.
- **C.** Arab Americans have a lower life expectancy compared to non-Arab and non-Hispanic Whites.
- **D.** There is no relationship between age and mortality rate.

Question 25

Which of the following are examples of how social changes in globalization have affected people of Arab descent?

- I. Ever since the terrorist attacks of September 11, 2001, Arab Americans have been subject to increased rates of prejudice and hate crimes.
- II. The rise of social media usage and western democracy in the Arab region contributed to the Arab Spring, a period of civil unrest.
- III. Egyptian textile factory workers gathered to protest low wages and diminished job security, slowing production to a halt.

- **A.** I only
- **B.** II only
- **C.** I and II only
- **D.** II and III only

Question 26

Which of the following statements is most consistent with racial formation theory as it applies to Arab Americans?

- **A.** An Egyptian immigrant to the United States is classified by the government as being "White" on the basis of his place of origin.
- **B.** An Egyptian immigrant to the United States is classified as "White" on the basis of her place of origin, but identifies as "Black or African American" due to her dark skin color.
- **C.** A second-generation Arab American considers himself to be White due to his phenotypic traits.
- **D.** Race is a dynamic social construct, and thus, a static classification of an Arab American as "White" is inadequate.

Questions 27 - 30 do not refer to a passage and are independent of each other.

Question 27

A survey was performed on self reported health, mortality, and internet usage in 5000 Brazilian adults between 1980 and 2010. Which of the following would be expected?

- **A.** Due to suburbanization, the average Brazilian has greater access to healthcare and perceives better health.
- **B.** Due to globalization, the rate of internet usage to access health information increased in Brazil, but later than in America.
- **C.** Due to urbanization, lowered rates of infectious disease are reflected in decreased mortality in Brazil.
- **D.** Compared to America, validity of self rated health is more likely to reflect the proportion of internet users accurately in Brazil.

Question 28

A third-generation Mexican American is similar to a natural-born Mexican who recently immigrated to the United States in terms of:

- I. the racial stereotypes they endure.
- II. their ethnicity.
- III. their race.

- **A.** I and II only
- **B.** I and III only
- **C.** II and III only
- **D.** I, II, and III

Question 29

An American expert in the field of robotic surgery wishes to conduct a study with a fellow expert in Japan to assess the efficacy of their methods and determine techniques they might be able to learn from one another to better serve their patient populations. Each physician measures their patients' quality of life before and after surgery. This is an example of which of the following?

- **A.** A comparison of two cohort studies, representing increased globalization in medicine.
- **B.** A comparison of two cross-sectional studies, representing increased multiculturalism in medicine.
- **C.** A single cross-sectional study, representing technological advancements in medicine.
- **D.** An observational study, representing increased healthcare equity.

Question 30

A young couple acquires the resources to leave a rural town in a developing country and settle in a cosmopolitan city in the United States. What are some push and pull factors, respectively, that may have led this family to migrate?

- ○ **A.** Poor economic conditions in their home country was a pull factor, and greater economic opportunity in the United States was a push factor.

- ○ **B.** Poor economic conditions in their home country was both a pull factor and a push factor.

- ○ **C.** The presence of a support system in their home country was a pull factor, and poor economic conditions in their home country was a push factor.

- ○ **D.** Greater economic opportunity in the United States was a pull factor, and poor economic conditions on their home country was a push factor.

Passage 6 (Questions 31-34)

Health has strong positive externalities and plays an important role in promoting social and economic development. Thus, improving the population health is one of the most important social objectives of most governments. A common approach to achieve this goal is to set up a health system to guarantee that all residents suffering from illness can access basic medical services, and to guarantee the equity in the distribution of health. Although more expenditure on health does not guarantee better health outcomes, governments usually focus on the operational measure of promoting equality in government health expenditure (GHE). Unfortunately, too often GHE is disproportionately distributed via tax reform measures and medical insurance systems.

Tax Reform

The federal government has the ability to reform tax law, thus reducing local governments' tax revenues. Yet, local governments' responsibilities of providing public services, including medical services, remain unchanged. Citizens often criticize excessive taxes and support reforms that lower tax rates. However, the effect that this has on local hospitals and public health efforts can be detrimental to a community.

Medical Insurance Systems

Another source of the regional disparity in GHE lies in the structure of the healthcare financing system. Countries have two general options when it comes to medical insurance: control or capitalism. Free market medical insurance has the advantage of competition amongst insurance companies so that consumers have a range of coverage options. Government-subsidized insurance makes medical insurance more affordable to low income families but may place a large cost on middle class families.

This passage was adapted from "Disparity and Convergence: Chinese Provincial Government Health Expenditures." Pan J, Wang P, Qin X, Zhang S. *PLoS ONE.* 2013. 8(8) doi:10.1371/journal.pone.0071474 for use under the terms of the Creative Commons CC BY 3.0 license (http://creativecommons.org/licenses/by/3.0/legalcode).

Question 31

The rapid advancement in medical care has resulted in a significant financial strain for many countries. Assuming the value of healthcare declines in the coming years, which of the following theories may be at play?

- ○ **A.** Malthusian theory
- ○ **B.** Marxist theory
- ○ **C.** Olduvai theory
- ○ **D.** Demographic theory

Question 32

Publicly funded hospitals are required to provide emergency medical care to any person that needs it. Yet, many citizens are unable to afford visits to a primary care doctor. Compared to countries where medical care is not a right, citizens are experiencing:

○ **A.** absolute poverty.

○ **B.** probable mortality.

○ **C.** relative deprivation.

○ **D.** improved morality.

Question 33

Profits for hospitals are often dependent on the average income of citizens utilizing the hospital. Which of the following shifts would improve profits?

○ **A.** Urbanization

○ **B.** Gentrification

○ **C.** Globalization

○ **D.** Industrialization

Question 34

Stratification of a populace, as is done through the United States census, forces individuals to delineate their race. How would a multiracial individual respond to such a survey, and what effect may that have on the results?

○ **A.** He or she would choose the race that is most genetically accurate, so as to not bias the results.

○ **B.** He or she would choose the race that is most socially accepted, so the results may have biased external validity.

○ **C.** He or she would choose the race that he or she identifies with the most, so the results may have biased internal validity.

○ **D.** He or she would choose the race he or she identifies with the most, so the results may have biased external validity.

Passage 7 (Questions 35-38)

In a study on stereotype threat, experimenters tested whether stereotypical situations would affect low-status group members' performance more strongly than high-status group members. Gender was used as a proxy of chronic social status, with men being viewed as part of the dominant group due to the historical asymmetry between men and women (i.e., the chronic status acquired through socialization processes). A small apparatus was built for measuring fine motor skills for this experiment, including a wooden platform, a plastic wand, a metal washer combination, and a bent metal rod providing a winding track. A loud buzzing sound and a red light alerted participants when the washer touched the rod, which indicated a hit. Fine motor skill tasks generally lead to men and women performing equally well.

Participants were randomly assigned to one of three experimental conditions. The first condition was a control condition and did not refer to gender. In two other conditions, gender stereotypes were evoked. In the men superiority condition the experimenters indicated that usually "men succeed more on this task than do women". In the female superiority condition the same instruction was used, except the words men and women were reversed. Figure 1 summarizes the results of this study. A second study was conducted, aimed to extend this result on another hierarchical social group. The procedure, materials, and task were identical to experiment 1. In this study, participants were asked the question "How important is it for you to be a male/a female?" Participants answered on a scale ranging from not at all (1) to very important (5).

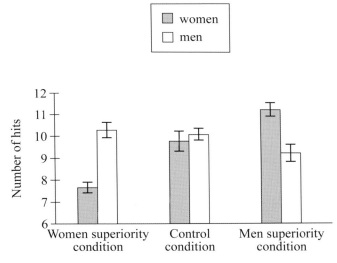

Figure 1 Average number of hits of each experimental group

This passage was adapted from "The Influence of Chronic and Situational Social Status on Stereotype Susceptibility." Pillaud et al. *PLoS ONE*. 2015. 10(12) doi:10.1371/journal.pone.0144582 for use under the terms of the Creative Commons CC BY 4.0 license (https://creativecommons.org/licenses/by/4.0/legalcode).

Question 35

In the first study, the experimenters assumed a historical discrepancy in status between men and women. Which of the following factors most contributes to this difference in status?

- **A.** Hidden curriculum
- **B.** Religion
- **C.** Class consciousness
- **D.** Urbanization

Question 36

Based on the results shown in Figure 1, what is the expected relationship between a person's income and the effect of stereotype threat on that person?

A.

B.

C.

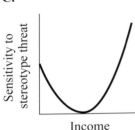

D.

Question 37

The experimenters hypothesized that similar results could be replicated using race instead of gender. Which of the following contributes LEAST to the formation of race ?

- **A.** Physical differences
- **B.** Stereotypes
- **C.** Conditioning
- **D.** Culture

Question 38

Another study found that family members tended to be similarly affected by stereotype threat. What is the best explanation for this finding?

- **A.** Social reproduction
- **B.** Cultural values
- **C.** Cultural diffusion
- **D.** Intergenerational mobility

Passage 8 (Questions 39-44)

The ageing population poses a tremendous challenge to understanding the sources of inequalities in health. Though they appear to be far removed, childhood conditions are known to be inextricably linked with adult health, and, in turn, on health in later life. The Long Arm of Childhood Conditions hypothesis is often tested using recollection of childhood circumstances, but such subjective recall can yield potentially inaccurate or possibly biased inferences. Researchers tested the Long Arm hypothesis on three outcomes in later life, arrayed from objective to subjective health, namely: gait speed, episodic memory, and mental health.

Investigators used the English Longitudinal Study of Ageing 2006 enriched with retrospective life history (N = 5,913). To deal with recall problems two solutions, covariate measurement and endogenous treatment models, were applied. Retrospective childhood material lack includes growing up without running hot or cold water, fixed bath, indoor lavatory, or central heating. Adjustment was made for an extensive set of confounders including sex, age, adult health, wealth, education, occupation, social support, social connections, chronic conditions, smoking, drinking, and physical exercise. It was found that material poverty when growing up shows no association with health when growing old, assuming accurate recall. Once recall problems were controlled, researchers found that childhood material poverty changes inversely with later life health. Namely, a poorer childhood goes with slower gait, poorer memory, and more depression in later life. This result provides a further impetus to eliminate child poverty.

This passage was adapted from "Growing Up in Poverty, Growing Old in Infirmity: The Long Arm of Childhood Conditions in Great Britain." Tampubolon G. *PLoS ONE*. 2015. 10(12) doi:10.1371/journal.pone.0144722 for use under the terms of Creative Commons CC BY 4.0 license (http://creativecommons.org/licenses/by/4.0/legalcode).

Question 39

In combination with income and occupation, which of the following is a determinant of socioeconomic status?

- **A.** Age
- **B.** Gender
- **C.** Education
- **D.** Race

Question 40

Which of the following factors may have precluded children living in poverty from obtaining adequate health care?

- **A.** Social exclusion
- **B.** Social inequality
- **C.** Spatial inequality
- **D.** Spatial exclusion

Next ▶

Question 41

The No Child Left Behind Act was an important introduction to public education and helped to counteract generational poverty. This act was in contrast to which of the following concepts?

○ **A.** Democracy

○ **B.** Meritocracy

○ **C.** Theocracy

○ **D.** Federacy

Question 42

Which of the following changes during childhood may have biased the study?

○ **A.** Puberty

○ **B.** Horizontal mobility

○ **C.** Vertical mobility

○ **D.** Intergenerational mobility

Question 43

Which of the following diseases may be present in adult participants whom experienced childhood poverty?

○ **A.** Alzheimer's disease, which is characterized by impairments in memory.

○ **B.** Parkinson's disease, which is characterized by impairments in movement.

○ **C.** Huntington's disease, which is characterized by changes in personality.

○ **D.** Normal pressure hydrocephalus, which is characterized by incontinence, trouble walking, cognitive and mood changes.

Question 44

Which of the following is an appropriate definition of material poverty as used in the passage?

○ **A.** Absolute poverty, including the absence of clothing and other resources

○ **B.** Absolute poverty, including the absence of food and water

○ **C.** Relative poverty, including the absence of clothing and other resources

○ **D.** Relative poverty, including the absence of food and water

Questions 45 - 48 do not refer to a passage and are independent of each other.

Question 45

Less residential segregation would lead to which of the following effects?

○ **A.** A greater movement of people between different areas of the city.

○ **B.** Residents exercise less outdoors to avoid being victimized.

○ **C.** An increase in expensive housing in wealthy neighborhoods.

○ **D.** A chronic activation of stress processes due to continual fear of crime.

Question 46

Which of the following individuals has the greatest power, as defined in sociology?

○ **A.** A prestigious physician, now retired at old age

○ **B.** A woman leading a respected local grass-roots organization

○ **C.** A former leader of a region-wide gang, now incarcerated

○ **D.** A supply chain manager for an oil company

Question 47

Which of the following is an example of spatial inequality?

○ **A.** In the United States, no one under the age of 18 is allowed to vote.

○ **B.** The western portion of a large city has no major hospitals in it.

○ **C.** Under the Jim Crow laws in the U.S., racial segregation of public spaces was encoded in the law.

○ **D.** Aging professionals have a harder time getting hired by technology companies.

Question 48

Anna grew up in a poor neighborhood in New York City with few good schools. With hard work and studying, she eventually became a successful lawyer. Which of the following best describes Anna's situation before and after becoming a lawyer?

○ **A.** Residential segregation; intergenerational mobility

○ **B.** Residential segregation; intragenerational mobility

○ **C.** Social inequality; intergenerational mobility

○ **D.** Social inequality; intragenerational mobility

Passage 9 (Questions 49-52)

Heather, raised in an upper-middle class household, successfully managed depressive episodes through medication and counseling during post-secondary education. She went on to become successful partner in a law firm. Julia, reared in a blue-collar household, struggled with depression and later, heart palpitations. Unlike Heather, who had more comprehensive insurance coverage, Julia was forced to drop out of college to work as a server in a small restaurant to avoid accruing further debt from medical bills.

Major depressive disorder (MDD) and cardiovascular disease (CVD) are leading burdens of disease worldwide, and there is increasing recognition that the two are related. There is growing evidence to suggest that these negative health outcomes are related to social and economic factors. To investigate this phenomenon, data were collected through self-report using Beck Depression Inventory-II, socioeconomic status, and social cohesion surveys of residents 18 years of age and older from rural areas of Tuanfeng, in central China. Analysis supported the hypothesis that levels of depression were negatively correlated to socioeconomic status and social cohesion.

In another study, researchers investigating the relationship between CVD and MDD revealed that participants with a MDD diagnosis were significantly more at risk for CVD, and that this difference was further pronounced in those with comorbid generalized anxiety. These groups exhibited decreased heart rate variability, a marker of autonomic inflexibility, when compared to non-diagnosed participants.

Important to understanding these differences is the concept of Social Determinants of Health. If social factors are risk factors for poor health, then social inequality represents the "causes of the causes." Social determinants not only contribute to risk and resilience in health, but are also important considerations for interventions beyond the individual. These issues should be addressed not only by those within the health sector and by psychiatrists, but also by intersectoral policy action and government.

Question 49

Which of the following is best illustrated by Julia's, but not Heather's experience?

○ **A.** Social reproduction, in relation to health care costs and insurance

○ **B.** Absolute poverty, in regards to her economic status compared to the upper class

○ **C.** Self-fulfilling prophecy, because Julia maintained her social class

○ **D.** Lack of power, as Julia had decreased access to health care

Question 50

The findings in the passage would be most useful in drawing conclusions about which of the following?

○ **A.** An American woman's risk of cardiovascular disease based on her socioeconomic status

○ **B.** A Chinese woman's risk of generalized anxiety given a prior MDD diagnosis

○ **C.** An American woman's risk of cardiovascular disease based on her HRV

○ **D.** A Chinese woman's risk of MDD given her reported strength of social support network

Question 51

Which of the following statements is least supported by the findings in the passage?

○ **A.** Implementing financial assistance programs in rural China will decrease MDD prevalence in that population.

○ **B.** Sustainable community development projects that increase social cohesion will thereby decrease negative health outcomes.

○ **C.** Lower-class Chinese children are more likely to experience psychiatric illness than those in the middle-class.

○ **D.** A reduction in socioeconomic risk factors for psychiatric illness may reduce CVD prevalence.

Question 52

In Tuanfeng, waste management is handled locally. These positions are held by members of the lower-class who must reside in company housing at the edge of the county, in close proximity to the disposal facilities. This is an example of:

　　I. residential segregation.

　　II. environmental injustice.

　　III. division of labor.

○ **A.** I only

○ **B.** II only

○ **C.** I and II only

○ **D.** I, II, and III

Next ▶

Passage 10 (Questions 53-56)

Studies have shown that negative life events occur more frequently and earlier among those in disadvantaged neighborhoods, and they are powerful potential triggers in producing stress-related health effects. A research group hypothesized that negative life events may be geographically clustered and that these events mediate the relation between neighborhood characteristics and health outcomes. To assess this indirect relationship, a clustered representative sample of Chicago residents (n = 3,105) was analyzed from the Chicago Community Adult Health Survey (CCAHS). The survey elicited individual level data about negative life events, neighborhood conditions, sociodemographics, and health outcomes.

Respondents were asked about their experience of 16 specific negative life events in the last 5 years. Examples of events include a lost job, death of a child, legal trouble, and physical assault. Events were classified as respondent-directed or other-directed (i.e., events that affected the self primarily through their impact on others). The subjects' health outcomes were evaluated by asking them to self-rate overall health, anxiety, and depression. The researchers then modeled paths between different datasets to look at various similarities between groups, correlations between individual-level characteristics and life events, and locations of life events. The results show that the neighborhood characteristic strongly predicts a recent negative life event, and a recent life event strongly predicts the health outcome. By contrast, direct associations of the neighborhood variable with health are smaller.

This passage was adapted from "Negative Life Events Vary by Neighborhood and Mediate the Relation between Neighborhood Context and Psychological Well-Being." King K, Ogle C. *PLoS ONE*. 2014. 9(4) doi: 10.1371/journal.pone.0093539 for use under the terms of the Creative Commons CC BY 4.0 license (https://creativecommons.org/licenses/by/4.0/legalcode).

Question 53

Why would the researchers collect information on the people the participants interact with, in addition to number of life events?

○ **A.** Characteristics of individuals' organizations affect the risk of experiencing a negative life event, and thus it is a source of error.

○ **B.** Characteristics of individuals' networks affect the risk of experiencing a negative life event, and thus it is a source of error.

○ **C.** Characteristics of individuals' organizations affect the risk of experiencing a negative life event, and thus it is a confounding variable.

○ **D.** Characteristics of individuals' networks affect the risk of experiencing a negative life event, and thus it is a confounding variable.

Question 54

Subjects were also asked about levels of anomie. Based on the information in the passage and the principles of strain theory, what responses were most likely?

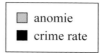

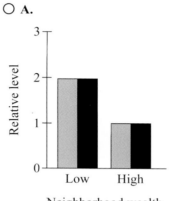

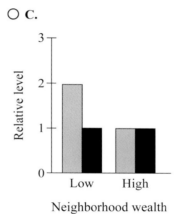
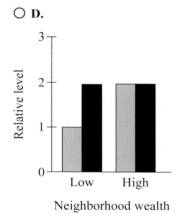

Question 55

The researchers decide to perform case studies on two respondents: a young woman whom belongs to a minority religious group, and an elderly man whom belongs to a major religious group, the LGBT community, and is African-American. What result will they likely find?

○ **A.** Poorer overall health in the female, due to the principle of intersectionality.

○ **B.** Better overall health in the female, due to the principle of intersectionality.

○ **C.** Poorer overall health in the female, because she belongs to a higher socioeconomic status.

○ **D.** Better overall health in the female, because she belongs to a higher socioeconomic status.

Question 56

If this study took place in a society with a caste system, what effect would the life events most likely have on respondents' social mobility?

○ **A.** According to the downward drift hypothesis, the respondents would continually spiral toward worse health.

○ **B.** A caste system is the opposite of a class system, and, thus, life events would have no effect on upward social mobility.

○ **C.** Life events would trigger downward social mobility.

○ **D.** Negative life events would trigger horizontal social mobility.

Questions 57 - 59 do not refer to a passage and are independent of each other.

Question 57

Many women of low socioeconomic status do not have equal access to breast cancer screening and treatment options. This most relates to the concept of:

○ **A.** social capital.

○ **B.** cultural capital.

○ **C.** social reproduction.

○ **D.** social exclusion.

Question 58

Social theorist Karl Marx argued in favor of a collective awareness based on class. The failure to recognize poverty as the product of an oppressive class system has been called:

○ **A.** a class consciousness.

○ **B.** a false consciousness.

○ **C.** absolute poverty.

○ **D.** relative poverty.

Question 59

A family doctor who works for a busy clinic in Los Angeles that caters to a wealthy clientele moves back home to take care of his aging mother in rural Texas, where he opens his own private practice and caters to the needs of an underserved patient population. The social change that the doctor undergoes represents which of the following?

    I. Horizontal mobility

    II. Vertical mobility

   III. Intergenerational mobility

   IV. Intragenerational mobility

○ **A.** I only

○ **B.** II only

○ **C.** I and IV only

○ **D.** II and III only

STOP. If you finish before time is called, check your work. You may go back to any question in this test.

ANSWERS & EXPLANATIONS for Test 1B can be found on p. 166.

LECTURE

Relationships and Behavior

TEST 2A

Time: 95 minutes
Questions 1–59

DIRECTIONS: Most of the questions in this test section are grouped with a passage. Read the passage, then select the best answer to each question. Some questions are independent of any passage and of one another. Select the best answer to each of these questions. If you are unsure of an answer, rule out incorrect choices and select from the remaining options. Indicate your selection beside the option you choose.

Passage 1 (Questions 1-5)

Maladaptive disgust responses are tenacious and resistant to exposure-based interventions.

In a similar vein, laboratory studies have shown that conditioned disgust is relatively insensitive to Conditioned Stimulus (CS)-only extinction procedures. The relatively strong resistance to extinction might be explained by disgust's adaptive function to motivate avoidance from contamination threats (pathogens) that cannot be readily detected and are invisible to the naked eye. Therefore, the mere visual presentation of unreinforced disgust-eliciting stimuli might not be sufficient to correct a previously acquired threat value of the CS.

Researchers tested whether the efficacy of CS-only exposure can be improved by providing additional safety information about the CS. For the CSs, they included two neutral items, a pea soup and a sausage roll, whereas for the Unconditioned Stimulus (US) they used one video clip of a woman vomiting and a neutral one about glass blowing. The additional safety information was conveyed by allowing actual contact with the CS or by observing an actress eating the food items representing the CS. When additional safety information was provided by allowing direct contact with the CS, there was a relatively strong post-extinction increase in participants' willingness to eat the CS. This beneficial effect was still evident at one-week follow up.

Also, self-reported disgust was lower at one-week follow up when additional safety information was provided. The findings help explain why disgust is relatively insensitive to CS-only extinction procedures, and provide helpful starting points to improve interventions that are aimed to reduce distress in disgust-related psychopathology.

This passage was adapted from "Optimising Extinction of Conditioned Disgust." Bosman RC, Borg C, de Jong PJ. *PLoS ONE*. 2016. 11(2) doi:10.1371/journal. pone.0148626 for use under the terms of the Creative Commons CC BY 4.0 license (http://creativecommons.org/licenses/by/4.0/legalcode).

Question 1

Prior to exposure to the unconditioned stimulus, the conditioned response is:

○ **A.** disgust.

○ **B.** a neutral response.

○ **C.** a pathogen.

○ **D.** vomiting.

Question 2

Which of the following techniques could be used to prevent extinction?

○ **A.** Shaping by decreasing exposure to the vomiting video after successive avoidance of the CS.

○ **B.** Shaping by demonstrating appropriate avoidance of the CS.

○ **C.** Modeling by decreasing exposure to the vomiting video after successive avoidance of the CS.

○ **D.** Modeling by demonstrating appropriate avoidance of the CS.

Question 3

The passage focuses on the principles of operant conditioning. Which of the following techniques in operant conditioning can decrease the frequency of a behavior?

  I.   Positive reinforcement

  II. Positive punishment

  III. Negative reinforcement

  IV. Negative punishment

○ **A.** I only

○ **B.** I and II only

○ **C.** II and IV only

○ **D.** I, II, III and IV

Question 4

In a follow up experiment, researchers attempted to condition participants to eat moldy bread. Which of the following is true regarding this experiment?

○ **A.** The behavior would be difficult to condition, and only some participants would be capable.

○ **B.** Pairing the behavior to a non-aversive stimulus would be the least effective means to achieve a response.

○ **C.** The ethics board would never approve of the study.

○ **D.** The behavior could be conditioned, but would dissipate over time due to instinctual drift.

Question 5

In a follow up experiment, researchers assessed the effect of modeling. Which of the following statements is most accurate?

○ **A.** Modeling is a process in associative learning, and it would be important to use the same "model" with each participant.

○ **B.** Modeling is a process in associative learning, and it would be important to use different "models" with each participant.

○ **C.** Modeling is a process in observational learning, and it would be important to use the same "model" with each participant.

○ **D.** Modeling is a process in observational learning, and it would be important to use different "models" with each participant.

Passage 2 (Questions 6-9)

Amyotrophic Lateral Sclerosis (ALS) is a neurodegenerative disease that involves the progressive degeneration of upper and lower motor neurons. ALS has traditionally been considered as a condition affecting exclusively the motor system, with no repercussions on the cognitive domain. However, numerous studies have now challenged this view, demonstrating the presence of significant cognitive impairment, predominantly in the realm of executive functions.

Structural and functional neuroimaging have demonstrated that ALS is associated with abnormalities localized mainly in the frontal lobes. The frontal syndrome that appears to characterize up to 50% of ALS has been noted to be similar to the profile that characterizes patients with frontotemporal dementia (FTD). Moreover, 5–15% of ALS patients develop a full blown FTD.

FTD is characterized by deficits in social cognition and changes in social behavior. Processes of theory of mind (ToM) are now recognized as fundamentally impaired in the disease. ToM can be defined as the ability to attribute mental states such as intentions and beliefs to others in order to understand and predict their behavior and to behave accordingly. It has been recently proposed that the severe social and behavioral problems that often characterize FTD may at least partially be the result of a significant impairment in ToM.

15 patients with ALS were tested using an experimental protocol that distinguishes between private (non-social) intentions and social intentions. The performance of patients with ALS and healthy controls significantly differed on the comprehension of social context only, with an impairment in patients with ALS. Single case analysis confirmed the findings at an individual level. A subset of patients with FTD reported that difficulty in the social domain causes them to be ridiculed by those around them.

This passage was adapted from "Evidence of Social Understanding Impairment in Patients with Amyotrophic Lateral Sclerosis." Cavallo M, Adenzato M, MacPherson SE, Karwig G, Enrici I, et al. *PLoS ONE*. 2011. 6(10). doi:10.1371/journal.pone.0025948 for use under the terms of the Creative Commons CC BY 3.0 license (http://creativecommons.org/licenses/by/3.0/legalcode).

Question 6

One study group hypothesized that mirror neurons in individuals with ALS die as the disease progresses. Which of the following experimental results would validate this hypothesis?

I. When an ALS patient lifts a cup, the neurons do not fire.

II. When an ALS patient watches someone lift a cup, the neurons do not fire.

III. When an ALS patient thinks about lifting a cup, neurons fire but the action cannot be completed.

- A. II only
- B. I and II only
- C. I and III only
- D. I, II and III

Question 7

Patients who struggle with ToM may choose to undergo behavioral therapy in order to improve functioning in social situations. Rewards for improvement in the social domain are sometimes given to these patients after completing a number of tasks, but they never know after which task the reward will be presented. This is an example of:

- A. variable-interval partial reinforcement.
- B. variable-ratio partial reinforcement.
- C. variable-interval continuous reinforcement.
- D. variable-ratio continuous reinforcement.

Question 8

Based on the findings in the last paragraph, if patients stopped putting themselves in social situations, this would best be described as a product of:

- A. positive reinforcement.
- B. negative reinforcement.
- C. positive punishment.
- D. negative punishment.

Question 9

If individuals with social deficits are provided with a rewarding stimulus following the appropriate completion of every social interaction, which of the following is NOT true?

- A. The behavior learned with this type of reinforcement will be most resistant to extinction.
- B. This is the quickest way to establish a behavior.
- C. The reinforcement could be positive or negative.
- D. Providing a stimulus to dictate future behavior is a central tenant of operant conditioning.

Questions 10 - 13 do not refer to a passage and are independent of each other.

Question 10

A patient with chronic back pain comes to the hospital for his weekly injection. His pain lessens at the sight of the needle. How does this relate to classical conditioning?

- ○ **A.** The needle is a conditioned stimulus, and pain relief is a conditioned response.
- ○ **B.** The needle is a neutral stimulus, and pain relief is a conditioned response.
- ○ **C.** The needle is an unconditioned stimulus, and pain relief is an unconditioned response.
- ○ **D.** The needle is a neutral stimulus, and pain relief is an unconditioned response.

Question 11

After Kelly was caught sneaking out of her house to go to a party, her parents decided to make Kelly take out the trash for one week. This is an example of:

- ○ **A.** negative punishment.
- ○ **B.** positive punishment.
- ○ **C.** negative reinforcement.
- ○ **D.** positive reinforcement.

Question 12

A minority patient has been seeing a new Caucasian physician for several visits and has had a negative experience every time. Now this patient refuses to see any Caucasian physicians. This response is likely a result of which kind of learning?

- ○ **A.** Stimulus generalization
- ○ **B.** Classical conditioning
- ○ **C.** Avoidance conditioning
- ○ **D.** Stimulus discrimination

Question 13

Which of the following examples would most likely prove difficult to change via conditioning?

- ○ **A.** An innate drive for a pet to attack upon experiencing a predictive stimulus
- ○ **B.** A behavior taught to a pet through the use of a variable-interval reinforcement schedule
- ○ **C.** A behavior taught to a pet through the use of continuous reinforcement schedule
- ○ **D.** A behavior taught to a pet through the use of a fixed-ratio reinforcement schedule

Passage 3 (Questions 14-16)

Circadian clocks are vital to sleep-wake cycles, mating, hibernation, and seasonal migration. There have been several studies on the role of circadian clocks in the regulation of associative learning and memory processes in both vertebrate and invertebrate species.

Previous results have shown that following differential classical conditioning in the cockroach, in an olfactory discrimination task, formation of short-term and long-term memory is under strict circadian control. In contrast, there appeared to be no circadian regulation of the ability to recall established memories.

Researchers attempted to verify these results with a modified experimental design. Conditioning involved placing animals that had been isolated from food and water for 6–7 days in a cylindrical plastic container with two odor choices on opposite sides of the arena. Peppermint, which is an aversive odor, was associated with a standardized slice of apple as a reward. In subsequent trials, a reduction in the number of visits to vanilla prior to acquiring the apple near the peppermint was taken a measure of learning. The results are summarized in Figure 1.

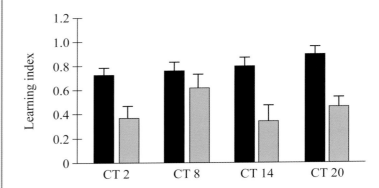

Figure 1 Learning at different circadian times (CT) immediately following training and 48 hours later

This passage was adapted from "Effect of Circadian Phase on Memory Acquisition and Recall: Operant Conditioning vs. Classical Conditioning." Garren MV, Sexauer SB, Page TL. *PLoS ONE*. 2013. 8(3) doi:10.1371/journal.pone.0058693 for use under the terms of the Creative Commons CC BY 3.0 license (http://creativecommons.org/licenses/by/3.0/legalcode).

Question 14

Cockroaches trained during CT8 were:

- ○ **A.** more likely to undergo associative learning than cockroaches trained during CT2.
- ○ **B.** more likely to undergo associative learning than cockroaches trained during CT14.
- ○ **C.** more likely to undergo observational learning than cockroaches trained during CT20.
- ○ **D.** less likely to learn than all other cockroaches.

TEST 2A

Question 15

The timepoint "5 Min" in Figure 1 is indicative of:

○ **A.** acquisition.

○ **B.** extinction.

○ **C.** shaping.

○ **D.** motivation.

Question 16

Which of the following statements is LEAST true concerning associative learning?

○ **A.** Continuous reinforcement allows for rapid learning but also rapid extinction.

○ **B.** Reinforcement schedules can be used to modify learning and extinction rates.

○ **C.** Fixed-interval reinforcement is the most effective reinforcement schedule.

○ **D.** Variable-ratio reinforcement results in slow extinction.

Passage 4 (Questions 17-20)

Environmental cues that are repeatedly paired with drugs develop the ability to produce conditioned responses through associative learning. Drug-associated cues can elicit a variety of responses thought to be relevant for the development of addiction, such as drug craving, physiological arousal, emotional reactivity, and attentional bias. These responses are believed to facilitate drug-seeking behavior in drug-dependent populations and elicit relapse in recently abstinent individuals. Conditioned drug responses have been demonstrated in human drug users for several substances, including methamphetamine, nicotine, alcohol, and cocaine.

Strengthening associations

One factor thought to contribute to the strength of conditioning is the number of conditioning trials. This has been observed in humans using cues paired with either food or drug rewards. For example, in non-dependent daily cigarette smokers, more pairings between an auditory cue (a neutral tone) and smoking resulted in a greater urge to smoke and larger changes in physiological measures, such as heart rate and blood pressure, in response to the cue. Similarly, in non-dependent daily cigarette smokers, an increased number of training sessions between neutral tones paired with smoking cigarettes resulted in greater preference for the tones than fewer training sessions.

De novo associations

When studying populations with an established history of drug use, researchers have little control over participants' previous drug exposures, their associated cues and contexts, or the memories related to the drug using experience. Studies with healthy volunteers address some of these problems. A recent study examined the acquisition of *de novo* drug-cue associations in healthy young adults. This procedure involved pairing neutral audio-visual cues with either methamphetamine (MA; 20 mg oral) or placebo (PBO), two times each. Methamphetamine was chosen as the drug because it has been shown to reliably elicit positive mood ratings. Conditioning was measured with assessments of behavioral preference, attentional bias, emotional reactivity towards the MA-paired cue, and subjective "liking" of the cue. Conditioned responses were detected on all measures except cue "liking."

This passage was adapted from "Acquisition of Conditioning between Methamphetamine and Cues in Healthy Humans." Cavallo JS, Mayo LM, de Wit H. 2016. *PLoS ONE* 11(8). doi:10.1371/journal.pone.0161541 for use under the terms of the Creative Commons CC BY 4.0 license. (https://creativecommons.org/licenses/by/4.0/legalcode)

Question 17

The studies mentioned in paragraph 2 examine which process of associative learning?

○ **A.** Extinction

○ **B.** Acquisition

○ **C.** Spontaneous recovery

○ **D.** Stimulus generalization

Question 18

During the course of the study mentioned in paragraph 3, the audio-visual cue acts:

- ○ **A.** first as an unconditioned stimulus, then as a conditioned stimulus.
- ○ **B.** first as a conditioned stimulus, then as an unconditioned stimulus.
- ○ **C.** first as a neutral stimulus, then as a conditioned stimulus.
- ○ **D.** first as a neutral stimulus, then as an unconditioned stimulus.

Question 19

Which piece of information, if shown to be true, would best support the hypothesis presented in paragraph 1?

- ○ **A.** Individuals in a weight-loss study who are placed on a strict diet report higher desire to break from their diet after being presented with a slideshow of fast-food logos.
- ○ **B.** A week into a smoking cessation program that relies on exposure to graphic anti-tobacco ad campaigns, participants drastically decreased the average number of cigarettes smoked per day.
- ○ **C.** Students in a community with a high rate of methamphetamine use are shown to be more susceptible than peers from other areas to methamphetamine addiction.
- ○ **D.** Individuals in an alcohol rehabilitation program experience headaches and trembling hands within one week of abstinence from alcohol.

Question 20

Past studies involving addiction have relied mostly on populations with an established history of drug use. When using healthy young adults to study *de novo* associations as described in paragraph 3, the researchers may be:

- ○ **A.** decreasing the external validity for studying the unconditioned response.
- ○ **B.** decreasing the internal validity for studying stimulus generalization.
- ○ **C.** minimizing the confounding effects of spontaneous recovery.
- ○ **D.** controlling for other variables to study the effects of stimulus discrimination.

Passage 5 (Questions 21-25)

A study was designed to assess the effect of gene knockout for NMDA receptors (*NR1*) in the midbrain on the conditioned response to smoking stimuli. Nicotine from smoking tobacco produces one of the most common forms of addictive behavior and has major societal and health consequences. It is a well-documented phenomenon that, in the process of quitting smoking, smokers are challenged by the urge to smoke at certain times of the day and at certain locations. An example of a location could be when they pass a particular road on their ride home. This concept was assessed in a mouse model.

The knockouts were created and assessed for conditioned place preference (CPP). The CPP test utilizes two chambers: one preferred and one non-preferred. Due to their natural tendency to avoid bright environments, mice showed significant initial preference for the dark chamber (Figure 1). To induce conditioned place preference, mice from the mutant and control groups were all injected with either nicotine or with saline and then placed in one of the two chambers. Nicotine injections were paired with the non-preferred chamber and saline injections were paired with the preferred chamber. After four days of conditioning, during which mice were given one injection of nicotine and one injection of saline each day, CPP was tested on the fifth day. Each mouse was allowed to move freely between all the chambers. The results are summarized in Figure 1.

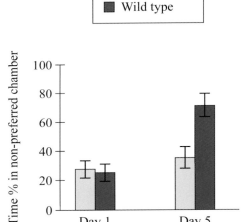

Figure 1 CPP in knockout and wild type mice

Question 21

The first paragraph mentions a type of learning known as:

- ○ **A.** classical conditioning.
- ○ **B.** kinesthetic learning.
- ○ **C.** observational learning.
- ○ **D.** operant conditioning.

Question 22

Which of the following would be considered a neutral stimulus for a smoker whom shows CPP?

- ○ **A.** A bar
- ○ **B.** A car
- ○ **C.** A smokers' lounge
- ○ **D.** The shower

Question 23

Which of the following is absent in the knockout mice?

- ○ **A.** The unconditioned stimulus
- ○ **B.** The conditioned stimulus
- ○ **C.** The unconditioned response
- ○ **D.** The conditioned response

Question 24

In another experiment, researchers assessed the processes of operant conditioning. The wild type mice were conditioned to develop an addiction to nicotine, but then the nicotine dose was increased to a level believed to induce nausea. This would result in:

- ○ **A.** addiction.
- ○ **B.** acquisition.
- ○ **C.** extinction.
- ○ **D.** recovery.

Question 25

Other than the *NR1* gene, knockout mice and wild type mice were not genetically identical. Which of the following biases may have been present in the research design?

- ○ **A.** A lack of internal validity, because the study could not be applied to humans.
- ○ **B.** A lack of external validity, because the mice likely were euthanized.
- ○ **C.** A predisposition to publication bias, because there is a greater likelihood for statistical significance.
- ○ **D.** A potential for confirmation bias, because other genes may have been involved.

Questions 26 - 29 do not refer to a passage and are independent of each other.

Question 26

A woman cries during a sad scene in a movie. She is experiencing:

- ○ **A.** observational learning.
- ○ **B.** an innate behavior.
- ○ **C.** vicarious emotions.
- ○ **D.** depression.

Question 27

A child is very bothered by the itchiness of a wool sweater, but after wearing it for an hour she no longer notices the discomfort. This is called:

- ○ **A.** sensitization.
- ○ **B.** habitation.
- ○ **C.** dishabituation.
- ○ **D.** learning.

Question 28

Although considered inappropriate in present society, aggression is an important evolutionary trait. Which of the following graphs likely depicts the relationship between aggression and survival?

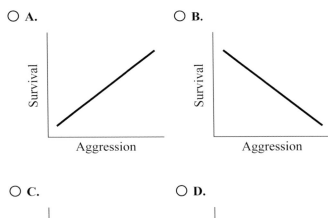

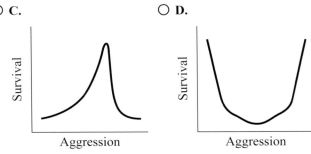

Question 29

Our prehuman ancestors relied on the formation of social groups for all of the following EXCEPT:

○ **A.** grooming.

○ **B.** mating.

○ **C.** defense.

○ **D.** foraging.

Passage 6 (Questions 30-34)

Adolescence (10–19 years old) is a critical period of rapid physical and psychosocial changes. It is also during adolescence that sex-differential mortality and morbidity patterns begin to emerge. For girls pregnancy complications associated with early pregnancy, childbearing and unsafe abortion, HIV/AIDS and infectious diseases all account for significant mortality. Adolescent boys engage in more health harming behaviors than girls such as early and heavy smoking, alcohol and illicit drug use and are more likely than girls to engage in early and unprotected sexual behaviors.

While there are many factors that explain sex differentials in mortality and morbidity, a key determinant is gender inequality. Gender inequalities manifest in different ways, such as unequal access to resources, power, education and discriminatory socio-cultural practices. While gender inequalities affect the lives of both boys and girls, generally they disproportionately disadvantage girls. At the root of many gender inequalities are gender norms that prescribe different status, power and opportunities to girls and boys according to culturally appropriate versions of masculinities and femininities. These gender norms shape the way adolescents interact, form relationships, and engage in sexual and reproductive practices as well as most all social behaviors.

Global data indicate that gender norms are commonly reflected in adolescents' personal gender attitudes. Studies conducted with young men from low- to middle-income countries (LMICs) further reflect the complexity of gender attitudes where some might eschew harmful gender discriminatory practices but at the same time endorse unequal gender division of labor in the household or other inequitable gender norms. Gender attitudes that endorse norms that perpetuate gender inequality are thought to be harmful to both boys and girls. Among young men, endorsement of stereotypical masculinity norms prescribing male dominance and toughness have been associated with substance use, violence and delinquency, and lower male engagement in caregiving and household chores.

This passage was adapted from "Understanding Factors that Shape Gender Attitudes in Early Adolescence Globally: A Mixed-Methods Systematic Review." Kagesten A, Gibbs S, Blum RW, Moreau C, Chandra-Mouli V, et al. *PLoS One*. 2016. 11(6) doi:10.1371/journal.pone.0157805 for use under the terms of the Creative Commons CC BY 4.0 license (http://creativecommons.org/licenses/by/4.0/legalcode).

Question 30

According to information contained in the passage, which of the following social behaviors is less likely to be displayed by boys from LMIC than high income countries?

○ **A.** Aggression

○ **B.** Altruism

○ **C.** Mate choice

○ **D.** Attachment

Question 31

Attractiveness would NOT be displayed through which of the following nonverbal communications?

- ○ **A.** Hand-holding
- ○ **B.** Smiling
- ○ **C.** Light touch
- ○ **D.** Words expressing love and support

Question 32

Which of the following changes to the culture of LMICs would likely help reduce gender discriminatory practices through observational learning?

- ○ **A.** Male members of older generations begin involving women in making household decisions and support their desire for education.
- ○ **B.** Male members of older generations tell their sons to treat their spouses with more respect.
- ○ **C.** The government mandates a particular percentage of jobs be filled by female applicants.
- ○ **D.** Laws banning domestic abuse are strengthened and more commonly enforced.

Question 33

One method of reducing harmful male behavior discussed in paragraph one is to provide payments for each month that the boys screen negative for drug use. This is an example of:

- ○ **A.** fixed-ratio reinforcement.
- ○ **B.** variable-ratio reinforcement.
- ○ **C.** fixed-interval reinforcement.
- ○ **D.** variable-interval reinforcement.

Question 34

Which of the following studies would best determine the societal influences that impact gender discrimination and unequal division of labor?

- ○ **A.** A longitudinal questionnaire of 10 males over a 30-year period that asked questions about their views of female participation in the workforce.
- ○ **B.** A case-control study of 100 males and 100 females in high- and low-income countries where half of each of the study population is provided education about the benefits of gender equality.
- ○ **C.** A cross-sectional survey of 250 males and 300 females about their participation in various aspects of civil and professional life.
- ○ **D.** A longitudinal questionnaire of 300 women about their role in child-rearing responsibilities.

Passage 7 (Questions 35-38)

Are people more selfish if they can passively allow for a selfish allocation of resources, rather than actively having to implement it? This question speaks to a variety of different choice situations, as decisions about resource allocation often vary by whether they require active involvement or not.

People may be more likely to walk by a charity solicitor on the street than to refuse to give to a solicitor whom knocks on their door. An employer may passively allow for inflation to erode workers' real wages, even if she would not be willing to actively cut nominal wages. Citizens face governmental policies about redistributive matters that vary by the involvement they require, such as whether being an organ donor requires active registration or not, or whether declarations of taxable income require more or less active statements.

Researchers investigated whether individuals are more prone to act selfishly if they can passively allow for an outcome to be implemented (omission) rather than having to make an active choice (commission). In most settings, active and passive choice alternatives differ in terms of factors such as the presence of a suggested option, costs of taking an action, and awareness.

The experiment was a binary trade-off game where the participant has the choice of giving $15 to the subject and $1.5 to the recipient (the selfish choice) or giving $10 to each the subject and the recipient (the fair choice). Subjects are randomized to omission or commission groups where the omission group is further randomized to a fair default or a selfish default. In this paradigm, 43.8% of the commission group and 63.7% of the omission group favored the selfish choice. The results were not statistically significant.

This passage was adapted from "Is There an Omission Effect in Prosocial Behavior? A Laboratory Experiment on Passive vs. Active Generosity." Gartner M, Sandberg A. *PLoS ONE*. 2017. 12(3) doi:10.1371/journal.pone.0172496 for use under the terms of the Creative Commons CC BY 4.0 license (http://creativecommons.org/licenses/by/4.0/legalcode).

Question 35

How does the concept of inclusive fitness relate to the findings in the study?

- ○ **A.** The fair choice benefits both groups, since more money is earned.
- ○ **B.** The selfish choice benefits both groups, since more money is earned.
- ○ **C.** The commission group is evolutionarily more prone to altruistic behavior.
- ○ **D.** The omission group is evolutionarily more prone to altruistic behavior.

Question 36

In many countries, the concept of sharing is deeply ingrained in citizens. This is a(n):

○ A. means of promoting capitalism.

○ B. example of socialism.

○ C. mechanism of informal social control.

○ D. type of free will.

Question 37

Under the dramaturgical approach, a selfish participant would:

○ A. present his back-stage self when asked if he made the fair or selfish choice.

○ B. present his front-stage self when asked if he made the fair or selfish choice.

○ C. utilize impression management to ensure others did not think he was selfish.

○ D. utilize nonverbal communication to convey his behaviors.

Question 38

Which of the following biases may have resulted in poor generalizability of this study?

○ A. Acquiescence bias

○ B. Confirmation bias

○ C. Social desirability bias

○ D. Sponsor bias

Passage 8 (Questions 39-43)

Smoking is one of the leading preventable causes of early death, disease and disability. In addition, smoking is a major contributor to socioeconomic inequalities in health since smoking-attributed mortality accounts for more than a half of the difference in mortality rates between social strata in middle age. Smoking is typically taken up in adolescence, and early nicotine exposure directly increases risks of later nicotine dependence. Given that the major risk period for smoking initiation is mostly over by the age of twenty, understanding how environmental and individual risk factors contribute to smoking initiation in adolescence is a crucial step in designing appropriate intervention and prevention strategies.

Among environmental factors, socioeconomic status (SES), a combination of factors including income, education and occupation, have been shown to impact health due to lifestyle choices. For example, smoking is more common among people of lower education and lower SES levels. Crucially, while smoking rates among adults and adolescents are in decline in many western countries, these changes do not occur equally across different socioeconomic levels. Adults with at least some college education had a significantly greater decline in smoking prevalence than those whose highest level of education is high school or less. Among individual factors, personality traits described by the Five Factor Model (FFM), have been associated with a variety of health behaviors, including smoking. A study conducted on an elderly population showed that current smokers had higher levels of neuroticism, and lower levels of agreeableness and conscientiousness than former smokers, and those who never smoked had lowest levels of neuroticism and highest levels of agreeableness and conscientiousness of all groups. Higher openness and higher neuroticism have been associated with lifetime-smoking, and higher conscientiousness appears to protect against smoking progression and persistence in adults.

This passage was adapted from "The Associations of Personality Traits and Parental Education with Smoking Behaviour Among Adolescents." Yanez A, Leiva A, Estela A, and Cukic I. *PLoS ONE*. 2017. 12(3) doi:10.1371/journal.pone.0174211 for use under the terms of the Creative Commons CC BY 4.0 license (http://creativecommons.org/licenses/by/4.0/legalcode).

Question 39

Excess consumption of alcohol, similar to smoking, can result in significant long-term health consequences. Disulfiram, a medication used to treat alcoholism by inducing vomiting upon alcohol consumption, most likely works through:

○ A. classical conditioning.

○ B. operant conditioning.

○ C. extinction.

○ D. spontaneous recovery.

Question 40

Individuals from low SES who are reimbursed by their health insurance companies when they do not test positive for nicotine are likely receiving a:

- ○ **A.** reward.
- ○ **B.** punishment.
- ○ **C.** secondary reinforcement.
- ○ **D.** primary reinforcement.

Question 41

When reviewing the results of the study conducted in the elderly population, a graduate student identifies with feelings of loneliness and hopelessness described by the study participants. The student is exemplifying:

- ○ **A.** modeling.
- ○ **B.** observational learning.
- ○ **C.** vicarious emotions.
- ○ **D.** nonverbal communication.

Question 42

A recent study showed that consumption of cigarettes may be higher among officials in countries that outlaw smoking compared to officials in other countries. The increased rate of smoking may be a result of:

- ○ **A.** the iron law of oligarchy.
- ○ **B.** formal organization.
- ○ **C.** perspectives on bureaucracy.
- ○ **D.** characteristics of an ideal bureaucracy.

Question 43

Which of the following studies would have best identified individuals most at risk for addictive smoking behavior?

- ○ **A.** A cross-sectional survey that identified individuals that are most likely to use opioid drugs.
- ○ **B.** A longitudinal survey that tracks use of alcohol over time.
- ○ **C.** An interventional trial that tested a novel anti-drug abuse medication.
- ○ **D.** A survey that identified individuals at risk for self-esteem and body image difficulties.

Questions 44 - 47 do not refer to a passage and are independent of each other.

Question 44

A patient describes her workplace as an organization. Which of the following characteristics is most likely true of this patient's workplace?

- ○ **A.** The workplace employs over 20 members.
- ○ **B.** Members of the workplace share a common goal.
- ○ **C.** The workplace is registered with 3 governmental organizations.
- ○ **D.** The employee handbook places a particular emphasis on workplace efficiency.

Question 45

Which of the following is LEAST likely to occur within a bureaucracy?

- ○ **A.** Methods to remove the bureaucracy's "higher-ups" are excessively convoluted and difficult to enact.
- ○ **B.** The hierarchical nature is removed in order to better execute the bureaucracy's goals.
- ○ **C.** Employee training emphasizes leaving emotion out of bureaucratic decisions.
- ○ **D.** The bureaucracy's employees rank efficiency as their number one priority.

Question 46

Which of the following changes is least consistent with becoming a more ideal bureaucracy?

- ○ **A.** The purchase of 100 potted plants to increase employee morale
- ○ **B.** Preventing store managers from making decisions on bathroom sizes
- ○ **C.** Promoting regional managers to the same level as marketing specialists with respect to advertisement decisions
- ○ **D.** Redirecting sponsorship money from a national sports team to numerous local teams

Question 47

Dogs must differentially interpret which of the following nonverbal communications that has a different meaning in animals than humans?

- ○ **A.** Showing teeth
- ○ **B.** Ovulatory pheromones
- ○ **C.** Head tilt
- ○ **D.** Playing fetch

Passage 9 (Questions 48-51)

The directionality and mutuality of friendship ties is not always clear, which can significantly limit the ability of individuals to engage effectively in situations where cooperation is essential to success. A student can rate an individual highly as a friend while their "friend" might rate them as an acquaintance. As peer-support programs emerge as a highly effective and empowering tool to change an individual's behavior in various domains including smoking cessation, weight loss, diabetes management or alcohol misuse, the potential shortcomings of perceived social connections should be investigated.

A study was designed to examine the ability of students to comprehend the reciprocity of friendships. Students that were enrolled in an applied management course were instructed to complete a self-report survey. The survey asked participants to score every other participant using a numerical scale with 0 being "I do not know this person" and 5 being "one of my best friends." Data on overlapping social groups was also collected as a "mutuality variable". Figure 1 shows the statistical trend resulting from the mutuality variable. Mutuality is a measurement of mutual friends amongst individuals. As the value of mutuality increases, the total number of mutual friends amongst participants increases as well. The probability of a reciprocal tie refers to the chance of two students rating one another similarly on the survey.

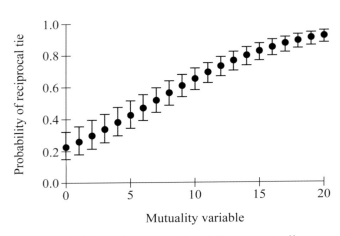

Figure 1 Probability of reciprocal in relation to mutuality

This passage was adapted from "Are You Your Friends' Friend? Poor Perception of Friendship Ties Limits the Ability to Promote Behavioral Change." Almaatouq A, Radaelli L, Pentland A, Shmueli E. *PLoS ONE*. 2016.11(3) doi: 10.1371/journal. pone.0151588 for use under the terms of the Creative Commons CC BY 4.0 license (https://creativecommons.org/licenses/by/4.0/legalcode).

Question 48

In the context of this investigation, an individual listing another as "one of my best friends" would primarily see him or her as a member of a:

- **A.** microsociological primary social group.
- **B.** microsociological secondary social group.
- **C.** macrosociological primary social group.
- **D.** macrosociological secondary social group.

Question 49

To enhance his or her rating on the survey, an individual would utilize which of the following techniques?

- **A.** Impression management
- **B.** A dramaturgical approach
- **C.** Use of a backstage self
- **D.** Group polarization

Question 50

Suppose the researchers were only interested in the survey data produced by two individuals rating one another on the survey. What type of microsociological grouping would the researchers utilize and would the use of self report impact the final data collected amongst these smaller groups?

- **A.** A dyad and the use of self report would have impacted the accuracy of the data via observer bias.
- **B.** A triad and the use of self report would have impacted the accuracy of the data via observer bias.
- **C.** A dyad and the use of self report would have impacted the accuracy of the data via subject bias.
- **D.** No microsociological grouping and self report would have no impact upon the final results.

Question 51

Suppose two individuals rated one another highly on the survey but possessed few mutual friends. Which image best illustrates the location of this data point in Figure 1?

○ **A.**

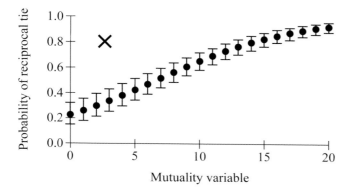

○ **B.**

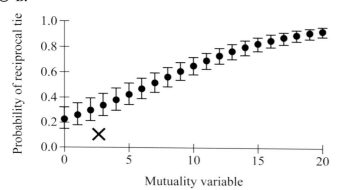

○ **C.**

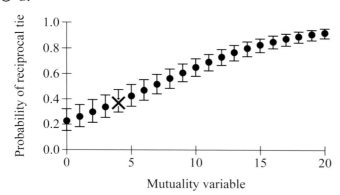

○ **D.**

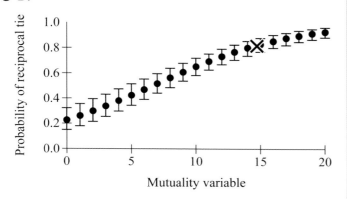

Passage 10 (Questions 52-55)

Dishonest behavior amongst medical students is an ongoing threat to medical education. Medical schools combat this problem by requiring identification prior to exams, limiting the number of students allowed out of the room during exams, and having "secret shopper" students whom inform professors of any observed cheating.

Recent empirical evidence shows that working in an unsupervised, isolated situation under competition can promote dishonest behavior. However, could working in a common space in the presence of colleagues affect cheating? Researchers examined how familiar-peer influence, supervision, and social incentives affect worker performance and dishonest behavior.

First, researchers investigated if working in the presence of peers is an effective mechanism to constrain dishonest behavior compared to an isolated work situation (Experiment 1). Second, researchers found that the mere suspicion that another peer is cheating is not enough to increase individual cheating behavior to the level seen in an isolated situation (Experiment 2). This would suggest that reputation holds great importance in a student's self-image and acts as a strong social incentive. Third, researchers showed that when the suspicion of dishonesty increases with multiple peers behaving dishonestly, the desire to increase social standing is sufficient to nudge individuals' behavior back to cheating at the same levels as in isolated situations (Experiment 3).

This passage was adapted from "Peer Effects in Unethical Behavior: Standing or Reputation?" Pascual-Ezama D, Dunfield D, Gil-Gómez de Liaño B, Prelec D. *PLoS ONE*. 2015. 10(4) doi:10.1371/journal.pone.0122305 for use under the terms of the Creative Commons CC BY 4.0 license (http://creativecommons.org/licenses/by/4.0/legalcode).

Question 52

The description of peer influence (final paragraph) suggests that cheating behavior is most influenced by which of the following principles?

○ **A.** Social facilitation and obedience

○ **B.** Stigma and de-individualization

○ **C.** The bystander effect and conformity

○ **D.** Social loafing and social control

Question 53

A participant in the experiments grew up in a lower class neighborhood. His upbringing determines his:

○ **A.** embodied status.

○ **B.** ascribed status.

○ **C.** achieved status.

○ **D.** master status.

Question 54

A medical student struggling to maintain his or her grades is experiencing:

○ **A.** role conflict.

○ **B.** role strain.

○ **C.** role exit.

○ **D.** role clarity.

Question 55

Which of the following types of social support is most relevant to a medical student seeking a mentor for career counseling?

○ **A.** Emotional support

○ **B.** Tangible support

○ **C.** Informational support

○ **D.** Companionship support

Questions 56 - 59 do not refer to a passage and are independent of each other.

Question 56

Recent studies indicate that pregnancy and parturition lead to changes in the brain that impair recognition of social cues. Which of the following may be a confounding variable in this experiment?

○ **A.** Education level

○ **B.** Use of exogenous hormones

○ **C.** Age of participants

○ **D.** Score on measure of expression interpretation

Question 57

A woman hopes to elevate her status in her group of friends. Which of the following would be most effective?

○ **A.** Bake cookies for her friends.

○ **B.** Plan a trip to the Caribbean.

○ **C.** Get married.

○ **D.** Have a pool installed at her home.

Question 58

Casey decided to adopt her nephew after his parents passed away. This behavior can best be described as:

○ **A.** inclusive fitness.

○ **B.** social support.

○ **C.** reproductive success.

○ **D.** mating behavior.

Question 59

Which of the following is least advantageous to the individual?

○ **A.** Attraction

○ **B.** Altruism

○ **C.** Attachment

○ **D.** Aggression

STOP. If you finish before time is called, check your work. You may go back to any question in this test.

ANSWERS & EXPLANATIONS for Test 2A can be found on p. 194.

Relationships and Behavior

TEST 2B

Time: 95 minutes
Questions 1–59

DIRECTIONS: Most of the questions in this test section are grouped with a passage. Read the passage, then select the best answer to each question. Some questions are independent of any passage and of one another. Select the best answer to each of these questions. If you are unsure of an answer, rule out incorrect choices and select from the remaining options. Indicate your selection beside the option you choose.

Passage 1 (Questions 1-4)

Previous research has documented social contagion in obesity-related health behaviors, but less is known about the social processes underlying these patterns. Given these relationships are strongest among married partners, survey data was collected from spouses answering on behalf of themselves and their partners in order to explore potential social mechanisms influencing obesity. Values are reported in Table 1.

Table 1 Sample Characteristics for Partnered Adults (n = 215)

Obesity-related variables	Respondent average value	Partner average value
Body measurements		
Body mass index (BMI)	27.53	28.85
Ideal body size*	3.67	—
Current body size*	—	4.67
Obesity-related behaviors		
Physical activity**	2.83	3.04
Produce consumption***	3.42	3.06
Fast food consumption****	4.98	5.73

*Based on Collins Adult Scale; **days/week; ***times/day; ****days/month

Significant correlations between respondent and partner BMI indicated body congruence within marital partnerships. A potential mechanism for the above-mentioned congruence is that respondents are influenced by their partners' behaviors. Statistical analyses revealed partners' exercise habits were significantly and positively related to that of the respondents, and standardized partner fast food consumption was a positive significant predictor of respondent fast food consumption. A positive significant correlation was also found between respondents' labels of themselves and their partners as "athlete" or "non-athlete." Results controlled for health, socioeconomic status, and education.

Partner convergence may also occur via the normative body size hypothesis, wherein a partner's body size influences the respondent's behaviors and ideal body size. The effects of partner body size on respondent's produce consumption were nonsignificant. Although partner body size did achieve significance in predicting the number of respondent visits to fast food restaurants, partner fast food consumption was a significantly larger predictor of this than partner body size. To provide an additional test of the normative body size hypothesis, the effects of partner body size and partner BMI on respondents' ideal body size were tested. Neither partner body size nor partner BMI were significantly associated with respondent ideal body size.

This passage was adapted from "Partner Influence in Diet and Exercise Behaviors: Testing Behavior Modeling, Social Control, and Normative Body Size." Perry B, Ciciurkaite G, Brady CF, Garcia J. *PLoS ONE*. 2016. 11(12) doi: 10.1371/journal.pone.0169193 for use under the terms of the Creative Commons CC BY 4.0 license (https://creativecommons.org/licenses/by/4.0/legalcode).

Question 1

The results from the passage best support which of the following conclusions?

- ○ **A.** Married couples engage in the same obesity-related health behaviors.
- ○ **B.** Body congruence within marital partnerships is due to partners influencing each others' health-related behaviors.
- ○ **C.** A high degree of behavioral social contagion is present within marital partnerships.
- ○ **D.** A behavior modeling mechanism may explain obesity-related health behaviors among married partners.

Question 2

Which of the following additions to a respondent and his/her partner would best allow for the formation of a triadic group?

- ○ **A.** A lifelong friend of both the respondent and partner
- ○ **B.** The respondent's father
- ○ **C.** A long-time neighbor of both the respondent and partner
- ○ **D.** A co-worker of both the respondent and partner

Question 3

Mating behavior theory would suggest that respondents are likely to choose partners labelled as an "athlete" because:

- ○ **A.** Athletes are likely to look attractive and will thus receive more attention from respondents.
- ○ **B.** Athletes are subconsciously perceived as being more capable than non-athletes in protecting the respondent and potential offspring.
- ○ **C.** The label may be a proxy by which the respondent can assess the genetic makeup and prospective parenting ability of the partner.
- ○ **D.** Mass media outlets favorably portray the "athletic build" as opposed to a "non-athletic build."

Question 4

Which of the following behaviors, if reported by a respondent in survey data, could best be described as a sanction?

- ○ **A.** A respondent refused to speak to his/her partner.
- ○ **B.** A respondent purposely chooses to not work out with his/her partner.
- ○ **C.** Every time his/her partner exercises, the respondent also chooses to exercise.
- ○ **D.** A respondent smiled at his/her partner in recognizing that they returned from the gym.

Passage 2 (Questions 5-8)

Elderly populations are particularly susceptible to functional disability (FD), which is characterized by an inability to perform day-to-day activities without long-term assistance. While research has shown exercise to be an effective way to prevent FD in an aging population, it is unclear whether getting exercise from a sports organization yields the same preventative utility as does exercising alone. In addition to the physiological benefits of exercising, social networks and social support, which have been linked to improved health outcomes, are more easily obtained through joining an organization.

Researchers investigated factors associated with FD by analyzing responses to self-reported questionnaires mailed to individuals aged 65 years or older. Of the six included municipalities, a random sampling method was used in the two larger municipalities while a complete census was used in the four smaller municipalities. Individuals introduced to the study were followed for a 4-year period.

Based on questionnaire responses, subjects were split into 4 groups. Subjects not participating in a sports organization were classified either as "Exercise Alone" (EA) if they exercised more than once-a-month or as "Sedentary" (S) if they exercised once-a-month or less. Subjects participating in a sports organization were classified as either an "Active Participant" (AP) or a "Passive Participant" (PP) based on the same exercise frequency criteria that were used for the non-participants.

Cox's proportional hazards model was used to calculate the hazard ratio (HR) of FD over 4 years. The HR is defined as the ratio of the probability of developing a FD within a particular group compared to that of a reference group. There were 1,888 subjects (16.3%) in the AP group, 2,548 subjects (22.0%) in the EA group, 447 subjects (3.9%) in the PP group and 6,698 subjects (57.8%) in the S group. Mean age was lowest in the AP group and highest in the S group, with a difference of 2.8 years. Ten times more people in the PP group exercised once-a-month compared to the S group. 34% of the AP group and 20% of the PP group reported wearing some aspect of an organization uniform.

Setting the AP group's HR as reference (1.00), the EA group and the S group displayed significantly higher HR levels than that of the AP group's, at 1.29 and 1.65, respectively. No significant difference from reference was seen in the PP group.

This passage was adapted from "Participation in Sports Organizations and the Prevention of Functional Disability in Older Japanese: The AGES Cohort Study." Kanamori S, Kai Y, Kondo K, Hirai H, Ichida Y et al. *PLoS ONE*. 2012. 7(11) doi: 10.1371/journal.pone.0051061 for use under the terms of the Creative Commons CC BY 3.0 license (http://creativecommons.org/licenses/by/3.0/legalcode).

Question 5

Researchers would classify the relationships between the subjects within the AP and PP groups as part of a:

- ○ **A.** primary group.
- ○ **B.** secondary group.
- ○ **C.** social network.
- ○ **D.** group.

Question 6

Which piece of information would most support the conclusion that, in relation to the EA group, the AP group should have had a higher HR than was reported in paragraph 5?

- ○ **A.** Nearly twice the people in the EA group exercised almost every day compared to the AP group.
- ○ **B.** The AP group included 16.3% of subjects, while the EA group included 22.0% of subjects.
- ○ **C.** Subjects in the EA group were already predisposed to a functional disability.
- ○ **D.** Subjects in the AP group and the EA group performed different exercises.

Question 7

Based on the result described in paragraph 4, which of the following study follow-ups could the researchers undertake to assess the appearance of a fad?

- ○ **A.** Ask members of the AP group the length of time that they wore a uniform.
- ○ **B.** Ask members of both the PP and AP groups what aspects of an organization uniform they wore.
- ○ **C.** Ask members of the PP group when they started and stopped wearing a uniform.
- ○ **D.** Ask members of both the PP and AP groups why they wore a uniform.

Question 8

A coach of a sports team is likely to exhibit role exit due to:

    I. choosing not to play his/her best friend due to the friend's lack of athletic ability.

    II. persistent pressure on the coach to win games.

    III. a lucrative offer to coach for a different team.

- ○ **A.** I only
- ○ **B.** II only
- ○ **C.** I and II only
- ○ **D.** I, II, and III

Questions 9 - 12 do not refer to a passage and are independent of each other.

Question 9

Which of the following observations of a sports organization would be consistent with the iron law of oligarchy?

- ○ **A.** The organization owners begin to enforce rules more strictly.
- ○ **B.** Methods to replace upper management become excessively burdensome.
- ○ **C.** Members of the organization quit due to disagreements with the owners.
- ○ **D.** The sports organization merges with two other sports organizations.

Question 10

A recent study showed that football players tend to perform better during games than during practice. This is likely due to:

- ○ **A.** social facilitation.
- ○ **B.** social loafing.
- ○ **C.** group polarization.
- ○ **D.** peer pressure.

Question 11

A recent riot in a Midatlantic city in the United States is estimated to have cost nearly $9 million. Which of the following contributes to the behavior of participants in riots?

- ○ **A.** Bystander effect
- ○ **B.** Deindividuation
- ○ **C.** Inclusive fitness
- ○ **D.** Self-presentation

Question 12

Which of the following best demonstrates the violation of a folkway?

- ○ **A.** A man boarding an uncrowded bus sits directly next to another passenger.
- ○ **B.** Two people engage in an incestuous relationship.
- ○ **C.** John is the only person in his neighborhood that does not practice recycling.
- ○ **D.** A group of students arrives late to a school function.

Passage 3 (Questions 13-16)

Diabetes Mellitus (DM) patients tend to show a low adherence rate to non-pharmacological (diet and physical exercise) and pharmacological treatments (insulin and/or oral anti-diabetic medication) aimed at maintaining metabolic control. Clinical-metabolic control includes blood glucose, blood pressure, and cholesterol control. Studies suggest that social support (SS) may be associated with treatment adherence. SS involves individuals and their social networks that help to satisfy their needs and provide resources.

Study 1 analyzed perceived social support of 162 patients with type 2 diabetes mellitus. 58% of participants were women and 42% were men. 70.4% were married. 70% were overweight, and 35.5% practiced regular physical activity. Participants were asked to fill out the Social Support Network Inventory to assess type of social network and perceived social support. High levels of perceived SS were observed, with relatives as the main source, followed by health professionals and support groups. No significant differences were found in mean SS with regard to gender or marital status. Patients who were part of a support group had higher perceived SS.

Study 2 used the same sample population but analyzed the relationship among social support, adherence to both types of treatment, and metabolic control. Participants filled out the Diabetes Self-care Activities Questionnaire to assess adherence to diet and exercise recommendations and the Morisky Test to assess medication treatment adherence. Social support was directly correlated with adherence to both types of treatment. Patients who were part of a support group showed significantly higher treatment adherence than those not part of a support group. Adherence to diet and exercise was lower than medication adherence on average and was inversely correlated with body mass index (BMI). Medication adherence was inversely correlated with blood pressure. No correlations were observed between blood glucose control and adherence variables.

This passage was adapted from "Relationships among social support, treatment adherence and metabolic control of diabetes mellitus patients." Gomez-Villas Boas L C, Foss M C, Foss de Freitas M C, Pace A E. *Revista Latino-Americana de Enfermagem.* 2012. 20(1) doi: 10.1590/S0104-11692012000100008 for use under the terms of the Creative Commons CC BY 3.0 license (http://creativecommons.org/licenses/by/3.0/legalcode).

Question 13

Based on the results of Study 2, researchers infer that DM patients who have recently joined a support group may start consciously trying to adhere to their treatments so that existing members perceive them in a positive light. This most closely relates to:

- ○ **A.** groupthink.
- ○ **B.** impression management.
- ○ **C.** social facilitation.
- ○ **D.** social loafing.

Next ►

Question 14

A follow-up study showed that diabetic patients who reported concern about negative stereotypes of diabetes such as obesity and low self-control had a higher body mass index than diabetic patients who were not concerned. This relates to:

○ **A.** a stereotype threat that led to individual discrimination.

○ **B.** individual discrimination that led to a stereotype threat.

○ **C.** a stereotype threat that led to a self-fulfilling prophecy.

○ **D.** a self-fulfilling prophecy that led to a stereotype threat.

Question 15

Based on the results of Study 2, which type of learning might new members of support groups be experiencing in order to alter their adherence to treatments?

○ **A.** Observational learning

○ **B.** Operant conditioning

○ **C.** Classical conditioning

○ **D.** Spontaneous recovery

Question 16

How could researchers alter the study to analyze how medication treatment adherence is affected by patient conformity versus patient obedience, respectively?

○ **A.** Use the Morisky Test to determine medication treatment adherence after being scolded by a physician versus after participating in a support group, respectively.

○ **B.** Use the Morisky Test to determine medication treatment adherence after participating in a support group versus after being scolded by a physician, respectively.

○ **C.** Use the Diabetes Self-care Activities Questionnaire to determine how the patient feels about conformity and obedience.

○ **D.** Use the Diabetes Self-care Activities Questionnaire to determine diet and exercise adherence.

Passage 4 (Questions 17-22)

Researchers designed a study to determine whether and how the social networks of people with long-term conditions are associated with emotional well-being and with changes in emotional well-being over time. Patients representing two different long-term disease groups (chronic heart disease (CHD) and diabetes) were mailed questionnaires to assess details of personal social networks and emotional well-being. In order to characterize the extent of each participant's network, participants were asked to place as many members of their network that they considered relevant into predefined relationships types (out of 10: e.g., immediate family, extended family, neighbors, work relationships). An emotional well-being score was constructed by combining responses across two items, each rated on a scale of zero (extremely unhappy/dissatisfied) to 10 (extremely happy/satisfied): 'Taking all things together, how happy would you say you are?' and 'All things considered, how satisfied are you with your life as a whole nowadays?' Follow-up took place 12 months after baseline data collection. Results are displayed in Figure 1.

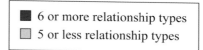

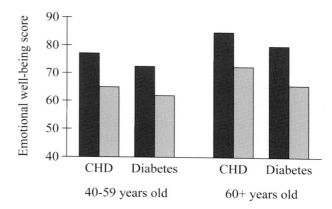

Figure 1 Average emotional well-being score by quantity of relationship types

In a follow-up study using the same participant groups, researchers examined the effect of network member social support on emotional well-being. To quantify the contribution to illness management (labelled illness work) made by members of each network, participants were distributed a questionnaire to assess perceived contribution (from 1 = not at all to 5 = a lot) of each member to each of 13 aspects of illness work. Each member's ratings were then summed across the items and to obtain overall scores for each network.

This passage was adapted from "The Contribution of Social Networks to the Health and Self-Management of Patients with Long-Term Conditions: A Longitudinal Study." Reeves D, Blickem C, Vassilev I, Brooks H, Kennedy A, et al. *PLoS ONE*. 2014. 9(6) doi:10.1371/journal.pone.0098340 for use under the terms of the Creative Commons CC BY 4.0 license (https://creativecommons.org/licenses/by/4.0/legalcode).

Question 17

A common stereotype of individuals with chronic diseases is an inability to engage in strenuous exercise. Participants from the follow-up study that joined group exercise classes may report lower emotional well-being scores due to:

- **A.** role conflict.
- **B.** peer pressure.
- **C.** stereotype threat.
- **D.** agents of socialization.

Question 18

Which of the following aspects from the study could allow the researchers to assess the impact that involvement in a formal organization has on emotional well-being?

- **A.** The quantity of network members from organizations consisting of five or more members
- **B.** The quantity of hours the participant spent interacting with peers at the workplace
- **C.** The quantity of network members from goal-oriented groups with clear rules governing behavior
- **D.** The quantity of network members from organizations registered with the government

Question 19

Participants displaying which of the following behaviors would be applying a game theoretic approach?

- **A.** Participants always take medications on time in order to minimize the risk of illness.
- **B.** Participants regularly seek medical consultation in order to maximize their reward/move ratio.
- **C.** Participants seek medications that optimize between cost and emotional well-being.
- **D.** Participants determine the likelihood of others providing them care before caring for themselves.

Question 20

The follow-up study revealed a positive relationship between illness work and emotional well-being. If social loafing later developed amongst participant social circles, reported emotional well-being is likely to:

- **A.** decrease, because group members expect others to fully care for the participant.
- **B.** decrease, because network members contribute less work since are no longer expecting anything in return.
- **C.** increase, because network size is likely to grow in response to social loafing.
- **D.** increase, because measures of participant self-efficacy are likely to increase.

Question 21

A co-worker is most likely to be part of a participant's:

- **A.** primary group.
- **B.** secondary group.
- **C.** social network.
- **D.** bureaucracy.

Question 22

Which conclusion is best supported by the findings in Figure 1?

- **A.** The quantity of members in a participant's network is positively related to emotional well-being.
- **B.** The number of relationship types has a greater effect on emotional well-being in the older participant group.
- **C.** CHD and diabetes patients would benefit from increasing the number of relationship types they have in their network.
- **D.** CHD patients show a correlation between diversity in their webs of social interaction and emotional well-being.

Passage 5 (Questions 23-26)

"Pain" is a subjective experience, commonly modeled by the biopsychosocial approach. A study was designed to identify specific types of negative body image that would worsen a perceived pain level. A total of 25 healthy right-handed students (9 males, 16 females) participated in this study, in which a rubber hand illusion was used to evoke a negative body image. This illusion is a body ownership illusion in which individuals start to feel that the fake hand is their own hand when a hidden real hand and a rubber hand placed in front of them are touched simultaneously.

For the purpose of this study, the following types of rubber hands were created: a normal rubber hand that would not make the participants feel uncomfortable (Normal); an injured rubber hand to make the participants feel uncomfortable by the sight of an injury (Injured); a hairy rubber hand to make the participants feel uncomfortable about being seen by others (Hairy); and a distorted rubber hand to make the participants feel uncomfortable because their body does not conform to the established idea of what a body should look like (Distorted). In addition, for each type of rubber hand, the study provided both illusion and no illusion conditions.

Pain thresholds were measured by applying stimuli to the back of the left forearm by a thermal stimulator. Participants were instructed to press the switch on the remote control in the right hand the moment they felt pain so that the temperature would not be increased further.

The pain thresholds for the eight conditions are shown in Figure 1.

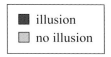

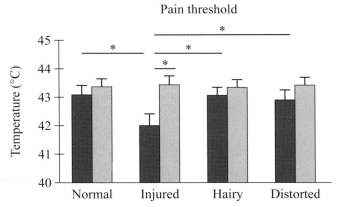

Figure 1 Pain threshold under each condition (Note: an asterisk (*) indicates that a statistically significant difference between the two conditions)

This passage was adapted from "Negative Body Image Associated with Changes in the Visual Body Appearance Increases Pain Perception." Osumi et al. *PLoS ONE.* 2014. 9(9) doi:10/1371/journal.pone.0107376 for use under the terms of the Creative Commons CC BY 4.0 license (https://creativecommons.org/licenses/by/4.0/legalcode).

Question 23

Suppose the experiment was performed in the presence of an audience. Which of the following is the best interpretation of how impression management might affect the test results?

- ○ **A.** The individual will record a high pain threshold temperature to purposefully appear exceptional to others.
- ○ **B.** The individual will reach optimal arousal and record a very high pain threshold temperature.
- ○ **C.** The individual will either record a very low or very high pain threshold temperature due to group polarization.
- ○ **D.** The individual will press the switch at a median pain threshold temperature, in order to conform to the group.

Question 24

Suppose a subject from the study accidentally burns his left hand and appears to press an imaginary switch with his right hand. In this experiment, the removal of the thermal stimulator from the left forearm unintentionally acted as which of the following?

- ○ **A.** Conditioned Stimulus
- ○ **B.** Conditioned Response
- ○ **C.** Positive Punishment
- ○ **D.** Negative Reinforcement

Question 25

In the study, the scientists theorized that a fear of nonconformity might modulate pain response. What statement does NOT correctly identify a concept related to conformity?

- ○ **A.** Peer Pressure
- ○ **B.** Groupthink
- ○ **C.** Social Facilitation
- ○ **D.** Deindividuation

Question 26

How might experimenters best utilize the concept of cultural relativism in improving this study?

- ○ **A.** Only recruit subjects raised in the same culture.
- ○ **B.** Recruit a diverse variety of subjects from a multitude of cultures.
- ○ **C.** Consider creating new hand models for different cultures.
- ○ **D.** Use a different measure of pain threshold.

Questions 27 - 30 do not refer to a passage and are independent of each other.

Question 27

A patient who pays for his own healthcare at a private clinic believes they are unwell, and a specific medication will improve his condition. He visits a physician to request the medication. The physician performs a series of diagnostic tests and prescribes physical therapy instead. The patient is dissatisfied with their care. Which of the following concepts best applies to this scenario?

○ **A.** The physician feels role conflict.

○ **B.** The patient feels role strain.

○ **C.** Role exit has occurred to the patient.

○ **D.** The physician has ascribed a new role to the patient due to their access to health information.

Question 28

Jason had several emotional outbursts at his new job. He only decided to enroll in anger management classes because his boss indicated that if he does not get control of his temper, he will be fired. This is an example of:

○ **A.** conformity.

○ **B.** obedience.

○ **C.** socialization.

○ **D.** punishment.

Question 29

Groupthink occurs as a result of:

○ **A.** variations in power distribution among group members.

○ **B.** members avoiding group discord.

○ **C.** bias generated from generalized perceptions of out-groups.

○ **D.** dissenting expressed opinions within the group.

Question 30

A group of apartment residents meet to discuss the rules for a new common space. Each person comes to the meeting with a few abstract ideas that seem reasonable, and after a three hour meeting, a list of rigid policies has been generated. This was likely the product of:

○ **A.** groupthink.

○ **B.** group polarization.

○ **C.** peer pressure.

○ **D.** the bystander effect.

Passage 6 (Questions 31-34)

Propensity for risky behavior in adolescents is thought to reflect a maturational imbalance between reward processing and cognitive control systems that affect decision-making. This propensity is particularly increased when in peer groups. A study was designed to investigate risk-taking behavior and effects of peer influence in 18-19 year old male adolescents. Subjects underwent an fMRI (functional magnetic resonance imaging) scan while taking part in a simulated driving task. The subject controlled a car which moved along a track through 20 intersections with traffic lights. The goal was to reach the end of the track as quickly as possible. As the car approached the intersection, the traffic light turned yellow and the subject made a decision whether to stop and wait for a red light to turn green (with a short 3 second delay). Conversely, the subject could choose to pass the intersection without braking (for no delay) and take the risk of a car crash (with a longer 6 second delay). A decision to Not Stop could be seen as engaging in risky behavior.

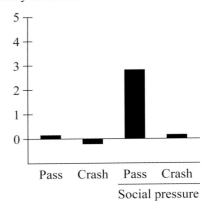

Figure 1 Outcome-related fMRI activation

Figure 1 shows average effect size of fMRI activation related to either a Pass or Crash outcome, following a decision to Not Stop. Social pressure was applied in the form of a hypothetical peer competition, in which subjects were randomly told their scores would be compared to their peers' scores and the results presented at school. After the experiment, the subjects were divided into low and high risk-taking groups according to the risk-taking rates they exhibited during the task. Figure 1 displays data obtained from analysis of the entire sample. A 0 corresponds to low fMRI activation (and thus low usage of) the caudate nucleus. A 5 corresponds to a high level of activation under the specified condition.

This passage was adapted from "Risk-Taking Behavior in a Computerized Driving Task: Brain Activation Correlates of Decision-Making, Outcome, and Peer Influence in Male Adolescents." Vorobyev V, Kwon MS, Moe D, Parkkola R, Hämäläinen H. *PLoS ONE.* 2015. 10(6) doi: 10.1371/journal.pone.0129516 for use under the terms of the Creative Commons CC BY 4.0 license (https://creativecommons.org/licenses/by/4.0/legalcode).

Question 31

The data contained in Figure 1 best support what conclusion?

- **A.** For low risk-takers, conformity decreases the subjective value of a successful outcome.
- **B.** For high risk-takers, peer pressure increases the subjective value of a successful outcome.
- **C.** For both high and low risk-takers, conformity increases the subjective value of a successful outcome.
- **D.** For both high and low risk-takers, peer pressure increases the subjective value of a successful outcome.

Question 32

The subjects whose data are presented in Figure 1 represent which group?

- **A.** A sample of 18-19 year old male high risk-takers going through Piaget's Concrete Operational stage from a population of 18-19 year old males in the U.S.
- **B.** A sample of 18-19 year old male high and low risk-takers going through Piaget's Formal Operational stage from a population of 18-19 year old males in the U.S.
- **C.** A population of male adolescents going through Piaget's Concrete Operational stage taken from a sample of all male adolescents in the U.S.
- **D.** A population of 18-19 year old males going through Piaget's Formal Operational stage taken from a sample of 18-19 year old male adolescents in the U.S.

Question 33

Instead of describing a hypothetical peer competition, the researchers allow subjects to watch several peers complete the task before them. These peers were (secretly) directed beforehand to stop at every red light. If the subjects overall stop at red lights more frequently thereafter, they are exhibiting:

- **A.** groupthink.
- **B.** group polarization.
- **C.** conformity.
- **D.** social mores.

Question 34

Adults are found to be less affected by peer pressure than adolescents in this driving task. Which graph best captures this finding?

- **A.**

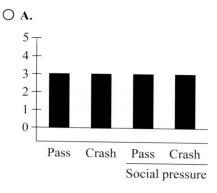

- **B.**

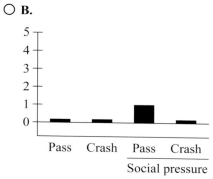

- **C.**

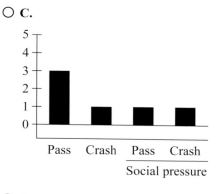

- **D.**

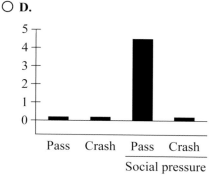

Passage 7 (Questions 35-38)

It has been demonstrated that interaction at the level of body movements plays a crucial role in the success of social exchanges. Motor coordination of interacting people influences social cognitive functioning; for example, it impacts feelings of connectedness or interpersonal rapport and communication. Abnormal movements during social interactions have been reported in patients with schizophrenia, which may in part explain their interpersonal deficits. Moreover, such abnormal movements may be the earliest sign of schizophrenia and may be used as a marker for earlier diagnostics of this illness that affects almost one percent of the world population.

Researchers examined intentional and unintentional social motor coordination in participants oscillating hand-held pendulums from the wrist. The control group consisted of twenty healthy participant pairs, while the experimental group consisted of twenty participant pairs with one participant suffering from schizophrenia.

To investigate unintentional social coordination, each pair of participants performed three 90 second trials each containing three 30 second segments completed continuously. For each trial, participants were instructed to oscillate their pendulum at a self-selected comfort tempo and maintain it while they were looking (second trial) or not looking (first and third trials) at the oscillatory movements of their partner.

To investigate whether schizophrenia affects intentional social coordination, the same pairs of participants were then instructed to perform together in-phase or anti-phase swinging of their wrist pendulums for 60 seconds.

The results showed that unintentional social motor coordination was preserved, while intentional social motor coordination was impaired. In intentional coordination, the schizophrenia group displayed coordination patterns that had lower stability and in which the patient never led the coordination. A coupled oscillator model suggests that the schizophrenia group coordination pattern was due to a decrease in the amount of available information together with a delay in information transmission. The study thus identified relational motor signatures of schizophrenia and opens new perspectives for detecting the illness and improving social interactions of patients.

This passage was adapted from "Impairments of Social Motor Coordination in Schizophrenia." Varlet M, Marin L, Raffard S, Schmidt RC, Capdevielle D, et al. *PLoS ONE*. 2012. 7(1) doi:10.1371/journal.pone.0029772 for use under the terms of the Creative Commons CC BY 3.0 license (http://creativecommons.org/licenses/by/3.0/legalcode).

Question 35

If researchers analyzed the brains of people with schizophrenia, they may notice defects in:

- A. the amygdala.
- B. mirror neurons.
- C. Broca's area.
- D. the brainstem.

Question 36

Based on the study, which of the following would be expected if the researchers tested siblings of participants with schizophrenia?

   I. Monozygotic twins will have the greatest concordance of schizophrenia and are most likely to struggle with intentional coordination.

   II. Dizygotic twins will have a high rate of concordance of schizophrenia and are likely to struggle with intentional coordination.

   III. Non-twin siblings will have no increased risk of schizophrenia and are most likely to perform normally on the intentional coordination task.

- A. I only
- B. III only
- C. I and II only
- D. I, II, and III

Question 37

Which type of social behavior is likely impaired in the control group?

- A. Dominance behavior is impaired.
- B. Mating behavior is impaired.
- C. Nonverbal communication is impaired.
- D. The control group does not show impairment in social behavior.

Question 38

Which of the following correctly identifies a group process that may be impaired in schizophrenia?

- A. Group polarization, where the attitudes of a group become stronger than they were in the individuals alone.
- B. The bystander effect, where group members work less vigorously than they would on their own.
- C. De-individualization, where a person performs better when he knows he is being watched.
- D. Social loafing, where peers increase a behavior.

Passage 8 (Questions 39-42)

In the classic black sheep effect (BSE), an ingroup deviant member is usually evaluated more negatively than the corresponding outgroup deviant. Based on literature on BSE, people tend to derogate a negative ingroup member more than a similar outgroup member in order to protect the group from the threat that the deviant poses to their social identity. Studies testing this effect have tended to rely on self-reported reactions to imagined scenarios where the BSE would occur.

The present study proposes a new method to investigate the BSE by considering the behavioral and physiological reactions to unfair behavior in a realistic group-setting. Physiological reactions to unfair behavior included the measurement of participant's blood pressure to examine the possibility of any tangible health side-effects of the BSE. The study involved 52 university students in a minimal group setting who performed a modified version of the competitive reaction time (CRT) task adapted to be played in groups of four people. The classic BSE was replicated for evaluation but not for the behavioral reactions (retaliate to aggression) to deviants. A negative relationship emerged in the ingroup deviant condition between the level of behavioral derogation and the systolic blood pressure level.

The study showed a BSE toward the ingroup anti-normative member, evaluating him more negatively with respect to the outgroup anti-normative member. Figure 1 exemplifies these findings.

Blood Pressure data obtained from participants is presented in Figure 2. People successful in controlling their aggressive behavior in a group setting incur the possibly unhealthy consequence of increased state of arousal activation testified by a higher level of SBP than people who allow themselves to participate in aggressive behavior.

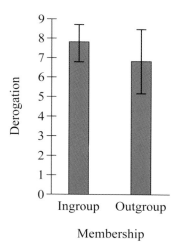

Figure 1 Derogation as function of membership ("Ingroup" vs. "Outgroup")

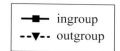

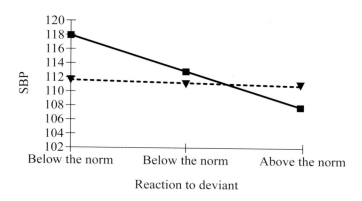

Figure 2 Moderation effects of membership (Ingroup vs Outgroup) on the relationship between the strength of reaction to deviant and the SBPs

This passage was adapted from "Reactions to Ingroup and Outgroup Deviants: An Experimental Group Paradigm for Black Sheep Effect." Rullo M, Presaghi F, and Livi, S. *PLoS ONE*. 2014. 10(5) doi:10.1371/journal.pone.0125605 for use under the terms of the Creative Commons CC BY 4.0 license (https://creativecommons.org/licenses/by/4.0/legalcode).

Question 39

Based on the information provided in the passage, what feature of the experimental design poses the largest threat to external validity?

○ **A.** The sample size and demographics of the participants in the study

○ **B.** The ineffective use of a competitive reaction time task

○ **C.** The use of SBP as a dependent variable

○ **D.** The lack of psychological data on the participant's personal accounts of the study

Question 40

Which statement is most supported by the data in Figure 2?

○ **A.** BSE directly affected blood pressures.

○ **B.** Blood pressure was affected most in ingroup deviants.

○ **C.** Blood pressure was affected most in outgroup deviants.

○ **D.** Blood pressure was affected most in non-deviants.

Question 41

Is it reasonable to assume that participants who do not deviate will always have higher blood pressure?

○ **A.** Yes, because SBP was always higher in participants who did not deviate due to blood pressure's complementary relationship with stress.

○ **B.** Yes, because SBP was always higher in participants who did deviate due to blood pressure's complementary relationship with stress.

○ **C.** No, because non-deviates do not have higher SBP levels and increased blood pressure is linked to stressful behavior.

○ **D.** No, because blood pressure is individual and some deviants may still have higher SBP levels than some non-deviants.

Question 42

The BSE suggests that groups treat divergent ingroup members more harshly than divergent outgroup members. This paradigm could be construed as a symptom of:

○ **A.** group polarization.

○ **B.** deindividuation.

○ **C.** ethnocentrism.

○ **D.** socialization.

Questions 43 - 46 do not refer to a passage and are independent of each other.

Question 43

The Implicit Association Test (IAT) was developed to measure implicit feelings about race and ethnicity. Which of the following is likely true?

○ **A.** A person may overcome subconscious prejudice by focusing on avoiding bias.

○ **B.** People of different races likely have the same biases.

○ **C.** Racial bias is always age-specific.

○ **D.** Racial bias is never a problem in society.

Question 44

Ashley believes that all Chinese people enjoy the taste of rice. This is an example of:

○ **A.** positive stereotype.

○ **B.** negative stereotype.

○ **C.** neutral stereotype.

○ **D.** stereotype threat.

Question 45

A group of researchers wish to test the influence of various agents of socialization on an individual's decision making skills. Which of the following is NOT considered an agent of socialization, and should not be used in the experiment?

○ **A.** Family

○ **B.** Radio

○ **C.** Religion

○ **D.** Emotion

Question 46

While a student is studying in the school library, she tears a few pages out of a library book and slips them in to her bag so that she can have exclusive access to that content. This behavior is an example of:

○ **A.** deviance.

○ **B.** Antisocial Personality Disorder.

○ **C.** the back stage self.

○ **D.** foraging behavior.

Passage 9 (Questions 47-52)

People who are obese are often perceived as lazy, unsuccessful, and weak-willed. These beliefs about individuals with obesity are often translated into negative attitudes, discrimination, and verbal and physical assaults.

A total of 6,157 participants were drawn from the Health and Retirement Study (HRS), a nationally representative longitudinal study of Americans ages 50 and older. Starting in 2006, participants received a psychosocial questionnaire that included items about the experience of different types of discrimination, including weight discrimination. The 2006 assessment was used as the baseline, and the obesity data from the 2010 assessment was used as follow-up to have the longest longitudinal interval between assessments. Participants who completed the discrimination measure and had weight and height at both the 2006 and 2010 assessments were, on average, 66.51 years old, had an average of 12.83 years of education, and were 84.7% white, 12.8% African-American, and 2.5% other ethnicities (self-reported).

In addition to weight, participants could also have attributed discrimination to their ancestry, sex, race, age, physical disability, other aspects of physical appearance, and/or sexual orientation. A total of 513 participants (8%) reported that they had been discriminated against because of their weight. Among participants who were not obese at baseline, those who reported weight discrimination were approximately 2.5 times more likely to be obese by follow-up than those who did not report weight discrimination (Table 1). This effect was specific to weight discrimination; the other types of discrimination were largely unrelated to reported obesity. That is, none of the other types of discrimination assessed were associated with becoming obese between the two assessments (Table 2).

Table 1 Likelihood that an Individual Will Become or Remain Obese Given Exposure to Weight Discrimination.

Discrimination	Percentage (%)	Became obese	Remained obese
Weight	8.0	2.54	3.20

Table 2 Likelihood that an Individual Will Become or Remain Obese Given Exposure to Selected Types of Discrimination.

Discrimination	Percentage (%)	Became obese	Remained obese
Race	10.2	0.83	1.18
Ancestry	6.2	1.25	0.73
Sex	13.6	1.20	1.30
Age	30.0	1.31	0.89

Question 47

The data in the passage best support which of the following conclusions?

- A. Weight discrimination is the most prevalent discrimination among the HRS population.
- B. All types of discrimination result in significantly increased risk for becoming obese.
- C. Weight discrimination causes further gains in individuals who are overweight.
- D. Weight discrimination in this study was the result of an in-group mentality.

Question 48

One would expect this study design and data analysis to be LEAST biased if which of the following were true?

- A. The study team members each had an average of 20 years of education.
- B. The study team was comprised of 5 males and 4 females.
- C. The study team members had an average BMI that fell into the overweight classification.
- D. The study team members had an average BMI that fell into the underweight classification.

Question 49

If individuals who participate in weight discrimination believe that all people who are obese are lazy, unsuccessful, and weak-willed, this can be described as all of the following EXCEPT:

- A. stereotyping.
- B. discrimination.
- C. stigma.
- D. prejudice.

Question 50

Obese individuals have reported that in situations when they have been subject to verbal assault in crowded, public places, no one has come to their defense. However, in less populated settings of only one or two onlookers, someone will usually step in. This is a result of:

- A. the bystander effect.
- B. social loafing.
- C. social facilitation.
- D. groupthink.

Question 51

If it were the policy of a hospital not to admit patients who were obese to the emergency room, this would be an example of:

○ **A.** individual prejudice.

○ **B.** institutional prejudice.

○ **C.** individual discrimination.

○ **D.** institutional discrimination.

Question 52

A follow-up study hypothesized that individuals from all over the world who are overweight and obese will socialize more with individuals who are also overweight and obese. This hypothesis was likely based on:

○ **A.** ingroup mentality.

○ **B.** outgroup mentality.

○ **C.** social facilitation.

○ **D.** ethnocentrism.

Passage 10 (Questions 53-56)

Many of the personality and behavioral traits, for example, social imperviousness, directness in conversation, lack of imagination, affinity for solitude, and difficulty displaying emotion that are known to be sensitive to context and reference group also appear in questionnaire-based assessments of autistic traits. Therefore, two experiments investigated the effects of specifying contexts and reference groups when assessing autistic traits in autistic and non-autistic participants.

Experiment 1 utilized 124 autistic and 124 non-autistic participants whom completed the Autism Phenotype Questionnaire (APQ). Two question sets were used. In the "with autistic people" question set, "people" were specified as "autistic people;" for example, the item "I like being around other people" appeared as "I like being around autistic people." In the "with non-autistic people" question set, "people" were specified as "non-autistic people;" for example, the item "I like being around other people" appeared as "I like being around non-autistic people." Both autistic and non-autistic participants self-reported having more autistic traits; when the context was specified as the participants' in-group, participants reported having fewer autistic traits. Experiment 2 utilized 82 autistic and 82 non-autistic participants whom completed the Social Responsiveness Scale in much the same way as the APQ was used in Experiment 1. When the reference group on the Social Responsiveness Scale (SRS) was specified as the participants' out-group, autistic participants reported having more autistic traits; when the reference group was their in-group, autistic participants reported having fewer autistic traits. Non-autistic participants appeared insensitive to reference group on the Social Responsiveness Scale.

Exploratory analyses suggested that when neither the context nor the reference group is specified (for assessing autistic traits on the Autism-Spectrum Quotient), both autistic and non-autistic participants use the majority ("non-autistic people") as the implied context and reference group.

This passage was adapted from "Specificity, contexts, and reference groups matter when assessing autistic traits." Gernsbacher MA, Stevenson JL, Dern S. *PLoS ONE*. 2017. 12(2) doi:10.1371/journal.pone.0171931 for use under the terms of the Creative Commons CC BY 4.0 license (http://creativecommons.org/licenses/by/4.0/legalcode).

Question 53

Outside of the scope of the study, which of the following may bias diagnosis of autism based on symptomatology?

○ **A.** Norms

○ **B.** Anomie

○ **C.** Taboo

○ **D.** Fad

Question 54

In what way may the questionnaire differ for individuals from Western or Eastern cultures?

- ○ **A.** Western cultures focus on collective emotions, whereas Eastern cultures focus on individual emotions.
- ○ **B.** Western cultures focus on individual emotions, whereas Eastern cultures focus on collective emotions.
- ○ **C.** Western cultures focus on individual mood, whereas Eastern cultures focus on collective mood.
- ○ **D.** Western cultures focus on collective mood, whereas Eastern cultures focus on individual mood.

Question 55

An individual biased by the reference group on the SRS may:

- ○ **A.** have prejudice against autistic people.
- ○ **B.** discriminate against autistic people.
- ○ **C.** not show any prejudice.
- ○ **D.** have lower intelligence.

Question 56

Previous research has indicated that individuals with autistic traits may fail to form traditional attachment relationships. This research may have been conducted by:

- ○ **A.** John Watson.
- ○ **B.** Carl Rogers.
- ○ **C.** Sigmund Freud.
- ○ **D.** Mary Ainsworth.

Questions 57 - 59 do not refer to a passage and are independent of each other.

Question 57

Which of the following graphs is a proper depiction of the interplay between power, prestige, and class?

○ **A.**

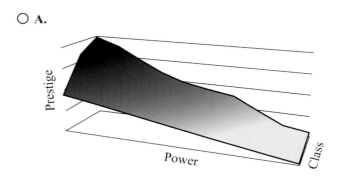

○ **B.**

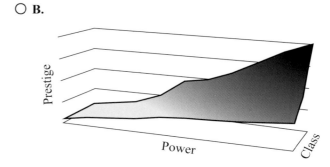

○ **C.**

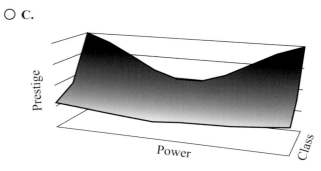

○ **D.**

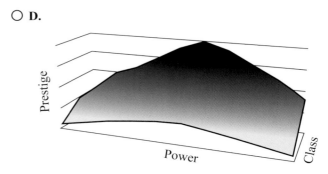

Question 58

A medical student on her psychiatry rotation notices that she and other students dislike working with patients struggling with addiction. This is an example of:

○ **A.** prejudice.

○ **B.** stigma.

○ **C.** discrimination.

○ **D.** a stereotype.

Question 59

When shopping, minority women often report that they are frequently followed by employees whom assume they are shoplifting. This is an example of:

○ **A.** prejudice on the basis of power.

○ **B.** prejudice on the basis of class.

○ **C.** discrimination on the basis of power.

○ **D.** discrimination on the basis of class.

STOP. If you finish before time is called, check your work. You may go back to any question in this test.

ANSWERS & EXPLANATIONS for Test 2B can be found on p. 194.

Identity and the Individual

TEST 3A

Time: 95 minutes
Questions 1–59

DIRECTIONS: Most of the questions in this test section are grouped with a passage. Read the passage, then select the best answer to each question. Some questions are independent of any passage and of one another. Select the best answer to each of these questions. If you are unsure of an answer, rule out incorrect choices and select from the remaining options. Indicate your selection beside the option you choose.

Passage 1 (Questions 1-5)

The US racial/ethnic academic achievement gap is a well-documented social inequality. Explanations for these gaps tend to focus on the influence of socioeconomic resources, neighborhood and school characteristics, and family composition in patterning socioeconomic inequalities. In addition to the complexity that arises from race/ethnicity, socioeconomic status, and intersections between them, different patterns in academic and non-academic outcomes by gender have also received longstanding attention. In contrast to explanations for socioeconomic inequalities, gender differences have been mainly attributed to social conditioning and stereotyping within families, schools, communities, and the wider society.

Researchers examined inequalities across several eighth grade academic and non-academic outcomes at the intersection of race/ethnicity, gender, and socioeconomic status. Five outcome variables were selected to examine the study aims: two measures relating to non-cognitive academic skills (perceived interest/competence in reading and math) and three measures capturing socioemotional development (internalizing behavior, locus of control, and self-concept).

Additional variables were used to classify students into classes of individual and contextual advantage or disadvantage. Individual advantage was defined as a family in an upper-middle class or higher socioeconomic status group. Contextual advantage was measured at the school and neighborhood level. At the school-level, contextual advantage was measured as the percentage of students eligible for free school meals and the percentage of students from a racial/ethnic background other than White non-Hispanic. To capture the neighborhood environment, a variable was included which measured the level of safety of the neighborhood in kindergarten, first, third, fifth and eighth grades. The results of the study are shown in Table 1.

Table 1 Psychosocial Factors Affecting Academic and Non-Academic Performance by Family (Individual) and Neighborhood (Contextual) Resources. Positive Coefficients Represent Factors that Played a Larger Role Than in the Reference Group

	Class 1: Individually and contextually disadvantaged Coeff	Class 2: Individually wealthy, contextually disadvantaged Coeff	Class 3: Individually and contextually wealthy Coeff	Class 4: Individually disadvantaged, contextually wealthy Coeff
Perceived interest / Competence, reading				
White boys	Reference	Reference	Reference	Reference
White girls	0.16	0.17	0.37*	0.42*
Black boys	0.16	−0.08	−0.50*	−0.13
Black girls	0.29	0.28	0.22	0.31
Hispanic boys	0.01	−0.24*	−0.17	−0.14
Hispanic girls	0.13	0.18	0.26*	0.17
Locus of control				
White boys	Reference	Reference	Reference	Reference
White girls	0.37	0.08	0.13*	0.06
Black boys	0.09	0.17	−0.05	0.13
Black girls	−0.15	0.14	0.25	−0.21
Hispanic boys	0.01	0.08	−0.02	−0.07
Hispanic girls	0.10	0.13	−0.03	0.06

* statistically significant

Question 1

Eighth-grade students that perform in the top 10% of their class often describe themselves as hard-working. Being hard-working is most likely a:

- ○ **A.** trait.
- ○ **B.** personality.
- ○ **C.** hereditary factor.
- ○ **D.** behavior.

Question 2

Research findings indicate higher levels of achievement when the teacher is the same race as the student because:

- ○ **A.** both the student and the teacher belong to the same in-group.
- ○ **B.** both the student and the teacher have shared all the same experiences.
- ○ **C.** of the racial hostility between students and teachers of different races.
- ○ **D.** the reduction in role stain experiences by the teacher.

Question 3

Which of the following would be most useful in determining the effect of the environment on socioemotional development?

- ○ **A.** Heredity study
- ○ **B.** Twin study
- ○ **C.** Temperament study
- ○ **D.** IQ test

Question 4

Multiple factors may contribute to a student's perceived competence in reading and math. These factors are likely to include:

    I. openness to experience.

    II. conscientiousness.

    III. neuroticism.

- ○ **A.** I only
- ○ **B.** II only
- ○ **C.** I and II only
- ○ **D.** I, II, and III

Question 5

Which of the following statements best describes the findings in Table 1?

- ○ **A.** Variations in perceived interest in math and reading can best be attributed to within class gender differences.
- ○ **B.** Variations in locus of control can best be attributed to within class racial/ethnic differences.
- ○ **C.** Variations in perceived interest in math and reading can best be attributed to between class gender differences.
- ○ **D.** Variations in locus of control can best be attributed to between class racial/ethnic differences.

Passage 2 (Questions 6-9)

Piaget proposed that children attribute biological (e.g., being alive) and psychological (e.g., having knowledge) properties to inanimate objects such as clouds, which is known as children's animism. These imaginary agents, or imaginary companions (IC), also participate in activities with children. Two types of ICs are generally observed: a stuffed animal and an invisible friend. The phenomenon of having an IC is commonly observed in young children with approximately half interacting with the ICs as they would a real friend.

Given these considerations, it is possible that children may have an agent perception system that responds to imaginary and invisible agents by which they attribute biological and psychological properties to ICs. Specifically, this tendency would be observed in children with ICs but not in those without ICs. In order to compare children with and without ICs, children were introduced to an invisible agent named "Hikaru" by a researcher and then given a sequence of questions about the biological (e.g., "Does X walk?"), psychological (e.g., "Can X feel happy?"), and perceptual (e.g.,"Can X see things?") properties of the agent. Children less than six years old with ICs (IC group, N=26) and without ICs (NIC group, N= 24) participated in the first study. The results are shown in Figure 1.

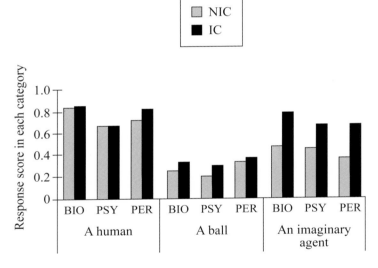

Figure 1 Results of Study 1 where response score is the proportion of "yes" to "no" responses

Since IC children may attribute biological and psychological properties to any invisible item, researchers conducted a second study in which IC (N= 17) and NIC (N = 17) children were given questions about an imaginary (invisible) stone.

This passage was adapted from "My Neighbor: Children's Perception of Agency in Interaction with an Imaginary Agent." Moriguchi Y, Shinohara I. *PLoS ONE*. 2012. 7(9) doi:10.1371/journal.pone.0044463 for use under the terms of the Creative Commons CC BY 3.0 license (http://creativecommons.org/licenses/by/3.0/legalcode).

Question 6

James Marcia expanded on Erikson's work by describing specific types of identity that occur in which of Erikson's stages?

- ○ **A.** Stage 1
- ○ **B.** Stage 3
- ○ **C.** Stage 5
- ○ **D.** Stage 7

Question 7

The deviation between IC and NIC depicted in Figure 1:

- ○ **A.** shows that children with IC give external attributions to imaginary agents.
- ○ **B.** shows that children with IC give internal attributions to imaginary agents.
- ○ **C.** shows that children with NIC give external attributions to imaginary agents.
- ○ **D.** shows that children with NIC give internal attributions to imaginary agents.

Question 8

If the study was repeated on children from a small tribe in Africa, which of the following changes to the design may be required?

- ○ **A.** The questions should focus on the collectivist feelings of the imaginary agent.
- ○ **B.** More children should be sampled so the results can reach statistical significance.
- ○ **C.** Children should not be sampled in their native language.
- ○ **D.** Children should be sampled over many time points to determine if the results are stable over time.

Question 9

Which of the following additional questions would determine if the children ascribe an internal or external locus of control to the imaginary agent?

- ○ **A.** Who is Hikaru's best friend?
- ○ **B.** Does Hikaru play with you?
- ○ **C.** Does Hikaru eat breakfast?
- ○ **D.** Who controls Hikaru's future in life?

Next ▶

Passage 3 (Questions 10-13)

It has been suggested that the personality of patients with malignant tumors may have an effect on tumor progression. In one study, researchers conducted a personality inventory in 3,003 outpatients and compared the personality of patients with malignant tumors to the personality of patients with non-malignant tumors.

603 outpatients diagnosed with malignant tumors (M group) and 2400 outpatients (non-M group) were enrolled in this study and completed the Japanese Maudsley Personality Inventory (MPI). MPI comprises 80 items assessing three personality fields: introversion/extroversion (E-score), neurotic tendencies (N-score), and lying tendencies (L-score), all of which are evaluated on a 45-point scale. A higher E-score and N-score indicate greater extroversion and neurotic tendency, respectively. A higher L-score indicates a greater lying or exhibitionistic tendency.

Of the 3,000 patients investigated in this study, 1,190 were men and 1,810 were women. Average E-score was roughly 30 points in the M group and 26 points in the non-M group, although this difference was not significant. Average N-score was 15 points in the M group and 18 points the non-M group. Again, this difference was not significant. Average L-score was 22 points in the M group, significantly higher than that in the non-M group (12 points). Investigation across age and sex categories revealed no significant differences in E-, N-, and L-scores between the M group and the non-M group.

The results of this study showed that personality of patients with malignant tumors was slightly more extroverted and less neurotic than patients with nonmalignant tumors. Researchers suggest this may reflect the desire of patients with malignant tumors to establish positive relationships and to lead an ordinary life in order to suppress the fear of their illness and death and to adopt a mindset of conquering their cancer and seeking a quality of life higher than that imagined by their doctors.

This passage was adapted from "Personalities of outpatients with malignant tumors: a cross-sectional study." Wang Z, Sakakibara T, Kasai Y. *World Journal of Surgical Oncology*. 2012. 3(187) doi: 10.1186/1477-7819-10-187 for use under the terms of the Creative Commons CC BY 3.0 license (http://creativecommons.org/licenses/by/3.0/legalcode).

Question 10

The researchers from this study would most agree with which of the following personality theories?

- O **A.** Psychoanalytic theory
- O **B.** Behaviorist theory
- O **C.** Humanist theory
- O **D.** Biological theory

Question 11

Based on the researchers' interpretation of the results, patients with malignant tumors who establish positive relationships and suppress fear most likely have:

- O **A.** an internal locus of control.
- O **B.** a locus of control.
- O **C.** an external locus of control.
- O **D.** a reference group.

Question 12

Which statement best summarizes how the researchers would describe the relationship between behavior and malignant tumors?

- O **A.** There is no relationship between behavior and the existence of a malignant tumor.
- O **B.** Patients with malignant tumors tend to be extroverted and less neurotic because they desire a higher quality of life.
- O **C.** Patients with malignant tumors tend to be introverted and neurotic because they fear death.
- O **D.** Patients with malignant tumors tend to be extroverted and more neurotic because they desire a higher quality of life.

Question 13

Researchers attributed the personality of patients with malignant tumors to the patients' desire to obtain a higher quality of life. This attribution is most consistent with:

- O **A.** attribution theory.
- O **B.** personality attribution.
- O **C.** dispositional attribution.
- O **D.** situational attribution.

Questions 14 - 16 do not refer to a passage and are independent of each other.

Question 14

Which of the following twin studies would be the most helpful for testing the biological theory of personality?

○ **A.** Monozygotic twins raised apart

○ **B.** Monozygotic twins raised in the same household

○ **C.** Dizygotic twins raised apart

○ **D.** Dizygotic twins raised in the same household

Question 15

Behaviorist theory of personality involves all of the following EXCEPT:

○ **A.** learning experiences.

○ **B.** observable behaviors.

○ **C.** psychological drives.

○ **D.** environmental influences.

Question 16

When children are forming their understanding of identity, they often imitate:

○ **A.** one another.

○ **B.** television characters.

○ **C.** siblings.

○ **D.** strangers in public.

Passage 4 (Questions 17-20)

Recently, perfectionism has been viewed as a multidimensional personality trait related to psychological difficulties, distortions of interpersonal relations, and an erroneous relationship to success. According to this model, perfectionism is a three-dimensional construct including self-oriented, other-oriented, and socially-prescribed perfectionism.

Self-oriented perfectionism reflects one's tendency to define high or unreachable personal standards of achievement. Other-oriented perfectionism concerns individuals whom have high expectations for those in their social environment. Socially-prescribed perfectionism is related to perceived environmental pressures. Socially-prescribed perfectionists perceive pressure from others to hold excessively high standards of achievement.

Perfectionism has also been extensively examined in the literature on giftedness. If perfectionism is a personality facet that can be useful for the expression of talent with high levels of accomplishment, it can also be associated with anxious feelings if one's standards of accomplishment are never met. Gifted children may require particular support because of their strong tendency to be tense and anxious, but only a few empirical studies exist to support this point of view.

Using self-report measures with 132 children, researchers hypothesized that intellectually-gifted children express a higher level of perfectionism and anxiety. The results pointed out a paradox: the gifted group obtained a higher self-oriented perfectionism score than the control group in 6th grade, but presented the same level of anxiety. In contrast, the gifted group showed the same level of perfectionism than non-gifted 5th graders, but reported a higher anxiety level. Thus, the interplay between perfectionism and anxiety appears to be more complex than a simple linear relationship in giftedness.

This passage was adapted from "Perfectionism and Anxiety: A Paradox in Intellectual Giftedness?" Guignard J-H, Jacquet A-Y, Lubart TI. *PLoS ONE*. 2012. 7(7) doi:10.1371/journal.pone.0041043 for use under the terms of the Creative Commons CC BY 3.0 license (http://creativecommons.org/licenses/by/3.0/legalcode).

Question 17

Assuming perfectionism is a trait, which of the following is NOT true?

○ **A.** Perfectionism is constant over a lifetime.

○ **B.** Perfectionism is innate.

○ **C.** Perfectionism is not always desirable.

○ **D.** Perfectionism can emerge during schooling.

Next ▶

Question 18

The authors likely favor which approach to psychopathology?

- **A.** A biological approach
- **B.** A physiological approach
- **C.** A psychosocial approach
- **D.** A biopsychosocial approach

Question 19

Individuals who were identified as "gifted" by researchers may have personality disorders in:

- **A.** cluster A.
- **B.** cluster B.
- **C.** cluster C.
- **D.** cluster D.

Question 20

Assuming the results found in the 5th graders are bidirectional, which of the following drugs may decrease giftedness?

- **A.** Fluoxetine, a selective serotonin reuptake inhibitor
- **B.** Gabapentin, a GABA analogue
- **C.** Levodopa, the (L) enantiomer of dopamine
- **D.** Modafinil, a dopamine transporter blocker

Passage 5 (Questions 21-25)

The prevalence of child and adolescent obesity has risen substantially over the past 30 years. In developed countries, 23.8% of boys and 22.6% of girls were overweight or obese in 2013 (defined as a body-mass-index (BMI) greater than 25 or 30, respectively), with indications that increased trends are set to continue. Obesity in childhood has a wide range of serious complications that include an increased risk of premature mortality and physical morbidity in later life.

Several factors that relate to diet, physical activity and sedentary behavior have been found to predict the accumulation of body fat in childhood and adolescence. These include a lack of awareness and false beliefs about nutrition, residence in metropolitan cities, and accessibility to convenience stores and recreational physical activity facilities.

Other research demonstrates correlations between personality traits and BMI levels. In school-age children (age 6 to 12 years), high levels of introversion, neuroticism and emotionality, and low levels of conscientiousness correlate to a higher BMI.

These findings demonstrate that personality is important for BMI across the lifespan, and researchers have begun to explore potential moderators of observed associations. Some research indicates such associations are potentially moderated by parental personality characteristics. Specifically, parental conscientiousness was significant moderator for girls' adult BMI levels, and parental neuroticism was important moderator for boys' adult BMI levels.

Personality is thought to contribute to BMI because individuals with particular personality traits are more or less likely to engage in health-comprising and health-confronting behaviors. Indeed, research in child and adolescent samples has found that personality relates to dietary intake, participation in extracurricular sports, and sedentary behaviors such as television viewing. Other research notes childhood BMI could be mediated by changes in personality traits overtime. In a two-year follow-up study paradigm, researchers concluded that decreased persistence across the two-year time interval was correlated with a higher BMI at follow-up and increased in BMI across the two-year time interval.

This passage was adapted from "Personality and Body-Mass-Index in School-Age Children: An Exploration of Mediating and Moderating Variables." Allen MS, Vella SA. PLoS ONE. 2016. 11(8) doi: 10.1371/journal.pone.0158353 for use under the terms of the Creative Commons CC BY 4.0 license (http://creativecommons.org/licenses/by/4.0/legalcode).

Question 21

Which of the following groups of psychologists would be most likely to question the results from the two-year follow-up study?

- **A.** Trait theorists
- **B.** Psychoanalysts
- **C.** Humanistic psychologists
- **D.** Attribute-constancy psychologists

Question 22

A social cognitive theorist would most likely describe the personalities of the 6 to 12 year-olds described in the passage as influenced by:

○ **A.** an attempt to attain self-actualization.

○ **B.** learned experiences of others that are applied in novel situations.

○ **C.** triadic reciprocal causation between behaviors, latent biases, and genetic influences.

○ **D.** a causative interaction in which a combination of environmental and genetic factors influence behavior.

Question 23

Studies linking obesity-related behaviors to residence in metropolitan cities and accessibility to physical activity centers are best exemplifying which of the following processes?

○ **A.** Role-taking

○ **B.** Situational attribution

○ **C.** External locus of control

○ **D.** Fundamental attribution error

Question 24

The validity of the results at end of paragraph 4 would be best supported if which of the following control variables were considered:

○ **A.** adult BMI levels.

○ **B.** children personality traits.

○ **C.** aspects of the child's reference group.

○ **D.** characteristics of the child's self-concept.

Question 25

A follow-up study ascertains a positive correlation between measures of childhood psychological distress and adult BMI levels. What would a psychologist following Carl Rogers' tenants be most likely to suggest increases a child's BMI level later in life?

○ **A.** A difference between the child's view of their own personality and what the child wants to be like

○ **B.** An incongruence between in-group expectations and personal desires

○ **C.** An overlap between self-concept, actual self, and ideal self

○ **D.** Inheritance of parental personality characteristics

Questions 26 - 29 do not refer to a passage and are independent of each other.

Question 26

Danielle doubts whether she will play well at volleyball tryouts to make the school team. Danielle is struggling with:

○ **A.** self-esteem.

○ **B.** self-efficacy.

○ **C.** self-concept.

○ **D.** locus of control.

Question 27

Maria meets her birth mother for the first time after being raised by adoptive parents since she was born. Maria recognizes that she has many similarities with her mother. What personality theory does this support?

○ **A.** Psychoanalytic theory

○ **B.** Biological theory

○ **C.** Behaviorist theory

○ **D.** Social cognitive theory

Question 28

A study found that children who act out and rebel as teenagers are still likely to act very similar to their parents as adults. What is this final state of acting like their parents an example of?

○ **A.** Imitation

○ **B.** Role-taking

○ **C.** Social comparison

○ **D.** Becoming part of the in-group

Question 29

A recent study found that if patients with malignant tumors participate in support groups, their reported self-esteem increased significantly. The support group is an example of:

○ **A.** an out-group.

○ **B.** an in-group.

○ **C.** imitation.

○ **D.** role-taking.

Passage 6 (Questions 30-34)

Once one has lived in another culture, discovering and embracing exotic music, food and traditions, one may return to one's heritage culture only to find that 'home' is not what one remembered it to be. Acculturation, or adjustment to a new culture, necessitates an exchange between two different cultures: the heritage culture, from which an individual or their parents are from, and a host or mainstream culture, which the acculturating individual has moved to.

One particular type of sojourner that has received research attention is the Third Culture Individual (TCI). TCIs are individuals that have spent a significant part of their developmental years outside the parent's culture. TCIs identify less with a particular cultural group and more with people whom have experienced and grown up with a similar third culture background, and are more likely to hold a 'worldview.' Some TCIs see themselves as excelling at shifting between cultural systems, but they also tended to blend their cultural identities into one overarching identity. TCIs grow up learning to juggle different sets of cultural rules, and, as a result, their developmental process is different from people whom grew up in a more homogenous environment. While peers in the host and heritage culture have already internalized the norms, TCIs are still trying to figure out what the rules are.

Transitioning between cultures may cause a disruption in identity development; indeed, certain fundamental developmental tasks (e.g. identity achievement) that are usually mastered in adolescence in monocultural children may be delayed until the twenties and thirties in TCIs. Even at later stages of life, TCIs report feeling as if they "did not fit in," along with higher levels of social difficulty.

This passage was adapted from "When You Have Lived in a Different Culture, Does Returning 'Home' Not Feel Like Home? Predictors of Psychological Readjustment to the Heritage Culture." Altweck L and Marshall T. *PLoS ONE*. 2015. 10(5) doi:10.1371/journal.pone.0124393 for use under the terms of the Creative Commons CC BY 4.0 license (http://creativecommons.org/licenses/by/4.0/legalcode).

Question 30

TCIs are most likely to spend an extended period of time in which of the following of Erikson's stages?

- ○ **A.** Stage 2
- ○ **B.** Stage 4
- ○ **C.** Stage 5
- ○ **D.** Stage 7

Question 31

Vygotsky's theory of development would most likely support which of the following statements about Third Culture Individuals?

- ○ **A.** Social and cultural factors influence the interactions of TCIs with others that promote the acquisition of culturally valued beliefs and behaviors.
- ○ **B.** TCIs never fully resolve the crisis of identity versus role confusion during late adolescence.
- ○ **C.** TCIs, unlike monocultural individuals, are less likely to experience sexual urges for members of their heritage culture.
- ○ **D.** Compared to monocultural individuals, TCIs are more likely to volunteer with their community.

Question 32

Would a child that spent the ages of 2-18 growing up in Europe, but now attends college in the United States, be expected to display greater postconventional morality compared to a child that grew up in the United States?

- ○ **A.** Yes, because the individual would be able to incorporate expectations from multiple cultures when determining how to act in social settings.
- ○ **B.** Yes, because the individual has a greater 'worldview' compared to a young adult that was only raised in the United States.
- ○ **C.** No, because the individual would be unaware of all of the norms of the host culture.
- ○ **D.** No, because the individual would only be aware of the norms of the heritage culture but not the host culture.

Question 33

A subsequent research study suggested that TCIs do not fully integrate into their heritage community because members of the heritage community are unlikely to invite them to community events. TCIs most likely explain their lack of full integration through:

- ○ **A.** dispositional attribution.
- ○ **B.** situational attribution.
- ○ **C.** fundamental attribution error.
- ○ **D.** self-serving bias.

Question 34

As suggested by paragraph three of the passage, monocultural children are LEAST likely to enter which of the following stages earlier in adulthood than TCIs?

- ○ **A.** Identity diffusion
- ○ **B.** Identity moratorium
- ○ **C.** Identity foreclosure
- ○ **D.** Identity achievement

Passage 7 (Questions 35-38)

Reports of physical and sexual abuse in childhood are more frequent in patients diagnosed with affective disorders (depression, bipolar disorder, and anxiety disorder), substance-related disorders, and schizophrenic disorders than in the healthy population. The present study sets out to evaluate reported positive and negative life events from early childhood to adulthood in patients with mental illnesses. Researchers examined whether negative life experiences are positively associated with these diagnoses in adulthood, and if early childhood and adolescence were 'sensitive periods', that is, whether these diagnoses were more closely related to negative experience in these developmental periods.

A total of 151 patients with diagnoses of alcohol-related disorders (n = 45), schizophrenic disorders (n = 52), and affective disorders (n = 54) completed a 42-item self-rating retrospective scale (Traumatic Antecedents Questionnaire, TAQ). The TAQ assesses personal positive experiences (competence and safety) and negative experiences (neglect, emotional, physical and sexual abuse, and more) during four developmental periods, (ages 0–6, 7–12 13–18, and ≥ 19). 63 subjects without any history of mental illness served as controls and also took the TAQ. The subjects were asked to score on a frequency/intensity scale the degree to which it describes their experience: 0 ("never or not at all"), 1 ("rarely or a little bit"), 2 ("occasionally or moderately"), 3 ("often or very much"), and DK ("don't know").

Negative experiences and emotional abuse were more frequent in patients than in controls, with adolescence as the most susceptible period. This suggests that negative experiences in adolescence play a role in identity and personality development. Emotional neglect and abuse were encountered more often in late childhood and adolescence than in early childhood. Physical abuse was more often reported by patients with alcohol-related disorders and with schizophrenic disorders than among controls. The reports of physical abuse generally increased across developmental periods. If sexual abuse was experienced, it occurred particularly in later developmental periods, especially in female patients after puberty.

This passage was adapted from "Negative and Positive Childhood Experiences Across Developmental Periods in Psychiatric Patients with Different Diagnoses—an Explorative Study." Saleptsi E, Bichescu D, Rockstroh B, Neuner F, Schauer M, et al. *BMC Psychiatry*. 2004. 4(40) doi: 10.1186/1471-244X-4-40 for use under the terms of the Creative Commons CC BY 2.0 license (http://creativecommons.org/licenses/by/2.0/legalcode).

Question 35

Which personality theory best describes the findings of the study, assuming that genetics plays no part in the development of the disorders in the study?

- ○ A. Biological theory
- ○ B. Behaviorist theory
- ○ C. Psychoanalytic theory
- ○ D. Humanistic theory

Question 36

Based on the study results, patients who experienced abuse primarily in adolescence would likely be fixated in which of Freud's developmental periods?

- ○ A. Latent stage
- ○ B. Genital stage
- ○ C. Identity vs. role confusion
- ○ D. Autonomy vs. shame and self doubt

Question 37

Which finding of the study best correlates with Erik Erikson's stages of development?

- ○ A. Adolescence is the most sensitive period to negative experiences since it is characterized by the identity vs. role confusion stage.
- ○ B. Adolescence is the most sensitive period to negative experiences since it is characterized by the integrity vs. despair stage.
- ○ C. Adolescence is the least sensitive period to negative experiences since it is characterized by the genital stage of psychosexual development.
- ○ D. Adolescence is the least sensitive period to negative experiences regardless of developmental stage.

Question 38

In a new study, researchers asked patients with psychological disorders to state whether they attributed their personalities to their negative experiences during their development. Patients who attributed their personalities to negative experiences most likely have:

- ○ A. a positive self-efficacy.
- ○ B. an external locus of control.
- ○ C. an internal locus of control.
- ○ D. a negative self-efficacy.

Passage 8 (Questions 39-43)

Achieving ego-integrity is supposed to be associated with achieving wisdom and less death anxiety. In contrast, a person experiences despair if he or she experiences regret about the life he or she has led, and has feelings of sadness, failure and hopelessness. It is suggested that despair is related to psychological distress, depressive symptoms, loneliness, and isolation.

Information on ego-integrity and despair is scarce and a valid questionnaire to assess ego-integrity and despair among cancer patients is lacking. Such a questionnaire is important, because it is hypothesized that patients who do not achieve ego-integrity and have a high level of despair can experience more psychological problems and death anxiety, have fewer personal and interpersonal resources for facing cancer, and are more vulnerable to developing depressive symptoms.

The Northwestern Ego-Integrity Scale (NEIS)—a questionnaire targeting ego-integrity and despair—was developed based on research in the general population. Researchers evaluated psychometric characteristics of the NEIS on ego-integrity (the experience of wholeness and meaning in life, even in spite of negative experiences) and despair (the experience of regret about the life one has led, and feelings of sadness, failure and hopelessness) among cancer patients.

The majority of all items of the NEIS were completed by patients and single item missing rate was below 2%. The ego-integrity subscale was not significantly associated with quality of life, distress, anxiety, or depression. The despair subscale correlated significantly with quality of life, distress, anxiety and depression.

This passage was adapted from "Psychometric Characteristics of a Patient Reported Outcome Measure on Ego-Integrity and Despair among Cancer Patients." Kleijn G, Post L, Witte BI, Bohlmeijer ET, Westerhof GJ, et al. *PLoS ONE.* 2016. 11(5) doi:10.1371/journal.pone.0156003 for use under the terms of the Creative Commons CC BY 4.0 license (http://creativecommons.org/licenses/by/4.0/legalcode).

Question 39

Prior to the stage mentioned in the passage, an individual likely achieves:

- **A.** autonomy vs. shame.
- **B.** generativity vs. stagnation.
- **C.** initiative vs. guilt.
- **D.** intimacy vs. isolation.

Question 40

In what way may the environment have biased the results of the study?

- **A.** Subconscious feelings about the environment are capable of shaping behavior.
- **B.** If a participant's reference group has achieved ego integrity, he is more likely to report ego integrity.
- **C.** An overcast day may have made participants more likely to report despair.
- **D.** A dark environment may have made participants more fearful.

Question 41

Previous research has shown that a supportive social network is important during elderly years. How could researchers test the effect of social networks on the model used in the passage?

- **A.** Use the NEIS to sample an entire family.
- **B.** Differentiate the members of a social network with very low or very high NEIS scores.
- **C.** First sample the participants, then utilize the NEIS to sample friends and family.
- **D.** By sampling more individuals, researchers could improve the statistical significance of the data.

Question 42

Which different types of identities could be used to further categorize participants?

- I. Gender identity
- II. Racial identity
- III. Class identity

- **A.** I only
- **B.** II only
- **C.** I and II only
- **D.** I, II, and III

Question 43

If a large proportion of the participants suffered from Parkinson's disease, the results would show more participants with:

- **A.** ego integrity.
- **B.** despair.
- **C.** depression.
- **D.** psychological illness.

Questions 44 – 47 do not refer to a passage and are independent of each other.

Question 44

Which of the following is NOT used to diagnose a psychological disorder using the DSM-5?

- ○ **A.** Checklist of symptoms
- ○ **B.** Behaviors identified by the clinician
- ○ **C.** Behaviors identified by the patient
- ○ **D.** Cultural ideas

Question 45

A woman in her twenties describes periods of low mood interspersed with bursts of intense excitement and hyperactivity that go on for a few days at a time. Which of the following is NOT true about her condition(s)?

- ○ **A.** Her symptoms fall into the category of mood disorders.
- ○ **B.** She has two distinct disorders—depression and mania.
- ○ **C.** A single diagnosis of depressive disorder would not be an appropriate.
- ○ **D.** There is a strong genetic component driving her symptoms.

Question 46

An adult is struggling with impulse control and delaying gratification. The adult's therapist theorizes that this patient was overindulged by his parents as an infant, and this overindulgence and need for instant gratification has persisted and become a pervasive part of this individual's personality. This therapist likely endorses the theory of personality development put forth by:

- ○ **A.** Erik Erikson.
- ○ **B.** Lev Vygotsky.
- ○ **C.** Sigmund Freud.
- ○ **D.** Jean Piaget.

Question 47

Which of the following personality traits is NOT a part of the popular five-factor model?

- ○ **A.** Neuroticism
- ○ **B.** Narcissism
- ○ **C.** Agreeableness
- ○ **D.** Conscientiousness

Passage 9 (Questions 48-51)

Childhood maltreatment has been increasingly recognized as a major public health problem in high-income countries. Adverse childhood experiences comprise acts of commission of sexual, physical, and emotional abuse, as well as acts of omission, such as emotional and physical neglect and witnessing intimate partner violence. The experience of being harmed by persons who should provide support and protection leads to severe neurobiological, somatic, and mental damage in the developing child, compromising the ability to cope with somatic and psychic stressors throughout his or her lifespan.

Yet, not all individuals affected by stressful life events, such as childhood adversities, suffer from psychological distress, such as post-traumatic stress syndromes, or medical disorders later in their lives. Hence, researchers aimed to determine the association between resilient coping and distress in participants with and without reported childhood adversities.

A representative community sample (N = 2508) between 14-92 years (1334 women; 1174 men) was examined by the short form of the Childhood Trauma Questionnaire, the Brief Resilience Coping Scale, standardized scales of distress, and for somatoform symptoms. Childhood adversity was associated with reduced adjustment, social support, and resilience. It was also strongly associated with increased distress and somatoform complaints. Resilient coping was not only associated with lower distress; it also buffered the effects of childhood adversity on distress. Subjects with high resilience show less distress and somatoform symptoms despite reported childhood adversities in comparison to those with low resilient coping abilities.

This passage was adapted from "Childhood Adversities and Distress—The Role of Resilience in a Representative Sample." Beutel ME, Tibubos AN, Klein EM, Schmutzer G, Reiner I, et al. PLoS ONE. 2017. 12(3) doi:10.1371/journal.pone.0173826 for use under the terms of the Creative Commons CC BY 4.0 license (http://creativecommons.org/licenses/by/4.0/legalcode).

Question 48

Of the negative outcomes associated with childhood adversity, which of the following symptoms would be expected?

- ○ **A.** Reduced resilience
- ○ **B.** Psychological stress
- ○ **C.** Frequent infections
- ○ **D.** Headaches

Question 49

Which of the following psychological disorders attributed to child abuse was previously well-known but recently debunked and modified in the DSM V?

- ○ **A.** Conversion disorder
- ○ **B.** Somatization disorder
- ○ **C.** Dissociative identity disorder
- ○ **D.** Major depressive disorder

Question 50

Freud described a series of defense mechanisms for dealing with stress. Which of the following coping mechanisms may be exhibited by participants at the time of adversity?

○ **A.** Passive aggression, subtle hostility toward the attacker

○ **B.** Humor, laughing at the situation

○ **C.** Displacement, focusing negative emotions on another person or object

○ **D.** Intellectualization, using logic to deal with situation

Question 51

Although not mentioned in the passage, a history of childhood abuse often results in the development of post-traumatic stress disorder (PTSD). Which of the following treatments would be LEAST effective for PTSD?

○ **A.** Anti-depressants

○ **B.** Anti-anxiety medications

○ **C.** Cognitive behavioral therapy (CBT)

○ **D.** Dialectical behavioral therapy (DBT)

Passage 10 (Questions 52-55)

Schizophrenia patients have been widely reported to have a heavier smoking pattern when compared with general population and patients with other mental disorders. This association may be due to smoking's ability to alleviate symptoms of schizophrenia and reduce side effects of antipsychotics.

Researchers sought to examine the smoking pattern among male Chinese schizophrenia patients in Singapore. The study also attempted to investigate the possible mechanisms for their heavy smoking pattern by examining the association of smoking with symptomatology of schizophrenia and with antipsychotics usage and their side effects. Male patients with schizophrenia were recruited from the Institute of Mental Health (IMH) in Singapore. Two independent study samples were recruited: Sample-A was recruited between 2005 and 2008 and consisted of 604 male patients with schizophrenia; Sample-B was recruited between 2008 and 2012 and consisted of 535 male patients. A total of 535 healthy male controls were also recruited from the community in Singapore between 2008 and 2012 to serve as a reference comparison group. The smoking patterns of the two samples were compared to that of the healthy males. This comparison of smoking patterns can be seen in Table 1.

All participants were assessed with the Structured Clinical Interview for DSM-IV-TR (SCID) and Positive and Negative Syndrome Scale (PANSS) by clinicians and research psychologists, who were trained on the administration of the instruments. Demographic and smoking information was collected during an interview. The extra-pyramidal side effects (EPS) of antipsychotics were assessed by two instruments: Abnormal Involuntary Movement Scale (AIMS) and Simpson-Angus Scale (SAS) instrument. Based on AIMS score, patients were classified as tardive dyskinesia, which is a chronic movement disorder characterized by repetitive, involuntary and purposeless movements. Based on SAS score, patients were classified to have drug-induced Parkinsonism, a syndrome characterized by extrapyramidal rigidity, tremor at rest, and postural instability, if the score is more or equal to 3.

Table 1 Smoking Characteristics

	Sample-A N = 604	Sample-B N = 535	Healthy controls N = 535	Risk ratio (RR)/ difference
Ever smoker	50.9%	54.1%	29.5%	1.83
Current smoker	37.9%	42.4%	16.8%	2.52
Ex-smoker	13.4%	12.7%	12.8%	1.00
Cessation rate	26.9%	23.5%	43.3%	0.54
Current smoking status	—	—	—	—
Non-smoker	62.1%	55.3%	82.6%	—
Light smoker	13.4%	14.4%	11.6%	—
Heavy smoker	13.9%	24.5%	3.0%	—
Missing	10.6%	5.8%	2.8%	—
Smoking starting age	—	24.1	24.0	0.1

Question 52

According to the results, were patients with schizophrenia more likely to smoke and does this support the hypothesis that smoking reduces the side effects of antipsychotics?

- O **A.** Yes, schizophrenia patients were more likely to smoke, no this does not support that smoking reduces the side effects of antipsychotics.
- O **B.** Yes, schizophrenia patients were more likely to smoke, yes this does support that smoking reduces the side effects of antipsychotics.
- O **C.** No, schizophrenia patients were not more likely to smoke, no this does not support that smoking reduces the side effects of antipsychotics.
- O **D.** No, schizophrenia patients were not more likely to smoke, yes this does support that smoking reduces the side effects of antipsychotics.

Question 53

A male, Chinese patient with schizophrenia has begun to take lots of time off work they used to be enthusiastic about. What type of symptom are they exhibiting?

- O **A.** Positive
- O **B.** Depression
- O **C.** Negative
- O **D.** Genetic

Question 54

If smoking does reduce the side-effects of antipsychotics, how is this most likely to be accomplished?

- O **A.** The nicotine would improve the side effects.
- O **B.** The nicotine could induce dopamine release in pre-frontal cortex and could also decrease hepatic clearance of antipsychotics, as such EPS could be alleviated by smoking.
- O **C.** The nicotine could induce dopamine release in pre-frontal cortex and could also increase hepatic clearance of antipsychotics, as such EPS could be alleviated by smoking.
- O **D.** There is no way that smoking would reduce the side-effects of antipsychotics.

Question 55

Judging from the results of the study, would it be appropriate for a doctor to encourage a schizophrenia patient to take up smoking socially?

- O **A.** Yes, because the results of the study show that cigarettes help schizophrenics.
- O **B.** Yes, because there is a chance it will decrease symptoms from anti-psychotic medication.
- O **C.** No, because the results of the study show that cigarettes are more harmful then beneficial.
- O **D.** No, because the negative effects of cigarettes are known while the positive effects are unknown.

Questions 56 - 59 do not refer to a passage and are independent of each other.

Question 56

Jane is terrified of heights and thus refuses to work in a building with more than two stories. Jane can best be diagnosed with:

○ **A.** generalized anxiety disorder.

○ **B.** social phobia.

○ **C.** panic disorder.

○ **D.** specific phobia.

Question 57

A recent study found that when individuals who have been in traumatic motor vehicle accidents are given a certain type of antidepressant, they experience relief from depressive symptoms and chronic pain. This type of medication would be especially useful for:

○ **A.** depressive disorder.

○ **B.** somatoform disorder.

○ **C.** mood disorder.

○ **D.** post-traumatic stress disorder.

Question 58

Which of the following situations could be appropriately labeled as representative of a psychological disorder?

○ **A.** A competitive swimmer gets so nervous before races that she has difficulty breathing, and sometimes drops out of meets.

○ **B.** An individual cannot leave his house without engaging in a ritual of checking that the door is locked two separate times.

○ **C.** A grieving person feels extremely sad in the weeks following a loved one's loss.

○ **D.** A sufferer of epilepsy experiences intermittent seizures while at work.

Question 59

Max and his friends go to a busy restaurant on a Saturday evening and did not have a good experience with their waitress. Max thinks that she must not be a very nice person in general, but he did not know that she had recently lost her home. Max's judgment is an example of:

○ **A.** fundamental attribution error.

○ **B.** dispositional attribution.

○ **C.** situational attribution.

○ **D.** personality attribution error.

STOP. If you finish before time is called, check your work. You may go back to any question in this test.

ANSWERS & EXPLANATIONS for Test 3A can be found on p. 220.

LECTURE

Identity and the Individual

TEST 3B

Time: 95 minutes
Questions 1–59

DIRECTIONS: Most of the questions in this test section are grouped with a passage. Read the passage, then select the best answer to each question. Some questions are independent of any passage and of one another. Select the best answer to each of these questions. If you are unsure of an answer, rule out incorrect choices and select from the remaining options. Indicate your selection beside the option you choose.

Passage 1 (Questions 1-4)

There have been a number of studies that have looked at personality trait correlates of health and illness as well as tobacco usage. They have nearly all been cross-sectional, correlational studies that have looked at the relationship between self-reported smoking habits and personality traits. Most recent studies have used tests that assess the Big Five dimensions of personality, which include neuroticism which assesses emotional sensitivity, instability, and proneness to anxiety and depression; extraversion which assesses sociability, gregariousness, positive affect and excitement seeking; openness-to-experience which assesses curiosity, imaginativeness, and a preference for new experiences; agreeableness which concerns compassion, empathy, modesty and tender-mindedness; and conscientiousness which concerns being ambitious, dutiful, reliable and self-disciplined.

Results of the surveys have shown that Extraverts, Neurotics and those Open-to-Experience tend to smoke more while those who are Agreeable and Conscientious tend to smoke less. Most previous research in the area has established Conscientiousness as a protective factor of a number of health conditions and as a predictor of longevity. Two facets of trait Conscientiousness, namely industriousness and self-control were both equally highly correlated with tobacco use. Neuroticism also was associated with increased risk of progression from ever-smoking to daily smoking and persistent daily smoking while Conscientiousness was associated with decreased risk of lifetime cigarette use, progression to daily smoking, and smoking persistence.

One implication of these findings is helping people try to give up smoking. This may mean for Extraverts encouraging some other activities which satisfy their need for stimulation. Similarly, it could involve encouraging people to be more conscientious in their monitoring and regulation of the smoking, as well as trying to encourage those with high openness scores to seek safer, alternative substitutes for tobacco. This suggests that those trying to help or advise smokers quit the habit adapt their suggested treatment regime to the personality profile of the individuals.

This passage was adapted from "The Big-Five Personality Traits, Maternal Smoking during Pregnancy, and Educational Qualifications as Predictors of Tobacco Use in a Nationally Representative Sample." Cheng H, Furnham A. *PLoS ONE*. 2016. 11(1) doi:10.1371/journal.pone.0145552 for use under the terms of the Creative Commons CC BY 4.0 license (http://creativecommons.org/licenses/by/4.0/legalcode).

Question 1

A study surveys participants of a smoking reduction class at the beginning and end of the three-month treatment period. Which of the following plots would likely represent changes in personality, according to trait theory?

○ A.

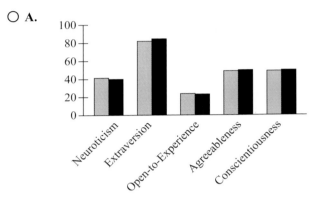

○ B.

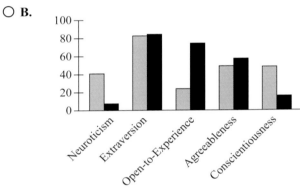

○ C.

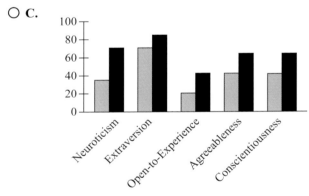

○ D.

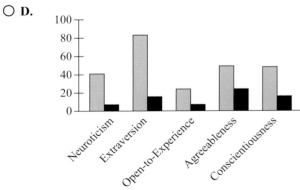

Question 2

Which of the following statements would best support the hereditary perspective concerning self-reported smoking habits and personality?

- A. High scores of agreeableness are often found in individuals that have stable family units consisting of non-smokers.
- B. Conscientiousness and extraversion often show opposite relationships in the same individual, but only after psychotherapy for smoking.
- C. Mutations in the *MAOA* gene often result in aggressive behaviors, increasing neuroticism, and making an individual more likely to smoke.
- D. Those with higher Open-to-Experience scores have a higher level of T_3 and lower resting metabolic rate, leading to less smoking.

Question 3

Individuals that have a high need for stimulation are likely to have:

- A. a strong sense of social identity.
- B. identify with two ethnicities simultaneously.
- C. large social groups.
- D. be more open to variations in sexual orientation.

Question 4

Information contained in the passage would suggest that individuals with high neuroticism are at higher risk for:

- A. obsessive-compulsive disorder.
- B. post-traumatic stress disorder.
- C. bipolar disorder.
- D. schizophrenia.

Passage 2 (Questions 5-10)

Substance abuse, including alcohol, by students is prevalent at U.S. colleges and universities. National surveys of individuals aged 18-25 indicate 52% report lifetime use, 31% report usage within the prior twelve months and 21% within the past month. Further, 58% of alcohol drinking adolescents report using alcohol and marijuana (MJ) simultaneously.

Early-onset marijuana users demonstrate poorer attention, cognitive inhibition and abstract reasoning, all of which are critical skills needed to function and succeed in a college environment. A large longitudinal study confirmed that adolescent-onset marijuana users showed the largest full scale IQ drop between childhood and adulthood. Because substance use patterns tend to cluster among students, it is important to recognize that their influence on academic outcomes may have separable additive or synergistic effects.

It is important to note that alcohol and marijuana are not the only factors that contribute to poor academic achievement. A variety of other mediating and/or comorbid factors such as socioeconomic status, mental health, cultural and family values, stress handling capability, peer pressure, intelligence quotient (IQ), personality traits, and tobacco smoking can play a major role in determining academic performance in college students. Scientists aimed to examine the effects of concurrent alcohol and marijuana use on academic performance in a large sample of college students over a two year period.

They found that substance-use clusters identified across individuals in our study were relatively stable across semesters. Students fell into three clusters: 1) no-low alcohol + MJ, 2) low MJ + moderate/high alcohol, and 3) moderate/high alcohol + MJ. After controlling for a variety of demographic and clinical characteristics, cluster 3 students (who were moderate/heavy users of both substances) had poorer grades than their peers who consumed little or no alcohol/marijuana.

This passage is adapted from "Longitudinal Influence of Alcohol and Marijuana Use on Academic Performance in College Students." Meda S, Gueorguieva R, Pittman B, Rosen R, Aslanzadeh F, et al. *PLoS ONE*. 2017. doi:10.1371/journal.pone.0172213 for use under the terms of the Creative Commons CC BY 4.0 license (http://creativecommons.org/licenses/by/4.0/legalcode).

Question 5

Which of the following studies would be conducted by researchers to quantify the role of genetics in predisposing individuals to smoke marijuana?

- A. A study with two monozygotic females that attended the same high school and local state university.
- B. A study with two monozygotic males that attended the same high school but different colleges.
- C. A study with one dizygotic male and one dizygotic female that attended the same high school and local state university.
- D. A study with one dizygotic male and one dizygotic female that attended the same high school but different colleges.

Question 6

In a follow-up study, researchers found that college students were more likely to smoke marijuana if their parents had shared their previous experiences smoked marijuana in college. This finding supports which of the following theories of development?

○ **A.** Psychoanalytic theory

○ **B.** Biological theory

○ **C.** Biopsychosocial theory

○ **D.** Behaviorist theory

Question 7

Students that fell into cluster 3 in the study are also likely to have increased rates of which of the following disorders?

   I. Prescription drug abuse

   II. Anxiety

   III. Eating disorders

○ **A.** I only

○ **B.** II only

○ **C.** II and III only

○ **D.** I, II, and III

Question 8

Evidence has shown that students whom do not normally smoke marijuana will try the drug if the host of the party also smokes. This exemplifies which of the following explanations of behavior?

○ **A.** Bystander effect

○ **B.** Social loafing

○ **C.** Social facilitation

○ **D.** Peer pressure

Question 9

Which of the following pieces of additional information would most challenge theories that rationalize alcohol and marijuana use in college students?

○ **A.** A student begins her morning with five cups of coffee while at college, but only three cups when at home over the summer.

○ **B.** A student drinks alcoholic beverages most nights of the week while at college, but abstains from drinking while home over the summer.

○ **C.** Some students are able to achieve high GPAs, even when drinking heavily each weekend in college.

○ **D.** A student with severe test anxiety uses a prescription medication to relax before taking exams in college.

Question 10

Which of the following is LEAST likely to be an explanation for the change in performance over time for the group of cluster 2 students?

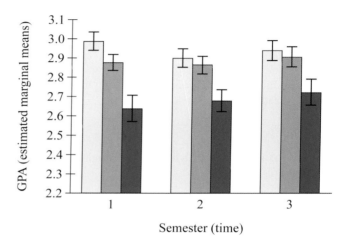

○ cluster1 (no-low alcohol + MJ)
○ cluster2 (low MJ + moderate-high alcohol)
○ cluster3 (moderate-high alcohol + MJ)

○ **A.** Students consuming moderate-to-high levels of alcohol and no marijuana develop tolerance to the effects of alcohol.

○ **B.** Students consuming moderate-to-high levels of alcohol and no marijuana regulate their behavior to only drink when there are no upcoming exams.

○ **C.** Students consuming moderate-to-high levels of alcohol and no marijuana chose to switch to less academically challenging courses.

○ **D.** Students consuming moderate-to-high levels of alcohol and no marijuana showed lower attendance and reported less time studying than their peers that did not drink or smoke.

Questions 11 - 14 do not refer to a passage and are independent of each other.

Question 11

Numerous theories have been used to describe personality development. Which of the following perspectives focuses on learned experiences and behavioral choices?

○ **A.** Behaviorist theory

○ **B.** Humanistic theory

○ **C.** Psychoanalytic theory

○ **D.** Social cognitive theory

Question 12

Which of the following examples best illustrates the humanistic theory?

○ **A.** A doctor reads a biography of a cancer survivor to gain better insight into how he could discuss end of life care in a patient-centric approach.

○ **B.** A student reads the assigned textbook but not suggested reading in order to make time for extracurricular activities.

○ **C.** A lawyer prepares for that day's legal proceedings by reviewing a case immediately before entering the court room.

○ **D.** A journalist drafts a news article but fails to identify two inaccuracies.

Question 13

Morbidity and Mortality conferences, where doctors and allied health professionals discuss medical errors that resulted in patient harm, are an example of:

○ **A.** self-actualization.

○ **B.** social cognitive theory.

○ **C.** observational learning.

○ **D.** psychoanalytic theory.

Question 14

A fourth-year medical student displays confidence in clinical knowledge when teaching first-year medical students, but often has difficulty answering clinical questions from an attending physician. This student most likely shows changes in behavior due to:

○ **A.** personality differences between teaching and answering clinical questions.

○ **B.** anxiety level differences between teaching and answering clinical questions.

○ **C.** temperament differences between teaching and answering clinical questions.

○ **D.** heredity differences between teaching and answering clinical questions.

Passage 3 (Questions 15-18)

Dialysis is a method of removing waste from blood when the kidneys cannot perform this task sufficiently, for example in patients with chronic kidney disease (CKD). Compared to healthy people, patients with CKD participate less in jobs and social activities since dialysis places substantial psychosocial demands on patients. In Study 1, researchers examined the differences between employed versus unemployed pre-dialysis patients. Of 109 patients, 59% were employed and 41% were unemployed. Employed patients were significantly younger than unemployed patients, but there were no significant differences based on other demographic qualifiers. Working patients' mean importance rating score with respect to working was 5.8 out of 7 and unemployed patients' score was 5.2 out of 7.

In Study 2, researchers examined the pre-dialysis patients' illness and treatment perceptions in association with perceived autonomy and self-esteem. Perceived autonomy was assessed as 'heath related autonomy' (i.e. 'My health stops me from doing the things I want to do') and 'global autonomy' (i.e. 'I can do the things that I want to do'). The mean global autonomy score was 1.2 (Range scores = 0-3) and the mean score on the health related autonomy item was 1.1 (Range scores = 0-3). The mean self-esteem score was 78.2 (Range scores = 46-98). High educated patients had higher self-esteem compared to patients with a low and moderate educational level. Researchers then measured to what extent patients believe their illness affects their daily life (consequences), extent to which patients believe their illness is chronic (timeline), and to what extent they believe their illness to be positively influenced by the treatment (treatment control) and by themselves (personal control). Results of this part of Study 2 are shown in Figure 1.

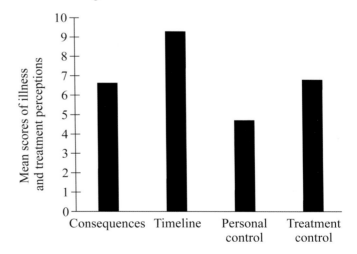

Figure 1 Mean scores of illness and treatment perceptions of pre-dialysis patients

This passage was adapted from "Pre-Dialysis Patients' Perceived Autonomy, Self-esteem and Labor Participation: Associations with Illness Perceptions and Treatment Perceptions. A cross-sectional study." Jansen DL, Grootendorst DC, Rijken M, Kaptein AA, Boeschoten EW, et al. *BMC Nephrology*. 2010. 11(35) doi: 10.1186/1471-2369-11-35 for use under the Creative Commons CC BY 3.0 license (http://creativecommons.org/licenses/by/3.0/legalcode).

Question 15

How could researchers alter Study 2 in order to compare patients' self-efficacy to their desire to work?

- O **A.** Asking patients to what extent they feel their illness affects their ability to work.
- O **B.** Asking patients to what extent they would like to work and feel able to work.
- O **C.** Asking patients how they perceive themselves and perceive their ability to work.
- O **D.** Asking patients how they perceive themselves.

Question 16

Which theorist would hypothesize that combining CKD and its treatment with paid work will stimulate a positive sense of self, and what changes to Study 1 would test this hypothesis?

- O **A.** Humanistic theorist; maintaining the same independent variable, and adding a question that asks if working makes/would make patients feel more fulfilled.
- O **B.** Social cognitive theorist; maintaining the same independent variable, and adding a question that asks if working makes/would make patients feel more fulfilled.
- O **C.** Humanistic theorist; maintaining the same dependent variable, and adding a question that asks if working makes/would make patients feel more fulfilled.
- O **D.** Social cognitive theorist; maintaining the same dependent variable, and adding a question that asks if working makes/would make patients feel more fulfilled.

Question 17

A follow-up study found that educated CKD patients were more motivated than less educated patients to continue working despite the demands of dialysis. Based on this and the results of Study 2, researchers would most likely conclude that:

- O **A.** less educated patients have a positive self-concept but tend to judge themselves more negatively than higher educated patients.
- O **B.** less educated patients have a negative self-concept but tend to judge themselves more positively than higher educated patients.
- O **C.** educated patients have a positive self-concept and tend to judge themselves more positively than lower educated patients.
- O **D.** educated patients have a negative self-concept but tend to judge themselves more positively than lower educated patients.

Question 18

Based on the results of Study 1, a researcher who agrees with the situational approach to explaining behavior would most likely conclude that unemployed patients consider:

- O **A.** working to be important but impossible due to dialysis.
- O **B.** working to be not very important because dialysis is the most important thing in their lives.
- O **C.** dialysis to be more important than working.
- O **D.** their self-efficacy to be too low to work.

Next ▶

Passage 4 (Questions 19-22)

The development of vaccines is one of the most important advances in the history of medicine. In recent years, however, vaccination has declined in many regions of the world, especially vaccination against Measles, Mumps and Rubella (MMR). Research has indicated that one contributor to this particular decline appears to have been the publication concerning a possible link between the MMR vaccination and the appearance of autism. Though this publication was proven to be fabricated and has since been discredited, anti-vaccine conspiracy theories have grown in popularity.

To counteract these theories, researchers investigated the motivations behind anti-vaccine conspiracy theories. Study 1 was designed to test the predictions that belief in anti-vaccine conspiracy theories would be associated with decreased vaccination intentions. Participants, who were all parents, were presented with a scenario depicting a fictitious child and asked to imagine that they were faced with the decision to have this child vaccinated against a specific disease. They were given information about the disease and the vaccination and were asked to indicate their intention to have the child vaccinated. Afterwards, they were asked to rate the effect of four factors on their decision to vaccinate or not vaccinate the child. These four factors were the perceived risk of vaccination, feeling powerless to understand medical literature, disillusionment with western medicine, and inherent trust in authorities.

This passage is adapted from "The Effects of Anti-Vaccine Conspiracy Theories on Vaccine Intentions." Jolley D and Douglas K. *PLoS ONE*. 2014. 9(2) doi:10.1371/journal.pone.0089177 for use under the terms of the Creative Commons CC BY 4.0 license (http://creativecommons.org/licenses/by/4.0/legalcode).

Question 19

If participants of Study 1 differed in their degree of scientific literacy, which outcome would be most likely?

- **A.** Participants whose scientific literacy played a central role would be more affected by trust in authorities regarding their decision to vaccinate or not.
- **B.** Participants whose scientific literacy played a central role would be less affected by trust in authorities regarding their decision to vaccinate or not.
- **C.** Participants whose scientific literacy played a central role would not be affected by the potential dangers of vaccination when deciding to vaccinate or not.
- **D.** Participants whose scientific literacy played a central role would be more affected by powerlessness of choice when deciding to vaccinate or not.

Question 20

Participants that chose to have the child vaccinated in order to maintain the 95% vaccination rate recommended to maintain herd immunity most likely have achieved which stage of Kohlberg's moral reasoning?

- **A.** Preconventional morality stage of universal ethics
- **B.** Postconventional mortality stage of social contract
- **C.** Conventional morality stage of rule following
- **D.** Postconventional morality stage of social disapproval

Question 21

Participants that ranked powerlessness to interpret the medical literature as the greatest reason for avoiding vaccination would likely agree with which of the following statements?

- **A.** Individual beliefs do not play a role in determining whether a study participant would have vaccinated a child.
- **B.** Individual beliefs play the sole role in determining whether a study participant would have vaccinated a child.
- **C.** Study participants weigh each individual belief equally when determining whether to vaccinate a child or not.
- **D.** Varying beliefs likely affect whether a study participant would have vaccinated a child, but are unlikely to be the sole factor.

Question 22

Study participants were asked about the vaccination of children aged 4-6. According to Freud's theory, these children are likely:

- **A.** undergoing toilet training.
- **B.** exploring the concept of boy versus girl.
- **C.** strengthening their concept of friends and peer groups.
- **D.** learning the necessary skills to nurse.

Passage 5 (Questions 23-26)

Bipolar I disorder (BD) causes severe psychological and financial strain on patients, their family members, and the public health care administration system. In addition, it causes substantial disability. It has been reported that patients with bipolar I disorder show reduced task performance at work. They are also at a high risk of suicide, with 50% attempting suicide and 6% to 20% committing suicide.

According to psychological behaviorism theory, the etiological factors underlying BD are past psychosocial factors, current psychosocial factors, current transient organic factors, and basic behavioral repertoires. Researchers sought to identify psychosocial factors related to the onset of bipolar I disorder. To do so, the Bipolar Disorder Etiology Scale (BDES), based on psychological behaviorism, was developed and validated.

The main task in the development of the BDES was composing items not related to symptoms themselves, but rather to behavioral tendencies affecting the symptoms as etiological factors, especially in the case of basic behavior repertoires. Using the BDES, common factors related to both major depressive disorder (MDD) and BD and specific factors related only to BD were investigated. The BDES measures 17 factors based on psychological behaviorism hypotheses.

The scale was administered to 113 non-clinical control subjects, 30 subjects with MDD, and 32 people with BD. Subscales on which MDD and BD groups scored higher than controls were classified as common factors, while those on which the BD group scored higher than MDD and control groups were classified as specific factors.

Twelve common factors influence both MDD and BD, and one specific factor influences only BD. Common factors included the following: learning grandiose self-labeling, learning dangerous behavior, reinforcing impulsive behavior, exposure to irritability, punishment of negative emotional expression, lack of support, sleep problems, antidepressant problems, positive arousal to threat, lack of social skills, and pursuit of short-term pleasure. The BD-specific factor was manic emotional response.

This passage was adapted from "Validation of the Bipolar Disorder Etiology Scale Based on Psychological Behaviorism Theory and Factors Related to the Onset of Bipolar Disorder." Park JW, Park KH. *PLoS ONE*. 2014. 9(12) doi: 10.1371/journal.pone.0116265 for use under the terms of the Creative Commons CC BY 4.0 license (http://creativecommons.org/licenses/by/4.0/legalcode).

Question 23

Which of the following theories correctly describes behaviorism theory as it relates to personality?

- **A.** Personality is a genetic predisposition toward a certain behavior.
- **B.** Personality is dynamic and highly dependent on evolved characteristics.
- **C.** Personality is a product of the environment and a learned characteristic.
- **D.** Personality can be trained through repeated exposures.

Question 24

Classified as a mood disorder, which of the following features must be present to diagnose BD?

- **A.** Anxiety
- **B.** Depression
- **C.** Mania
- **D.** Suicidality

Question 25

Assuming imitation played a significant role in the identity formation of the BD participants, which of the following may describe a parent of a person with BD?

- **A.** Dismissive, self-absorbed, unreliable
- **B.** Amicable, popular, formidable
- **C.** Ornery, strong-willed, dependable
- **D.** Impulsive, grandiose, self-centered

Question 26

A similar test was developed for OCD. Which of the following may summarize this new test?

- **A.** Behaviors like poor response to anxiety and perfectionism would be recorded.
- **B.** Impulsive behavior and obsessive thoughts would be recorded.
- **C.** Checklists would be used to develop the questionnaire.
- **D.** The questionnaire would probe for symptoms of repetitive behavior.

Questions 27 - 30 do not refer to a passage and are independent of each other.

Question 27

A student finds that when she asks for regular feedback, she both improves the quality of her work and finds that her mentors appear to trust her work more. This best illustrates which of the following ideas?

○ **A.** Social cognitive theory

○ **B.** Observational learning

○ **C.** Reciprocal causation

○ **D.** Self-actualization

Question 28

A pediatrician discovers that a subset of his patients is only able to correctly administer insulin injections at first with his guidance. This subset of patients is best represented within which of the following psychological classifications?

○ **A.** Reference group

○ **B.** Freud's latent stage

○ **C.** Vygotsky's zone of proximal development

○ **D.** Erikson's developmental stage of autonomy vs. shame and doubt

Question 29

Which of the following is not a type of identity?

○ **A.** Racial identity

○ **B.** Socioeconomic identity

○ **C.** Gender identity

○ **D.** Personal identity

Question 30

A pediatric psychiatrist notes that several of her patients take medications mostly because they are afraid of the consequences involved in disobeying their parents' orders. What stage of Kohlberg's theory of moral development would these patients best fit into?

○ **A.** Preconventional level

○ **B.** Conventional level

○ **C.** Trust vs. mistrust

○ **D.** Obedience vs. disobedience

Passage 6 (Questions 31-34)

The admissions committee at a medical school wished to examine the associations between empathy and big five personality traits among medical students. Empathy is an essential element in medical practice, which promotes positive physician-patient communication and is associated with improved patient satisfaction, treatment adherence, and clinical outcomes.

A cross-sectional study was conducted. A total of 530 clinical medical students became the final subjects. Hierarchical regression analysis was performed to explore the effects of big five personality traits on empathy.

In the first phase, students responded to the Big Five Inventory (BFI) to assess personality. In the second phase, students responded to the Interpersonal Reactivity Index (IRI) and the Big Five Inventory (BFI), and demographic characteristics were distributed.

Big five personality traits accounted for 19.4%, 18.1%, 30.2% of the variance in three dimensions of empathy, namely, perspective taking, empathic concern, and personal distress, respectively. Specifically, agreeableness had a strong positive association with empathic concern, and a moderate association with perspective taking. Neuroticism had a strong positive association with personal distress and was modestly associated with perspective taking. Openness to experience had modest associations with perspective taking and personal distress. Conscientiousness had a modest association with perspective taking.

This passage was adapted from "Associations Between Empathy and Big Five Personality Traits Among Chinese Undergraduate Medical Students." Song Y, Shi M. *PLoS ONE*. 2017. 12(2) doi:10.1371/journal.pone.0171665 for use under the terms of the Creative Commons CC BY 4.0 license (http://creativecommons.org/licenses/by/4.0/legalcode).

Question 31

In the first phase, researchers based their framework on which of the following theories of personality?

○ **A.** Humanistic theory

○ **B.** Behaviorist theory

○ **C.** Dispositional theory

○ **D.** Psychoanalytic theory

Question 32

What is the best explanation for the results of the study ?

○ **A.** Empathetic concern is likely stable over a lifetime and predicted by agreeableness.

○ **B.** Empathetic concern is not stable over a lifetime but is predicted by agreeableness.

○ **C.** Empathetic concern is likely stable over a lifetime and predicted by conscientiousness.

○ **D.** Empathetic concern is not stable over a lifetime but is predicted by conscientiousness.

Question 33

Under the Freudian model of personality, which of the following is most responsible for empathy?

- ○ **A.** The unconscious
- ○ **B.** The id
- ○ **C.** The ego
- ○ **D.** The superego

Question 34

The correlations found by researchers suggest all of the following EXCEPT:

- ○ **A.** an empathetic student may have a neurotic in-group.
- ○ **B.** an empathetic student may have a conscientious reference group.
- ○ **C.** an empathetic student may imitate an agreeable student.
- ○ **D.** an empathetic student may have a strong internal locus of control.

Passage 7 (Questions 35-38)

Chronic cocaine use has been associated with impairments in social cognition, self-serving and antisocial behavior, and socially relevant personality disorders (PD). Together, these specific social characteristics of chronic cocaine users resemble the broad concept of Machiavellianism, which is described as social attitude characterized by cynical beliefs, interpersonal manipulation, and pragmatic morality. Despite the apparent relationship between Machiavellianism and stimulant use, no study has explicitly examined this personality concept in cocaine users so far.

In the frame of the longitudinal Zurich Cocaine Cognition Study, the Machiavellianism Questionnaire (MACH-IV) was assessed in 68 recreational and 30 dependent cocaine users, as well as in 68 psychostimulant-naïve controls at baseline. Additionally, three closely related personality dimensions from the Temperament and Character Inventory (TCI)—cooperativeness, (social) reward dependence, and self-directedness—and the screening questionnaire of the Structured Clinical Interview for DSM-IV Axis II Personality Disorders (SCID-II) were acquired.

Both recreational and dependent cocaine users showed significantly higher Machiavellianism than controls, while dependent cocaine users additionally displayed significantly lower levels of TCI cooperativeness and self-directedness. Moreover, in cocaine users, higher Machiavellianism correlated significantly with lower levels of cooperativeness and self-directedness, with less prosocial behavior, and with higher cluster B PD personality disorder scores.

These results were again replicated at 1-year follow-up. However, Machiavellianism was not correlated with measures of cocaine use severity. Both recreational and dependent cocaine users displayed pronounced and stable Machiavellian personality traits. The lack of correlations with severity of cocaine use and its temporal stability indicates that a Machiavellian personality trait might represent a predisposition for cocaine use that potentially serves as a predictor for stimulant addiction.

This passage was adapted from "Stable Self-Serving Personality Traits in Recreational and Dependent Cocaine Users." Quednow BB, Hulka LM, Preller KH, Baumgartner MR, Eisenegger C, et al. *PLoS ONE*. 2017. 12(3) doi:10.1371/journal.pone.0172853 for use under the terms of the Creative Commons CC BY 4.0 license (http://creativecommons.org/licenses/by/4.0/legalcode).

Question 35

Which of the following personality disorders may be associated with Machiavellianism?

- ○ **A.** Antisocial personality disorder
- ○ **B.** Obsessive-compulsive personality disorder
- ○ **C.** Paranoid personality disorder
- ○ **D.** Schizotypal personality disorder

Question 36

According to the trait perspective:

○ **A.** the amount of Machiavellianism is constant over a lifetime but varies from person to person.

○ **B.** the amount of Machiavellianism is constant over a lifetime and is either present or not.

○ **C.** the amount of Machiavellianism varies over a lifetime and varies from person to person.

○ **D.** the amount of Machiavellianism varies over a lifetime and is either present or not.

Question 37

Under the Freudian paradigm of personality, which of the following would be responsible for drug abuse?

○ **A.** Self

○ **B.** Id

○ **C.** Superego

○ **D.** Ego

Question 38

Based on the findings in the passage, cocaine abuse may be associated with a(n):

○ **A.** high self-esteem.

○ **B.** high self-efficacy.

○ **C.** internal locus of control.

○ **D.** external locus of control.

Passage 8 (Questions 39-44)

Understanding the factors that influence eating behavior can pave the way for targeted interventions. This can encourage healthier eating and ultimately improve quality of life. Investigating health perceptions and real-world eating behavior may elucidate what potential this social norm manipulation might have as an intervention strategy to encourage healthier eating.

A study investigated whether people change their food preferences and eating behavior in response to health-based social norms. 120 participants rated a series of healthy and unhealthy food images. After each rating, participants viewed a rating that ostensibly represented the average rating of previous participants. In fact, these average ratings were manipulated to convey a particular social norm. Participants either saw average ratings that favored healthy foods, favored unhealthy foods, or did not see any average ratings. Participants then re-rated those same food images after approximately ten minutes and again three days later.

In addition to the rating experiment, researchers also investigated potential additional consequences of this novel social norm manipulation. After the norm manipulation, participants were given the chance to take as many pieces of candy as they wanted from a jar. This jar was weighed before participants arrived and after they left to determine the amount of candy each participant took. The experimenters predicted that participants whom show an increased preference for unhealthy foods would consume more candy.

Participants exposed to a healthy social norm consistently reported lower preferences for unhealthy foods as compared to participants in the other two conditions. This preference difference persisted three days after the social norm manipulation. However, health-based social norm manipulations did not influence the amount of candy participants took. Although health-based social norm manipulations can influence stated food preferences, in this case they did not influence subsequent eating behavior.

This passage was adapted from "Social Norms Shift Preferences for Healthy and Unhealthy Foods." Templeton EM, Stanton MV, Zaki J. *PLoS ONE*. 2016. 11(11) doi:10.1371/journal.pone.0166286 for use under the terms of the Creative Commons CC BY 4.0 license (https://creativecommons.org/licenses/by/4.0/legalcode).

Question 39

The study found that the average rating of previous participants affected a participant's preference for healthy foods. The previous participants are acting as which of the following?

○ **A.** In-group

○ **B.** Out-group

○ **C.** Reference group

○ **D.** Primary group

Question 40

A longitudinal study reveals that an individual's food preferences tend to change minimally during the span of his or her life. This finding best supports the validity of which of the following personality theories?

- ○ **A.** Trait theory
- ○ **B.** Psychoanalytic theory
- ○ **C.** Behaviorist theory
- ○ **D.** Humanistic theory

Question 41

A nutritionist wishes to incorporate the results of these studies into improving the health of one of her overweight clients. According to the findings, which of the following actions would be most effective?

- ○ **A.** Giving the client one-on-one counseling on eating habits and weight loss strategies, and then following up with the client every two weeks.
- ○ **B.** Encouraging the client's friends and families to eat healthier, to act as a positive influence on the client.
- ○ **C.** Exposing the client to previously unknown social norms that encourage healthier eating.
- ○ **D.** Asking the client to rate pictures of food items as healthy or unhealthy, and then asking them to re-rate the pictures 10 days later.

Question 42

The experimenters decide to do a follow-up experiment to study the mediating effect of mood disorders on social norm manipulation. Participants with which of the following symptoms should NOT be included in this study?

- ○ **A.** Loss of interest in activities and disruptions in eating patterns
- ○ **B.** Alternating between feelings of extreme happiness and sadness
- ○ **C.** A deficiency in serum levels of monoamine neurotransmitters
- ○ **D.** Attention seeking behavior and inability to maintain stable relationships

Question 43

Suppose that the participants in this study were recruited from a single university. Which psychosocial stage would most of participants belong to?

- ○ **A.** Integrity vs. despair
- ○ **B.** Intimacy vs. isolation
- ○ **C.** Industry vs. inferiority
- ○ **D.** Initiative vs. guilt

Question 44

Which of the following is a biomedical interpretation of the results of the study?

- ○ **A.** Eating behavior is not influenced by social norms because it has a strong genetic basis.
- ○ **B.** Eating behavior is not influenced by social norms because it is affected by a combination of psychological and social influences.
- ○ **C.** Eating behavior is not influenced by social norms because the study does not accurately model social norm manipulation.
- ○ **D.** Eating behavior is not influenced by social norms because a preference for candy is not representative of all food preferences.

Next ▶

Questions 45 - 48 do not refer to a passage and are independent of each other.

Question 45

Although neurons have limited regenerative potential, special cells can be implanted to promote regeneration. Which of the following would be most effective?

○ **A.** Pluripotent stem cells of endoderm origin

○ **B.** Pluripotent stem cells of mesoderm origin

○ **C.** Pluripotent stem cells of ectoderm origin

○ **D.** Pluripotent stem cells of mesenchymal origin

Question 46

β-amyloid plaques and neurofibrillary tangles (hyperphosphorlyated tau proteins) are associated with which neurodegenerative disease?

○ **A.** Alzheimer's disease

○ **B.** Amyotrophic lateral sclerosis

○ **C.** Korsakoff's syndrome

○ **D.** Parkinson's disease

Question 47

John thinks he hears a voice in his head telling him how to act. This can be described as a:

○ **A.** delusion.

○ **B.** hallucination.

○ **C.** disorganized thought.

○ **D.** negative symptom.

Question 48

Which of the following psychological disorders is most common?

○ **A.** Anxiety disorders

○ **B.** Bipolar disorder

○ **C.** Depression

○ **D.** Schizophrenia

Passage 9 (Questions 49-52)

Breast cancer is the most common cancer among women in the United States. The improvement in treatment quality combined with America's aging population has led to an increase in breast cancer survivors the past decade. Previous studies have found that 35%-38% of all breast cancer patients experience significant emotional distress, anxiety or other depression following their diagnosis.

A study examined the associations between breast cancer diagnosis and the diagnoses of anxiety or depression among 4,164 hospitalized breast cancer cases matched with 4,164 nonbreast cancer controls using 2006-2009 inpatient data obtained from the Nationwide Inpatient Sample database. Women without a primary breast cancer diagnosis were matched 1:1 to women with primary breast cancer diagnosis on age at admission, race/ethnicity, length of stay, insurance type, residential income, and discharge disposition.

The study examined two separate outcomes: 1) Diagnoses of mental health disorders in breast cancer inpatients comparing cases with matched non-breast cancer controls; and 2) In-hospital mortality among breast cancer patients, defined as death during hospitalization using a sample of breast cancer cases. Data collected can be seen in Table 1.

Table 1 Results of Breast Cancer Cases and Control Groups in Categories Diagnosed Depression, Diagnosed Anxiety, Race/Ethnicity, Residential Income, and Insurance Type

	Cases N = 4,164	Controls N = 4,164
Diagnosed depression		
No	3,809	3,585
Yes	355	579
Diagnosed anxiety		
No	3,992	3,918
Yes	172	246
Race/Ethnicity		
White	2,375	2,387
Black	407	381
Hispanic	203	229
Other	167	163
Residential income		
Q1-lowest	958	1,133
Q2	977	1,138
Q3	963	977
Q4-highest	1,174	812
Insurance type		
Private	2,055	1,711
Medicare	1,554	1,790
Medicaid	333	336
Other	222	327

This passage was adapted from "Depression and Anxiety Disorders among Hospitalized Women with Breast Cancer." Vin-Raviv N, Akinyemiju T, Galea S, and Bovbjerg D. *PLoS ONE*. 2015. 10(6) doi: 10.1371/journal.pone.0129169 for use under the terms of the Creative Commons CC BY 4.0 license (https://creativecommons.org/licenses/by/4.0/legalcode).

Question 49

Based on the results of the study, were hospitalized patients with breast cancer more or less likely than non-breast cancer patients to be diagnosed with depression and why might this be?

- A. More likely, because they will receive more attention than other patients.
- B. More likely, because they are more likely to get depressed.
- C. Less likely, because they are less depressed than other patients.
- D. Less likely, because of a lack of oncologists collaborating with mental health physicians on treatment plans.

Question 50

A patient is found to have excessive sympathetic nervous system activation. What disorder is this patient most likely to have?

- A. Anxiety
- B. Depression
- C. Anxiety and depression
- D. Neither anxiety nor depression

Question 51

What is a category not considered in matching that could have the biggest effect on the reliability of the results?

- A. Genetic predisposition
- B. Personality
- C. Financial situation
- D. Temperament

Question 52

Is the biopsychosocial model or the biomedical model a better approach to understanding anxiety and depression?

- A. Biomedical because of the underlying biological processes that cause depression and anxiety are extremely important.
- B. Biomedical because in order to understand psychological conditions both biological and external factors are important.
- C. Biopsychosocial because the underlying biological processes that cause depression and anxiety are extremely important.
- D. Biopsychosocial because in order to understand psychological conditions both biological and external factors are important.

Next ▶

Passage 10 (Questions 53-56)

Depression in the elderly can coexist and be easily confused with dementia and general debility due to ill health. Unpublished data from the authors using the Philadelphia Geriatric Morale Scale (PGC) diagnostic system show a nationwide prevalence of about 12% sub-clinical (level 1–2) and 2% clinical (level 3–5) depression.

A study examined the relationship between morale measured by the PGC and disability, social support, religiosity, and personality traits. A low score on the PGC signifies low morale. Instruments predicting morale were then tested against PGC domains.

The study utilized a cross-sectional survey with a multistage cluster sampling design. Instruments used were disability via the WHO Disability Score-II, social support via the Duke Social Support Scale, the Lubben Social Network Scale, the Medical Outcomes Study Social Support Survey, religiosity via the Revised Intrinsic- Extrinsic Religious Orientation Scale, and personality via the Ten-Item Personality Inventory. Effects of confounders such as gender, age, and ethnicity were checked using binary logistic regression.

For PGC domains, attitude toward aging and lonely dissatisfaction trended together, while agitation did not. Disability, social support, religiosity, and personality strongly influenced morale measures.

This passage was adapted from "Assessment of Factors Influencing Morale in the Elderly." Loke SC, Abdullah SS, Chai ST, Hamid TA, Yahaya N. *PLoS ONE*. 2011. 6(1) doi:10.1371 journal.pone.0016490 for use under the terms of the Creative Commons CC BY 3.0 license (http://creativecommons.org/licenses/by/3.0/legalcode).

Question 53

An elderly man with a low PGC may be diagnosed with which psychological disease?

- ○ **A.** An anxiety disorder
- ○ **B.** A mood disorder
- ○ **C.** A personality disorder
- ○ **D.** A trauma-related disorder

Question 54

Which of the following personality perspectives may the researchers favor?

- ○ **A.** Biological theory
- ○ **B.** Psychoanalytic theory
- ○ **C.** Trait theory
- ○ **D.** Social cognitive theory

Question 55

Utilizing a biological framework, the elderly referenced in the first paragraph may have depletion in which of the following?

- ○ **A.** Epinephrine
- ○ **B.** GABA
- ○ **C.** Monoamines
- ○ **D.** Orexin

Question 56

Based on nationwide prevalence, which of the following disorders is most likely?

- ○ **A.** Anxiety
- ○ **B.** Depression
- ○ **C.** Dissociative disorders
- ○ **D.** Schizophrenia

Questions 57 - 59 do not refer to a passage and are independent of each other.

Question 57

Researchers studying Parkinson's disease attempted to document the mood of patients over the course of their diagnosis. Which of the following would be a confounding variable?

    I. Use of selective serotonin reuptake inhibitors (SSRIs)

    II. Disease related mood impairment

    III. Coexistence of a mood disorder

○ **A.** I only

○ **B.** I and II only

○ **C.** I and III only

○ **D.** I, II, and III

Question 58

A doctor wishes to investigate a patient's family history in order to see which psychological disorders she is most at risk for. Which of the following diseases is LEAST important to look for?

○ **A.** Depression

○ **B.** Schizophrenia

○ **C.** Bipolar disorder

○ **D.** Post Traumatic Stress Disorder

Question 59

An individual fails to pay her rent on time, but in the same week, she receives a large promotion at work. She feels that her promotion was due to her intelligence, skill, and hard work, but concludes that her failure to pay rent on time was due to the fact that she was not feeling well that week. These explanations are an example of:

○ **A.** the fundamental attribution error.

○ **B.** dispositional attribution.

○ **C.** self-serving bias.

○ **D.** reciprocation theory.

STOP. If you finish before time is called, check your work. You may go back to any question in this test.

ANSWERS & EXPLANATIONS for Test 3B can be found on p. 220.

LECTURE

Thought and Emotion

TEST 4A

Time: 95 minutes
Questions 1–59

DIRECTIONS: Most of the questions in this test section are grouped with a passage. Read the passage, then select the best answer to each question. Some questions are independent of any passage and of one another. Select the best answer to each of these questions. If you are unsure of an answer, rule out incorrect choices and select from the remaining options. Indicate your selection beside the option you choose.

Passage 1 (Questions 1-4)

Memory is essential to many cognitive tasks including language. Apart from empirical studies of memory effects on language acquisition and use, there is a lack of sufficient evolutionary explorations on whether a high level of memory capacity is a prerequisite for language and whether language origin could influence memory capacity.

In line with evolutionary theories that natural selection refined language-related cognitive abilities, researchers advocated a coevolution scenario between language and memory capacity, which incorporated the genetic transmission of individual memory capacity, cultural transmission of idiolects, and natural and cultural selections on individual reproduction and language teaching.

To illustrate the coevolution dynamics, researchers adopted a multi-agent computational model simulating the emergence of lexical items and simple syntax through iterated communications. Simulations showed that: along with the origin of a communal language, an initially-low memory capacity for acquired linguistic knowledge was boosted; and such a coherent increase in linguistic understandability and memory capacities reflected a language-memory coevolution; and such coevolution stopped till memory capacities became sufficient for language communications.

Statistical analyses revealed that the coevolution was realized mainly by natural selection based on individual communicative success in cultural transmissions. This work elaborated the biology-culture parallelism of language evolution, demonstrated the driving force of culturally-constituted factors for natural selection of individual cognitive abilities, and suggested that the degree difference in language-related cognitive abilities between humans and nonhuman animals could result from a coevolution with language.

This passage was adapted from "Modeling Coevolution between Language and Memory Capacity during Language Origin." Gong T, Shuai L. *PLoS ONE*. 2015. 10(11) doi:10.1371/journal.pone.0142281 for use under the terms of the Creative Commons CC BY 4.0 license (http://creativecommons.org/licenses/by/4.0/legalcode).

Question 1

Which of the following areas of the brain must have also coevolved with the skills stated in the passage?

○ **A.** The frontal lobes and insula

○ **B.** The temporal lobes

○ **C.** The amygdala and entorhinal cortex

○ **D.** The occipital lobes

Question 2

Which of the following methods could be used to determine which neurobiological advancement mentioned in the passage preceded the other?

○ **A.** Examine brain specimens from human remains.

○ **B.** Examine vocal cord specimens from human remains.

○ **C.** Design an experiment to assess which advancement occurs first in primates.

○ **D.** Compare records timing tool usage and hieroglyphics.

Question 3

Prior to the evolution mentioned in the passage, individuals never surpassed which of Piaget's stages?

○ **A.** Concrete operational

○ **B.** Formal operational

○ **C.** Preoperational

○ **D.** Sensorimotor

Question 4

Although not explicitly mentioned in the passage, personality and executive function are very important in language and cognition. Which of the following brain regions controls these features?

○ **A.** Frontal lobes

○ **B.** Parietal lobes

○ **C.** Temporal lobes

○ **D.** Occipital lobes

Passage 2 (Questions 5-8)

As people age, the risk of developing dementia increases substantially. Delaying dementia onset by a few years would therefore have enormous benefits for the health and social care sectors, and would have large implications for the psychological well-being of the patients and their loved ones. It has been previously demonstrated that social, physical, and cognitive activity protects retired seniors from cognitive decline.

Researchers introduced voluntary work defined as 1) activities performed out of free will, 2) without receiving remuneration, 3) in a formal organization, and 4) benefiting others as a specific form of later-life activity that may protect retired seniors from cognitive complaints and dementia.

The theoretical tenet behind this assumption is that volunteering provides retired seniors with a clear time structure, increases social, physical, and cognitive activity, and allows them to participate in a collective purpose (all to varying degrees depending on the nature of the voluntary work). The unique combination of these aspects and forms of activity may subsequently, through social, physical, and cognitive mechanisms, lead to improved cognitive functioning and reduced dementia risks.

Three groups of seniors participated in a study: 1) no volunteering, 2) discontinuous volunteering, and 3) continuous volunteering. Researchers investigated the effect of voluntary work (discontinuously and continuously) on self-reported cognitive complaints and the likelihood of being prescribed an anti-dementia treatment after controlling for baseline and relevant background variables. The results indicated that seniors who continuously volunteered reported a decrease in their cognitive complaints over time, whereas no such associations were found for the other groups. In addition, they were 2 times less likely to be prescribed an anti-dementia treatment.

This passage was adapted from "Can Volunteering in Later Life Reduce the Risk of Dementia? A 5-Year Longitudinal Study Among Volunteering and Non-volunteering Retired Seniors." Griep Y, Hanson LM, Vantilborgh T, Janssens L, Jones SK, et al. *PLoS ONE.* 2017. 12(3) doi:10.1371/journal.pone.0173885 for use under the terms of the Creative Commons CC BY 4.0 license (http://creativecommons.org/licenses/by/4.0/legalcode).

Question 5

A student summarizes the results of the study as "volunteering causes decreased dementia." Which of the following types of problem solving did the student use?

○ **A.** Heuristics

○ **B.** Trial and error

○ **C.** Algorithm

○ **D.** Intuition

Question 6

A participant in the study who volunteers had an IQ of 124 during college. Which of the following is likely his IQ now?

○ **A.** 100

○ **B.** 115

○ **C.** 125

○ **D.** 140

Question 7

In what way may culture have biased the results?

○ **A.** In underdeveloped countries, the elderly are expected to volunteer.

○ **B.** In developed countries, the elderly are expected to volunteer.

○ **C.** In underdeveloped countries, cognitive decline in the elderly is expected.

○ **D.** In developed countries, cognitive decline in the elderly is expected.

Question 8

Which of the following cognitive changes is a normal part of aging and not a symptom of dementia?

○ **A.** Forgetting names of acquaintances

○ **B.** Not recognizing love ones

○ **C.** Delayed reaction time

○ **D.** Not remembering to eat meals

Questions 9 - 12 do not refer to a passage and are independent of each other.

Question 9

Which of the following theories of language development is correctly defined?

○ A. The nativist theory states language is learned from a native speaker.

○ B. The nativist theory states that language is innate.

○ C. The interactionist theory states that biology and psychology interact to form language.

○ D. The interactionist theory states multiple theories interplay to promote language development.

Question 10

Dementia is a progressive disease that gradually destroys the ability to recall recent and eventually remote events. In what way does this relate to the information-processing model?

○ A. Like a computer, the brain relies on proper coding and storage of material.

○ B. As the brain ages, it is normal to have cognitive slowing.

○ C. Information enters the brain but is incorrectly processed, so it is irretrievable later.

○ D. Dementia, including Alzheimer's disease, damages the hippocampus and other cortical regions.

Question 11

A young child who is homeschooled undergoes evaluation for a delay in language development. The psychologist suggests the child in scouting or sports groups. This approach utilizes which theory of language acquisition?

○ A. Nativist Theory

○ B. Interactionist Theory

○ C. Learning Theory

○ D. Relational Theory

Question 12

A patient with head trauma repeats words back to an individual but does not seem to comprehend them. Which area of the brain was most likely damaged?

○ A. Frontal lobe

○ B. Parietal lobe

○ C. Broca's area

○ D. Wernicke's area

Passage 3 (Questions 13-16)

Previous literature has shown that vehicle crash risk increases as drivers' off-road glance duration increases. Many factors influence drivers' glance duration, such as individual differences, driving environment, or task characteristics. Researchers examined the effect of glance sequence on glance duration among drivers completing a visual-manual radio tuning task and an auditory-vocal based multi-modal navigation entry task.

For the radio tuning task, there were two groups. In group 1, forty participants drove under an experimental protocol that required three button presses and rotation of a tuning knob to complete the radio tuning task. In group 2, forty participants completed the task with one less button press. The tasks are summarized in Figure 1.

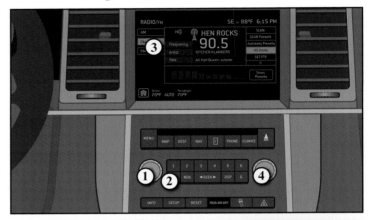

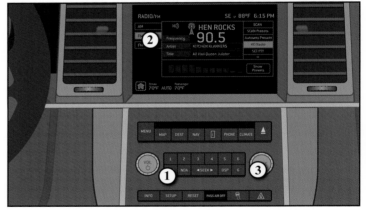

Figure 1 Group 1 task (top) and group 2 task (bottom)

For the navigation entry tasks, there was no protocol difference between the two data sets. The task required participants to press a button on the steering wheel to start the voice recognition system and to verbally enter the designated addresses in a series of steps. There were two trials and a different address for each trial. The navigation entry task consisted of six steps: (1) press the voice button, (2) say "Destination street address," (3) say "City name," (4) say "Street name," (5) say "House number," and (6) say "Yes" to confirm the entry.

This passage was adapted from "Does Order Matter? Investigating the Effect of Sequence on Glance Duration During On-road Driving." Lee J, Roberts SC, Reimer B, Mehler B. *PLoS ONE*. 2017. 12(12) doi:10.1371/ journal.pone.0171730 for use under the terms of the Creative Commons CC BY 4.0 license (http://creativecommons.org/ licenses/by/4.0/legalcode).

Question 13

Impairment in which of the following regions would affect the navigation task?

- ○ **A.** Occipital notch
- ○ **B.** Left inferior frontal gyrus
- ○ **C.** Subthalamic nucleus
- ○ **D.** Superior parietal lobule

Question 14

Which of the following is NOT expected to change the results of the experiment ?

- ○ **A.** Use of caffeine
- ○ **B.** Use of alcohol
- ○ **C.** High IQ
- ○ **D.** Low IQ

Question 15

Which methodology would best replicate the experiment?

- ○ **A.** Word association testing
- ○ **B.** Stroop testing
- ○ **C.** Field sobriety testing
- ○ **D.** Operational span testing

Question 16

Which approach to problem solving would be most effective in completing the radio-tuning and navigation tasks?

- ○ **A.** Analogies
- ○ **B.** Algorithms
- ○ **C.** Intuition
- ○ **D.** Heuristics

Passage 4 (Questions 17-22)

Counterfactual thinking (CFT) is a type of conditional reasoning that takes place when thinking about past events. In this context, most people automatically compare the actual outcome of the event with "what might have been" by generating hypothetical "if only" outcomes supposing an alternative event had taken place. The causal order effect, describes how, when faced with a hypothetical scenario involving a chain of events that has a negative outcome, most subjects tend to choose the first event in the scenario as the main determinant of the outcome.

A total of 40 schizophrenia patients and 40 controls completed a series of tests that assessed the influence of the causal order effect on counterfactual thinking and the ability to generate counterfactual thoughts and counterfactually derive inferences from a hypothetical situation.

The Counterfactual Inference Test (CIT) was administered as part of this study. The CIT consists of a set of four forced-choice questions; for each, two events with similar outcomes experienced by two subjects are presented. However, the circumstances between them differ such that in one the subjects should think "if only" to a greater extent than in the other. The questions represent interpretation of "upset", "regret", "rumination", and "avoidance". Each of the four questions describes a hypothetical social event and participants are given three possible answers: a normative answer (that is, the target counterfactual response), a non-normative response, and a "neither" response if the participant considers none of the previous options to be suitable.

Significant differences were found for the scenarios related to "regret" and "rumination". Regarding the "regret" item, a significant proportion of schizophrenia patients were unable to choose between the normative and the non-normative response, choosing the "neither" answer. In the case of the "rumination" item, a higher proportion of schizophrenia patients selected the non-normative response rather than choosing the normative response or the "neither" answer.

This passage was adapted from "Counterfactual Reasoning Deficits in Schizophrenia Patients." Contreras F, Albacete A, Castellví P, Caño A, Benejam B, Menchón JM. *PLoS ONE*. 2016. 11(2) doi:10.1371/journal.pone.0148440 for use under the terms of the Creative Commons CC BY 4.0 license (http://creativecommons.org/licenses/by/4.0/legalcode).

Question 17

Which of the following cognitive barriers is most consistent with the findings in patients with schizophrenia?

- ○ **A.** Confirmation bias
- ○ **B.** Fixation
- ○ **C.** Heuristics
- ○ **D.** Belief bias

Question 18

How is it possible for the average IQ to be the same between the control group and schizophrenia group?

○ **A.** There are eight types of intelligence, but none of them would be impaired by schizophrenia.

○ **B.** There are eight types of intelligence, and all of them would be impaired by schizophrenia.

○ **C.** An IQ test is not biased by psychiatric disorders.

○ **D.** An IQ test is biased by psychiatric disorders.

Question 19

The research design employed in the passage is a:

○ **A.** case-control.

○ **B.** cohort.

○ **C.** randomized control trial.

○ **D.** experimental.

Question 20

A psychological test relies on norm theory, which suggests the ease of imagining a different event determines the alternatives developed and affective component elicited. Which problem solving tool is associated with the greatest ease?

○ **A.** Algorithm

○ **B.** Analogies

○ **C.** Intuition

○ **D.** Trial and error

Question 21

Schizophrenia is an isolating disease because of its rarity and impairment in social interactions. How does this relate to the findings in the passage?

○ **A.** The passage describes how schizophrenia impairs verbal interactions.

○ **B.** The passage highlights how patients with schizophrenia may fail to behave in the normative manner.

○ **C.** The passage compares the behaviors of different psychological disorders including schizophrenia.

○ **D.** The passage indicates that as schizophrenia progresses, behavior deviates further from the norm.

Question 22

CFT has been shown in previous research to rely on deductive reasoning. Which of Piaget's stages is associated with completely functional deductive reasoning skills?

○ **A.** Sensorimotor

○ **B.** Pre-operational

○ **C.** Concrete operational

○ **D.** Formal operational

Passage 5 (Questions 23-26)

There is a growing interest in comparing the explanatory power of 'bright' and 'dark' side personality traits. 'Bright' traits are those attributable to the interpersonal behaviors exhibited when we are being purposeful, positive, and at our best. Dark side traits, however, are those that have the potential to derail our personal and professional lives, and emerge with greater frequency when we let our guard down. We reveal our dark side when our cognitive resources that inhibit and suppress maladaptive impulses are depleted because we are stressed, tired, or overworked.

In situations of prolonged interpersonal and emotional stress at work, employees can experience burnout. Conversely, under immense stress, some individuals demonstrate resilience and persevere in a relatively unwavering manner. Can certain dark side traits be beneficial in stressful situations by providing additional psychological resources or aiding the adaptive allocation of these in a way that manifests resilience?

Burnout is conceptualized as an internal and emotional response to external stressors that consume, exceed, and deplete our personal and social resources. Burnout is comprised of feelings of emotional exhaustion, depersonalization, and a lack of personal achievement. Resilience is a dynamic process, where an interaction occurs with the environment by negotiating and managing resources in response to the stressor. Resilience emerges from ordinary processes that serve to protect the efficacy of these resource allocation systems.

Resilience is hypothesized to be positively predicted by diligent personality. 'Bright' side analysis has revealed that having a highly conscientious personality is beneficial for resilience due to the task-orientated approach it elicits when dealing with stress. Conscientious personalities are often formed in cultures that emphasize relationships. Burnout, however, is hypothesized to be negatively predicted by bold personality. Bold personality will prevent burnout by reinforcing beliefs that one's work is meaningful and of a good quality, rather than promoting an underlying tenacity to persevere. Bold personalities are often formed in cultures that emphasize individual achievement.

This passage was adapted from "The Dark Side of Resilience and Burnout: A Moderation-Meditation Model." Treglown L, Palaiou K, Zarola A, Furnham A. *PLoS ONE.* 2016. doi:10.1371/journal.pone.0156279 for use under the terms of the Creative Commons CC BY 4.0 license (http://creativecommons.org/licenses/by/4.0/legalcode).

Question 23

Behaviors that differentiate 'bright' side and 'dark' side personality traits are likely to be processed in the:

○ **A.** frontal lobe.

○ **B.** occipital lobe.

○ **C.** temporal lobe.

○ **D.** parietal lobe.

Question 24

Additional research has shown that individuals with IQ scores at least two standard deviations above the mean are more likely to experience resilience than burnout. A possible IQ score of such an individual is:

- A. 92.
- B. 102.
- C. 128.
- D. 132.

Question 25

Individuals that experience resilience are LEAST likely to use which of the following problem-solving techniques to navigate stressful situations?

- A. Algorithm
- B. Analogies
- C. Heuristics
- D. Intuition

Question 26

Which of the following additional studies would be likely to identify the types of bias that are more common to individuals that experience burnout than individuals that experience resilience?

- A. A 10-year survey of working men and women that assessed how people incorporate new information into problem-solving
- B. A 1-year survey of men that assessed belief perseverance and overconfidence
- C. A 9-year survey of retired men and women that assessed financial stability and its impact on emotional well-being
- D. A 7-year survey of working women that assessed whether they believed that their failures resulted from internal or external factors

Questions 27 - 30 do not refer to a passage and are independent of each other.

Question 27

Which of the following does NOT describe a feature of an IQ test?

- A. Score is constant over a lifetime.
- B. Score is normalized against matched controls.
- C. Score is reproducible.
- D. Score is not confounded by learning disabilities.

Question 28

Genes and the environment both are at play in cognitive development. Which of the following experiments could study the relationship between the environment and genetics and their effect on cognitive development?

- A. Compare monozygotic twins raised in the same environment and different environments.
- B. Compare dizygotic twins raised in the same environment and different environments.
- C. Compare the genes of children raised in the same environment.
- D. Compare the genes of children raised in different environments.

Question 29

Under the Cannon-Bard theory of emotion, which two events occur simultaneously?

- A. Perception of the eyes and physiological response
- B. Perception of the eyes and psychological response
- C. Physiological response and psychological response
- D. Perception of the eyes, physiological response and psychological response

A new program is initiated for preschool-aged children from low income families. The effect of the program on IQ is shown below. What do these results suggest?

Group	IQ
Low income, before program (n = 15)	88
Low income, after program (n = 15)	98
High income, before program (n = 15)	102
High income, after program (n = 15)	103

○ **A.** Intelligence is mostly genetically determined.

○ **B.** Intelligence can be potentiated by cultural influences.

○ **C.** High income children are not able to benefit from the program.

○ **D.** The program allows low income children to intellectually catch up to high income children.

Passage 6 (Questions 31-34)

The effects of poverty on child health are cumulative and also affect multiple contexts of children's lives including cognitive and social-emotional development. In an initial study, researchers found a negative association between diarrhea burden and three measurements of cognitive function in children who had undergone full surveillance for diarrhea over their first two years of life. As poor gastrointestinal health has been associated with poverty, the researchers concluded that a lack of resources had deleterious effects on the children's cognitive development. However, one question to be raised is whether the main association adequately controlled for confounding factors.

In a follow-up study, researchers recruited the families of 365 children, who answered questions about domestic psycho-social stimulation and cognitive function to determine if any confounding variables possibly affected the results of previous studies. Researchers sought to examine the impact of poverty on cognitive scores at five years of age by identifying the possible causal pathways through which poverty affects cognition. The cognitive performance at five years old, measured by the Wechsler Pre-School and Primary Scale of Intelligence Revised instrument (WPPSI-R), enabled researchers to consider the mediating effect of psychosocial stimulation and a wide range of household environment, neighborhood environment, child health, and nutritional status variables.

The data analyzed were collected at two points. A team of field workers visited households twice a week to collect data on birth weight, parasitic infection, diarrhea, nutritional status, mother's schooling and sanitary conditions. Psychosocial stimulation and cognitive performance were measured two years later in the household by a licensed psychologist, who also collected data on pre-school attendance and family purchasing power.

Inadequate psychosocial stimulation, undernutrition and infections are more common among poor children, and psychosocial stimulation, along with the physical quality of the home environment, is recognized as mediating the effect of socioeconomic status on children's cognitive development. Unfavorable socioeconomic conditions, a poorly educated mother, an absent father, poor sanitary conditions at home and in the neighborhood, and a low birth weight were negatively associated with cognitive performance at five years of age, while strong positive associations were found with high levels of domestic stimulation and nursery school attendance.

This passage was adapted from "Determinants of Cognitive Function in Childhood: A Cohort Study in a Middle Income Context." Santos D, O Assis AM, Bastos ACS, Santos LM, Santos CAST, et al. *BMC Public Health*. 2008. 8(202) doi:10.1186/1471-2458-8-202 for use under the terms of the Creative Commons CC BY 3.0 license (http://creativecommons.org/licenses/by/3.0/legalcode).

Question 31

If a participant underwent cognitive testing and scored significantly below average after controlling for psychosocial stimulation and environmental causes, which of the following explanations would be most likely?

- ○ **A.** Lead exposure produced cognitive deficits.
- ○ **B.** The child must have a genetic disorder, like a viral infection producing diarrhea.
- ○ **C.** The mother likely abused drugs and alcohol during gestation.
- ○ **D.** The child might suffer from a genetic learning disability, like phenylketonuria.

Question 32

One of the researchers suspects that native language is a confounding variable and believes it should be controlled for on the WPPSI-R. About which determinant of cognitive development is the author concerned?

- ○ **A.** The researcher is concerned that cultural determinants, including language, which is used to transmit culture, can affect the validity of the results of the study.
- ○ **B.** The researcher believes that the biological differences in the way language is processed will influence cognitive functioning.
- ○ **C.** The researcher hypothesized that language would have a dramatic effect on the environmental conditions of the children in the study.
- ○ **D.** The researcher suspects that native speakers might have a psychological advantage and so wished to control for this variable to ensure validity.

Question 33

The follow-up study attempts to understand how the environment influences cognition, as measured by the WPPSI-R instrument. Which of the following participants would likely have been excluded?

- ○ **A.** A child who does not show symptoms of diarrheal disease
- ○ **B.** A child who has Down syndrome
- ○ **C.** A set of twins
- ○ **D.** A child whose parents have an advanced education

Question 34

Stress has been proposed as a confounding variable that could also mediate the effects of poverty on cognitive development as described in the passage. What role would stress play in the follow-up study?

- ○ **A.** Stress is not related to cognitive development and would not likely produce a significant effect in this study.
- ○ **B.** Stress differentially affects the physiology of people of different socioeconomic statuses, so its role in cognitive development cannot be elucidated.
- ○ **C.** Stress could also be a mediating factor because prolonged stress due to poverty can lead to elevated cortisol levels and affect the participant's ability to do well on standardized tests.
- ○ **D.** Children under the age of seven, like those in the follow-up study, do not experience stress and are unlikely to be affected by increased stress due to poverty.

Passage 7 (Questions 35-38)

Pharmacological cognitive enhancement (PCE) in healthy individuals is often legitimated by the assumption that PCE will become widespread and desirable for the general public in the near future. This assumption was questioned as PCE is not equally safe and effective in everyone. Additionally, the willingness to use PCE is strongly personality-dependent, likely preventing a broad PCE epidemic.

One study investigated whether the cognitive performance and personality of healthy individuals with regular, nonmedical methylphenidate (MPH) use for PCE differ from stimulant-naïve controls. Twenty-five healthy individuals using MPH for PCE were compared with 39 age-, sex-, and education-matched healthy controls regarding cognitive performance and personality, which was assessed by a comprehensive neuropsychological test battery including social cognition, prosocial behavior, decision-making, impulsivity, and personality questionnaires. Selected results of various tests between the control and PCE user group are shown in Figure 1.

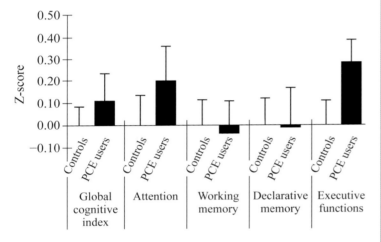

Figure 1 Comparative Z-scores between the PCE users and non-users

Recently abstinent PCE users showed no cognitive impairment but superior strategic thinking and decision-making. PCE users displayed higher levels of trait impulsivity, novelty seeking; and Machiavellianism combined with lower levels of social reward dependence and cognitive empathy. PCE users reported a smaller social network and exhibited less prosocial behavior in social interaction tasks. In line with this personality pattern, they behaved more opportunistically in social interaction tasks, showed less cognitive empathy, and reported having a smaller social network. PCE users showed a highly specific personality profile that shares a number of features with illegal stimulant users.

This passage was adapted from "Pharmacological Cognitive Enhancement in Healthy Individuals: A Compensation for Cognitive Deficits or a Question of Personality?" Maier, L., Wunderli, M. D., Vonmoos M., Rommelt A. T., Baumgartner M. R., et al. *PLoS ONE*. 2015. 10(6) doi: 10.1371/journal.pone.0129805 for use under the terms of the Creative Commons CC BY 4.0 license (https://creativecommons.org/licenses/by/4.0/legalcode).

Question 35

Based on Figure 1, what part of the brain would be most closely associated with the category that had the biggest effect between PCE users and stimulant-naive individuals?

- A. Parietal lobe
- B. Frontal lobe
- C. Temporal lobe
- D. Cerebral cortex

Question 36

Based on information from the study, which of the following traits would a PCE user be most likely to possess?

- A. Increased emotional intelligence
- B. Intuition
- C. High IQ
- D. Overconfidence

Question 37

The traits that are underdeveloped in PCE users are usually acquired at which stage of development?

- A. Sensorimotor
- B. Formal operational
- C. Concrete operational
- D. Preoperational

Question 38

What type of mechanism is the most likely to play a role in the improvement of patients who respond well to PCE?

- A. Incentive theory
- B. Negative feedback system
- C. Drive reduction theory
- D. Environmental influences

Passage 8 (Questions 39-43)

Sex differences have been demonstrated in the onset and severity of schizophrenia with men being more severely affected. Estrogen may act as a neuroprotective factor in women with schizophrenia, but little is known about the role of testosterone in men with schizophrenia. The peak in age-of-onset during adolescence suggests a link between exposure to increased androgens and development of schizophrenia in at-risk men. The evidence for a relationship with testosterone is strengthened by reports of increased negative symptoms and worse cognitive function in association with low endogenous testosterone levels in men with schizophrenia.

Researchers predicted that testosterone levels may affect other neurocognitive processes that are more central to the illness, such as executive control, attention, emotion processing, and regulation. They performed a study to test whether circulating testosterone levels were correlated with brain activation during cognitive-emotional processing in men with schizophrenia. They used fMRI to assess brain activation in 18 men with schizophrenia and 22 age-matched healthy men while participants were asked to categorize words as "positive," "neutral," or "negative" as the words appeared on a screen. This activity is thought to activate dorsal prefrontal executive control brain regions associated with emotion regulation. These results are shown in Figure 1. The researchers also measured total serum testosterone levels on the morning of the experiment (Figure 2).

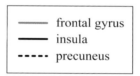

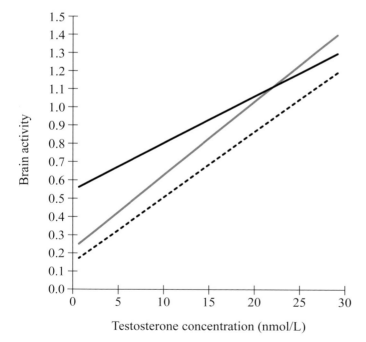

Figure 1 Brain activation in males with schizophrenia measured by contrast as seen on the fMRI

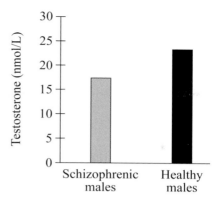

Figure 2 Serum testosterone levels in males with and without schizophrenia

This passage was adapted from "Testosterone Is Inversely Related to Brain Activity during Emotional Inhibition in Schizophrenia." Vercammen A, Skilleter AJ, Lenroot R, Catts SV, Weickert CS, et al. *PLoS ONE*. 2013. 8(10): e77496. doi:10.1371/journal. pone.0077496 for use under the terms of the Creative Commons CC BY 3.0 license (http://creativecommons.org/licenses/by/3.0/legalcode).

Question 39

The results of Figure 2 could be explained by all of the following EXCEPT:

- **A.** testosterone improves the ability of the brain to regulate emotions.
- **B.** the biological mechanisms of schizophrenia reduce testosterone production.
- **C.** the genes that regulate testosterone production share promoter regions with the genes involved in schizophrenia.
- **D.** testosterone contributes to the biological changes that cause the onset of schizophrenia.

Question 40

If a man with schizophrenia experiences a difficult separation from a significant other, he will most likely:

- **A.** experience his symptoms of schizophrenia worsen in the days after the break up.
- **B.** experience his symptoms of schizophrenia worsen in the months after the break up.
- **C.** experience his symptoms of schizophrenia improve in the days after the break up.
- **D.** experience his symptoms of schizophrenia improve in the months after the break up.

Question 41

Which of the following is an example of an interventional study that researchers could perform to further explore the relationship between testosterone and schizophrenia?

○ **A.** Track and record levels of testosterone in males with schizophrenia over the period of a year and look for a correlation between testosterone levels and severity of symptoms

○ **B.** Measure testosterone levels in males with schizophrenia as they are shown different emotional stimuli

○ **C.** Administer testosterone to males with schizophrenia to see if their symptoms improve

○ **D.** Compare serum testosterone levels of females with schizophrenia to levels of males with schizophrenia

Question 42

Compared to Figure 1, the data from males without schizophrenia would most likely:

○ **A.** show brain activation in different regions of the brain.

○ **B.** show brain activation in the same regions of the brain.

○ **C.** show no correlation between testosterone and brain activity.

○ **D.** show a negative correlation between testosterone and brain activity.

Question 43

In addition to the frontal gyrus, insula, and precuneus, researchers from the passage might also be interested in studying all of the following EXCEPT:

○ **A.** the hypothalamus.

○ **B.** the amygdala.

○ **C.** the prefrontal cortex.

○ **D.** the cerebral cortex.

Questions 44 - 47 do not refer to a passage and are independent of each other.

Question 44

Which of the following most accurately describes the relationship between genetic and environmental influences on a child's cognitive development?

○ **A.** Inherited factors provide a guideline for cognitive development while early childhood experiences, like preschool, shape cognitive function.

○ **B.** The environment plays little role in development because inherited factors are primarily responsible for the development of cognitive function.

○ **C.** As mentioned in the passage, environmental factors play an essential role in the development of cognitive function, so hereditary factors are negligible.

○ **D.** Inherited factors and environmental factors act antagonistically to one another with respect to cognitive development.

Question 45

Which of the following would an IQ score best predict?

○ **A.** Career advancement

○ **B.** Career choice

○ **C.** Class schedule

○ **D.** Class rank

Question 46

Which theory of emotion argues that a stimulus initiates first a physiological and then an emotional response?

○ **A.** James-Lange theory

○ **B.** Cannon- Bard theory

○ **C.** Schachter-Singer theory

○ **D.** Opponent process theory

Question 47

TORCH infections are a group of infectious disease that can be transmitted from the mother to fetus in utero and can cause characteristic birth defects, severe illness and cognitive delay. Which concept describes the outcome of TORCH Syndrome?

○ **A.** Hereditary influence on intelligence

○ **B.** Environmental influence on intelligence

○ **C.** Hereditary influence on psychological disease

○ **D.** Environmental influence on psychological disease

Passage 9 (Questions 48-51)

Investigators studying fear and Parkinson's disease (PD) designed a trial to compare PD patients with and without freezing of gait (FOG). FOG describes a phenomenon where patients suddenly freeze while walking and feel unable to continue moving. Using virtual reality, fourteen patients with PD and freezing of gait (Freezers) and 17 PD without freezing of gait (Non-freezers) were first instructed to walk across a plank that was located on the ground (LOW). Then, using virtual reality to induce fear, they were asked to walk across a plank above a deep pit (HIGH). Seven patients classified as Freezers completed this study twice, once while on their dopaminergic medications (ON) and once after twelve hours off of their medications (OFF). These medications are the typical treatment regimen for early PD patients. The results of the ON-OFF trial are presented in Table 1.

Table 1 Comparison of Freezing Characteristics for Freezers on Medication and 12 hours off Medication

	Freezers (OFF n = 7)		Freezers (ON n = 7)	
	Low	High	Low	High
Percent of each trial spent frozen	2.09	81.6	0	51.88
Total number of freezing episodes	3.00	111.0	0	26.00
Average number of freezing episodes per trial	0.40	15.9	0	3.80
Average duration of each freezing episode (sec)	0.58	7.5	0	7.91

Freezers were also compared to Non-freezers in both virtual environments. Investigators aimed to discover if Freezers reported higher levels of fear compared to Non-freezers. Researchers then measured reported levels of fear when walking across the HIGH plank compared to the LOW plank. The results are shown in Figure 1.

One important question that arises with this study is whether freezing precedes fear or if fear does in fact lead to a freeze episode. An important finding to note is that patients perceive a fear-producing situation and signs ranging from heart rate increases to panic attacks (ex. fainting, shortness of breath) occur. These have been identified during freezing episodes.

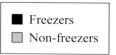

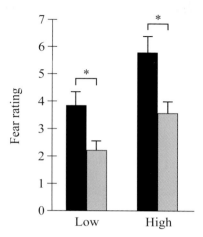

Figure 1 Fear ratings after participants walked across the plank (Freezers, n = 14; Non-freezers, n = 17).

This passage was adapted from "Does Anxiety Cause Freezing of Gait in Parkinson's Disease?" Ehgoetz Martens KA, Ellard CG, Almeida QJ. *PLoS ONE.* 2014. 9(9): e106561. doi:10.1371/journal.pone.0106561 for use under the terms of the Creative Commons CC BY 4.0 license (http://creativecommons.org/licenses/by/4.0/legalcode).

Question 48

If the temporal lobe, including the amygdala, was ablated in these study participants, what results might one expect in Table 1 for the Freezers off of their dopaminergic medications?

- **A.** Increased freezing episodes and duration due to fearfulness
- **B.** Increased freezing episodes and duration due to ANS hyperfunction
- **C.** Decreased freezing episodes and duration due to ANS hypofunction
- **D.** Decreased freezing episodes and duration due to fearlessness

Question 49

The finding in the last paragraph most closely supports which theory of emotion?

- **A.** Schachter-Singer theory
- **B.** James-Lange theory
- **C.** Cannon-Bard theory
- **D.** Two-factor theory

Question 50

Which of the following is least consistent with the findings in Figure 1?

○ **A.** Patients experience more cortisol release in the HIGH virtual environment.

○ **B.** Patients have decreased blood pressure in the HIGH environment which leads to fainting.

○ **C.** Patients should experience a decrease in heart rate moving from the HIGH to LOW environment.

○ **D.** Patients who are Non-freezers are less likely to experience weight gain and sleep disturbances than Freezers.

Question 51

Another study measured FOG at baseline and when patients were performing a difficult cognitive task. Which of the following best explains the conclusion that motor functioning and cognition are processed simultaneously rather than individually?

○ **A.** Cognition and motor functioning are processed serially—if the system gets overloaded by processing the cognitive task, there is not enough processing capacity to perform the motor task alongside the cognitive task.

○ **B.** Cognition and motor functioning are processed serially—if the patient experiences FOG, they cannot move past the motor component to process the cognitive task.

○ **C.** Cognition and motor functioning are processed in parallel—if the system gets overloaded by processing the cognitive task, there is not enough processing capacity to perform the motor task alongside the cognitive task.

○ **D.** Cognition and motor functioning are processed in parallel—if the patient experiences FOG, they cannot move past the motor component to process the cognitive task.

Passage 10 (Questions 52-56)

Adults view one another as mentalistic agents whose behavior is driven by intention, emotion, and belief. Humans routinely represent others' inner thoughts and feelings so as to interpret and predict their action. Infant research using spontaneous-response tasks has established that such a mentalising ability emerges much earlier than previously thought. The early development of mental state attribution suggests its fundamental role in social interaction.

Emerging evidence has indicated infants' early sensitivity to acoustic cues in music. One study examined infants' development of emotional cognitive understanding of music with a violation of-expectation paradigm.

Twelve- and 20-month-olds were presented with emotionally concordant and discordant music-face displays on alternate trials. The 20-month-olds, but not the 12-month-olds, were surprised by emotional incongruence between musical and facial expressions, suggesting their sensitivity to musical emotion.

In a separate non-music task, only the 20-month-olds were able to use an actress's affective facial displays to predict her subsequent action. Interestingly, for the 20-month-olds, such emotion-action understanding correlated with sensitivity to musical expressions measured in the first task. These two abilities, however, did not correlate with family income, parental estimation of language and communicative skills, and quality of parent-child interaction. The findings suggest that sensitivity to musical emotion and emotion-action understanding may be supported by a generalized common capacity to represent emotion from social cues, which lays a foundation for later social-communicative development.

This passage was adapted from "Infants' Sensitivity to Emotion in Music and Emotion-action Understanding." Siu T-SC, Cheung H. *PLoS ONE.* 2017. 12(2). doi:10.1371/journal.pone.0171023 for use under the terms of the Creative Commons CC BY 4.0 license (http://creativecommons.org/licenses/by/4.0/legalcode).

Question 52

The ability of infants to interpret adult facial expression is:

○ **A.** adaptive because this is an important evolutionary trait.

○ **B.** adaptive because the faces are congruent with musical emotion.

○ **C.** maladaptive because infants rely on adults for vitality.

○ **D.** maladaptive because the faces are incongruent with musical emotion.

Question 53

20-month-olds, compared to 12-month-olds were able to activate which brain region?

○ **A.** Amygdala

○ **B.** Cortex

○ **C.** Hypothalamus

○ **D.** Thalamus

Question 54

Which statement best summarizes the findings of the study?

○ **A.** Prior to 20 months of age, infants' acoustic centers are not fully developed.

○ **B.** Recognizing emotions like fear and anger is possible in infancy.

○ **C.** After one year of age, humans develop the ability to recognize emotional cues.

○ **D.** Parents can effectively predict if a child is capable of emotion recognition.

Question 55

The study in the passage is most supported by which of the following theories of emotion?

○ **A.** James-Lange

○ **B.** Cannon-Bard

○ **C.** Schachter-Singer

○ **D.** Three Factor

Question 56

Based on the passage, infants are utilizing which component of emotion?

○ **A.** Personal

○ **B.** Physiological

○ **C.** Behavioral

○ **D.** Cognitive

Questions 57 - 59 do not refer to a passage and are independent of each other.

Question 57

Fear is associated with:

○ **A.** elevated dopamine.

○ **B.** elevated serotonin.

○ **C.** elevated GABA.

○ **D.** elevated epinephrine.

Question 58

Which of the following incorrectly defines a theory of emotion?

○ **A.** James-Lange theory is also known as the two factor theory.

○ **B.** Cannon-Bard theory is a physiological-based theory.

○ **C.** Schachter-Singer theory relies on a cognitive appraisal.

○ **D.** Facial-feedback theory suggests emotions can be triggered by facial expressions.

Question 59

A recent study of smokers found the 90% believe that smoking is bad for their health. Which term describes this finding?

○ **A.** Avoidance

○ **B.** Classical conditioning

○ **C.** Denial

○ **D.** Cognitive dissonance

STOP. If you finish before time is called, check your work. You may go back to any question in this test.

ANSWERS & EXPLANATIONS for Test 4A can be found on p. 246.

TEST 4A

Thought and Emotion

TEST 4B

Time: 95 minutes
Questions 1–59

DIRECTIONS: Most of the questions in this test section are grouped with a passage. Read the passage, then select the best answer to each question. Some questions are independent of any passage and of one another. Select the best answer to each of these questions. If you are unsure of an answer, rule out incorrect choices and select from the remaining options. Indicate your selection beside the option you choose.

Passage 1 (Questions 1-6)

According to self-determination theory (SDT), motivation results from the degree to which a person perceives the fulfillment of three basic psychological needs: the need for autonomy, competence, and relatedness. Intrinsic motivation is then the result of the fulfillment of those three needs, while thwarting of those needs would result in controlled motivation. Although SDT acknowledges that the three basic psychological needs contain both a cognitive and an affective component, there are only few SDT studies that have focused on the explicit role of emotions in the motivation generative mechanism.

A study was designed to address this issue by investigating how individual differences in the extent to which people are able to differentiate between different specific emotions, known as emotion differentiation, affect the emotion-motivation relationship. People low in emotion differentiation (poor differentiators) have difficulty disentangling different emotions of the same valence and therefore have the tendency to distinguish emotions based on the sense that they are pleasant or unpleasant. Conversely, people high in emotion differentiation (good differentiators) experience emotions in a differentiated manner and are therefore capable of clearly distinguishing different emotions of the same valence.

The researchers' main goal was to study the impact of emotion differentiation on motivation. They focused on the relationship between different specific negative emotions and intrinsic motivation for people who are good negative differentiators compared to people who are poor negative differentiators, as well as the relationship between the specific positive emotions and intrinsic motivation. The findings showed that the relationship between enthusiasm, cheerfulness, optimism, contentedness, gloominess, miserableness, uneasiness, calmness, relaxation, tenseness, depression, worry on one hand and intrinsic motivation on the other hand was moderated by positive emotion differentiation for the positive emotions and by negative emotion differentiation for the negative emotions, but both to a greater extent in poor differentiators.

This passage was adapted from "Relating Specific Emotions to Intrinsic Motivation: On the Moderating Role of Positive and Negative Emotion Differentiation." Vandercammen L, Hofmans J, Theuns P. *PLoS ONE*. 2014. 9(12) doi: 10.1371/journal. pone.0115396 for use under the terms of the Creative Commons CC BY 4.0 license (http://creativecommons.org/licenses/by/4.0/legalcode).

Question 1

Which of the following theories is LEAST applicable to the study?

- A. Incentive theory
- B. Drive reduction theory
- C. Cognitive theory
- D. Need-based theory

Question 2

The main purpose of including good differentiators in the study is:

- A. to provide a control to which the poor differentiators can be compared.
- B. to allow the researchers to assess the role of emotional differentiation.
- C. to allow the sample to reflect variability seen in the general population.
- D. to provide a group not affected by the cognitive aspect of emotion.

Question 3

Based on the hypothesis in the last paragraph, which of the following would most likely be true of a good differentiator?

- A. Relaxation and cheerfulness would act equally as motivators.
- B. Uneasiness would act as a stronger motivator than it would for a poor differentiator.
- C. Enthusiasm would act as a stronger motivator than cheerfulness.
- D. Universal emotions would be perceived as equivalent motivators.

Question 4

Which of the following statements does NOT point to a potential weakness of the study design?

- A. While the study demonstrates correlation, there is no evidence of causation.
- B. The researchers did not include a control group.
- C. Self-reported emotion can lead to discrepancies in results.
- D. There was no control for the adaptive nature of emotions.

Question 5

Based on the passage, which of the following theories of emotion best explains a good differentiator experiencing the physiological aspect of emotion before emotional feeling, but using both aspects for perception of the emotion?

○ **A.** Cannon-Bard theory of emotion

○ **B.** Schachter-Singer theory of emotion

○ **C.** James-Lange theory of emotion

○ **D.** Adaptive theory of emotion

Question 6

Which statement best explains how this study demonstrates the role of biological processes in perceiving emotion?

○ **A.** Recollection of emotions similar to previous emotions affects emotional differentiation.

○ **B.** A broad spectrum of emotions was perceived, requiring physiological responses.

○ **C.** The temperament of participants affected their decision making process.

○ **D.** Research participants are unaware of the role their emotions are playing in motivation.

Passage 2 (Questions 7-10)

Facial features differ in the amount of expressive information they convey. Specifically, eyes are argued to be essential for fear recognition, while smiles are crucial for recognizing happy expressions. In three experiments, researchers tested whether expression modulates the perceptual saliency of diagnostic facial features and whether the feature's saliency depends on the face configuration.

Participants were presented with masked facial features or noise at perceptual conscious threshold. The task was to indicate whether a pair of eyes (experiments 1-3A) or a mouth (experiment 3B) was present. The expression of the face and its configuration (i.e. spatial arrangement of the features) were manipulated. Experiment 1 compared fearful with neutral expressions, while experiments 2 and 3 compared fearful versus happy expressions.

The detection accuracy data was analyzed using Signal Detection Theory (SDT), to examine the effects of expression and configuration on perceptual precision and response bias, separately. Across all three experiments, fearful eyes were detected better than neutral and happy eyes. Eyes were more precisely detected than mouths, whereas smiles were detected better than fearful mouths. The configuration of the features had no consistent effects across the experiments on the ability to detect expressive features, but facial configuration consistently affected the response bias. Participants used a more liberal criterion for detecting the eyes in canonical configuration and fearful expression. The results suggest that expressive features are perceptually more salient due to changes at the low-level visual properties, with emotions affecting perception through top-down processes, as reflected by the response bias.

This passage was adapted from "The Perceptual Saliency of Fearful Eyes and Smiles: A Signal Detection Study." Elsherif MM, Saban MI, Rotshtein P. *PLoS ONE*. 2017. 12(3) doi:10.1371/journal.pone.0173199 for use under the terms of the Creative Commons CC BY 4.0 license (http://creativecommons.org/licenses/by/4.0/legalcode).

Question 7

Based on the results in the study, which of the following graphs would be most appropriate to display the results?

○ **A.**

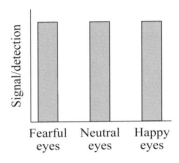

Fearful Neutral Happy
eyes   eyes   eyes

○ **B.**

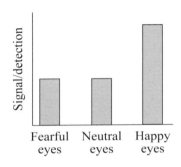

Fearful Neutral Happy
eyes   eyes   eyes

○ **C.**

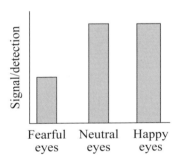

Fearful Neutral Happy
eyes   eyes   eyes

○ **D.**

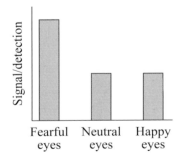

Fearful Neutral Happy
eyes   eyes   eyes

Question 8

All of the emotions mentioned in the passage are:

    I. universal.

    II. adaptive.

    III. required.

○ **A.** I only

○ **B.** III only

○ **C.** I and II only

○ **D.** I and III only

Question 9

Which of the following hormones is NOT associated with an early stress response?

○ **A.** Insulin

○ **B.** Epinephrine

○ **C.** Norepinephrine

○ **D.** Cortisol

Question 10

Separate research has shown that perception of faces is often subconscious, meaning it enters a less evolved portion of the brain before reaching the cortex. How does this adaptation relate to the theories of emotion?

○ **A.** It supports the James-Lange theory because the psychological component does not occur.

○ **B.** It supports the Cannon-Bard theory because the physiological component does not occur.

○ **C.** It supports the Schachter-Singer theory because the physiological component does not occur.

○ **D.** It does not support any particular theory but indicates that emotional response to faces is an adaptive trait that emerged very early in human evolution.

Questions 11 - 14 do not refer to a passage and are independent of each other.

Question 11

In order to test the drive-reduction theory of motivation in rats, a researcher could:

- ○ **A.** allow addicted rats to self-administer morphine tablets.
- ○ **B.** provide the rats with a new toy only if they squeak.
- ○ **C.** treat the rats with a sedative drug.
- ○ **D.** administer diuretics to the rats to increase the need to urinate.

Question 12

Which branch of the nervous system is most involved in emotional processing?

- ○ **A.** Somatic nervous system
- ○ **B.** Enteric nervous system
- ○ **C.** Autonomic nervous system
- ○ **D.** Peripheral nervous system

Question 13

Like humans, canines rely on facial cues to respond to dangerous stimuli. If his owner appears afraid, a dog will:

- ○ **A.** appraise the situation as dangerous.
- ○ **B.** appraise the situation as safe.
- ○ **C.** mirror his owner's body language.
- ○ **D.** defend his owner.

Question 14

Presidential approval ratings rapidly fluctuate and seem to have little to do with presidential policy. Which of the following best explains this observation?

- ○ **A.** Peripheral route processing in the elaboration likelihood model.
- ○ **B.** Central route processing in the elaboration likelihood model.
- ○ **C.** Peripheral route processing in the social-cognitive model.
- ○ **D.** Central route processing in the social-cognitive model.

Passage 3 (Questions 15-18)

Accumulating evidence suggests traumatic experience can rapidly alter brain activation associated with emotion processing. However, little is known about the acute changes in emotion neurocircuits that underlie PTSD symptom development. To examine acute alterations in emotion circuit activation and structure that may be linked to PTSD symptoms, thirty-eight participants performed a task of appraisal of emotional faces as their brains were functionally and structurally studied with MRI at both two weeks and three months after motor vehicle collision.

The Shifted-Attention Emotion Appraisal Task (SEAT) was used to examine activation in brain regions associated with implicit emotional processing, attention modulation of emotion, and cognitive appraisal. In brief, subjects viewed a grayscale composite picture depicting an emotional face on an indoor or outdoor scene. On each trial, subjects determined whether: (a) the face was male or female (Male/Female) to probe implicit emotional processing, (b) the scene was indoor or outdoor (Indoor/Outdoor) to probe attention modulation of emotion, or (c) whether they liked or disliked the face (Like/Dislike) to probe modulation of emotion by cognitive appraisal. Each trial lasted 1.5 seconds, and intertrial intervals were randomized from 3 to 8 seconds. Fourteen trials for each trial type and 10 trials each of the control condition (uncompounded face or place) were divided into 3 runs of about 7 minutes per run in each session.

The probable PTSD group had greater activation than the non-PTSD group in dorsal and ventral medial prefrontal cortex (dmPFC) while appraising fearful faces two weeks after trauma and in left insular cortex three months after trauma. Changes over time in dmPFC activation and in PTSD symptom severity were also significantly positively correlated in the probable PTSD group. A significant time by group interaction was found for volume changes in left superior frontal gyrus (SFG) that partially overlapped the dmPFC active region. Between two weeks and three months, left SFG volume decreased in probable PTSD survivors.

This passage was adapted from "Preliminary Study of Acute Changes in Emotion Processing in Trauma Survivors with PTSD Symptoms." Wang X, Xie H, Cotton AS, Duval ER, Tamburrino MB, et al. *PLoS ONE*. 2016. 11(7) doi:10.1371/journal.pone.0159065 for use under the terms of the Creative Commons CC BY 4.0 license (http://creativecommons.org/licenses/by/4.0/legalcode).

Question 15

Which of the following is necessary for dmPFC activation following face exposure in the probable PTSD group?

- ○ **A.** The participant appraises the stressor as a cataclysmic event.
- ○ **B.** The participant fails to appraise the stressor as a cataclysmic event.
- ○ **C.** The participant appraises the stressor as a personal event.
- ○ **D.** The participant fails to appraise the stressor as a personal event.

Question 16

Which of the following correctly describes feelings of discomfort that patients with PTSD may experience?

- ○ **A.** Drive
- ○ **B.** Need
- ○ **C.** Emotion
- ○ **D.** Attitude

Question 17

What non-pharmacologic intervention would NOT benefit patients with PTSD?

- ○ **A.** Diet
- ○ **B.** Exercise
- ○ **C.** Relaxation
- ○ **D.** Spirituality

Question 18

Which of the following results would be expected in participants who had normal activation of the SFG?

- ○ **A.** Increased connections between the amygdala and hypothalamus.
- ○ **B.** Hippocampus with increased number of gyri.
- ○ **C.** Amygdala of standard shape and size.
- ○ **D.** Excess of parasympathetic signals.

Passage 4 (Questions 19-22)

Categorization of everyday sounds is a crucial aspect in the perception of the surrounding world. However, it constitutes a poorly explored domain in developmental psychology. Researchers sought to understand the nature and logic of the construction of auditory cognitive categories for natural sounds during development.

Eighty-two children (6–9 years), 20 teenagers (12–13 years), and 24 young adults participated in the study. Perception and categorization of everyday sounds was assessed based on a task composed of 18 different sounds belonging to three a priori categories: non-linguistic human vocalizations, environmental sounds, and musical instruments. Select results are shown in Figure 1.

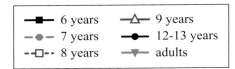

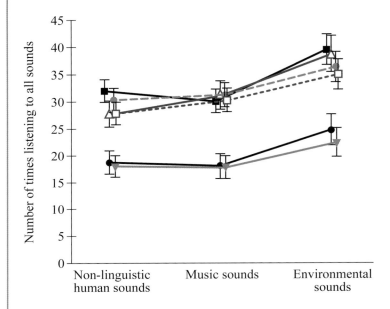

Figure 1 Frequency of listening to sounds by age group

Children listened to the sounds more times than older participants, built significantly more classes than adults, and used a different strategy of classification. Analysis of the auditory categorization performed by 6-year-old children showed that this age constitutes a pivotal stage, in agreement with the progressive change from a non-logical reasoning based mainly on perceptive representations to the logical reasoning used by older children.

This passage was adapted from "Perception of Everyday Sounds: A Developmental Study of a Free Sorting Task." Berland A, Gaillard P, Guidetti M, Barone P. *PLoS ONE.* 2015. 10(2) doi:10.1371/journal.pone.0115557 for use under the terms of the Creative Commons CC BY 4.0 license (http://creativecommons.org/licenses/by/4.0/legalcode).

Question 19

Assuming participants had an affective response to each type of sound, which sound likely evoked the strongest response?

- ○ **A.** Linguistic sounds
- ○ **B.** Non-linguistic human sounds
- ○ **C.** Musical sounds
- ○ **D.** Environmental sounds

Question 20

In a follow-up experiment, researchers attempted to influence participants' attitudes about certain sounds. Which slow, yet effective, technique should be employed?

- ○ **A.** Foot-in-the-door
- ○ **B.** Door-in-the-face
- ○ **C.** Role-playing
- ○ **D.** Cognitive dissonance

Question 21

Although not explored in this experiment, in what way may role-playing have modified the results?

- ○ **A.** Role-playing is common in childhood but less common in teenage years and adulthood.
- ○ **B.** Role-playing may have distracted adult listeners for each sound type.
- ○ **C.** Role-playing may have distracted young listeners for each sound type.
- ○ **D.** Role-playing could not have biased the results.

Question 22

Which of the following is an accurate assessment of the results presented in the final paragraph?

- ○ **A.** Young children have less preconceived attitudes about the sounds making it more difficult to categorize them.
- ○ **B.** Children lack the cognitive ability to categorize sounds.
- ○ **C.** Children struggle with the Gestalt concept of symmetry.
- ○ **D.** Adults are most skilled with the Gestalt concept of continuity.

Passage 5 (Questions 23-26)

According to decades of research on affective motivation in the human brain, approach motivational states are supported primarily by the left hemisphere and avoidance states by the right hemisphere. The underlying cause of this specialization, however, has remained unknown.

Researchers conducted the first test of the Sword and Shield Hypothesis (SSH), according to which the hemispheric laterality of affective motivation depends on the laterality of motor control for the dominant hand (i.e., the "sword hand," used preferentially to perform approach actions) and the non-dominant hand (i.e., the "shield hand," used preferentially to perform avoidance actions).

Researchers measured alpha-band power (an inverse index of neural activity) in right- and left-handed participants during resting-state electroencephalography and analyzed hemispheric alpha-power asymmetries as a function of the participants' trait approach motivational tendencies. Stronger approach motivation was associated with more left-hemisphere activity in right-handers but with more right-hemisphere activity in left-handers. The alpha-band power is depicted in Figure 1.

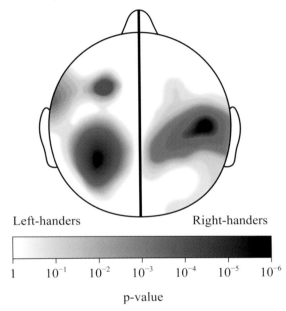

Figure 1 Statistical significance of the approach motivation and hemisphere interaction of resting alpha-band power

The hemispheric correlates of approach motivation reversed between right- and left-handed participants, which is consistent with the way they typically use their dominant and non-dominant hands to perform approach and avoidance actions. In both right- and left-handed participants, approach motivation was lateralized to the same hemisphere that controls the dominant hand. This covariation between neural systems for action and emotion provides initial support for the SSH.

This passage was adapted from "Motivation and Motor Control: Hemispheric Specialization for Approach Motivation Reverses with Handedness." Brookshire G, Casasanto D. *PLoS ONE*. 2012. 7(4) doi:10.1371/journal.pone.0036036 for use under the terms of the Creative Commons CC BY 3.0 license (http://creativecommons.org/licenses/by/3.0/legalcode).

Question 23

Which of the following factors that influence motivation was tested by the SSH?

- ○ **A.** Need
- ○ **B.** Want
- ○ **C.** Instinct
- ○ **D.** Drive

Question 24

Researchers could have used which of the following to assess the handedness of drives?

- ○ **A.** Water deprivation
- ○ **B.** Social deprivation
- ○ **C.** Monetary reward
- ○ **D.** Conditioned response

Question 25

Like the SSH, needs are motivators that are often studied. Which of the following is NOT classically a need?

- ○ **A.** Food
- ○ **B.** Water
- ○ **C.** Money
- ○ **D.** Self-actualization

Question 26

Which of the following sociocultural motivators may have biased the study?

- ○ **A.** Peer-pressure may cause children to modify their handedness.
- ○ **B.** Elementary school teachers used to retrain left-handers to use their right hand instead.
- ○ **C.** A baseball player that is left-handed has an advantage against a right-handed pitcher.
- ○ **D.** Many common items favor right-handers including scissors and doorknobs.

Questions 27 - 30 do not refer to a passage and are independent of each other.

Question 27

Arousal is paramount to motivation. Which of the following techniques would NOT promote arousal?

- ○ **A.** Administration of caffeine
- ○ **B.** Simulation of an attack
- ○ **C.** Meditation prior to task
- ○ **D.** A task performed in new environment

Question 28

Which of the following is an example of a man using the foot-in-the-door technique?

- ○ **A.** Coercing a friend to loan him $20
- ○ **B.** Convincing a coworker to do a series of increasingly larger tasks for him
- ○ **C.** Working his way up at a fortune 500 company
- ○ **D.** Obtaining a job interview by speaking to the receptionist

Question 29

A study shows that academic performance is enhanced by moderate levels of stress. Which theory of motivation best supports this finding?

- ○ **A.** Drive-reduction theory
- ○ **B.** Incentive theory
- ○ **C.** Cognitive theory
- ○ **D.** Need-based theory

Question 30

Theories of PTSD focus on a failure of cognitive appraisal. This is applicable to the:

- ○ **A.** James-Lange theory.
- ○ **B.** Schachter-Singer theory.
- ○ **C.** Cannon-Bard theory.
- ○ **D.** Cognitive behavioral theory (CBT).

Passage 6 (Questions 31-36)

Even though there is a high market demand for Science, Technology, Engineering, and Mathematics (STEM) graduates, the combination of a declining interest of high school students for STEM studies and the low success rates of first-year college students remains problematic. To better understand the STEM first-year experience and to identify targets for effective interventions, empirical research on academic achievement and retention in STEM programs is essential. Various motivational factors have been found to be important predictors of first year academic achievement and study persistence.

Academic self-concept is a subjective judgment of one's perceived ability in an academic or learning context. Three distinct models have been proposed to describe the relationship between academic self-concept and academic achievement: the skill development model (academic achievement determines academic self-concept), the self-enhancement model (academic self-concept determines achievement) and the reciprocal effects model (achievement and self-concept mutually reinforce each other).

Researchers investigated whether different motivational and academic self-concept profiles could be discerned between male and female first-year college students in STEM and whether differences in early academic achievement were associated with these student groups. Gender differences were found in this study: male students with high levels of academic self-concept and internal motivation had higher academic achievement compared to male students with low levels on both motivational and academic self-concept profiles. Male students with high internal motivation profiles performed better than those with high external motivation profiles. Female students had lower academic self-concept in general, but their motivational profiles were not associated with academic achievement.

This passage was adapted from "Profiling First-Year Students in STEM Programs Based on Autonomous Motivation and Academic Self-Concept and Relationship with Academic Achievement." Van Soom C, Donche V. *PLoS ONE*. 2014. 9(11): e112489. doi:10.1371/journal.pone.0112489 for use under the terms of the Creative Commons CC BY 3.0 license (http://creativecommons.org/licenses/by/3.0/legalcode).

Question 31

According to Maslow's hierarchy of needs, high achieving STEM students are likely to have all of the following EXCEPT:

- **A.** supportive friends and family.
- **B.** a stable housing situation.
- **C.** access to adequate food and water.
- **D.** a sense of self-fulfillment.

Question 32

Which of the following factors that influence motivation has the LEAST influence on academic self-concept?

- **A.** Instinct
- **B.** Arousal
- **C.** Drive
- **D.** Need

Question 33

A group of researchers want to study the link between academic self-concept and levels of academic stress. They measure academic self-concept on a scale from 1-5, with 1 being the lowest score. Their results would most likely resemble which of the following figures?

○ **A.**

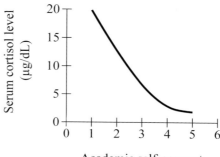

○ **B.**

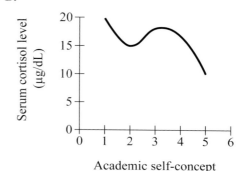

○ **C.**

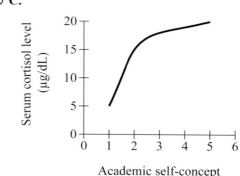

○ **D.**

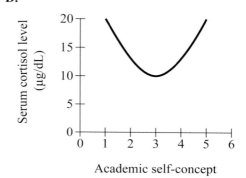

Question 34

Allen is a pre-med student because he is interested in the science of human health. Richard is a pre-med student because he wants to have a stable, well-paying career. If both students possess high academic self-concept, who is more likely to get better grades in his pre-med requirement classes?

- ○ A. Allen because he is motivated by an intrinsic motivator.
- ○ B. Richard because he is motivated by an intrinsic motivator.
- ○ C. Allen because he is motivated by an extrinsic motivator.
- ○ D. Richard because he is motivated by an extrinsic motivator.

Question 35

The finding that female STEM students scored lower on academic self-concept is most consistent with which of the following behaviors?

- ○ A. Female scientists are less likely to be published in high-impact journals.
- ○ B. Female programmers are less likely to be named team leaders on projects.
- ○ C. Female engineers are less likely to ask for promotions.
- ○ D. Female doctors are less likely to be sued for malpractice.

Question 36

Which conclusion is best supported by the study in the passage?

- ○ A. Boosting the internal motivation of students makes them do better in school.
- ○ B. Programs that want to help STEM students succeed should consider ways to support students' academic self-worth.
- ○ C. The creation of an incentive system that rewards good grades will increase academic performance among STEM students.
- ○ D. The success of students in the humanities is also correlated to strong internal motivation and high academic self-concept.

Passage 7 (Questions 37-40)

Intertemporal choices—involved decisions which trade off instant and delayed outcomes—are often made under stress. It remains unknown, however, whether and how psychosocial stress affects intertemporal choice. Researchers subjected 142 healthy male subjects to a laboratory stress or control protocol, and asked them to make a series of intertemporal choices either directly after stress, or 20 minutes later (resulting in four experimental groups). Based on theory and evidence from behavioral economics and cellular neuroscience, researchers predicted a bidirectional effect of stress on intertemporal choice, with increases in impatience or present bias immediately after stress, but decreases in present bias or impatience when subjects are tested 20 minutes later. However, the results showed no effects of stress on intertemporal choice.

A subsequent study was performed to determine if the stressor was sufficient to elicit a stress response in participants. The participants were exposed to the same psychosocial stressor used in the original experiment. The task included a job interview where participants were asked a variety of questions. Both the control and experimental groups were asked the same questions. But, only the experimental group was frequently interrupted by the interviewer. Physiological measures of stress were obtained throughout the task and the results are shown in Figure 1.

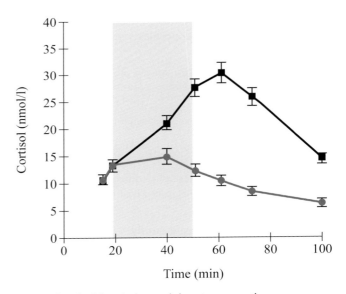

Figure 1 Cortisol levels in participants across time.

This passage was adapted from "No Effects of Psychosocial Stress on Intertemporal Choice." Haushofer J, Cornelisse S, Seinstra M, Fehr E, Joëls M, et al. *PLoS ONE*. 2013. 8(11) doi:10.1371/journal.pone.0078597 for use under the terms of the Creative Commons CC BY 4.0 license (https://creativecommons.org/licenses/by/4.0/legalcode).

Next ▶

Question 37

Which of the following conclusions is supported by Figure 1?

- **A.** The procedure did not produce a stress response.
- **B.** The findings in the first experiment were inaccurate.
- **C.** The findings in the first experiment were flawed by poor internal validity.
- **D.** The findings in the first experiment were not flawed by procedural errors.

Question 38

If researchers measured epinephrine and norepinephrine instead of cortisol, the results would:

- **A.** be essentially identical to those in Figure 1.
- **B.** be essentially identical to those in Figure 1 for epinephrine but not for norepinephrine.
- **C.** be essentially identical to those in Figure 1 for norepinephrine but not for epinephrine.
- **D.** be dissimilar to Figure 1, but it is impossible to predict the exact shape of the curve.

Question 39

The first experiment was investigating which type of response to stress?

- **A.** Emotional
- **B.** Behavioral
- **C.** Physiological
- **D.** Psychological

Question 40

Which of the following could have served as the stressor in the experiment?

- **A.** Mindfulness meditation
- **B.** Intense exercise
- **C.** A written exam
- **D.** A threat to the participant's social status

Passage 8 (Questions 41-44)

Aversive stressful experiences are often associated with increased anxiety and a predisposition to develop mood disorders. Negative stress also suppresses adult neurogenesis and restricts dendritic architecture in the hippocampus, a brain region associated with anxiety regulation. The effects of aversive stress on hippocampal structure and function have been linked to stress-induced elevations in glucocorticoids. Normalizing corticosterone levels prevents some of the deleterious consequences of stress, including increased anxiety and suppressed structural plasticity in the hippocampus. Researchers examined whether a rewarding stressor, namely a sexual experience, also adversely affects hippocampal structure and function in adult rats. Adult male rats were exposed to a sexually-receptive female once (acute), once daily for 14 consecutive days (chronic), or not at all (naïve), and levels of circulating glucocorticoids were measured. The results are shown in Figure 1.

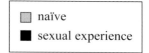

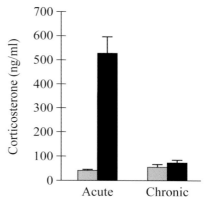

Figure 1 Acute and chronic sexual experience effect on corticosterone levels in mice

Then, separate cohorts of sexually experienced rats were injected with the thymidine analog bromodeoxyuridine in order to measure cell proliferation and neurogenesis in the hippocampus. In addition, brains were processed using Golgi impregnation to assess the effects of sexual experience on dendritic spines and dendritic complexity in the hippocampus. Finally, to evaluate whether sexual experience alters hippocampal function, rats were tested on two tests of anxiety-like behavior: novelty suppressed feeding and the elevated plus maze.

Question 41

Which conclusion is best supported by the findings in Figure 1?

○ **A.** Acute sexual experience exposure is associated with elevation in corticosterone.

○ **B.** Acute sexual experience exposure is associated with depression in corticosterone.

○ **C.** Chronic sexual experience exposure is associated with elevation in corticosterone.

○ **D.** Chronic sexual experience exposure is associated with depression in corticosterone.

Question 42

How could researchers decrease the likelihood of normalizing corticosterone levels?

○ **A.** They could expose the rats to a different stress-inducing task.

○ **B.** They could use a different method to sample corticosterone levels.

○ **C.** They could increase exercise in the rats, lowering the physiological response to stress.

○ **D.** They could promote meditative behavior in the rats, lowering the physiological response to stress.

Question 43

Theories of stress and motivation are often not applicable to animal models. But, if researchers assume that rats and humans are cognitively similar, which of the following would be true?

○ **A.** The cataclysmic stress on the rats likely resulted in increased stress hormones.

○ **B.** The rats used primary and secondary appraisals to assess the severity of the stressor.

○ **C.** Sex is a source of external motivation in the incentive theory, so rats would be motivated to perform this behavior.

○ **D.** In Maslow's hierarchy of needs, sex is near the top and is therefore highly motivating.

Question 44

If the study was modified to assess changes in the amygdala as opposed to the hippocampus, what hypothesis would this test?

○ **A.** Does exposure to stress modify the structure or portions of the brain that deal with emotion?

○ **B.** Do changes in the parts of the brain that deal with memory formation cause changes in the parts of the brain that deal with emotion?

○ **C.** Does the frontal cortex allow the brain to "re-wire" and react differently to the same stressor in different situations?

○ **D.** Does exposure to stress alter the area of the brain associated with memory formation?

Questions 45 - 48 do not refer to a passage and are independent of each other.

Question 45

A tourist who is afraid of heights moves away from the edge of a roof top. Which of the following is most likely motivating this movement?

○ **A.** Drive

○ **B.** Instinct

○ **C.** Need

○ **D.** Arousal

Question 46

Which of the following situations is most likely to involve a long lasting change in attitude?

○ **A.** A medical student attends a lecture in order to get free breakfast.

○ **B.** A religious extremist watches a sermon given by a member of a more liberal branch of the same religion.

○ **C.** A physician reads a study from a respected medical journal, which contradicts his current protocols.

○ **D.** A recovering alcoholic is ordered into a twelve step program by a judge.

Question 47

An intertemporal choice task included the choice between a monetary offer of either $5 immediately or $10 in three months. A woman who states she is often very patient chooses the $5. This is an example of:

○ **A.** the drive reduction theory.

○ **B.** the foot-in-the-door phenomenon.

○ **C.** cognitive dissonance.

○ **D.** central route processing.

Question 48

Publication bias describes the bias in scientific literature where only statistically significant results are usually published. This means that results like those in the first experiment are usually not available for meta-analyses. Which cognitive bias(es) may occur in a meta-analysis if the publication bias had occurred prior?

    I. Confirmation bias

    II. Causation bias

    III. Self-serving bias

○ **A.** I only

○ **B.** III only

○ **C.** I and II only

○ **D.** I, II and III

Passage 9 (Questions 49-52)

Prolonged experiences of stress are related to poor individual health and associated with substantial financial costs for society. As a result, the development of cost effective stress prevention or stress management approaches has become an important endeavor of current research efforts. Music has been shown to beneficially affect stress-related physiological, as well as cognitive, and emotional processes. Thus, the use of listening to music as an economic, non-invasive, and highly accepted intervention tool has received special interest in the management of stress and stress-related health issues.

Researchers sought to thoroughly examine music effects across endocrine, autonomic, cognitive, and emotional domains of the human stress response. Sixty healthy female volunteers were exposed to a standardized psychosocial stress test after having been randomly assigned to one of three different conditions prior to the stress test: 1) relaxing music ('Miserere', Allegri) (RM), 2) sound of rippling water (SW), and 3) rest without acoustic stimulation (R). Salivary cortisol and salivary alpha-amylase (sAA), heart rate (HR), respiratory sinus arrhythmia (RSA), subjective stress perception and anxiety were repeatedly assessed in all subjects. Researchers hypothesized that listening to RM prior to the stress test, compared to SW or R, would result in a decreased stress response across all measured parameters.

The three conditions significantly differed regarding cortisol response to the stressor, with highest concentrations in the RM and lowest in the SW condition. After the stressor, sAA baseline values were reached considerably faster in the RM group than in the R group. HR and psychological measures did not significantly differ between groups. These findings indicate that music listening impacts the psychobiological stress system. Listening to music prior to a standardized stressor predominantly affected the autonomic nervous system (in terms of a faster recovery), and to a lesser degree the endocrine and psychological stress response.

This passage was adapted from "The Effect of Music on the Human Stress Response." Thoma MV, La Marca R, Brönnimann R, Finkel L, Ehlert U, et al. *PLoS ONE*. 2013. 8(8) doi:10.1371/journal.pone.0070156 for use under the terms of the Creative Commons CC BY 3.0 license (http://creativecommons.org/licenses/by/3.0/legalcode).

Question 49

Experimenters used the Trier social stress test (TSST) as the stressor, which includes five components. First, participants are given 5 minutes to prepare a presentation then 5 minutes to present the information, and finally 5 minutes of difficult mental math problems. The TSST is a:

- ○ **A.** personal stressor.
- ○ **B.** cataclysmic stressor.
- ○ **C.** daily stressor.
- ○ **D.** physical stressor.

Question 50

Which of the following components of stress was NOT considered by researchers?

- ○ **A.** The long lasting physiologic response
- ○ **B.** The component of fear
- ○ **C.** The rapid physiologic response
- ○ **D.** The component of anxiety

Question 51

Which of the following physiologic markers to stress could have been measured in addition to those already assessed by researchers?

- ○ **A.** Cortisol
- ○ **B.** Dopamine
- ○ **C.** Heart rate
- ○ **D.** Sweat

Question 52

A college student struggling with stress near the end of the semester reads these findings and hopes to apply them to his life but never makes the effort to download any calming music. This is an example of:

- ○ **A.** associative learning.
- ○ **B.** blind faith.
- ○ **C.** cognitive dissonance.
- ○ **D.** doublethink.

Passage 10 (Questions 53-56)

Previous research has found that stressful life events are correlated with the incidence of cancer, as well as cancer survival. However, the role of parental care and life stressors in breast cancer progression and survival has not been well studied. Researchers investigated whether these factors may be linked to biological prognostic variables, including lymph node involvement, which is a signature of a progressed cancer.

234 women with breast cancer were eligible for the study and approached by a clinical psychologist or research assistant a few hours following surgery to inquire about their willingness to participate. 167 accepted the offer (67 refused due to a lack of time, fatigue or pain related to post-operative complications). Two interviews were conducted. The first interview explored parental relationships, and the second interview gathered information on 61 life events that can be further divided into six areas (work, financial problems, health, bereavement, emigration, and loss of sentimental life). Patients were asked to indicate how many times in their life they experienced each event.

The researchers controlled for patient ethnicity, current socioeconomic status, and age. Analysis of the data found that the absence of optimal parental relationships is associated with an increased risk of lymph node involvement. An optimal relation with a least one parent was found to decrease the risk of lymph node involvement, but no difference between the effect of one or two parental relationships was established. The frequency of positive lymph node status among patients with either a singular or no occurrence of a life stressor compared to the frequency among patients with repeated life stressors is presented in Figure 1.

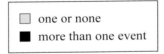

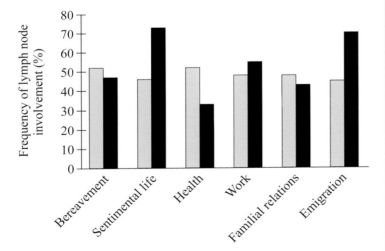

Figure 1 Frequency of lymph node involvement based on number and type of life stressors experienced

Question 53

Controlling for patient characteristics means that the researchers:

○ **A.** utilized a variety of information including background data from patients when constructing a sample.

○ **B.** conducted statistical analyses, when establishing a relationship between the variables.

○ **C.** factored the emotional effect of stress on patients when analyzing the data.

○ **D.** adjusted for factors in the sample that could be confounding variables.

Question 54

Which of the following conclusions concerning the progression of breast cancer is best supported by the research in the passage?

○ **A.** The study provides evidence that emigration and financial problems are positively correlated with lymph node involvement among breast cancer patients.

○ **B.** The study provides evidence that repeated health care problems cause a lower rate of lymph node involvement among breast cancer patients.

○ **C.** The study provides evidence that repeated emigration, but not health care problems, are positively correlated with cancer progression among breast cancer patients.

○ **D.** The study provides evidence that repeated emigration and financial problems are causes of lymph node involvement among breast cancer patients.

Next ▶

Question 55

Given the information in the passage, what limitations of the study pose the LEAST threat to the legitimacy of conclusions?

- ○ **A.** The percent of the sample excluded
- ○ **B.** The self-selecting nature of the sample
- ○ **C.** The lack of a cancer-free control group
- ○ **D.** The use of questionnaires

Question 56

Which participant recruitment method utilizes the foot-in-the-door method of persuasion?

- ○ **A.** The research assistant initially proposes a 500 question interview, planning to be rejected and then offers the shorter survey, which is the study.
- ○ **B.** The research assistant asks the patient to complete a five question survey on their hospital visit before asking the patient to participate in the study.
- ○ **C.** If the patient initially rejects the proposal, the research assistant reminds the individual that good natured patients are invited to the study comply.
- ○ **D.** If the patient initially rejects the proposal, the research assistant asks them three more times, with lengthy explanations on the value of the study and the necessity of full participation in between each request.

Questions 57 - 59 do not refer to a passage and are independent of each other.

Question 57

Researchers investigate the difference between infants who take to breast feeding and those who do not. This study design may reveal a deficit in which of the following factors that influence motivation?

- ○ **A.** Drive
- ○ **B.** Need
- ○ **C.** Arousal
- ○ **D.** Instinct

Question 58

A study found that when people are rewarded for their actions, they are 56% less likely to change their actions in the future. Of what theory of motivation is this an example?

- ○ **A.** Operant conditioning
- ○ **B.** Drive reduction
- ○ **C.** Need-based
- ○ **D.** Incentive

Question 59

A teaching assistant is nervous about giving a lecture on his thesis work. Which of the following psychological effects is most likely to happen?

- ○ **A.** Anxiety
- ○ **B.** Increased confidence
- ○ **C.** Improved attention
- ○ **D.** Short-term memory impairment

STOP. If you finish before time is called, check your work. You may go back to any question in this test.

ANSWERS & EXPLANATIONS for Test 4B can be found on p. 246.

Biological Correlates of Psychology

TEST 5A

Time: 95 minutes
Questions 1–59

DIRECTIONS: Most of the questions in this test section are grouped with a passage. Read the passage, then select the best answer to each question. Some questions are independent of any passage and of one another. Select the best answer to each of these questions. If you are unsure of an answer, rule out incorrect choices and select from the remaining options. Indicate your selection beside the option you choose.

Passage 1 (Questions 1-4)

Exposure to cigarette smoking affects the epigenome and could increase the risk of developing diseases such as cancer and cardiovascular disorders. Changes in DNA methylation associated with smoking may help to identify molecular pathways that contribute to disease etiology. Previous studies are not completely concordant in the identification of differentially methylated regions in the DNA of smokers.

Researchers performed an epigenome-wide DNA methylation study in a group of monozygotic (MZ) twins discordant for smoking habits to determine the effect of smoking on DNA methylation. They identified 22 CpG sites that were differentially methylated between smoker and non-smoker MZ twins by intra-pair analysis. They confirmed eight loci already described by other groups, located in the *AHRR*, *F2RL3*, *MYOG1*, and *CPLX1* genes, and also identified several new loci. *AHRR* is a tumor suppressor gene that is found in the gonads and pancreas. *F2RL3* is a GPCR that is activated by thrombin and trypsin. *MYOG1* is a transcription factor for the development of skeletal muscle. *CPLX1* encodes the gene for the complexin protein, which is a cytosolic protein that is used at the axon terminal for exocytosis.

Pathway analysis showed an enrichment of genes involved in GTPase regulatory activity. This study confirmed the evidence of smoking-related DNA methylation changes, emphasizing that well-designed MZ twin models can aid in the discovery of novel DNA methylation signals, even in a limited sample population.

This passage was adapted from "Novel Epigenetic Changes Unveiled by Monozygotic Twins Discordant for Smoking Habits." Allione A, Marcon F, Fiorito G, Guarrera S, Siniscalchi E, et al. *PLoS ONE*. 2015. 10(6) doi:10.1371/journal.pone.0128265 for use under the terms of the Creative Commons CC BY 4.0 license (http://creativecommons.org/licenses/by/4.0/legalcode).

Question 1

The hypermethylated CpG islands may result in:

- **A.** pruning of dendritic spines, decreasing neuronal connectivity.
- **B.** escape of the action potential down the axon.
- **C.** failure to transmit excitatory post synaptic potentials.
- **D.** altered resting membrane potential in affected neurons.

Question 2

Which of the following conclusions can be drawn from the results presented in the passage?

- **A.** Smoking behavior is predicted by genetic information that can be modified by DNA methylation.
- **B.** Although DNA is responsible for a large portion of neurobiology, environmental exposures can alter transcription.
- **C.** Smoking causes changes in DNA methylation.
- **D.** Cancer in the gonads or the pancreas is positively correlated with smoking and changes in behavior.

Question 3

Which of the following interventions may prevent initiation of smoking in children with predisposed temperament?

- **A.** Hypomethylation of the DNA sites mentioned in the passage
- **B.** Pairing smoking with a noxious stimulus
- **C.** Behavioral modification to reduce conditioning of positive feelings toward smoking
- **D.** Decrease exposure to parental smoking

Question 4

Previous research has shown that a protein similar to the one encoded by *F2RL3* is upregulated in patients with auditory hallucinations. How might the gene modify sensation?

- **A.** The protein encoded by *F2RL3* causes lasting changes in cytosolic proteins.
- **B.** The protein encoded by *F2RL3* translocates to the nucleus when it binds its target.
- **C.** The protein encoded by *F2RL3* is an ion channel that changes the membrane potential of the neuron.
- **D.** *F2RL3* is a regulatory gene that controls transcription of neuronal proteins.

Next ►

Passage 2 (Questions 5-9)

Autism spectrum disorder (ASD) affects about 1% of the population and is characterized by deficits in social communication alongside unusually narrow interests and repetitive behaviors. There are currently few effective behavioral or pharmacological treatments that can ameliorate core deficits in autism. In a study of the effects of imitation on stereotypic/repetitive behavior, children with ASD (N = 24) were videotaped in a playroom that featured 2 sets of the same toys and a seated, still-faced adult for 3 minutes. This was followed by a 3-minute period of the adult imitating all of the child's behaviors/actions. Another seated, still-face adult segment followed (3 min), and finally a spontaneous play period (3 min). The children ranged from 4 to 6 years of age and were classified as non-verbal based on the diagnostic assessment conducted before the experiment. The results of the study are presented in Table 1.

Table 1 Percentage of Time Certain Behaviors Occurred

Behavior	Imitation play	Spontaneous play
Non-repetitive object movements	32.7	33.4
Repetitive objects-to-face	6.3	16.8
Repetitive autistic-like vocalizations	6.7	24.4

One candidate pharmacological target of much current interest for autism and social behavior is the neuropeptide oxytocin. A study was conducted to examine how intranasal administration of oxytocin affects eye contact for adult males with ASD and controls in a real-time interaction with a researcher. Participants received an active intranasal oxytocin spray or a placebo. Sixty minutes later, the participants were asked to speak to a researcher at a remote location about their experience with the study, and the interaction was initiated as a semi-structured interview via video link designed to last about five minutes. Eye movements were tracked using a camera embedded in a LCD monitor, promoting more naturalistic participant behavior since it does not place restraints on participants such as a head mount or glasses. The results are shown in Figure 1. It has also been suggested that oxytocin therapy could promote longer lasting changes in social cognition through its action on dopaminergic neurons.

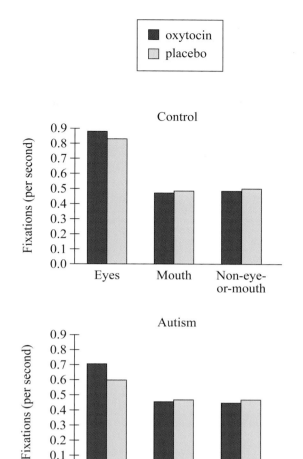

Figure 1 The effect of oxytocin on participants with ASD

This passage was adapted from "Imitation Can Reduce Repetitive Behaviors and Increase Play Behaviors in Children with Autism Spectrum Disorder." Field T, Hernandez-Reif M, Diego M, Corbin J, Stutzman M, et al. *Psychology*. 2014. 5 doi:10.4236/psych.2014.512157 for use under the terms of the Creative Commons CC BY 4.0 license (https://creativecommons.org/licenses/by/4.0/legalcode) and from "Oxytocin Increases Eye Contact During a Real-time, Naturalistic Social Interaction in Males with and without Autism." Auyeung B, Lombardo MV, Heinrichs M, Chakrabarti B, Sule A, et al. *Translational Psychiatry*. 2015. 5 doi:10.1038/tp.2014.146 for use under the terms of the Creative Commons CC BY 4.0 license (https://creativecommons.org/licenses/by/4.0/legalcode).

Question 5

Some researchers have suggested that repetitive autistic-like vocalizations are a means of self-stimulation in children with ASD. Which of the following, if true, would best support this hypothesis?

○ **A.** Repetitive autistic vocalizations increased when the study was completed in a room with soft music playing.

○ **B.** The children underwent the experiment immediately before their morning meal.

○ **C.** Findings did not differ significantly when the study was repeated in a room with two adults per child.

○ **D.** Children with ASD spent 36% of their time making repetitive autistic-like vocalizations in still-faced segment 2.

Question 6

The researcher found that in the second still-faced adult segment, children spent more time playing with toys. This finding demonstrates:

○ **A.** bottom-up processing.

○ **B.** top-down processing.

○ **C.** parallel processing.

○ **D.** neural plasticity.

Question 7

The data in Figure 1 were generated by monitoring subjects' eye contact with an interviewer in real time. Previous studies assessed subjects' tendency to gaze at static shapes resembling eyes following treatment with oxytocin. Static shapes could be used as substitutes for human eyes because perception follows:

○ **A.** psychosocial evolution.

○ **B.** interactionist theory.

○ **C.** Gestalt principles.

○ **D.** parallel processing.

Question 8

Before beginning clinical trials, a study analogous to the one described in paragraph 2 was conducted in mice. Suppose researchers wanted to repeat this study using individuals selected from a population of wild, captured mice, and bred selectively for a given trait. Which characteristic might they select for?

○ **A.** Low serum oxytocin.

○ **B.** Increased repetitive self-grooming behavior.

○ **C.** Low sociability.

○ **D.** It is unlikely that a natural population would yield useful test specimens.

Question 9

According to the passage, oxytocin may have a long-term effect on social behavior. If oxytocin therapy increases the enjoyment associated with future interview-like social exchanges, this may suggest that oxytocin:

○ **A.** acts as a depressant.

○ **B.** acts as a stimulant.

○ **C.** interacts with the reward pathway.

○ **D.** induces a hypnotic state.

Passage 3 (Questions 10-13)

Atrial fibrillation can cause depression and anxiety in patients, and depression and anxiety can initiate and perpetuate atrial fibrillation. Using psychiatric medications can reduce anxiety and may improve treatment outcomes in atrial fibrillation patients. Researchers analyzed the efficacy of anxiolytic medications in a new model of extreme anxiety in rats. In this model of extreme anxiety, forced apnea is combined with cold water vaporization in an inescapable situation to condition fear that triggers escape and avoidance behaviors. The number and latencies of jumps were measured, together with freezing time, which is defined by immobility for at least 4 seconds in the interval of 0 to 4 min. Decreased jumps and immobility time and increased time latency before the first jump are attributable to anxiopanicolytic properties of anxiety medications.

Investigators evaluated active (escape attempts) and passive (immobility/freezing) responses to rising water levels and determined the efficacy of subchronic versus acute administration of fluoxetine (FLX), a selective serotonin (5-HT) reuptake inhibitor. The results of this study are shown in Table 1.

In another study, researchers evaluated the same behavioral responses of the rats to determine the efficacy of a 1 mg/kg dose versus 3 mg/kg dose of diazepam (DZP), a benzodiazepine, in treating anxiety. The results of this study are shown in Table 2. The model of extreme anxiety used in these studies may improve investigation of anxiety disorder and its relationship to atrial fibrillation.

Table 1 Effects of Acute FLX Treatment (10 mg/kg IP) and Subchronic FLX Treatment (5 mg/kg/21 days)

Measures	Subchronic FLX				Acute FLX			
	Baseline (before treatment)		Test (after treatment)		Baseline (before treatment)		Test (after treatment)	
	Control	FLX	Control	FLX	Control	FLX	Control	FLX
Number of jumps	23	21	22	9	17	15	19	21
Latency before the first jump (s)	15	14	16	27	19	20	16	14
Immobility (s)	140	59	164	70	85	97	108	139

Table 2 Effects of Acute Diazepam Treatment (1 mg/kg, IP) and Acute Diazepam Treatment (3 mg/kg, IP)

Measures	Acute DZP (1 mg/kg)				Acute DZP (3 mg/kg)			
	Baseline (before treatment)		Test (after treatment)		Baseline (before treatment)		Test (after treatment)	
	Control	DZP	Control	DZP	Control	DZP	Control	DZP
Number of jumps	20	21	21	16	13.5	15.5	15	6
Latency before the first jump (s)	17	15	15	21	15.5	23.5	11	28
Immobility (s)	106	101	121	90	84	85.5	129.5	130

Question 10

Which of the following conclusions is best supported by the data in Table 1?

○ **A.** Atrial fibrillation patients with associated anxiety would best benefit from acute administration of FLX.

○ **B.** Subchronic treatment with FLX would most likely alleviate anxiety in a patient with an anxiety disorder.

○ **C.** Atrial fibrillation patients would benefit from the subchronic administration of FLX versus acute administration of FLX.

○ **D.** Both subchronic and acute administration of FLX could exacerbate anxiety symptoms in patients.

Question 11

As a 5- HT reuptake inhibitor, fluoxetine:

○ **A.** allows 5-HT to remain in the synapse and bind to receptors.

○ **B.** chemically mimics 5-HT to enhance its effects in the synapse.

○ **C.** facilitates binding of 5-HT to its receptors.

○ **D.** prevents the breakdown of 5-HT, thus allowing 5-HT to remain in the synapse.

Question 12

If the first study were changed to also test the effects of another 5-HT reuptake inhibitor, imipramine, how would this alter the experimental design of the study?

○ **A.** The existing dependent variables would change.

○ **B.** The reliability of the study would increase.

○ **C.** There would be another independent variable involved in the study.

○ **D.** The validity of the study would increase.

Question 13

Which of the following statements best describes the future implications of this study?

○ **A.** The model of extreme anxiety used would be ineffective at investigating anxiety disorder and its relationship to atrial fibrillation.

○ **B.** The model of extreme anxiety used may improve investigation of anxiety disorder and its relationship to atrial fibrillation.

○ **C.** The model of extreme anxiety used will prove the relationship between anxiety disorder and atrial fibrillation.

○ **D.** The model of extreme anxiety used needs improvement in order to support future investigations.

Questions 14 - 16 do not refer to a passage and are independent of each other.

Question 14

Research is often aimed at finding the "genes for smoking," although it is not proven that these are genetically encoded. Which of the following behaviors is most likely to have a genetic basis?

○ **A.** Aggression

○ **B.** Creativity

○ **C.** Hunger resulting in obesity

○ **D.** Infidelity to a spouse

Question 15

Which of the following modern behaviors is most likely to be passed down to future generations?

○ **A.** Texting while driving a car

○ **B.** Using contraceptives in sexual intercourse

○ **C.** Working overtime to get a promotion

○ **D.** Practicing extreme sports like sky diving

Question 16

In designing a similar experiment on behavioral genetics, for which of the following modifiers would be most difficult to control?

○ **A.** Genetics

○ **B.** Epigenetics

○ **C.** Prior environmental exposures

○ **D.** Behavior

Passage 4 (Questions 17-20)

According to the latest US surveys, 36% of the adult population is obese, and one third of adults report sleeping less than 6 hours per night, substantially less than the recommended 7–9 hours of sleep per night. Chronic sleep deprivation and obesity may be related in a bidirectional fashion, and they have similar consequences, including hypertension, diabetes, and cardiovascular disease. In addition, obesity and sleep deprivation have been linked to cognitive deficits. Obese individuals exhibit deficits in executive functions, including mental flexibility, planning, problem solving, and display impulsivity, as well as tend to favor immediate reward vs. long term gain. One hypothesis proposes that the "higher cortical functions" that control learning and executive function are no longer appropriately inhibiting feeding behavior in obese individuals. In turn, altered eating behavior in obesity may cause neurocognitive dysfunction. For example, a high-fat or high-carbohydrate meal can disrupt hippocampal function.

The Sleep Extension Study was a randomized, controlled, prospective study of sleep extension in chronically sleep-deprived obese individuals. Individuals were recruited by advertising for men and premenopausal women aged 18 to 50 years with a body mass index (BMI) between 30 and 55 kg/m² who reported sleeping less than 6.5 hours per night. Out of 121 individuals with baseline neuropsychological evaluation, 72 were randomized to the intervention group and 49 to the comparison group. Individuals in the intervention group were coached to increase sleep duration up to 7.5 hours per night, following a personalized sleep plan. The comparison group was asked to continue the existing short sleep habits. Sleeping habits were reviewed approximately every two months. Tests administered to participants were grouped into four cognitive ability domains: memory, attention, motor skills, and executive function. The results are shown in Figure 1.

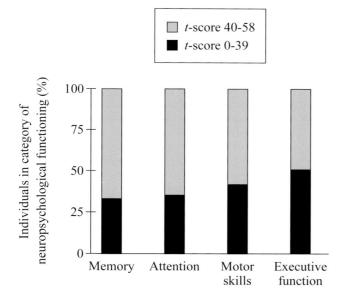

Figure 1 Domain Deficit Scores calculated from participant's responses to tests involving memory, attention, motor skills, and executive function

This passage was adapted from "Sleep Extension Improves Neurocognitive Functions in Chronically Sleep-Deprived Obese Individuals." Lucassen EA, Piaggi P, Dsurney J, Jonge L, Zhao X, et al. *PLoS ONE*. 2015. 9(1) doi: 10.1371/journal.pone.0084832 for use under the terms of the Creative Commons CC BY 4.0 license (https://creativecommons.org/licenses/by/4.0/legalcode).

Question 17

One possible link between participants obesity and sleep deficiency could be:

- ○ **A.** lack of delta waves in the fourth stage of sleep.
- ○ **B.** a dysregulation in participant's circadian rhythm.
- ○ **C.** a dysfunction in the suprachiasmatic nucleus in the hypothalamus.
- ○ **D.** more allotted time for wakefulness and thus more time for caloric consumption.

Question 18

Overweight, sleep deprived participants were most affected by what category of functioning and what biological faculty is this functioning most likely to affect?

- ○ **A.** Motor skills, depth perception
- ○ **B.** Motor skills, circadian rhythm
- ○ **C.** Executive functions, hypothalamus functioning
- ○ **D.** Executive functions, circadian rhythm

Question 19

Researchers aimed to assess the reversibility of possible deficits with sleep extension in a non-pharmacological way under real-life conditions. How would the researcher be able gauge participant improvement?

- ○ **A.** Test the participant's absolute threshold in all categories and see if it has improved with increased sleep.
- ○ **B.** Look at the difference threshold between the results before the study and after a period of time with increased sleep.
- ○ **C.** Compare participant's test results to the test results of the control group.
- ○ **D.** Complete all tests on participants again after a period of time with more sleep and compare results.

Question 20

The interaction between the environment and heredity play a critical role in psychological development, including the development of behavioral traits. What do the results of the study suggest relating to the obesity?

- ○ **A.** Support because participants with a genetic predisposition to obesity were more likely to be obese.
- ○ **B.** Deny because the way environment influences gene expression is through regulatory genes, which affect various steps from DNA to protein and thus alter gene expression.
- ○ **C.** Both support and deny because obesity is affected by both genetic and environmental factors.
- ○ **D.** Neither support nor deny because there is not enough information pertaining to heredity addressed in the study.

Passage 5 (Questions 21-25)

The effects of novelty on low-level visual perception were investigated in two experiments using a two-alternative forced choice tilt detection task. 17 participants (12 female; 15 right-handed) participated in the experiment on a voluntary basis.

For every participant, one geometric figure, or fractal, was randomly chosen to become familiarized. This 'familiar' image was presented for 20 seconds prior to the experiment, in order for participants to become familiarized with it. The 'novel' images were all unique fractals unknown to the observer.

A target, consisting of a Gabor patch, was preceded by a cue that was either a novel or a familiar fractal image. Participants had to indicate whether the Gabor stimulus was vertically oriented or slightly tilted. In the first experiment, tilt angle was manipulated; in the second, contrast of the Gabor patch was varied. The results are shown in Figure 1.

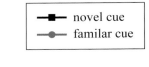

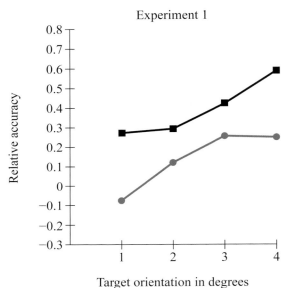

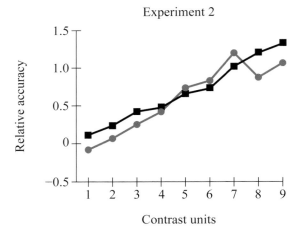

Figure 1 Effect of novel image cue on detection of orientation and contrast difference

This passage was adapted from "Novelty Enhances Visual Perception." Schomaker J, Meeter M. *PLoS ONE*. 2012. 7(12) doi:10.1371/journal.pone.0050599 for use under the terms of the Creative Commons CC BY 3.0 license (http://creativecommons.org/licenses/by/3.0/legalcode).

Question 21

Shown below is a Gabor patch like the one used in the experiment. Which of the following Gestalt principles most governs perception of this image?

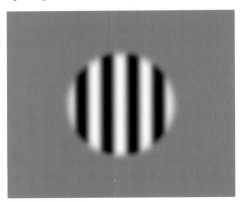

- ○ **A.** Symmetry
- ○ **B.** Linearity
- ○ **C.** Closure
- ○ **D.** Figure-ground

Question 22

Which perceptual skill was assessed by researchers?
- ○ **A.** Depth
- ○ **B.** Form
- ○ **C.** Motion
- ○ **D.** Constancy

Question 23

Use of which legal drug can increase attention and bias the results of the study?

○ **A.** Caffeine

○ **B.** Alcohol

○ **C.** Marijuana

○ **D.** Lidocaine, a cocaine derivative

Question 24

Suppose researchers found that one participant was completely incapable of recognizing any familiarity to the fractals. This person may have damage to which of the following brain regions?

○ **A.** The amygdala

○ **B.** The hippocampus

○ **C.** The frontal lobes

○ **D.** The temporal lobes

Question 25

Which of the following conclusions can be drawn from Figure 1?

○ **A.** Novel cues quickly become boring.

○ **B.** Compared to the contrast experiment, there was a greater variation between novel and familiar groups for the orientation experiment.

○ **C.** When there is a lack of constancy, the contrast of the Gabor patch is always easier to identify.

○ **D.** When there is a lack of constancy, the orientation of the Gabor patch is always easier to identify.

Questions 26 - 29 do not refer to a passage and are independent of each other.

Question 26

Which statement best illustrates the interaction between heredity and environment?

○ **A.** An adopted child takes on mannerisms of their adopted parents.

○ **B.** A brother and sister have similar reactions to emotional situations.

○ **C.** A person with congenital lack of photoreceptors has an expanded auditory cortex.

○ **D.** After a frightening experience, a child is afraid of sleeping.

Question 27

A "+" sign utilizes the Gestalt principle of:

○ **A.** similarity.

○ **B.** continuation.

○ **C.** proximity.

○ **D.** closure.

Question 28

A study shows that babies raised in middle class homes hear 70% more words in their first 24 months than babies raised in lower class homes. As a result, middle class children perform better in school than their lower income counterparts. What type of learning associated with these results is happening most during these 0-24 months?

○ **A.** Gestalt principles

○ **B.** Visual processing

○ **C.** Top-down processing

○ **D.** Bottom-up processing

Question 29

Which of the following is the most likely side effect that participants in this study experience in everyday life?

○ **A.** Decreased attention

○ **B.** Worsened depth perception

○ **C.** Worsened motion perception

○ **D.** Worsened visual processing

Passage 6 (Questions 30-34)

Hemianopia is defined as decreased vision in half of the visual field in one or both eyes. If it is bilateral, hemianopia is usually caused by a neurological injury or lesion since having symmetrical injury to both retinas would be rare. Bilateral left sided homonymous hemianopia would result in no left-sided vision perceived from either eye.

Researchers attempted a novel approach to vision rehabilitation that was based on passive auditory stimulation. Ten patients with either left or right-sided pure hemianopia received one hour of auditory stimulation on either their anopic or their intact side. The auditory stimuli were repetitive sequences of sound pulses emitted simultaneously via two loudspeakers. Immediately before and after auditory stimulation, as well as after a period of recovery, patients completed a simple visual task requiring detection of light flashes in total darkness. The results showed that one-time passive auditory stimulation on the side of the blind, but not of the intact side, induced an improvement in visual detections by almost 100% within 30 min after passive auditory stimulation. This enhancement in performance was reversible and was reduced to baseline 1.5 hours later. A non-significant trend of a shift of the visual field border toward the blind side was obtained after passive auditory stimulation. These results are compatible with the view that passive auditory stimulation elicited some activation of the residual visual pathways, which are known to be multisensory and may also be sensitive to unimodal auditory stimuli as were used here.

This passage was adapted from "Passive Auditory Stimulation Improves Vision in Hemianopia." Lewald J, Tegenthoff M, Peters S, Hausmann M. *PLoS ONE*. 2012. 7(5) doi:10.1371/ journal.pone.0031603 for use under the terms of the Creative Commons CC BY 3.0 license (http://creativecommons.org/licenses/by/3.0/legalcode)

Question 30

Which of the following is most likely true of participants prior to auditory stimulation?

- **A.** Participants have intact sensation and perception.
- **B.** Participants have intact sensation but impaired perception.
- **C.** Participants have impaired sensation but intact perception.
- **D.** Participants have impaired sensation and perception.

Question 31

Which threshold was lowered in patients in the study?

- **A.** Absolute threshold
- **B.** Difference threshold
- **C.** Significance threshold
- **D.** Weber threshold

Question 32

Which neurological phenomenon explains the findings of the study?

- **A.** Divided attention
- **B.** Selective attention
- **C.** Neural plasticity
- **D.** Stem cell activation

Question 33

Depth perception requires bilateral input from each retina in order to perceive small variations in location of an object. How would depth perception be affected in individuals with hemianopia?

- **A.** Depth perception will be essentially intact.
- **B.** Depth perception will only be intact in the parts of the visual field that are being perceived by participants.
- **C.** Depth perception will be extensively impaired, making participants perceive the world mostly in 2D.
- **D.** Not enough information is provided to comment on depth perception in participants.

Question 34

Improving which of the following normal processes may result in sustained improvement in vision in previously hemianopic patients?

- **A.** Increased activity of GABA
- **B.** Long-term potentiation
- **C.** Neuronal differentiation
- **D.** Regulatory genes

Passage 7 (Questions 35-39)

Light is the most important time cue for maintaining the 24 hour period of circadian rhythms in humans. In the Arctic and Antarctic Circles, deprivation of natural light occurs in winter. Some studies suggest that these suboptimal light conditions are deleterious to health, sleep and mood. An adequate light exposure pattern may help to prevent or even reverse health problems associated with circadian disruption.

In this study, two different populations of workers were compared. One group lives beneath the Equator in northern Brazil, and the other group lives within the Arctic Circle in northern Sweden. The hypothesis was that at an extreme latitude (Swedish workers) lack of natural light exposure affects sleep quality and may lead to depressive symptoms. Both Arctic and Equatorial workers reported how many hours per day on average they were exposed to natural light. Three independent indices related to sleep problems were obtained from the Karolinska Sleep Questionnaire. They included sleep quality, awakening problems, and sleepiness. At both sites, clinical depression was reported using the Work Ability Index or Hamilton Depression Subscale. The workers were split according to self-reported natural light exposure into short and long light exposure groups, according to the mean within each group. The study results are shown in Figure 1.

While Arctic workers reported more sleep problems on the questionnaires, electroencephalogram (EEG) studies revealed that many Equatorial workers rarely entered REM sleep. A higher proportion of Arctic workers complained that they were depressed compared with the Equatorial workers.

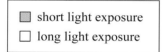

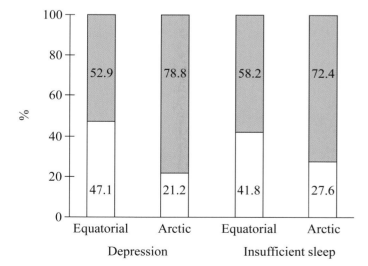

Figure 1 Percentage of workers reporting depression and insufficient sleep divided according to self-reported natural light exposure groups for Equatorial and Arctic groups.

This passage was adapted from "Natural Light Exposure, Sleep and Depression among Day Workers and Shiftworkers at Arctic and Equatorial Latitudes." Marqueze EC, Vasconcelos S, Garefelt J, Skene DJ, Moreno CR, et al. *PLoS ONE*. 2015. 10(4): e0122078. doi:10.1371/journal.pone.0122078 for use under the terms of the Creative Commons CC BY 4.0 license (http://creativecommons.org/licenses/by/4.0/legalcode).

Question 35

Different patterns of light exposure cause profound changes in sleepiness rankings on the Karolinska Sleep Questionnaire. People who have suffered from an aneurysm in the diencephalon do not experience increased wakefulness based on light. This is best explained by the finding that in these individuals:

- **A.** the suprachiasmatic nucleus becomes overactive in signaling to the pineal gland.
- **B.** the pineal gland begins producing excess melatonin.
- **C.** the optic nerve becomes more sensitive to changes in light.
- **D.** the connection between the hypothalamus and pineal gland is lost.

Question 36

Based on the passage, researchers should be most concerned about Equatorial workers experiencing which type of sleep disorder?

- **A.** Sleep terror disorder
- **B.** Nightmares
- **C.** Insomnia
- **D.** Narcolepsy

Question 37

Based on the findings in the passage, if Arctic workers were given a memory test, they would:

- **A.** outperform Equatorial workers because they achieve Stage 4 sleep.
- **B.** underperform relative to Equatorial workers because they only achieve Stage 4 sleep.
- **C.** outperform Equatorial workers because they achieve better REM sleep.
- **D.** underperform relative to Equatorial workers because they only achieve better REM sleep.

Question 38

Arctic workers in this study who self-report problems awakening and daytime sleepiness show a lack of delta waves on their EEG during sleep. They are likely not achieving which stage of sleep?

- ○ **A.** Stage 1
- ○ **B.** Stage 2
- ○ **C.** Stage 3
- ○ **D.** REM

Question 39

Many patients in this study reported using cocaine. They stated that it drastically reduces their daytime sleepiness and helps them stay productive while at work. Based on this result, the most likely mechanism of action for cocaine is:

- ○ **A.** increasing reuptake of serotonin.
- ○ **B.** blocking reuptake of norepinephrine.
- ○ **C.** blocking reuptake of acetylcholine.
- ○ **D.** increasing reuptake of dopamine.

Passage 8 (Questions 40-43)

The undergraduate years are a period of vulnerability when considering sleep problems and mental health. Sleep problems tend to worsen over time in undergraduate students, a finding which is concerning as even the time-limited experience of significant sleep problems is associated with reduced mental health outcomes.

Previous Research

In terms of mental health, approximately 25% of university students who did not report a mental health issue at a baseline assessment ultimately reported a mental health problem 2 years later; approximately 60% of students in that study experienced continuity in the report of at least one mental health issue over time. Approximately 50% of the students who reported continuous mental health issues across assessments did not seek mental health treatment. Taken together, these findings suggest that the sleep problems experienced by undergraduate students may not be inconsequential; they may develop into more significant problems over time and may have implications for mental health outcomes.

Current Investigation

Sixty-nine university students with generally healthy sleep habits completed questionnaires about sleep quality and mental health. Although participants did not report clinically concerning mental health issues as a group, global sleep quality was related to mental health. Regression analyses revealed that nighttime sleep duration and the frequency of nighttime sleep disruptions were differentially related to total problems and clinically-relevant symptoms of psychological distress. These results indicate that understanding relations between sleep and mental health in university students with generally healthy sleep habits is important not only due to the large number of undergraduates who experience sleep problems and mental health issues over time but also due to the potential to intervene and improve mental health outcomes before they become clinically concerning.

This passage was adapted from "Sleep and Mental Health in Undergraduate Students with Generally Healthy Sleep Habits." Milojevich HM, Lukowski AF. *PLoS ONE*. 2016. 11(6) doi:10.1371/journal.pone.0156372 for use under the terms of the Creative Commons CC BY 4.0 license (http://creativecommons.org/licenses/by/4.0/legalcode).

Next ▶

Question 40

In a follow up study, researchers found that a particular stage of sleep is associated with poor mental health. Excess time in which stage was likely recorded?

○ **A.** Stage 1

○ **B.** Stage 2

○ **C.** Stage 3

○ **D.** REM

Question 41

Participants with which of the following sleep-wake disorders are more likely to have mental illness?

○ **A.** Insomnia

○ **B.** Narcolepsy

○ **C.** Kleine-Levin syndrome (sleeping beauty syndrome)

○ **D.** Non-24-hour sleep-wake disorder

Question 42

According to information in the passage, participants taking which of the following drugs may be more at risk for mental illness?

○ **A.** Alcohol

○ **B.** Marijuana

○ **C.** Heroin

○ **D.** Crystal meth

Question 43

Based on the results of the study, a student with a mental disorder may benefit from which of the following rest-replacing techniques?

○ **A.** Psychotherapy

○ **B.** Hypnosis

○ **C.** Protein-rich diet

○ **D.** Meditation

Questions 44 - 47 do not refer to a passage and are independent of each other.

Question 44

Jet lag is a common complaint in individuals flying long distances. Which of the following techniques could prevent jet lag?

○ **A.** Sleeping on the plane

○ **B.** Gradually modifying bedtime to correspond to the new location

○ **C.** Use of light therapy

○ **D.** Ingesting melatonin immediately upon waking

Question 45

Which of the following drugs would be most effective in increasing sleep length and quality if prescribed to an overweight, sleep-deficient patient?

○ **A.** A stimulant

○ **B.** A depressant

○ **C.** A hallucinogen

○ **D.** A carcinogen

Question 46

Electronics use is positively correlated to poor sleep due to disruption of the circadian rhythms. Which of the following is a likely explanation?

○ **A.** Social interaction decreases wakefulness neurotransmitters in the pineal gland.

○ **B.** Social interaction increases sleep-promoting neurotransmitters in the pineal gland.

○ **C.** Light near the UV range on the visible spectrum promotes wakefulness.

○ **D.** Light near the IR range on the visible spectrum promotes wakefulness.

Question 47

If the Weber fraction for pain threshold was calculated to be 2/5, what change in stimulation would be required to detect a change from the original stimulus of 17.5 mA?

○ **A.** 1 mA

○ **B.** 7 mA

○ **C.** 10.5 mA

○ **D.** 0.4 mA

Passage 9 (Questions 48–51)

Pain has distinct sensory and affective (i.e., unpleasantness) dimensions and can induce an avoidance behavior. Thus, patients suffering from chronic neuropathic pain can develop psycho-social consequences. Breathing-controlled electrical stimulation (BreEStim), during which electrical stimulation is delivered during voluntary breathing, has been shown to selectively reduce the affective component of postamputation phantom pain.

A study was designed to investigate pain thresholds using BreEStim. Pain-free healthy subjects participated in the study. All subjects received BreEStim and conventional electrical stimulation (EStim) to two acupuncture points of the dominant hand in a random order. Painful, but tolerable electrical stimuli were delivered randomly during EStim but were triggered by effortful inhalation during BreEStim. Measurements of tactile sensation threshold, electrical sensation and electrical pain thresholds, thermal (cold sensation, warm sensation, cold pain and heat pain) thresholds were recorded from the thenar eminence of both hands. The electrical pain threshold (average = 17.5 mA) significantly increased after BreEStim and significantly decreased after EStim. There was no statistically significant change in other thresholds after BreEStim and EStim.

Memory mechanisms play an important role in the persistence of the awareness of chronic neuropathic pain as well as in the reinforcement of the associated distress. Traumatic injury resulting in spinal cord injury or amputation is usually a single event. However, the memory of the event could last for the rest of a person's life. When associated with a negative emotional context, pain (e.g., phantom pain after amputation) can be perceived as aversive, and re-triggered by a stressful life event.

This passage was adapted from "Modification of Electrical Pain Threshold by Voluntary Breathing-Controlled Electrical Stimulation (BreEStim) in Healthy Subjects." Li S, Berliner JC, Melton DH, Li S. *PLoS ONE*. 2013. 8(7) doi:10.1371/journal. pone.0070282 for use under the terms of the Creative Commons CC BY 3.0 license (http://creativecommons.org/licenses/by/3.0/legalcode).

Question 48

Based on the passage, which type of mental processing is most likely affected in phantom pain after amputation?

- A. Top-down processing
- B. Bottom-up processing
- C. Sensation
- D. Both top-down processing and bottom-up processing

Question 49

If memory plays a role in patients with phantom limb pain, this is most likely a result of what kind of memory storage?

- A. Sensory memory
- B. Short-term memory
- C. Working memory
- D. Long-term memory

Question 50

Which part of the study limits the conclusion that changes in pain threshold can alleviate postamputation phantom pain?

- A. The participants in the study were given pain stimuli on non-amputated limbs.
- B. The participants had control over BreEStim pain delivery, but not over EStim pain delivery.
- C. The researchers do not control for differences in perceived pain.
- D. The participants do not have an emotional component to the pain delivered.

Question 51

The researchers measured the threshold of sensation of various stimuli to establish:

- A. attention level.
- B. signal detection.
- C. difference threshold.
- D. absolute threshold.

Next ▶

Passage 10 (Questions 52-55)

In synesthesia, the input of one modality activates brain areas that are normally not involved in processing inputs of that modality. This activation can result in an additional sensory experience, for example, a color experience for a black letter or a spoken word. Some studies, most of them case-reports, suggest that synesthetes have an advantage in visual search and episodic memory tasks. To investigate this, a computerized test of consistency, conducted in the original test session and in a retest session two-to-three weeks later, confirmed the participants' synesthesia. Participants had to choose a color for each grapheme from a color palette with 144 different colors. For the synesthetes, consistency was r = 0.94 for hue, r = 0.85 for saturation and r = 0.58 for value (brightness). For the controls, consistency was r = 0.21 for hue, r = 0.26 for saturation and r = 0.24 for value. These results showed that the synesthetes in the trial truly had synesthesia.

Next, the groups were asked to perform a memory task. In the matrix memory test, participants had to learn two different matrices consisting of 50 randomly generated graphemes for later recall. One consisted of black digits while the other consisted of digits that were incongruent to the concurrents of each individual synesthete. The proportion of correctly reproduced matrix cells was analyzed. The results indicated that synesthesia does not seem to lead to a strong performance advantage. Rather, the superior performance of synesthetes observed in some case-report studies may be due to individual differences, a selection bias, or to a strategic use of synesthesia as a mnemonic. In order to establish universal effects of synesthesia on cognition, single-case studies must be complemented by group studies.

This passage was adapted from "Do Synesthetes Have a General Advantage in Visual Search and Episodic Memory? A Case for Group Studies." Rothen N, Meier B. *PLoS ONE*. 2009. 4(4) doi:10.1371/journal.pone.0005037 for use under the terms of the Creative Commons CC BY 3.0 license (http://creativecommons.org/licenses/by/3.0/legalcode).

Question 52

According to the data from the first study, synesthetes likely:

- A. have superior memory.
- B. have superior visual cortices.
- C. have a decreased Weber's fraction.
- D. have an increased absolute threshold.

Question 53

Which of the following is a possible hypothesis for the experiments in the passage?

- A. Synesthetes will perform better on memory tasks due to enhanced visual processing.
- B. Controls will perform better on memory tasks due to enhanced visual processing.
- C. Synesthetes will perform better on memory tasks due to enhanced semantic networks.
- D. Controls will perform better on memory tasks due to enhanced semantic networks.

Question 54

Which of the following techniques could universally improve performance on the second task?

- A. Expose participants to a stressful situation as memory is often enhanced in times of stress.
- B. Administer stimulant drugs like caffeine or amphetamines to participants.
- C. Recruit control participants with Alzheimer's disease, the synesthetes would perform better on the memory task.
- D. Recruit control participants with Alzheimer's disease, the controls would perform better on the memory task.

Question 55

Which of the following could correctly describe a physical basis for synesthesia?

- A. Cortical areas are cross activated due to a failure of neural pruning during development.
- B. Inheritance of a specific gene leads to production of a new protein that allows for synesthesia.
- C. The brain of participants with synesthesia likely have an increased number of gyri and sulci to processes increased information.
- D. Specific areas of tangled axons lead to diffuse electrical activation.

Question 56

What is the default state of consciousness?

○ **A.** Awake

○ **B.** Alert

○ **C.** Absorbing

○ **D.** Asleep

Question 57

Jane is taking a cumulative test for school. Which aspect of her memory is she utilizing the most?

○ **A.** Storage

○ **B.** Encoding

○ **C.** Retrieval

○ **D.** Working memory

Question 58

Damage to which of the following areas of the brain would most predispose a person to impairment in memory?

○ **A.** Suprachiasmatic nucleus of the hypothalamus, which contains ADH

○ **B.** Lateral geniculate nucleus of the thalamus, which has three major cell types

○ **C.** Pineal gland of the epithalamus, which produces melatonin

○ **D.** Nucleus of the subthalamus, which is primarily dopaminergic

Question 59

Edward was listening to music on his phone and accidentally tripped since he did not see a hole in the sidewalk. This accident can best be described by:

○ **A.** selective attention.

○ **B.** divided attention.

○ **C.** sensory imbalance.

○ **D.** perception loss.

ANSWERS & EXPLANATIONS for Test 5A can be found on p. 270.

Biological Correlates of Psychology

TEST 5B

Time: 95 minutes
Questions 1–59

DIRECTIONS: Most of the questions in this test section are grouped with a passage. Read the passage, then select the best answer to each question. Some questions are independent of any passage and of one another. Select the best answer to each of these questions. If you are unsure of an answer, rule out incorrect choices and select from the remaining options. Indicate your selection beside the option you choose.

Passage 1 (Questions 1-4)

Previous studies have shown that human sleep enhances the conversion of labile, recently acquired information into stable, long-term memories. This means that volunteers showed greater saving of memories when sleep, rather than nocturnal wakefulness, followed the learning process. Such consolidation effects of sleep have been found for declarative and procedural types of memory tasks. Bearing in mind that food intake produces many metabolic signals that can influence memory processing in humans (e.g. insulin), the present study addressed the question as to whether the enhancing effect of sleep on memory consolidation is affected by the amount of energy consumed during the preceding daytime. Compared to sleep, nocturnal wakefulness has been shown to impair memory consolidation in humans. Thus, a second question was to examine whether the impaired memory consolidation associated with sleep deprivation (SD) could be compensated by increased daytime energy consumption. Poor performance on memory tasks, such as those used in the present experiment, has been correlated with poor job performance, automobile accidents, and increased stress and anxiety, so variables affecting memory may contribute to poor quality of life and mortality.

To these end, 14 healthy normal-weight men learned a finger tapping sequence and a list of semantically associated word pairs. Learning was assessed after this training period. After the training period, standardized meals were administered, equaling either 50% or 150% of the estimated daily energy expenditure for each participant. In the morning, after sleep or wakefulness, memory consolidation was tested. Plasma glucose was measured before both learning and retrieval. Poly somnographic sleep recordings were performed by electroencephalography (EEG). The results of the learning tasks are shown in Table 1. These findings were independent of glucose levels.

Table 1 Relative Learning of Word Pairs and Sequences Post Sleep or SD

	Sleep + high energy	Sleep + low energy	SD + high energy	SD + low energy
Relative learning (%): word pairs	91.4 +/− 3.3	92.3 +/− 4.2	84.2 +/− 3.2	85.2 +/− 4.7
Relative learning (%): sequences	114.5 +/− 5.0	116.4 +/− 3.6	116.4 +/− 3.1	102.6 +/− 2.7

Question 1

For finger tapping sequences, which statement explains the findings in Table 1?

○ **A.** The relative learning is greater than 100% because learning improved between measurements, likely through attention and retrieval.

○ **B.** The relative learning is greater than 100% because learning improved between measurements, likely through rehearsal and encoding.

○ **C.** The relative learning is less than 100% because learning decreased between measurements, likely through attention and retrieval.

○ **D.** The relative learning is less than 100% because learning decreased between measurements, likely through inattention and forgetting.

Question 2

A follow-up study concludes that sustained learning of finger tapping sequences is significantly impaired in Alzheimer's disease and suggests that this measure be used to diagnose the illness. Which of the following scenarios may result in the misdiagnosis of Alzheimer's disease?

○ **A.** A young, obese patient with recent sleep deprivation.

○ **B.** A young, thin patient with recent sleep deprivation.

○ **C.** An elderly patient who consumes very few calories.

○ **D.** An elderly patient with a normal diet and sleep deprivation.

Question 3

A researcher wants to determine if the effects of the first study are confounded by any variables. Which conditions could interfere with the results?

○ **A.** Low IQ and obesity

○ **B.** Insomnia and Korsakoff's syndrome

○ **C.** Depression and anxiety

○ **D.** Low income and dyslexia

Question 4

According to the findings in Table 1, under which circumstances was there impairment in declarative memory?

○ **A.** There was no impairment in declarative memory.

○ **B.** There was impairment under sleep deprivation, regardless of energy intake.

○ **C.** There was impairment under sleep deprivation and with low energy intake only.

○ **D.** There was impairment but it was not statistically significant.

Passage 2 (Questions 5-8)

A recent study showed that many people spontaneously report vivid memories of events that they do not believe to have occurred. Counterintuitive as it might sound, people do not always believe that the events they remember actually occurred. Many people report having a memory that they know to be false, and in some cases, these memories can concern extremely significant experiences. For instance, there are documented cases of people with memories of severe childhood abuse having encountered incontestable proof that the events they recall could not possibly have happened.

Study 1

Researchers tested for the first time whether, after powerful false memories have been created, debriefing might leave behind nonbelieved memories for the fake events.

In Session 1, participants imitated simple actions, and in Session 2, they saw doctored video-recordings containing clips that falsely suggested they had performed additional (fake) actions. As in earlier studies, this procedure created powerful false memories. In Session 3, participants were debriefed and told that specific actions in the video were not truly performed.

Beliefs and memories for all critical actions were tested before and after the debriefing. Results showed that debriefing undermined participants' beliefs in their fake actions, but left behind residual memory-like content. These results indicate that debriefing can leave behind vivid false memories, which are no longer believed, and thus demonstrate for the first time that the memory of an event can be experimentally dissociated from the belief in the event's occurrence. These results also confirm that belief in and memory for an event can be independently-occurring constructs.

Study 2

Traumatic memories are of known importance to diseases like Post-Traumatic Stress Disorder (PTSD) and Adjustment Disorder. The fact that these memories may be altered has implications for the treatment of these diseases.

Researchers tested the hypothesis that altering these memories early on has effects on later symptom presentation. They found that in sexual assault victims, seeking medical or police assistance is associated with greater prevalence of later PTSD.

This passage was adapted from "Creating Non-Believed Memories for Recent Autobiographical Events." Clark A, Nash RA, Fincham G, Mazzoni G. *PLoS ONE*. 2012. 7(3) doi:10.1371/journal.pone.0032998 for use under the terms of the Creative Commons CC BY 3.0 license (http://creativecommons.org/licenses/by/3.0/legalcode).

Question 5

During session 2, which of the following memories are most likely to be forgotten?

○ **A.** False memories that occur at the beginning of the interaction.

○ **B.** False memories that occur at the middle of the interaction.

○ **C.** False memories that occur at the end of the interaction.

○ **D.** True memories that occur at the end of the interaction.

Question 6

Which of the following is a possible explanation for the findings in Study 2?

  I. Seeking medical and police assistance may cause an error in encoding and lead to false memories.

  II. Seeking medical and police assistance may cause an error in retrieval and lead to false memories.

  III. Victims seeking medical and police assistance had more traumatic experiences and are expected to later show psychopathology.

- ○ **A.** II only
- ○ **B.** III only
- ○ **C.** I and III only
- ○ **D.** II and III only

Question 7

In a subsequent experiment, scientists tested the effect of certain drugs on false memories in rats. In what way could they interpret these results?

- ○ **A.** Rats could be screened for false memories before and after drug administration.
- ○ **B.** Concentration of the drug can be measured in the brains of the rats.
- ○ **C.** Metabolites of the drug can be measured in the blood and urine of the rats and correlated to maze-running.
- ○ **D.** Activity in the limbic system can be measured through an electroencephalogram before and after the drug is administered.

Question 8

In a follow-up study, scientists determined that false memories may arise from consolidation of information from dreams. Which of the following stages of sleep is associated with dreams?

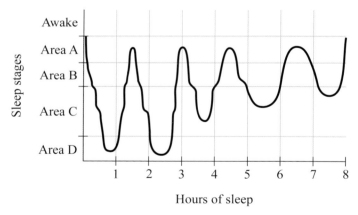

Hours of sleep

- ○ **A.** Area A
- ○ **B.** Area B
- ○ **C.** Area C
- ○ **D.** Area D

Questions 9 - 12 do not refer to a passage and are independent of each other.

Question 9

Alcohol addiction is a widespread problem that is associated with:

- ○ **A.** the reward pathway, comprising portions of the frontal lobe.
- ○ **B.** the reward pathway, comprising portions of the limbic system.
- ○ **C.** parallel pathways, which synchronously process information about the same stimulus.
- ○ **D.** mirror neurons, which fire when participants perform or observe a task.

Question 10

Which of the following is NOT associated with an increased rate of false memories?

- ○ **A.** Repetition
- ○ **B.** Fatigue
- ○ **C.** Chunking
- ○ **D.** Spreading activation

Question 11

It is found that the patient is only able to sleep an hour at a time. Which sleep stage is the patient lacking?

- ○ **A.** Stage 1
- ○ **B.** Stage 2
- ○ **C.** Stage 3
- ○ **D.** REM sleep

Question 12

Researchers design a study comparing the content of dreams to journals kept by subjects. The most likely hypothesis is that:

- ○ **A.** dreams occur during REM sleep.
- ○ **B.** dreams aid in the consolidation of memories.
- ○ **C.** dreams are due to random brain activity.
- ○ **D.** dreams are increased by stressful events.

Passage 3 (Questions 13-16)

In current research contexts, mindfulness is defined as nonjudgmental attention to experiences in the present moment. Mindfulness is cultivated in formal meditation practices, such as sitting meditation, walking meditation, and mindful movements. Mindfulness meditation has beneficial effects on a number of psychiatric, functional somatic, and stress-related symptoms and, therefore, has been increasingly incorporated into psychotherapeutic programs. The scientific bases of mindfulness involve attention, body awareness, the regulation of emotion, changes in self perspective, and the neural modulation of specific brain areas, including the anterior cingulate cortex (ACC), posterior cingulate cortex, (PCC), medial prefrontal cortex (MPFC), insula, temporo-parietal junction (TPJ), hippocampus, and amygdala.

A group of meditators (N = 10) was recruited from the Soto Zen Buddhist community. Individuals were required to meet the following inclusion criteria: 18 to 65 years old, long-term meditative practice (0.8 years meditating for an average of 1 hour daily), and no psychiatric disorder or pharmacologic treatment within one year before the study began. The healthy control group (N = 10) was recruited among hospital staff (comprising 4,800 workers: 700 doctors, 2,600 non-medical health professionals and 1,500 administrative and services personal), with an adjustment for gender, age, years of education, and ethnic group. Participants were assessed on the Hospital Anxiety Depression Scale (HADS), the Mini-Mental State Examination (MMSE), and the Mindful Attention Awareness Scale (MAAS). Participants also went through neuroimaging techniques such as magnetic resonance imaging (MRI), magnetic resonance spectroscopy (MRS), and diffusion weighted imaging (DWI). Findings of the study are represented in Table 1.

Table 1 Comparison of Psychological Variables in Non-meditator Healthy Controls and Meditators

Psychological variables	Non-meditator healthy controls (N = 10)	Meditators (N = 10)	Significance
Anxiety (HADS-anx) (mean, SD)	1.70 (0.94)	0.30 (0.48)	P = 0.002
Depression (HADS-dep) (mean, SD)	1.60 (0.51)	0.30 (0.48)	P = 0.001
Cognitive function (MMSE) (mean, SD)	35 (0)	35 (0)	P = 1
Mindfulness (MAAS) (mean, SD)	19.1 (2.98)	74.1 (5.32)	P = 0.001
Dopamine (mean, SD)	4.82 (0.32)	5.08 (0.29)	P = 0.003
Glutamate (mean, SD)	7.17 (0.80)	6.23 (0.93)	P = 0.004
Months of meditation in meditators (mean, SD, range)	—	190.80 (91.8); 96-360 months	—

This passage was adapted from "Brain Changes in Long-Term Zen Meditators Using Proton Magnetic Resonance Spectroscopy and Diffusion Tensor Imaging: A Controlled Study." Fayed N, del Hoyo YL, Andres E, Serrano-Blanco A, Bellon J, et al. *PLoS ONE*. 2013. 8(3) doi: 10.1371/journal.pone.0058476 for use under the terms of the Creative Commons CC BY 4.0 license (https://creativecommons.org/licenses/by/4.0/legalcode).

Question 13

Based on the results of the study, what type of memory is most likely to be improved in meditators?

- ○ **A.** Sensory memory, because mindfulness is significantly improved in meditators when compared to their control group.
- ○ **B.** Working memory, because mindfulness is significantly improved in meditators when compared to their control group.
- ○ **C.** Memory is not likely to be improved in meditators.
- ○ **D.** Memory is superior in non-meditators.

Question 14

The changes in meditators relative to the control group can most likely be biologically explained by:

- ○ **A.** excitatory postsynaptic potential.
- ○ **B.** neural plasticity.
- ○ **C.** long-term potentiation.
- ○ **D.** parallel processing.

Question 15

The researchers studied participants in their baseline state of consciousness: alert wakefulness. Would researchers expect the results of the study to be different in another state of consciousness?

- ○ **A.** Yes, results would be more pronounced if the study was done while participants were asleep.
- ○ **B.** Yes, results would be more pronounced if the study was done while participants were meditating.
- ○ **C.** No, the changes researchers found would be less pronounced in any other state of consciousness.
- ○ **D.** No, the changes researchers found were lasting neurological and behavioral changes that would not change based on state of consciousness.

Question 16

Active meditators were found to have decreased glutamate in the left thalamus. Which of the following is the best explanation for this observation?

- ○ **A.** Glutamate is the primary excitatory neurotransmitter in the brain.
- ○ **B.** The GABA system inhibits neuronal activity in the hippocampus.
- ○ **C.** Glutamate's role in the glutamine cycle and the glutamine cycle's role in neural activity.
- ○ **D.** The ability of the hippocampus to stimulate or inhibit neuronal activity in other structures.

Passage 4 (Questions 17-21)

Olfactory abilities are a flourishing field in psychiatry research. As the orbitofrontal cortex appears to be simultaneously implicated in odor processing and executive impairments, it has been proposed that olfaction could constitute a cognitive marker of psychiatric states. Researchers aimed to explore the links between olfaction and executive functions using two tasks of comparable difficulty. One of the tasks is known to rely on orbitofrontal cortex processing (i.e. a confabulation task), and the other is not associated with this area (i.e. stop-signal task).

Confabulation is the production of fabricated memories, which are usually seen in the context of certain memory disorders. The confabulation task presented 20 images to participants, and then after a 15 minute pause period, presented 120 more. Participants had to determine if any of the 120 later images appeared in the early group. The stop-signal task required participants to quickly identify images as animals, people, or objects. After certain images were presented, a "stop-signal" bell would ring, indicating that participants should not categorize that image.

Twenty recently sober alcoholic individuals and twenty paired controls took part in this experiment. Comorbidities and potential biasing variables were controlled for. The results of the experiment are shown in Figures 1, 2 and 3. The tests were designed such that high scores were superior on the olfaction and stop-signal tests, but a high score was a sign of impairment in the confabulation test.

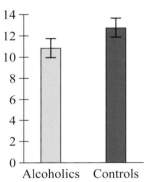

Figure 1 Olfaction score

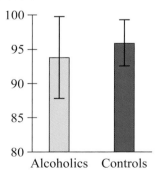

Figure 2 Stop-signal Score

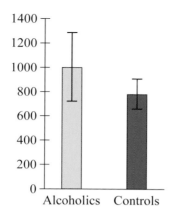

Figure 3 Confabulation Score

This passage was adapted from "Olfactory Impairment Is Correlated with Confabulation in Alcoholism: Towards a Multimodal Testing of Orbitofrontal Cortex." Maurage P, Callot C, Chang B, Philippot P, Rombaux P, et al. *PLoS ONE*. 2011. 6(8) doi:10.1371/journal.pone.0023190 for use under the terms of the Creative Commons CC BY 3.0 license (http://creativecommons.org/licenses/by/3.0/legalcode).

Question 17

Although the passage does not indicate that the alcoholic individuals had a definite neurological disorder, which of the following diagnoses is most likely in this group?

○ **A.** Schizophrenia

○ **B.** Korsakoff's syndrome

○ **C.** Alzheimer's disease

○ **D.** Stockholm syndrome

Question 18

If further research indicated that confabulation rates in alcoholics are amplified with time, what feature of memory may contribute to confabulation?

○ **A.** Rehearsal

○ **B.** Encoding

○ **C.** Decay

○ **D.** Retrieval

Question 19

Alcohol falls under which class of drug and is associated with which neurological effects?

○ **A.** Alcohol is a stimulant that causes vivid distortions in visual perception.

○ **B.** Alcohol is a depressant that causes cognitive slowing and impairment.

○ **C.** Alcohol is a hallucinogen that causes social disinhibition and promiscuity.

○ **D.** Alcohol is an antiseptic that is capable of killing bacterial.

Question 20

Based on the findings in Figure 1, alcoholic participants' sense of smell has an elevated:

○ **A.** absolute threshold.

○ **B.** difference threshold.

○ **C.** Weber fraction.

○ **D.** signal to noise ratio.

Question 21

Which of the following comorbidities were likely controlled for in this experiment?

    I. Age

    II. Alzheimer's disease

    III. Damage to the olfactory nerve

○ **A.** I only

○ **B.** I and II only

○ **C.** II and III only

○ **D.** I, II and III

Passage 5 (Questions 22-25)

The longitudinal rate and profile of cognitive decline in persons with stable, treated, and virally suppressed HIV infection is not established. To address this question, researchers quantified the rate of cognitive decline in a cohort of virally suppressed HIV positive persons using clinically relevant definitions of decline, and determined cognitive trajectories taking into account historical and baseline HIV-associated neurocognitive disorder (HAND) status.

96 HIV positive and 44 demographically comparable HIV negative participants underwent standard neuropsychological testing at baseline and 18-months follow-up. The results of the initial analysis are shown in Figure 1. HAND status was not dependent on age, gender, or viral load.

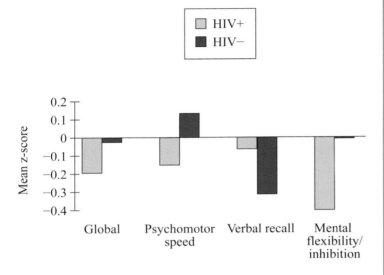

Figure 1 Global change score and select cognitive domain scores as a function of HIV status

Having HAND at baseline significantly predicted cognitive decline at follow up. Despite long-term viral suppression, researchers found mostly subclinical levels of decline in psychomotor speed and executive functioning (mental flexibility and cognitive inhibition), which are well-established markers of HAND progression. Moreover, 57% of the cohort was undergoing slow evolution of their disease, challenging the notion of prevalent neurocognitive stability in virally suppressed HIV infection.

This passage was adapted from "Cognitive Change Trajectories in Virally Suppressed HIV-infected Individuals Indicate High Prevalence of Disease Activity." Gott C, Gates T, Dermody N, Brew BJ, Cysique LA. *PLoS ONE*. 2017. 12(3) doi:10.1371/journal.pone.0171887 for use under the terms of the Creative Commons CC BY 4.0 license (http://creativecommons.org/licenses/by/4.0/legalcode).

Question 22

Assuming the decline mentioned in the study is reversible with administration of donepezil, an acetylcholinesterase inhibitor, neural plasticity must occur through:

- ○ **A.** neuronal mitosis.
- ○ **B.** axonal pruning.
- ○ **C.** synaptic development.
- ○ **D.** stem cell implantation.

Question 23

HIV can be transmitted across the placenta of an infected mother. The results of the study show what implications for a child born with HIV?

- ○ **A.** The results highlight the healthcare disparities of people with HIV.
- ○ **B.** The results suggest a child with HIV may struggle in school.
- ○ **C.** The results should be generalized to another population.
- ○ **D.** There are no implications because the cognitive decline only occurs in later years.

Question 24

Separate research has shown emotional blunting in participants with longstanding HIV. How would this support or refute the findings in the study?

- ○ **A.** It would support the passage because emotion can hinder memories.
- ○ **B.** It would support the passage because emotion can enhance memories.
- ○ **C.** It would refute the passage because emotion can hinder memories.
- ○ **D.** It would refute the passage because can enhance memories.

Question 25

Which of the following tools could participants utilize to aid in encoding memories?

- ○ **A.** The primacy effect
- ○ **B.** The recency effect
- ○ **C.** Weber's law
- ○ **D.** Hierarchies

Questions 26 - 29 do not refer to a passage and are independent of each other.

Question 26

Verbal recall has been shown to decay linearly over time. These results are summarized by which of the figures below?

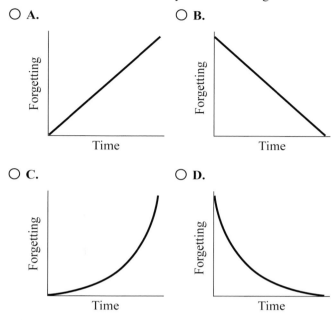

- ○ **A.**
- ○ **B.**
- ○ **C.**
- ○ **D.**

Question 27

A study examined the response of rats when exposed to extreme fear in the presence of food. Which of the following concepts most relates to the inability of rats to eat during periods of extreme fear?

- ○ **A.** Divided attention
- ○ **B.** Long-term potentiation
- ○ **C.** Sensory memory
- ○ **D.** Selective attention

Question 28

Through which mechanism are memories possible?

- ○ **A.** Neuronal mitosis
- ○ **B.** Neuronal meiosis
- ○ **C.** Long term potentiation
- ○ **D.** Post-synaptic excitation

Question 29

In one study, more than 80% of radiologists instructed to examine slides carefully for cancerous nodules on the lungs did not notice images of cartoon characters superimposed on the slides. This represents a failure of:

- ○ **A.** retrieval cues.
- ○ **B.** interference.
- ○ **C.** attention.
- ○ **D.** constancy of image.

Passage 6 (Questions 30-33)

The increasing number of older adults in western societies has brought to the forefront the important question of how to improve quality of life in older age. In particular, research has recently focused on factors that can help to reduce the negative effects of aging on cognitive functions. There is evidence that the ability to speak two or more languages improves cognitive performance, including memory, and that bilingualism may have some protective effect against dementia. Studies also indicate differential brain activation patterns in bilinguals compared to monolinguals. The results from a PET scanning study suggested that bilinguals showed increased activation in temporal structures and in left hemispheric inferior frontal brain areas when using the second language.

Memory retrieval relies on two different processes: recollection and familiarity. Recollection refers to the access of a memory while familiarity describes the strength of the memory, similar to the strength of a signal. Research suggests that cognitive control functions are related to recollection but not to familiarity. Scientists questioned the extent to which the enhanced cognitive control functions found in bilinguals may also benefit episodic memory, which refers to memories of personal experiences. A study investigating the effects of bilingualism on verbal and non-verbal memory performance concluded that the bilingual advantages were closely connected to the retrieval processes involving higher demands on cognitive processes.

This passage was adapted from "A Longitudinal Study of Memory Advantages in Bilinguals." Ljungberg JK, Hansson P, Andres P, Josefsson M, Nilsson L-G. *PLoS ONE*. 2013. 8(9): e73029. doi:10.1371/journal.pone.0073029 for use under the terms of the Creative Commons CC BY 3.0 license (http://creativecommons.org/licenses/by/3.0/legalcode).

Question 30

Which additional piece of information about the study design would be of most interest to researchers studying dementia?

- ○ **A.** The number of participants in the study
- ○ **B.** The age of participants in the study
- ○ **C.** How the study created conditions requiring higher cognitive load
- ○ **D.** Which methods were used to test verbal and nonverbal memory

Question 31

Unknown to the researchers conducting the study, nearly a fifth of participants suffer from some form of a sleep-wake disorder. How might this impact the results?

○ **A.** Performance on both verbal and nonverbal memory tests would be worse than expected.

○ **B.** Performance on verbal memory tests would be worse than expected, but nonverbal memory would not be significantly affected.

○ **C.** Performance on nonverbal memory tests would be worse than expected, but verbal memory would not be significantly affected.

○ **D.** Performance on neither verbal nor nonverbal memory tests would be significantly affected.

Question 32

Based on the passage, bilinguals are likely to perform better than monolinguals on which type of exam?

○ **A.** A written essay response

○ **B.** True/false questions

○ **C.** Multiple choice questions

○ **D.** Fill in the blank questions

Question 33

A polyglot is someone who can speak multiple foreign languages fluently. Compared to the brain of a monolingual individual, the brain of a polyglot would have:

○ **A.** more synaptic connections.

○ **B.** stronger synaptic connections.

○ **C.** higher concentrations of neurotransmitters.

○ **D.** larger neurons.

Passage 7 (Questions 34-37)

For decades, it has been commonly assumed that consolidated memories are not subject to further modification. However, this view has been challenged by animal studies suggesting that memories return to a fragile state when reactivated, making them susceptible to the same manipulations as the original consolidation process. A time-limited process of reconsolidation appears to be necessary to render reactivated memories stable again.

Manipulating memory reconsolidation provides a unique opportunity to change unwanted memories in a favorable manner. There is evidence that the administration of a beta-blocker after the reactivation of traumatic memories may reduce emotional responding to the traumatic event in Post-Traumatic Stress Disorder. A recent rodent study suggested comparable effects after a drug-free intervention, namely, learning new information after memory reactivation. Whether these findings can be translated to memories for events people experienced in their everyday life has important consequences for potential application in clinical, educational, or legal settings.

Researchers designed an experiment to examine whether autobiographical memories can be modified by learning new episodic material after memories have been reactivated. Participants memorized an Indian folk tale after they had recalled neutral and emotional experiences from their past. Another group of participants learned the story without prior reactivation of autobiographical memories. A third group recalled the personal experiences but did not learn the story afterwards; a fourth group neither reactivated the autobiographical memories, nor learned the story.

The researchers found that participants in the first group were impaired in their memory for the neutral, but not for the emotional, experiences one week later. The effect of learning the story depended critically on the preceding reactivation of the autobiographical memories since learning without reactivation had no effect. These results suggest that new learning impedes the reconsolidation of neutral autobiographical memories.

This passage was adapted from "New Episodic Learning Interferes with the Reconsolidation of Autobiographical Memories." Schwabe L, Wolf OT. *PLoS ONE.* 2009. 4(10): e7519. doi:10.1371/journal.pone.0007519 for use under the terms of the Creative Commons CC BY 3.0 license (http://creativecommons.org/licenses/by/3.0/legalcode).

Question 34

Which of the following best describes why the researchers included the group of participants that learned the Indian folk tale without prior reactivation of autobiographical memories?

○ **A.** To rule out the effect of memory consolidation on new learning

○ **B.** To study the role of new learning on memory consolidation

○ **C.** To account for the effects of learning the story on participants

○ **D.** To prevent the interference of learning on future memory reactivation

Question 35

How could the study design be changed to study the effect of new learning on non-declarative memories?

- ○ **A.** Have participants heat food in a microwave before learning the folk tale.
- ○ **B.** Have participants tell the examiner what they did last weekend before learning the folk tale.
- ○ **C.** Have participants draw the American flag before learning the folk tale.
- ○ **D.** Have participants describe to each other how they felt during a sad childhood event.

Question 36

Based on the results of the study, which of the following statements is most true?

- ○ **A.** With prior reactivation, new learning affects the conversion of working memory to short term.
- ○ **B.** With prior reactivation, new learning affects the conversion of short term memory to long term memory.
- ○ **C.** With prior reactivation, new learning affects the conversion of long term memory to working memory.
- ○ **D.** With prior reactivation, new learning affects the conversion of sensory memory to short term memory.

Question 37

Which of the following best describes why the study found that new learning affected the reconsolidation of neutral memories but not the reconsolidation of emotional memories?

- ○ **A.** Emotions are retrieval cues.
- ○ **B.** Emotional memories are more likely to have been retrieved repeatedly before the intervention.
- ○ **C.** Emotional memories are consolidated differently from neutral memories.
- ○ **D.** Emotional memories are more likely to use semantic networks.

Passage 8 (Questions 38-41)

Memory is critical to virtually all aspects of behavior, which may explain why memory is such a complex phenomenon involving numerous interacting mechanisms that operate across multiple brain regions. Many of these mechanisms cooperate to transform initially fragile memories into more permanent ones (memory consolidation). The process of memory consolidation starts at the level of individual synaptic connections, but it ultimately involves circuit reorganization in multiple brain regions.

Computational biology, or the use of biological data to create algorithms to describe biological relationships, is often used to study neural circuitry. Using computational biology, researchers studied whether there is an advantage in partitioning memory systems into subsystems that operate on different timescales. Individual subsystems cannot both store large amounts of information about new memories, and, at the same time, preserve older memories for long periods of time. Subsystems with highly plastic synapses (fast subsystems) are good at storing new memories but bad at retaining old ones, whereas subsystems with less plastic synapses (slow subsystems) can preserve old memories but cannot store detailed new memories.

Long-term memories are likely stored in the synaptic weights of neuronal networks in the brain. The storage capacity of such networks depends on the degree of plasticity of their synapses. Highly plastic synapses allow for strong memories, but these are quickly overwritten. On the other hand, less labile synapses result in long-lasting but weak memories. The present study investigates whether the trade-off between memory strength and memory lifetime can be overcome by partitioning the memory system into multiple regions characterized by different levels of synaptic plasticity and transferring memory information from the more to less plastic region.

This passage was adapted from "Efficient Partitioning of Memory Systems and Its Importance for Memory Consolidation." Roxin A, Fusi S. *PLoS Comput Biol*. 2013. 9(7) doi: 10.1371/journal.pcbi.1003146 for use under the terms of the Creative Commons CC BY 3.0 license (http://creativecommons.org/licenses/by/3.0/legalcode).

Question 38

The computational study is altered to investigate the efficiency of networks that related long-term memories are stored in. This change in study design would specifically allow the researchers to investigate whether:

- ○ **A.** synaptic plasticity is necessary for long-term memory storage.
- ○ **B.** spreading activation is an effective way to recall stored memories.
- ○ **C.** emotion plays a role in the consolidation of long-term memories.
- ○ **D.** long-term potentiation is increased when memory networks are formed.

Question 39

Which of the following is LEAST likely to aid in the retrieval of a memory that is consolidated in a slow subsystem?

- ○ **A.** Having a similar emotion to when the memory was learned
- ○ **B.** Being in the room where the memory was learned
- ○ **C.** Thinking about something related to the memory
- ○ **D.** Learning something similar to the memory

Question 40

A follow up study investigates the most effective method of encoding memories. The encoding of sensory memory will be:

- ○ **A.** enhanced by an increased number of sensory receptors.
- ○ **B.** worsened by an increased number of synapses.
- ○ **C.** equivalent whether a fear stimuli is present or not.
- ○ **D.** worsened by oversaturating the sensory receptors.

Question 41

The results from this study provide support for which of the following theories?

- ○ **A.** Long-term memories are stored in semantic networks.
- ○ **B.** Long-term potentiation is pivotal in the formation of memory.
- ○ **C.** Strong neural networks are necessary for memory consolidation.
- ○ **D.** Changes in synaptic connections underlie memory.

Questions 42 - 45 do not refer to a passage and are independent of each other.

Question 42

A bilingual individual has a dream in Spanish, her second language, about a recent job interview. When she sees her friends the next day, she tells them she had the interview in Spanish, when in reality it was in English. Which statement best explains what happened?

- ○ **A.** The Spanish interview is a constructed memory caused by interference from her dream.
- ○ **B.** The Spanish interview is a constructed memory caused by source confusion.
- ○ **C.** The Spanish interview is the result of the decay of the memory of the original interview.
- ○ **D.** The Spanish interview is the result of the memory of the original interview being erroneously stored.

Question 43

The consolidation of memory will vary most with which variable?

- ○ **A.** Gender
- ○ **B.** Race
- ○ **C.** Age
- ○ **D.** Ethnicity

Question 44

Researchers suspect that bilingualism protects cognitive control functions through increasing the brain's plasticity. According to this hypothesis, which other activities would also likely protect cognitive control functions?

- I. Reading
- II. Crossword puzzles
- III. Traveling to new places
- IV. Regular exercise

- ○ **A.** I and II only
- ○ **B.** II and III only
- ○ **C.** I, II, and III only
- ○ **D.** I, II, III, IV

Next ▶

Question 45

Studies have found that neurogenesis is reduced by negative stress. Which statement is NOT compatible with the term neurogenesis?

○ **A.** Neurogenesis is possible in the hippocampus, where memory formation allows for generation of new neurons.

○ **B.** Neurogenesis is synonymous with long term potentiation which allows for learning.

○ **C.** Induction of neurogenesis has a therapeutic role in neurodegenerative diseases like Alzheimer's disease.

○ **D.** Apart from embryonic development, neurogenesis is a rare event in humans.

Passage 9 (Questions 46-50)

Heart failure is classified using the New York Heart Association's (NYHA) Functional Classification system. The NYHA system classifies heart failure severity on the degree of shortness of breath and intensity of chest pain during physical activity. Class IV heart failure is the most serious, and oftentimes a heart transplant is the best treatment for recovery. In a recent case study, patients with class IV heart failure received heart transplants. In Case 1, the patient recovered normally after surgery. In Case 2, the patient experienced further cardiac issues. Doctors observed that the patient was forgetful and unfocused and attributed his poor health to his failure to follow the strict post-transplant treatment regimen. Doctors believe this was due to cognitive deficiencies caused by the heart failure.

Recent studies have reported that patients with class IV heart failure can have mild to severe cognitive deficits. As in Case 2, these deficits can have a large impact on the patient's ability to understand and to adhere to post-transplant treatment protocols. To develop a more detailed cognitive profile of such patients, investigators studied 207 heart transplant candidates with class IV heart failure. All patients underwent routine neuropsychological assessment of attention, memory, executive functions, and perceptive abilities. Executive functions were impaired in 70% of the participants, perception in 31%, memory in 51%, and attention in 26%. Overall, 36% of the participants had broad neuropsychological impairment.

Lack of sleep can also hinder adherence to treatment regimens in patients with class IV heart failure. In a separate study, subjects were given the paired-associate test, which is a standard test of declarative memory which consists of repeating pairs of related and unrelated words. Subjects were randomly assigned to one of two conditions. Subjects in the first condition learned the paired words at night and were tested for cued recall twelve hours later after a night of sleep. Subjects in the second condition learned the paired words in the morning and were tested for cued recall twelve hours later with no intervening sleep. An increase of 20.6% in long-term memory was found following sleep compared to the no-sleep group (p = 0.029).

This passage was adapted from "Neuropsychological Profile in a Large Group of Heart Transplant Candidates." Mapelli D, Bardi L, Mojoli M, Volpe B, Gerosa G, et al. *PLoS ONE*. 2011. 6(12); doi: 10.1371/journal.pone.0028313 and from "Sleep Improves Memory: The Effect of Sleep on Long Term Memory in Early Adolescence." Potkin KT, Bund WE. *PLoS ONE*. 7(8); doi: 10.1371/journal.pone.0042191 for use under the terms of the Creative Commons CC BY 3.0 license (http://creativecommons.org/licenses/by/3.0/legalcode).

Question 46

The main reason for testing the sleep group in the second study is:

○ **A.** to create a larger sample size in the study.

○ **B.** to minimize the effects of any confounding variables.

○ **C.** to provide the investigators with a comparison value for test performance with sleep.

○ **D.** to assess the effects of source monitoring on memory.

Question 47

In the second study, which type of interference could explain the sleep group's superior performance on the paired-associate test?

- **A.** Retroactive interference, because the paired words interfered with learning new material throughout the day
- **B.** Proactive interference, because the paired words interfered with learning new material throughout the day
- **C.** Retroactive interference, because remembering the paired words was prevented by learning new material throughout the day
- **D.** Proactive interference, because remembering the paired words was prevented by learning new material throughout the day

Question 48

Which statement illustrates a potential flaw in the design of the first experiment?

- **A.** There is no assessment of improper source monitoring in the cognitive evaluations.
- **B.** The study does not assess whether cognitive deficits affect adherence to treatment regimens post-transplantation.
- **C.** There is no group with demographics matched to the experimental group that holds the independent variable constant.
- **D.** While the measurements of rates of cognitive deficiencies were accurate, they were not precise.

Question 49

Which of the following statements about the second study is false?

- **A.** Lack of sleep impaired the recognition of paired words.
- **B.** The two groups in the study were tested under slightly different conditions.
- **C.** The paired-associate test is used to evaluate declarative memory.
- **D.** Intelligence is a potential confounder.

Question 50

Which of the following reasons could explain why participants taking the paired-associate test might have better recall of related word pairs compared to unrelated word pairs?

  I. Spreading activation
  II. Mnemonics
  III. Priming

- **A.** I only
- **B.** II only
- **C.** I and III only
- **D.** I, II, and III

Next ▶

Passage 10 (Questions 51-56)

For successful navigation in the environment, information about landmarks, spatial locations and routes has to be efficiently processed. While there is abundant evidence for spatial learning and memory decrements in patients with unilateral hippocampal lesions, remarkably little research has been done on spatial memory and learning in patients with Alzheimer's dementia (AD), in which relatively selective bilateral hippocampal atrophy is consistently reported in the early stages of the disease.

In spatial navigation, landmark recognition is crucial. Specifically, memory for objects placed at decision points on a route is relevant. Previous fMRI research in healthy adults showed higher medial-temporal lobe (MTL) activation for objects placed at decision points compared to non-decision points, even at an implicit level. Since there is evidence that implicit learning is intact in amnesic patients, the current study examined memory for objects relevant for navigation in patients with Alzheimer's dementia (AD).

21 AD patients participated with MTL atrophy assessed on MRI, as well as 20 age- and education-matched non-demented controls. All participants watched a 5 minute video showing a route through a virtual museum with 20 objects placed at intersections (decision points) and 20 at simple turns (non-decision points). The instruction was to pay attention to the toys (half of the objects) for which they were supposedly tested later. Subsequently, a recognition test followed with the 40 previously presented objects among 40 distractor items (both toys and non-toys). The results of the study are summarized in Figure 1.

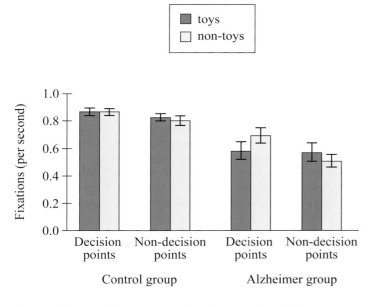

Figure 1 Recognition accuracy for the controls and the Alzheimer group for the toys and non-toys placed at decision points or non-decision points.

Question 51

Based on the study design, which of the following is NOT true about the application of these results to the general population?

○ **A.** The control population represents the performance of a sampling of elderly individuals.

○ **B.** AD patient data should not be considered generalizable to older individuals in a population.

○ **C.** The control data could generalize to individuals with age related cognitive decline.

○ **D.** The AD data could generalize to individuals with age related cognitive decline.

Question 52

In Alzheimer's disease, symptoms typically begin with the loss of the ability to form memories of recent events. If it was found that the first phase in memory formation is impaired, which of the following is preventing these individuals from forming new memories?

○ **A.** Sensory memory

○ **B.** Working memory

○ **C.** Long-term memory

○ **D.** Encoding

Question 53

Which of the following would be the biggest confounder of this study design?

○ **A.** All AD patients were recruited from the same doctor.

○ **B.** 9 AD patients did not report that they had neuroimaging prior to this study.

○ **C.** 2 control patients had a family history of Parkinson's disease.

○ **D.** 5 of the control patients withheld that they were severely alcoholic.

Question 54

The test described in the last paragraph required the individuals to learn a series of new toys, and this caused the majority of participants to forget the toys they had learned during the navigation task. This is an example of:

○ **A.** source monitoring.

○ **B.** proactive interference.

○ **C.** retroactive interference.

○ **D.** relearning.

Question 55

A patient becomes emotional when reaching a particular landmark, claiming it was an object he remembers from childhood. Based on evidence about emotions and memory, the research team is justified in assuming that:

- ○ **A.** the individual will remember this object better during testing.
- ○ **B.** the individual will remember this object poorly during testing.
- ○ **C.** there is no way to tell how his memory for this object will compare to other objects.
- ○ **D.** his response is a result of his age.

Question 56

Which of the following is LEAST likely to be true when an individual attributes a memory to a particular source?

- ○ **A.** There is a higher likelihood that an elderly individual will attribute the memory improperly.
- ○ **B.** Attributing a memory to the wrong source is always a misrepresentation or an act of deceit.
- ○ **C.** Attributing a memory to a certain source is mediated by declarative memory.
- ○ **D.** It is possible that this type of attribution can lead to the formation of false memories.

Questions 57 - 59 do not refer to a passage and are independent of each other.

Question 57

An individual with Post-Traumatic Stress Disorder (PTSD) would be most likely to reactivate his memory of the trauma when he feels:

- ○ **A.** tired.
- ○ **B.** depressed.
- ○ **C.** afraid.
- ○ **D.** lonely.

Question 58

In order to do well in a busy work environment, George must be able to have what type of attention:

- ○ **A.** conscious attention.
- ○ **B.** divided attention.
- ○ **C.** meditated attention.
- ○ **D.** selective attention.

Question 59

A recent study looked at twenty patients with associated brain damage restricted to the substantia nigra and severe motor impairment. What is the most likely similarity between the patients?

- ○ **A.** They all have Korsakoff's syndrome.
- ○ **B.** They all have Alzheimer's disease.
- ○ **C.** They all have Parkinson's disease.
- ○ **D.** They all have damage to the midbrain.

STOP. If you finish before time is called, check your work. You may go back to any question in this test.

ANSWERS & EXPLANATIONS for Test 5B can be found on p. 270.

WARM-UP

0

ANSWERS & EXPLANATIONS
Questions 1–5

ANSWER KEY
1. B
2. C
3. D
4. D
5. C

EXPLANATIONS FOR WARM-UP

Passage 1 (Questions 1-5)

1. **B is the best answer.** Culture shock occurs when a person is immersed in a culture different than his or her reference culture. A student from a small town who moves to a big city would experience a change in culture, so choice A is not the best answer. The war veteran may have experienced shock during war but is likely still immersed in his or her reference culture, which does not fit the definition of culture shock. Choice B is a possibility. Reverse culture shock is the culture shock that occurs when returning to a reference culture after being in a different culture for an extended period of time. This is what is occurring in choice C. Since reverse culture shock is a type of culture shock, choice C is not the best answer. A man who was in a coma for 10 years would wake up to a very different culture considering the rapid changes in technology that have occurred in the past 10 years. So, choice D is not the best answer.

2. **C is the best answer.** Transmission of culture occurs from one generation to the next and diffusion of culture occurs amongst one generation. In general, mass media is capable of diffusing and transmitting ideas. The reference to social media here is irrelevant. Mass media diffuses ideas by revealing how other cultures function. Mass media also transmits ideas by revealing the culture of past generations. So, choice C is the best answer.

3. **D is the best answer.** Globalization is the communication and integration of cultures around the world. Gentrification refers to the "flipping" of a neighborhood to conform to middle- or upper-class preference. This is relevant to urban renewal but not globalization so choice A is not a strong answer. Online video games may promote interaction between people from different countries, so choice B is a possible answer. International terrorism is a negative outcome of globalization. As countries interact more, acts of terror become more frequent. Choice C is relevant to globalization, but it does not necessarily promote globalization. Economic interdependence between sovereign nations certainly promotes globalization, so choice D is a possible answer. Between choice B and choice D, economic interdependence is the better answer because interdependence is forced communication and integration. Video games may not allow for communication and likely result in little integration of cultures. Choice D is always true but choice B is only sometimes true so choice D is the best answer.

4. **D is the best answer.** First decide if sex or gender is assigned and then if sex or gender is chosen. Sex is the biologically determined component, and gender is the identity component. The use of the word "chosen" is not quite appropriate, but a taboo like this may be used on the MCAT® so do not be distracted! This automatically rules out choices A and C. Deciding between choice B and D requires deciding which choice offers the better research design. The use of a questionnaire is generally considered a weak design. This study design is prone to bias including social desirability bias and response bias. Collecting real time data would avoid bias, so choice D is the best answer.

5. **C is the best answer.** Social stratification is the separation of groups usually based on income level but may refer to separation based on gender, race, or other demographics. There is no reason low-income individuals would be absolutely unable to participate in SNS groups. Public libraries offer access to the internet where low-income individuals could join SNS groups. Low-income may be an impedance, but choice A is too absolute and thus not a strong answer. Working class people may not have as much time to participate in SNS groups but there still would be some time to participate, so choice B is not a strong answer. Groups that require an invitation would certainly result in stratification. Individuals of different social groups would have no way of connecting and would not be invited to the private group. Choice C is a possible answer. Choice D is the opposite of what this question is looking for- it directly contradicts the concept of social stratification. So, choice D is not the best answer.

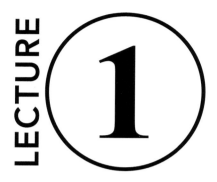

LECTURE

The Biopsychosocial Model, Society and Culture

TEST 1A

ANSWERS & EXPLANATIONS
Questions 1–59

LECTURE 1 ANSWER KEY

TEST 1A		TEST 1B	
1. A	31. D	1. B	31. A
2. B	32. C	2. B	32. C
3. A	33. D	3. C	33. B
4. B	34. C	4. C	34. C
5. D	35. C	5. C	35. A
6. A	36. A	6. A	36. B
7. B	37. A	7. D	37. C
8. D	38. D	8. B	38. A
9. D	39. D	9. A	39. C
10. B	40. B	10. B	40. A
11. C	41. C	11. C	41. B
12. C	42. D	12. C	42. C
13. C	43. B	13. C	43. D
14. A	44. A	14. C	44. B
15. A	45. D	15. D	45. A
16. D	46. C	16. C	46. B
17. B	47. A	17. A	47. B
18. C	48. B	18. D	48. B
19. B	49. C	19. A	49. A
20. A	50. A	20. C	50. D
21. B	51. A	21. A	51. C
22. D	52. C	22. B	52. C
23. D	53. B	23. D	53. D
24. D	54. A	24. A	54. A
25. D	55. C	25. C	55. B
26. B	56. D	26. D	56. B
27. B	57. B	27. B	57. D
28. A	58. B	28. B	58. B
29. C	59. D	29. A	59. C
30. C		30. D	

EXPLANATIONS FOR LECTURE 1

Passage 1 (Questions 1-4)

1. **A is the best answer.** Longitudinal studies follow the same group of people over time. The researchers studied the same subjects at age 11, and again at age 14, making this a longitudinal study. This makes Choice A a strong answer. Additionally, age is one of the major demographic categories (the others being race and ethnicity, immigration status, and gender) and the article that the passage was sourced from mentions that this was a longitudinal study in its title in the citation. In contrast, a cross-sectional study looks at the same variables and characteristics, in different groups of subjects, who are at different ages. Gerontology is the study of aging and the life course, and the researchers did not explore this in the study. Given these two facts, choice B is not the correct answer. Another type of study design is a case report. A case report is an in-depth analysis of a single subject or series of subjects, and an age cohort is defined as groups of people categorized by age range, which does not describe what the researchers did in this study, which makes choice C not the best answer. Finally, a meta-analysis study is one that combines the findings from multiple studies, and the notion of the social significance of aging is one that emphasizes the idea that aging is more complicated than simply the measured time since birth. This idea was not explored in the study, and so choice D can be eliminated.

2. **B is the best answer.** The study's findings do not in any way support nor disprove the conclusion proposed in choice A, so it can be eliminated. The study's findings are consistent with the phenomenon of teacher expectancy. Students' education and school experiences are affected by teacher's expectations, where teachers treat students differently according to preconceived ideas about their capabilities. This treatment, in turn, influences students' achievement. This conclusion, proposed in choice B, is supported by the data in Table 1 by the high OR score given to the "Teacher's Assessment" characteristic, making choice B the best answer. Choice C is the definition of teacher expectancy, except the roles of the student and teacher are reversed. It is the teacher who has the preconceived expectations, not the student. Thus, choice C is not the best answer. The purpose of education (formal and informal) is two-fold in a society. Education provides a formal structure during childhood and the transition to adulthood. It also provides an opportunity to instruct youth on the social norms, expectations for behavior, knowledge, and skills that they will need to operate within a society, and this is stated in choice D. However, because this conclusion can not be drawn based on the study's findings, choice D is not the best answer.

3. **A is the best answer.** Most sociological theories can be placed in two broad categories: microsociological or macrosociological. Microsociology focuses on individual, face-to-face, everyday social interactions. What is described in the question stem is an example of a microsociological theoretical approach to social structure, making choice A a strong answer. In contrast, macrosociology focuses on broad social structures that affect society. Conflict theory, choice B, and social constructionism, choice C, are macrosociological perspectives, and so both can be eliminated as answers. Conflict theorists view society in terms of competing groups that act according to their own self-interests, rather than according to the need for societal equilibrium. Social constructionism explains social structure through the idea of social constructs. For example, money is a social construct, as it is physically just a piece of paper or metal—however, society casts a value on it that makes it worth more than the paper itself. Choice D, rational choice theory, is neither a microsociological nor macrosociological approach. Rational choice theory assumes that people's actions are dictated by a rational consideration of alternatives. Individuals choose the action that is most likely to bring some type of profit. Again, this does not best describe the type of social interactions the student has with the other people in his or her life, because it is too specific and can not be substantiated, so choice D is not the best answer.

4. **B is the best answer.** Discrimination based on the results of the cognitive assessment contributes to an explanation of the study results. Discrimination is the action someone takes based on a prejudice—a generalization about a group or category of people. It is likely that teachers would categorize students as good or bad students based on the preliminary exam and act in a manner, intentionally or unintentionally, that perpetuates that belief. Therefore, we can eliminate choice A. Choice B describes the opposite of what would explain the study results. An out-group is a group that one does not identify with. Thus, the teacher would neither feel loyalty to an out-group nor favor those who come from one, making choice B the best answer. Choice C suggests in-group loyalty would affect the teacher's assessment. Loyalty toward a student from an in-group, a group with which an individual shares identity with, would help explain the research results, so choice C can be eliminated. Choice D addresses prejudice from the student's peers, who are from out-groups (the answer choice mentions they have a dissimilar background). This dissimilar background could involve having an attention disorder, using drugs, or having parents who have a lower education level than that which is average for that school's population. Prejudice can lead to discriminatory behaviors which would help explain the disparity between expected and attained education levels. Thus, choice D is not the best answer.

5. **D is the best answer.** The FAB hypothesis suggests that disciplines with a stronger focus in brilliance are likely to be much less diverse, especially with African Americans and women. According to paragraph one, there are societal stereotypes that portray the intelligence of African Americans and women in a negative light. According to social constructionism, humans construct a reality rather than inherit one. The information in the passage does not directly discuss created versus inherited reality, making choice A less likely to be the best answer. Symbolic interactionism is social constructionism on the micro-scale between two or just a few individuals. As with choice A, the passage does not directly discuss created versus inherited reality on either the macro- or micro-scale. Choice B can be eliminated. Functionalism suggests that factions of society work together, using their individual best skills to contribute to maintaining equilibrium in the face of environmental pressures. The passage does not directly discuss the contributions of various members of society to overall success. Choice C can be eliminated. Feminist theory explores the role of women in society, often from the viewpoint of being underrepresented. This is similar to the information in the passage about the underrepresentation of women and African Americans in fields that are thought to require "brilliance." Choice D is the best answer.

6. **A is the best answer.** Exchange theory dictates that behaviors within relationships are determined by individuals' expectations of reward or punishment. Increasing the rate of bonus payment from the state educational fund to universities that hire and tenure more African American physicists functions as a reward to the university. These additional hires would reduce the number of other spots to members of other ethnic groups, functioning as the exchange portion of the theory. Choice A seems to fit the principle of exchange theory, likely making it the best answer. Decreasing the number of Caucasian professors would not necessarily increase the number of physicists that were African Americans, as these spots that were vacated could go unfilled. Choice B is unlikely to be the best answer. Increased rates of advocacy from African American physicists would not support exchange theory, as the university would not receive some sort of compensation. Choice C can be eliminated. An increased rate of one-on-one interactions between African American physicists and universities describes the idea behind microsociology, which focuses on the smaller scale of social interactions between individuals. Choice D can be eliminated.

7. **B is the best answer.** Part of the existent culture suggests that women and African Americans may not share the same level of "brilliance" as other members of society. While this is false, the belief has been perpetuated over many generations. Material culture refers to physical objects that provide meaning in everyday life. The passage does not suggest a role for material objects in propagating the belief, eliminating choice A. Non-material culture is comprised of shared assumptions, ideas, and values that are passed along by members of a community. This fits the information provided in both the passage and the question stem, likely making choice B the best answer. Sanctions are a form of punishment imposed when a member of a community breaks a norm. The passage does not suggest any punishments are being applied, eliminating choice C. Folkways are norms governing casual interactions. The interactions being described in the passage are more professional in nature than personal, making choice D less likely than choice B to be the best answer.

8. **D is the best answer.** The first paragraph describes that women and African Americans are underrepresented in careers that require "a spark of brilliance." Gender is a social and psychological phenomenon that incorporates sex, gender identity, and gender expression. Being female would fit part of the definition of gender, eliminating choice A. Ethnicity incorporates race, eliminating choice B. Gender identify incorporates one's internal sense of self as male, female, both, or neither. Being female would fit this descriptor, eliminating choice C. The passage does not describe how age plays into the underrepresentation of women and African Americans into a particular part of the workforce, making choice D the best answer.

Stand-alones (Questions 9-12)

9. **D is the best answer.** The question stem describes conflict on a small scale. Therefore it is likely that the correct answer choice will include conflict theory as a possible explanatory theory, since it focuses on explaining social disruptions. Because functionalism describes how different elements work together to maintain social order and stability, it cannot explain social situations where a conflict is observed, eliminating choices A and B. Because social constructionism typically describes large-scale interactions, choice C is unlikely to be the best answer. Symbolic interactionism could also be used to describe the situation described because it focuses on small-scale interactions and focuses on individuals rather than social institutions. By process of elimination, choice D is the best answer.

10. **B is the best answer.** Conflict theory views society as a composite of numerous groups that compete with one another for power and resources, and act in their own self-interest rather than for the good of society as a whole. A key point to keep in mind about conflict theory is that it examines society on the macro-scale; it examines relationships between groups rather than relationships between individuals. In addition, conflict theory accounts for how and why societies change over time, but does not explain long-lasting stability. Choice A identifies that conflict is at the heart of conflict theory, but frames the conflict in terms of individuals. For this reason, it is not the most suitable answer. Choice B accurately identifies that competition is a central idea in conflict theory, and notes that this conflict takes place on the group scale. Choice C designates stability as the goal of the political leadership changes, which is not an attribute of conflict theory (stability is better explained by functionalism). Choice D (like choice A) explains the political leadership changes at the level of the individual. Choice B is the best answer because it correctly identifies both the level of analysis and the motives of actors according to conflict theory.

11. **C is the best answer.** Urbanization is the increase in the proportion of people living in urban areas. It is an example of a modern demographic trend. Healthcare is an example of a social institution. Microsociology focuses on small scale interactions between individuals. Since this question is focused on more large scale structures, choice A is not the best answer. Social psychology is the study of how people's thoughts and behaviors are affected by others. Because the question makes no mention of specific individuals, choice B is also not ideal. Macrosociology focuses on broad social structures that affect society. Both urbanization and healthcare are examples of broad social structures, so choice C is a very strong answer. Public sociology involves connecting elements of sociology with the non-academic public. The research question is unrelated to this idea, so choice D is fairly weak. Choice C is the best answer.

12. **C is the best answer.** Systematic error is constant across all participants whereas random error varies. The error introduced would occur with all participants because they all just attended a lecture on the subject. Choices B and D can be eliminated. Choice A is not the best answer because the situation is better explained by rational choice theory than by exchange theory. Rational choice theory suggests that people will always think logically when deciding on a course of action, and will weigh costs and benefits and choose the option that best suits their self-interest. So, choice C is the best answer.

Passage 3 (Questions 13-17)

13. **C is the best answer.** Socioeconomic status (SES) is determined by the relative income, wealth, education level, and occupation of an individual or group. Observing that Hispanics in New Mexico have a much lower annual income than other groups in New Mexico could show the presence of a disparity in healthcare as the result of a lower SES. Choice A does not make this distinction as it states that the two groups have a similar income, so it can be eliminated. Increasing the diversity in the physician workforce is one attempt at relieving some of the healthcare disparities experienced by minority groups. While this is a tempting answer, the healthcare disparities experienced by different ethnic groups are not as much a result of racial inequalities, as inequalities in social class and economic resources, so choice B is a weak answer. Lacking insurance has a direct effect on an individual's ability to obtain healthcare. If an individual cannot afford insurance because he or she is in a lower socioeconomic class, then this would contribute to the healthcare disparities experienced by Hispanics. Choice C is a strong answer. While being denied health care because of a lack of citizenship would ultimately support the observation seen in the passage of a higher rate of CRC mortality in Hispanic individuals, the lack of treatment is not the proposed mechanism for this observation. A decreased understanding of the risk of CRC and the need for regular screening would be a direct result of not having enough access to healthcare is a better explanation for the increased mortality rate, so choice D can be eliminated.

14. **A is the best answer.** When a sample is obtained for a research study, several conditions are taken into account to ensure the sample can be used with confidence. A large sample is obtained so the statistical analysis is able to detect minor differences. Researchers also attempt to ensure that the sample represents the population being sampled and that each group is similar to one another with the exception of the variable being tested. This allows the researchers to be confident that any difference between the groups is the result of the independent variable. If the researchers did not control for the age distribution in the samples, and the age of the participant has an effect on their level of CRC knowledge as shown in Table 1, then the results of the study are not nearly as strong as if age was controlled for. Choice A is a strong answer. Since age is not controlled for, the study needs to be repeated and the groups should be age-matched in order to have enough confidence in the effect of race on CRC knowledge. Since choice B claims that the effect of race is still strongly supported, it can be eliminated. If the sample did not control for age, it would weaken the original conclusions that race has a major effect on CRC knowledge. The sample is still flawed, and to conclude that Hispanics are equally educated would require a new sample with better controls. Choice C is too extreme of a conclusion and can be eliminated. While it is true that the knowledge difference between the age groups is not statistically significant, it can be seen from the data that a large difference between the two groups is still present. It is safe to assume that unequal distribution of ages between the two groups would have an effect on the results obtained, so choice D can eliminated.

15. **A is the best answer.** When sampling a population, it is important to obtain a sample that is as representative of that population as possible. If the researcher only sampled from patients at a CRC clinic, an over-representation of individuals with previous knowledge on the importance of screening would be obtained. A large portion of the population, especially the ones at the highest risk of not obtaining proper screening, will not be sampled and the results will not be as reliable as those performed in the original study, so choice A is a strong answer. By using a sampling procedure that factors out incomes, the researcher can be more confident that any differences observed between the two ethnic groups is not confounded by differences in socioeconomic status, so choice B would increase the confidence of the study and can be eliminated. Increasing sample size always increases the power of a sample and increases its ability to detect small differences. This means that increasing the sample size will provide the scientist with more confidence as well. Choice C can be eliminated. If the researcher introduces a way to eliminate a possible confounding variable, then he or she will be more confident in the conclusions drawn from a particular data set. In this case, that confounding variable is the effect of location, specifically how close an individual is to an urban setting where health education might be more accessible, has on the level of CRC knowledge. By testing for this variable, the researcher will have more confidence in the results, and choice D can be eliminated.

16. **D is the best answer.** Kinship is the social connection between family members and can be established either through bloodline, marriage, or adoption. A brother and sister would maintain their social bond despite the divorce of their parents. While it is possible that this bond could be broken if the parents separated the two siblings and refused to allow them to see or speak with one another, this is an extreme and unlikely situation, so choice A is probably not the best answer. Marriage is one way to form new bonds of kinship, even if the two parties are of completely different cultural backgrounds, so choice B can be eliminated. Adoption is one way to establish kinship, and whether the children were adopted from the same orphanage does not determine if this new social bond can be formed. Choice C can be eliminated. While entering into this formal agreement requires a social bond between the two neighbors, it is not the same type of bond that is experienced with kinship. Choice D is the best answer because it does not describe a situation of two individuals who are connected through bloodline, adoption, or marriage.

17. **B is the best answer.** While this passage shows that there are significant differences in the amount of medical knowledge between two different social groups, this is not necessarily the only cause of health disparities. Choice A is an extreme generalization that is not supported by the results of this specific study, so it can be eliminated. In contrast, choice B is a weaker conclusion that is more strongly supported by the results of the passage, which makes it a strong answer. There are many differences between the two groups sampled in this passage that are not addressed. Differing cultural practices are among one of those, and while certain culture-specific activities can represent unique risk factors, this is not a conclusion that can be drawn from the present study. Additionally, the passage only mentions an increase in the mortality from CRC experienced by Hispanics but does not mention an increase in the incidence of CRC, so choice C can be eliminated. While it is possible that Hispanic individuals are more prone to a more aggressive form of CRC, this study is not designed to investigate that hypothesis, so choice D can be eliminated. This leaves choice B as the best answer.

Passage 4 (Questions 18-22)

18. **C is the best answer.** Study 2 shows that people from rural areas are less likely to seek healthcare treatment than those from urban areas. Modernization is the transition from traditional, rural society to a modern, industrial one. Choice A is most definitely a true statement. Urban communities are more modern than rural communities. However, this choice fails to address any differences in healthcare between the two societies. The best answers are those that are both true statements and answer the question. Choice A does not answer the question, so it is a weak answer. If individuals from rural areas did indeed lead healthier lifestyles than those from urban areas, it might make sense that they have less reason to seek healthcare treatment. At first glance, choice B may seem like a strong answer. However, it does not agree with other details of the study. The data analyzed only included individuals who received CABG. This makes it very hard to conclude that one population is healthier than another, because all participants underwent a serious medical procedure. The best studies are designed using representative samples. The health of a patient undergoing CABG is not indicative of the health of the average person living in an area. Choice B is also a weak answer. A subculture is a culture shared by a smaller group of people who are also part of a larger culture but have specific cultural attributes that set them apart from the larger group. These attributes could include behavioral expectations or social norms. In this case, it is completely plausible that individuals from rural areas have different opinions regarding healthcare than do individuals from urban areas. Maybe people from rural areas view it as a sign of weakness to go to the doctor. These beliefs could impact their decisions on whether or not to seek healthcare treatment. Choice C is a strong answer. Social capital refers to any connections an individual has that may confer economic or personal benefits. It could be argued that personal connections may help a patient be seen by a healthcare provider. In the context of this question, it would also have to be assumed that individuals from urban areas have more social capital than those from rural areas. This is neither known nor stated in the passage. Choice D requires many assumptions to be correct. Since it is not as clear as choice C, choice C is the best answer.

19. **B is the best answer.** Urban decline is a decline in the standard of living in urban areas. Gentrification is an urban renewal pattern in which wealthy individuals purchase and restore cheap property in urban areas. This restoration functions to increase the standard of living, so choice A is a weak answer. Suburbanization refers to the large-scale movement of people from cities to suburbs, which are located just outside city lines. As more people leave the city, property values decrease and less money can be collected from property taxes. Since less money is available for maintenance and restoration, suburbanization does cause a decline in the standard of living in urban areas. Choice B is a strong answer. Health disparities are differences in healthcare or healthcare outcomes between different groups of people. The passage noted a relationship between urban living and healthcare, but offered no connection to urban decline. If anything, the finding that patients from urban areas received care from better-performing providers could be seen as a benefit of living in an urban community. This makes choice C a weak answer. Civil unrest is social disorder caused by a group of people in public due to a perceived injustice over resource distribution. This concept is unrelated to that of urbanization or urban decline. Civil unrest could affect urban areas, rural areas, or some combination of both. Since it is impossible to predict the location of civil unrest, choice D is also a weak answer.

20. **A is the best answer.** The results of the passage show that preferences for healthcare provider selection vary among rural and urban patients with different income levels. Though this is an acknowledgement of healthcare disparities between urban and rural areas, calling for government intervention to curb urbanization is quite a leap. An action like this would have far-reaching and unintended consequences. This is a good example of an answer selection that is beyond the scope of the passage. Choice A is a very strong answer. Choice B is a simple restatement of the results of the studies from the passage. This is most definitely consistent with the passage, so choice B is a weak answer. Choice C is basically a much softer version of the action proposed in choice A. Remember that softer language is often indicative of a more correct answer, or in this case an incorrect answer because the question asks which statement is NOT supported. The only reason to conduct a study pointing out that a problem like a healthcare disparity exists is to eventually find a solution to that problem. This statement is a logical next step given the information of the passage. Choice C is not the best answer. Spatial inequality is the unequal access to resources due to geographic distribution. This is consistent with the finding that rural areas have less access to quality healthcare resources than do urban areas. Choice D is a weak answer.

21. **B is the best answer.** Social institutions are systems that bring order to interpersonal interactions. They provide society with structure. A few examples of social institutions are government, education, religion, family, and medicine. The key to answering this question is to remember that Medicare is funded by the United States federal government. Also notice that many of the answer choices, while related to the question, are not examples of social institutions. Age is an example of a demographic, not a social institution, so choices A and D are weak answers. Government and economy are indeed examples of social institutions. One way that the government gives order to society is by providing services to its citizens. Medicare is an example of this. Choice B is a strong answer. Health disparities are related to social inequalities, not social institutions, so choice C is a weak answer.

22. **D is the best answer.** In the passage, the researchers are identified as functional theorists. Functionalism is the theory that factions of society work together to maintain stability. The correct answer choice should represent an aspect of this theory. Choice A depicts groups competing with each other instead of working together. This is a better example of conflict theory, which views society in terms of different groups competing for their own self-interests. As a result, choice A is a weak answer. Choice B again depicts individuals acting out of self-interest. This answer choice is closer to rational choice theory, which assumes that people's actions are dictated by the rational consideration of alternatives. Basically, this theory says that healthcare providers treat patients either because it makes them feel good or because they are paid to do so. Choice B is a weak answer. Choice C is a possible explanation of the findings of the passage that showed that patients from urban areas receive healthcare from better performing providers. However, nothing in the passage indicates that this is a belief held by the researchers. This answer choice also lacks any element of functionalism. While this answer choice may answer the question and match the passage, it is not necessarily a true statement. Choice C is a possibility. Choice D depicts groups working together to maintain society. This is consistent with the ideals of functionalism, making it a better supported answer than choice C. Choice D is the best answer.

Passage 5 (Questions 23-26)

23. **D is the best answer.** The study is looking at health information and self rated health, and to best answer this, the timescale of the study is important. While the question states that the internet came about in 1996, the study shows that the majority of people didn't use the internet to gain health information until 2010. The best answer to this question would reflect the gap between the introduction of the internet and its widespread usage. Choice A involves parts of culture that are based on ideas, morals, and beliefs. The internet is a tangible technological change and is part of material culture, so choice A is unlikely to be the best answer. Choice B is possible—the internet may have come as a shock to many people, but it doesn't have any effect on the study. The proportion of internet users is rising, and there is nothing to indicate that anyone was shocked. Choice C, assimilation, primarily refers to one culture taking up the practices of another. The internet was not part of anyone's culture prior to becoming part of American culture, so choice C is not the best answer. Choice D, culture lag, accurately reflects the time gap between the invention of the internet and usage by a majority of people, which is consistent with the definition of cultural lag. Choice D is the best answer.

24. **D is the best answer.** Choice A involves primarily youth, while the study is only concerned with adults, so this is unlikely to be the best answer. While choice B is plausible because patients are receiving less health information, knowing about conditions that are benign may make a patient feel less healthy, although the condition does not reduce their mortality. If a patient does not have knowledge of conditions that do not impact their mortality, they are likely to feel less ill and therefore more accurately perceive their health. Choice C also impacts individuals' access to health information but is accurately reporting a cause-effect relationship in a condition with high mortality. While the passage states that increased information may make patients more likely to be aware of previously non-existent conditions, the information in this choice is relevant, accurate, and important to a condition with high mortality, and is therefore likely to increase the accuracy of health predictions. Choice D is the best answer because individuals who are ill and believe themselves to be in poor health may report a more positive self-rated health because of the perceived effect of the supplements, although they do not actually effect their physical health.

25. **D is the best answer.** Internal validity refers to the methodology of the study—did the study accurately represent the population it is studying? External validity refers to the study's ability to help guide assumptions about other populations. Choices A and B are only applicable to the people who participated in the study and are probably not the best answer. Choice C represents something that would be reflected in the results, but is also accurate to the population, so it is not a threat to any kind of validity. Choice D deals with social epidemiology, or the distribution of health resource, and if other countries/ regions had less access to health information on the internet, this survey would be less likely to be valid to those populations.

26. **B is the best answer.** Figure 2 demonstrates several important findings from the study. First, respondents with internet access had lower mortality overall. Second, respondents with access to internet had little correlation between self rated health and mortality, because no matter what the self-rating is, mortality remained similar. While choice A might be accurate, this study does not gather any information about SES, and this choice is not relevant. Choice B indicates that medicalization decreases the validity of self rated health due to increased perception of conditions that do not affect mortality, and is the best answer. Because internet users have low validity of self rated health, it is reasonable to attribute that to medicalization due to increased information access. Choice C could explain why the internet usage group has lower mortality, but there are many potential confounders to this choice —individuals with internet access may also have access to better nutrition, education, and leisure time for physical activity. Choice D, while accurate, is not relevant to Figure 2, which only examines this correlation at one point in time.

27. **B is the best answer.** Assimilation is the integration of a person into a new culture. It would be facilitated by previous exposure to the culture such as by travel so choice A is not the best answer. Culture shock is the discomfort experienced by being immersed in a new culture. It can facilitate or hinder assimilation, so choice B is a possible answer. Comfort with the pop culture of a new society would facilitate assimilation by providing a framework for conversation and understanding norms. Choice C is not the best answer. Proficiency in the language used in the new culture would certainly facilitate communication which would facilitate assimilation. Choice D is not the best answer. This leaves choice B as the best answer.

28. **A is the best answer.** In order for a hypothesis to be considered testable, it must be falsifiable. As a general rule of thumb, hypotheses that speculate as to the existence of something are not considered falsifiable, because it is nearly impossible to commit a completely exhaustive search to prove that this idea or entity does not exist. Theoretically, it is possible for anything to be "hiding" somewhere in the world, waiting to be discovered. Choice A is the best answer because this does indeed present a falsifiable, and thus testable, hypothesis. The discovery of a single artifact attesting from the 19th century or earlier attesting to the existence of vaccines could prove this wrong. This hypothesis also includes a proper example of material culture; physical objects involved in carrying out a way of life. Choice B is not the best answer. This is not a testable hypothesis, because it would be impossible to confirm that there was not a single individual in ancient Rome that spoke out against the common religious practices of the society during that time. This hypothesis also does not concern material culture. It presents an example of symbolic culture, which is defined as shared ideas, beliefs, and values. Choice C is not the best answer, although it does state a testable hypothesis. The study of a single additional society in which polyandry (one woman being married to more than one man) is commonplace could falsify this hypothesis. This cultural institution would be considered symbolic culture, though. Choice D is not the best answer, because although it concerns material culture, it is not falsifiable. It is entirely possible that the ancient Greeks used anesthetics, but no evidence of this practice was among the artifacts discovered in later years.

29. **C is the best answer.** A taboo is a norm that, if violated, results in the most extreme of negative sanctions. Folkways are norms that govern casual interactions. Mores are norms that enforce the moral standards of society. Though choice A lists these norms in order of increasing sanctions upon violation, there is no evidence that a norm must move up this scale in order to become a taboo. As a result, choice A is a weak answer. It may be true that, at some level, humans are genetically programmed to avoid inbreeding. However, this explanation is very narrowly focused on biology, ignoring psychology and sociology. Remember that good answer choices are often consistent with the biopsychosocial approach. Even though choice B may be true, it may not be the best answer. Choice C alludes to the evolution of culture, which is the idea that behaviors that are beneficial to survival are more likely to be passed on. Since inbreeding does indeed result in offspring that have decreased fitness, this behavior is evolutionarily disadvantageous. It makes sense that its prevalence would decrease over time. This choice does integrate all disciplines of biology, psychology, and sociology, so it is a strong answer. Choice D mentions a possible sociological reason why inbreeding became taboo, but it makes no mention of biology. This makes choice D a weaker answer. Choice C is the best answer.

30. **C is the best answer.** This question tests the ability to recognize the key definition of a counterculture can be figured out without any historical context. A counterculture is a culture whose members subscribe to beliefs and cultural patterns not only different from but *in opposition to* the mainstream culture. Choice C is the only answer that focuses on opposition to mainstream social norms. While the other answer choices may all be true, none of them answer the question. Choice A describes a generic definition of a subculture, so choice C is a stronger answer to the question. Choice B describes the pursuit of multiculturalism, but does not highlight any conflict with existing mainstream culture in the 1960s, so it is not the best answer. Choice D describes the cultural legacies of the 1960s, but does not explicitly mention how these movements rejected the norms of 1960s mainstream culture; therefore choice C is still the best answer.

Passage 6 (Questions 31-34)

31. **D is the best answer.** According to functionalism, groups within society work together to maintain stability. The question stem does not imply that the increased presence of women in the workplace reflects a safer environment outside the workplace. Choice A is unlikely to be the best answer. Conflict theory states that society is made up of competing groups that act according to their own self-interests. Traditionally, the workplace has been male-dominated, so women and men could be seen as competing for the same jobs. Keep choice B, but consider the other answer choices. Exchange-Rational choice theory dictates that people's actions occur after rational consideration of alternatives. The question stem does not imply this, eliminating choice C. Feminist theory is closely related to conflict theory and focuses on the societal inequalities between men and women. This more closely matches the question stem, making choice D a better answer than choice B.

32. **C is the best answer.** The purpose of education is to help instruct youth on the social norms, expectations for behavior, knowledge, and skills they will need to operate within society. Members of a particular society may feel more comfortable with each other the more they learn about other groups of people, including their various cultures. Existential security, as implied by the passage, most likely means increased opportunities to pursue passions in work and personal life, in addition to a more civically involved society. It does not mean physical security, making choice A less likely to be the best answer. Education is not always evenly distributed across a population, as members of low income communities often do not receive the same access or level of education as members of wealthy populations. Choice B can be eliminated. Higher paying jobs that require more education could lead to more free time to pursue passions and allow other members of the household to enter the workplace. This sounds like existential security, as suggested by the passage, likely making choice C the best answer. It is not clear how a decreased incidence of childhood illness would improve existential security, eliminating choice D.

33. **D is the best answer.** As the level of existential security rises with the level of democracy, it is reasonable to assume that the definition of what constitutes a family would also broaden. Families consist of bonds of kin and marriage and make up a major organizing institution within society. The traditional form of the family has been two heterosexual parents with children. As a society becomes more democratic and open, the rates of divorce, number of non-traditional families, such as single-parent households and same-sex marriages, may also increase. This makes options I, II, and III part of the best answer, choice D.

34. **C is the best answer.** A population can often be broken down into various age cohorts, which may be provided as ranges of ages. Retirement planning is often a key part of middle adulthood, as individuals begin to set aside funds for future living costs. Children and adolescents are often not cognitively developed enough to plan the intricacies of saving money and may not be employed. Choices A and B are unlikely to be the best answer. Individuals that are aged 30-39 years old are likely working and earning an income. This would be an appropriate time for a society to encourage planning for retirement, making choice C the best answer. The elderly population suggested in choice D would be well beyond retirement for an economically-developed society, eliminating choice D.

Passage 7 (Questions 35-38)

35. **C is the best answer.** Spirituality describes believing in a higher power in the absence of a formal organization or named denomination, so options I and III are components of the best answer. A person can have intense spirituality, so option II should not be included. Choice C is the best answer.

36. **A is the best answer.** A church is not an extreme religious organization, so choice A is a possible answer. A cult is considered an extreme religious organization, and the term has a negative connotation. Choice B is not the best answer. A faction is a group within a church or denomination that is usually more extreme, so choice C is not the best answer. A sect is a more traditional group within a religious organization, so choice D is not the best answer.

37. **A is the best answer.** The DG is the dictator game. A dictatorship is when one person controls a government. The best answer should refer to one leader. Only choice A refers to one decision-maker, so choice A is the best answer.

38. **D is the best answer.** Secularization is a term that describes a decrease in power or presence of a religious organization. This means that a secular populace would be one that is less religious. The passage states that the TG results were independent of religion, so choices A and B can be eliminated. The passage indicates that religion was associated with non-selfish social choices on the DG and UG. An absence of religion could then be associated with selfish choices. This makes choice D most likely to be the best answer.

Passage 8 (Questions 39-42)

39. **D is the best answer.** The independent variable of an experiment is the one that is manipulated by the researchers and exerts an effect on the dependent variable, which is then measured. However, this passage discussed an observational study, not an experimental one. Kinship describes the social bonds that unite individuals into families. While this concept is relevant to the study, it was not a measured variable. Choice A isn't the best answer. Traits related to sexual maturity, reproduction, risk taking and family form were both data points that were collected as a part of this observational study. While this study shows these two variables are correlated, it cannot be said for certain that one causes the other. This would require a randomized, experimental study. There could be other factors that cause the link. Because neither variable can be correctly classified as independent, choices B and C are non-ideal. Observational studies do not contain independent variables, so choice D is the best answer.

40. **B is the best answer.** The question asks for a link between the presence of a stepparent and child abuse. While choice A could illuminate a potential conflict between stepparents and children, this idea is not part of the study and is beyond the scope of the passage. As a result, choice A is a weak answer. Choice B can be analyzed using the theory of inclusive fitness described in the passage. Since stepparents don't share any genes with their stepchildren, they do not receive any advantage in fitness by caring for them. It follows that, compared to genetic parents who do experience an advantage in fitness by caring for their children, stepparents could be more abusive. Choice B is a strong answer. Choice C fails to provide a link to child abuse. Also, SES is mentioned only very briefly in the passage, so choice C is a weak answer. Choice D could provide a potential link between stepparents and child abuse. It is conceivable that some religions encourage remarriage more than others and, at the same time, impart strict parental discipline. However, this idea was not mentioned at all in the passage. This makes choice D a weak answer.

41. **C is the best answer.** The question asks for a concept that is related to increased time spent in the educational system. Educational stratification refers to the separation of students into groups on the basis of academic achievement. This idea does not account for different periods of time spent in the educational system, so choice A is a weak answer. Teacher expectancy happens when teachers treat students differently according to preconceived ideas about their capabilities. Since the question makes no mention of the children's abilities, choice B is also a weak answer. Cultural capital refers to the set of non-monetary social factors that contribute to social mobility. The educational system is a place where these factors can be increased over time. Choice C is a strong answer. Social exclusion denotes how impoverished people are often excluded from opportunities available to others. The question does not mention anything about income level, so choice D is a weak answer choice.

42. **D is the best answer.** A confounding variable is a third variable that can explain or partially explain the link between two other variables. The effects of death and divorce could be a potential confounder to this study. No distinction was made between the two when evaluating family forms. Whether children have a divorced or dead parent could conceivably influence their development. Choice A is most likely true and thus not the best answer. Using the same thought process, it is conceivable that there is something different about parents who choose to remain single or remarry after widowhood or divorce that could impact their children's development. For example, different cultures experience dissimilar rates of second and third marriages. These cultures could also obey distinct norms related to raising children. Choice B is also not the best answer. Non-random sampling always introduces bias into a study. There could potentially be something different about those who choose to be interviewed than those who decline. This is called selection bias. Because of this, choice C is not the best answer. The researchers studied the effects of family form on child development. Choice D represents the researcher's hypothesis that was based on the theory of inclusive fitness. The idea is that the biological parent will be diverting some resources from parenting effort into their relationship with the new partner. The study was constructed in order to support this statement. Since it does not mention another variable, choice D is probably not correct and is the best answer.

Stand-alones (Questions 43-46)

43. **B is the best answer.** The hidden curriculum is the idea that schools also transmit cultural norms to their students in addition to providing a formal education. The question does not mention socialization or norms, so choice A is a weak answer. Teacher expectancy is the idea that teachers treat students differently due to preconceived notions about their abilities. In this case, students were assigned to different groups based on their abilities. It follows that expectations would differ for each group. Choice B is a strong answer. Educational segregation points out that disadvantaged groups receive a lower quality of education than do privileged ones. The question makes no mention of advantages or disadvantages, so choice C is a weak answer. Meritocracy is the ideal that individuals who work hard are rewarded with economic success. This is similar to the students who are more skilled at reading getting more attention from the teacher but a meritocracy has an economic component. The children have no economic incentive to improve reading. This means that choice D is probably not the best answer. Choice B is the best answer.

44. **A is the best answer.** Power allows individuals to exert their will over others, even in the presence of opposition. Authority is a specific type of power that is viewed as legitimate by the population. So the question asks for an individual who is able to exert his will over others in a way that is not viewed as legitimate. Choice A is very consistent with this. A robber can exert his will over others by threatening them with a gun. This behavior is illegal, so it is not viewed as legitimate. Choice A is a strong answer. A parking attendant can use his ability to write tickets in order to exert his will onto others. Even though not traditionally thought of as "authoritative figures," parking attendants are legally allowed to conduct this behavior. Choice B is not the best answer. Physicians are ethically not supposed to use their prescription writing privileges in order to control the behavior of others. As a result, this behavior is not really related to power or authority. Choice C is a weak answer. The surgeon general is able to influence the behavior of others through changes in health policy. However, like the case of the parking attendant, this behavior is legitimate, so this is a position of high authority. Choice D is not the best answer. Choice A is the best answer.

45. **D is the best answer.** Division of labor involves splitting work between different groups of people in a way that promotes specialization of tasks. Choice A is relevant to this concept because each restaurant employee focuses on one specific task, whether it is waiting tables, preparing food, or washing dishes. Choice B is also relevant because the labor is divided such that each friend specializes in one particular task, whether it is washing dishes or drying them. Choice C is relevant to the global division of labor, as each country specializes in the production of the good for which it has a comparative advantage, but they depend on each other for the production of the other good. Choice D is not relevant to the concept of division of labor because although the workload is split between the two friends, they do not specialize in any particular task. Given this information, choice D is the best answer.

46. **C is the best answer.** Choice A describes a capitalist economy. In capitalism, resources and the means to produce goods and services are privately controlled by individuals and organizations. The desire for profit drives commercial activity. This is not a strong answer because it can not be substantiated. On the other hand, it is true that socialist economies do tend to have a decreased wealth disparity, as described in choice B. Socialism is a system in which resources and the means of producing goods and services are managed collectively. A socialist economy relies on government regulation to match productive output to the demands of consumers. However, if there were increased numbers of these two groups of children, (the ones who do and the ones who do not reach their educational potential) an increased wealth disparity would be expected. So, choice B is not the best answer. The division of labor, in which an increasing number of individuals engage in work that is highly specific, is a reasonable consequence of a large difference between children who do and do not meet certain expectations, making choice C the best answer. Division of labor is a trend in current economic modernization. Those who excel in school may enter more management positions. And perhaps the children who fall behind in school would take more manual labor job positions, as in answer choice D. However, choice C encompasses a greater range of possibility, so choice D is not the best answer.

Passage 9 (Questions 47-52)

47. **A is the best answer.** Religiosity is the importance a community places on religious belief and practice. Figure 1 implies that those within the disaster region experienced an increase in religiosity because the area near the earthquake is a darker color. This makes choice A a strong answer. Choice B is not the best answer as it is a direct antithesis to the expected shift. Choice C is a weak answer because it is not supported by Figure 1. Choice D can be eliminated as the information needed to infer this shift is provided in Figure 1.

48. **B is the best answer.** The best answer to this question is one that contradicts the growth of religion within a community. Modernization gives individuals access to global resources. However, increased access to resources on differing faith-systems does not necessarily guarantee a change in faith amongst a population. Choice A is possible but probably not the best answer. Choice B is a strong answer as secularization is defined as a decreasing devotion to religious doctrine and practice. The passage also states that "secular people tend to turn to faith at times of national crisis". Fundamentalism refers to taking spiritual doctrine literally which would likely lead to an increase in faith. Choice D refers to the death rate within a population. As an increase in faith would not contradict proliferation of mortality within the population, choice D can be eliminated

49. **C is the best answer.** The passage specifies that the mortality rate was measured to observe the potential impact of decreased subjective health status amongst victims of the disaster. To do so, it would be beneficial to record each death over a set period of time. Crude mortality rate measures the total amount of deaths per one thousand individuals. A good example of this type of measurement can be seen in investigations of fatal diseases. A statement similar to: "one out of every one thousand individuals die from this disease" is an example of how crude mortality rates can be utilized. As a crude mortality rate would not provide specific enough data, choice A is not the best answer. Choice B would only provide the death rate for a specific demographic and can be eliminated as it would be too specific to serve much use to the researchers. Choice C is a strong answer as it would provide the total amount of deaths in the sample population. Choice D is not the best answer for the same reason as choice B and can be eliminated.

50. **A is the best answer.** Observational studies are utilized to measure variables without manipulating them. Cohort studies are utilized to observe population samples overtime. Cohort, cross-sectional, and case-control studies are all variations of observational studies. Mortality rates tend to be measured either in cohort investigations or period investigations. Choice A is a strong answer as it would be an effective tool for measuring the mortality rate over time. Choice B is not the best answer as cross sectional studies are only concerned with data at a specific point of time. Choice C can be eliminated as a case-control study would be more concerned with past events. Experimental studies intentionally introduce conditions that allow for measurement of the topic of interest. As the scientists were measuring observational data, choice D can be eliminated.

51. **A is the best answer.** Environmental justice refers to the idyllic equal treatment of each individual within a community by providing similar environmental and healthcare resources. Mistreatment of a group based on socioeconomic status would be can example of environmental injustice, making choice A a strong answer. Global inequality refers to disparities amongst nations when being compared to one another and is therefore too broad to address the question stem, allowing choice B to be eliminated. Spatial inequality refers to unequal access of resources available to a community due to geographical distribution. While the initial segregation of the area would be an example of spatial inequality, the question stem is instead asking the reader to focus on the rescue group's efforts. Due to this, choice C is not the best answer. Prejudice refers to a negative belief about a group of individuals. As prejudice refers to belief and not actual action, choice D can be eliminated.

52. **C is the best answer.** Push and pull factors refer to how events can impact immigration or emigration rates within a region. A push factor is generally negative and will dissuade people from immigrating to a region, while a pull factor is something positive that encourages immigration. A great way to think of this concept is in terms of food. If something is delicious, a child would pull in the plate for more. If something is not so delicious, a child might push the plate away. Natural disasters are considered a push factor, so choices B and D can be eliminated. Choice A is not the best answer as migration after an earthquake would not increase. Choice C is the best answer as an earthquake would act as a push factor that would decrease migration.

Passage 10 (Questions 53-56)

53. **B is the best answer.** The passage shows that enrollment in an HRA program leads to better health behaviors and a decreased mortality rate. The question asks for a finding that would undermine this. Choice A can be eliminated because it actually further validates the results of the study. Since the experimental group showed higher levels of fruit/vegetable/fiber intake after 2 years, this finding would make the intervention even more effective than previously believed. Choice B is a strong answer, as incidental deaths in the control group would artificially inflate the mortality rate, leading to the perception of a relationship that does not exist. Rational exchange theory states that individuals make decisions through cost-benefit analyses. This is consistent with choice C. However, the motivation of a researcher to conduct a study is unrelated to its results, so long as no bias is introduced into the experiment. This means that choice C is probably not the best answer. The hidden curriculum is the idea that schools transmit cultural beliefs beyond the stated goals of each institution. This term is more traditionally used to explain how schools teach children to conform to normal social behavior. Even if the term were expanded to apply to this study, it could be seen that healthcare professionals are acting as agents of socialization to their patients. However, when evaluating the effectiveness of HRA, all components, subliminal or otherwise, would ideally be included. As long as the effects of the hidden curriculum were assessed as part of the study, its presence would not invalidate the results. As a result, choice D is a weak answer choice. Choice B is the best answer.

54. **A is the best answer.** Conflict theorists view society in term of competing groups acting in the interest of their own self-interests. Choice A is a strong answer because it alludes to the competition of groups over scare resources. Factions of society working together to maintain stability is an idea that would be proposed by a functionalist, not a conflict theorist. Because of this, choice B is not the best answer. Conflict theory is concerned with conflict between groups, not internal conflict within an individual, so choice C is also a weak answer. Choice D states the findings of the study for the passage. Since it does not answer the question, choice D is probably not the best answer. Choice A is the best answer.

55. **C is the best answer.** The results of the study show that the HRA intervention leads to an increase in healthy behavior and a decrease in mortality. While it may true that more doctors will be needed to treat elderly patients in an aging society, the passage made no reference to the amount of doctors caring for elderly patients. As a result, choice A is beyond the scope of the passage, so it is not the best answer. The implementation of HRA involved multimodal interventions and the coordination of care. In the study, this was the independent variable. Healthy behavior and mortality rate were dependent variables. These dependent variables were used as measurements to assess the quality of care given to elderly patients. This makes the conclusion drawn in both choices B and C a good one. Choice B, however, offers an explanation for this conclusion that was not discussed in the study. Choice C is a better answer because it specifically mentions the variables of the experiment. While alluded to in the first paragraph, healthcare resources were also not part of the study. So even though it may be true, choice D is beyond the scope of the passage and is thus a weak answer. Choice C is the best answer.

56. **D is the best answer.** Population pyramids graph a population's age and sex cohorts. The y-axis depicts age, while the x-axis depicts population number. The center line divides males and females, with the male population shown on the left and the female population shown on the right. The passage states that the United States has an increasing elderly population. Choice A represents the population pyramid of an expanding society. Relatively, there are far more young people than older ones. This means that choice A can probably be eliminated. Choices B and C are not proper population pyramids. Conventionally, the graphs for each sex must start at the midline and work their way outward. In addition, even if the graphs were conventionally correct, they would be depicting populations where one gender predominates, both in total population and average lifespan. For both of these reasons, choices B and C are not the best answers. Choice D represents the population pyramid of a declining society. Older individuals make up a higher percentage of the population. This makes choice D the best answer.

Stand-alones (Questions 57-59)

57. **B is the best answer.** Choice A is not the best answer because it is referring to a measure of external validity rather than internal validity. The statement presented in choice A is a sensible statement to make, but it does not answer the question. External validity refers to the appropriateness of generalizing the results of the study to other situations, while internal validity is defined as the degree to which causality between the independent and dependent variables can be concluded. Choice B is the best answer because it describes the presence of a confounding variable that could certainly limit the researchers' ability to logically conclude a causal relationship between the two variables. A confounding variable is defined as a variable other than the independent variable that could be responsible for causing the observed effect on the dependent variable. This study is measuring teacher expectancy, which is defined as the teachers holding their own beliefs of students' capacity for achievement, and consciously or unconsciously transmitting these expectations to their students, leading to their expectations becoming self-fulfilling prophecies. According to teacher expectancy, the students' internalization of teachers' expectation affects their academic performance. Choice B presents a factor *other* than teacher expectancy responsible for students' poor performance, making this factor a confounder and posing a threat to internal validity. Choice C is not the best answer because random assignment is generally considered to be a measure of minimizing the effects of confounders and increasing rather than decreasing a study's internal validity. Choice D is not the best answer because this is also a measure that would increase internal validity by presenting the temporal conditions responsible for claiming causation. Temporality is a condition that must be met to claim a causal relationship between variables, and refers to the necessity of having the cause come chronologically before the effect. That is exactly what choice D presents, so choice D is not the best answer.

58. **B is the best answer.** A social group is defined as two or more individuals who interact with each other and share common characteristics and a sense of unity. A social institution can be described as a subset of a social group: it is a means to structure society by addressing a specific purpose or set of tasks. Government, family and religion are examples of social institutions. Because John and Mary closely interact with each other, they form a social group both before and after they get married. Answer choices A and C can be eliminated. John and Mary form a family, which is an example of a social institution. The question stem could mislead the reader to interpret that only once married and with children do John and Mary form a family. That would be the traditional definition of a nuclear family accepted for many generations. However it is generally accepted now that the concept of family is defined in many ways, and can include co-habitation, adoption and domestic partnerships. Additionally, a couple does not even need to have children to be considered a family. Therefore, John and Mary form a family in both of the situations described, so choice D can be crossed out, and choice B is confirmed to be the best answer.

59. **D is the best answer.** This question is simply asking for the strict definition of religion as given in a sociological context. It rewards the ability to discriminate between different classifications that a belief system can face in sociology. Choice B best describes a sect, or a religious group that typically broke off from a larger institution. Choice C best describes a cult. While generally seen in a negative context, the word cult can describe any more "radical" forms of religion. Choices A and D, while similar, have a key difference in their wording. Choice A makes a point to point out that members place their religious system first, and best describes the concept of "religiosity'. Choice D provides the strict definition of a religion, which is a well established group of individuals with a similar belief system. Note that all the variations provide beliefs that frame their member's life experiences.

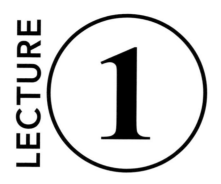

LECTURE

1

The Biopsychosocial Model, Society and Culture

TEST 1B

ANSWERS & EXPLANATIONS
Questions 1–59

Passage 1 (Questions 1-4)

1.   **B is the best answer.** This question states that the experiment was altered by preparing some of the participants with education on the biomedical model of health and illness. Recall that the biomedical approach focuses purely on the physical presentation and physical cause of illness. Therefore, if participants were educated on the biomedical approach, they would be more likely to report the case subjects' symptoms of depression as symptoms of a physical illness (in other words, somatically ill). If it wasn't immediately apparent that "somatically ill" is synonymous with "physically ill", remember that the "soma" of a neuron refers to the cell *body*, and that "somatic" was presented in the passage as opposing the definition of "psychological". Choice A is a distractor choice, as it has nothing to do with the added intervention of education on the biomedical approach to understanding illness. Additionally, perceived masculinity or femininity of the case subject was never mentioned in the passage as a dependent variable that was being collected. Choice B correctly recognizes that, according to the biomedical approach, physical symptoms would more likely be attributed to physical causes rather than emotional or psychological causes. Choice C states the converse of choice B, and is therefore incorrect. Choice D does not describe something that would necessarily happen after the intervention. Recall that the study design states that case subjects may be judged as displaying psychological symptoms, somatic symptoms, or both. Whether or not the participants rate the case subject as suffering from depression would depend on both the signs exhibited by the case subject, and the perspectives and background of the participant. Therefore, there is not enough information presented to make this assertion.

2.   **B is the best answer.** In simpler terms, the question first asks to think about which of the options best represents the way in which individuals come to take on a gender identity and take on the roles and values that are expected of them in their home society. A good way to go about finding the answer to this question would be through process of elimination. Choice A is inaccurate because this represents the source of gender identity as being far too limited. Lecture 1 emphasizes the pervasive interplay between biology, psychology, and sociology in determining learned behaviors, values, and worldviews. Choice B is best because it represents that gender identity is socially as well as biologically constructed. A great deal of roles or qualities associated with specific genders are arbitrary and were constructed by human actors, rather than being brute biological facts. Choice C would not be the best choice. A sufficiently large sample size would be meaningless if the Ito Sex Role Scale was created based on participants' answers to questions that did not make sense to them. Choice D is a choice that is not very relevant to the issue at hand. Material culture refers to physical objects that allow people to live out their lives, and symbolic culture refers the abstract aspects of culture such as beliefs and values. If anything, the Ito Sex Role Scale would be based on symbolic culture rather than material culture, which is the opposite of what choice D says.

3.   **C is the best answer.** For the Panic Disorder (PD) cases to be included in the evaluation, think back to the original hypothesis from the passage; participants scoring high in femininity would be more likely to recognize depressive symptoms as manifestations of *illness* compared to participants scoring low in femininity, and students scoring high in masculinity would be less likely to recognize depressive symptoms as manifestations of *illness* compared to participants scoring low in masculinity. This hypothesis, as it relates to Panic Disorder, would rely on the assumption of the study that Panic Disorder represents a state of disease. Choice A does present an issue as far as sample size and representativeness is concerned, but this does not threaten the viability of the study as much as choice C. Choice B is a distractor. The PD case is not a control group, rather, it represents the study taken in an entirely different direction. Choice C is the best answer for the following reason; if Panic Disorder is not perceived as a state of poor health according to the beliefs and values of the participants' home society and culture, it would be unlikely that any of the participants would recognize the case subject as ill, this giving the researchers to dependent variable to measure. Choice D is simply not a true statement. Without any knowledge of the symptoms of PD, the extreme language of this answer choice provides a clue as to why this would probably not be the best answer to an MCAT® question.

4.   **C is the best answer.** Skills in reading and interpreting figures are very important in answering this question. Choice A can be eliminated because we know nothing about the number of male versus female participants in the study; the y-axis of the graph is labeled as "psychological severity", which is not a field that could reveal any information about the composition of study participants. Choice B is a weaker answer because neither of the axes of the graph have any mention of chronology. Choice C is the best answer because this effectively accounts for the variable presented on each axis and their relation to one another. The line marked with diamonds refers to female study participants, and the line marked with circles refers to male study participants. The two groups on the x-axis refer to the gender of the case subject, and the y-axis refers to the severity of the psychological illness as rated by the study participants. The diamond bar is higher in the "girl case" region, and the circle bar is higher in the "boy case" region, indicating that participants rated psychological severity of the illness as high more often when they identified with the gender of the case subject. Choice D can be eliminated because it jumps to conclusions about causation. Recall that many conditions must be met in order to assert that a causal relationship between variables. All that this graph can tell, especially since there is not information about temporality, is that gender concordance between the participant and the test subject produces a pronounced effect in the recognition of illness. The reasons for this could be multifactorial and may have to do with the many ways that males and females express their particular qualities and differences, biologically or otherwise.

Passage 2 (Questions 5-10)

5. **C is the best answer.** Globalization describes the increased contact between individuals on an international scale. This contact is enacted through the exchange of ideas, products, services, and information. A variety of factors contributing to globalization have been identified, as well as a variety of perspectives on globalization, which attempt to describe the nature and effects of increased globalization. The hyper-globalist perspective argues that globalization entails a movement away from individual nations toward a single global society. However, this is a scholastic perspective, and it is not correct to say that "countries have a hyper-globalist perspective." Furthermore, even if an entire country carried this hyper-globalist outlook, the effect of such a perspective on the nutrition profile of refugees would be very difficult to quantify and generalize. Thus, choice A is not a strong answer. The transformationalist perspective argues that globalization causes new patterns of interdependent interactions but the outcomes cannot be predicted with any certainty. Again, this concept is a scholastic perspective and the effects on the refugee children would be difficult to quantify. Thus, choice B is not the best answer. One factor that contributes to globalization is economic interdependence, as corporations often conduct operations across multiple continents. It is reasonable to conclude that residents of a country that has had a high degree of contact with the US through economic conducts would have some similar living conditions and thus a similar nutritional profile among its citizens to the US. Thus, choice C is the best answer. Another factor that impacts globalization is communication technologies. Communication technologies allow an unprecedented type of interaction unbound by spatial constraints. These technologies significantly reduce the extent to which distance limits interactions. Therefore, the expected effect is that counties with strong communications infrastructure would have a similar nutritional profile among its citizens to the US, so choice D is not the best answer.

6. **A is the best answer.** After moving from one culture to another, it takes time to learn a new set of cultural norms and acceptable behaviors. The process by which an individual or group becomes part of a new culture is called assimilation. Assimilation occurs through a variety of means, including language acquisition and gaining knowledge about the social roles and rules of the newly adopted culture. It is reasonable that after a period of several years, as assessed by the change from cross-sectional to longitudinal study design, the subjects would be assimilated into their new US culture, including diet patterns and exercise habits. Thus, choice A is a strong answer. The current study is a cross-sectional design, in which the participants were all measured for certain characteristics at a single point in time. Thus, choice B can be eliminated. The presence of many subcultures within the U.S. has led to the rise of multiculturalism, the practice of valuing and respecting differences in culture. Multiculturalism includes the belief that the harmonious coexistence of separate cultures is a valuable goal, rather than encouraging all cultures to blend together through assimilation. Although multiculturalism is present in the US, it would not help to explain any homogeneity that arises. Thus, choice C is not the best answer. Additionally, the current study is a cross-sectional design, so choice D can also be eliminated.

7. **D is the best answer.** Emigrate means to leave one's country to live in another, while immigrate means to come into another country to live permanently. Although the rate of emigration or immigration may increase as relatives leave one's home country, this does not relate to the concept of relative deprivation presented in the question stem. Thus, choices A and B are not strong answers. The inability to meet minimal objective standards for living is defined as absolute deprivation, often synonymous with absolute poverty. This is different than relative deprivation. Relative deprivation refers to the feeling of disadvantage that arises when individuals compare themselves to others of similar status and feel that they possess relatively fewer resources and privileges. Thus, choice C is not the best answer. This feeling of inequality due to relative deprivation can spur the creation of social movements designed to promote a more equal society. A social movement describes a group of people who share an ideology and work together toward a specified set of goals. Social movements often arise among people who experience deprivation or alienation. The movement of refugees from one country to another can be seen as a social movement. Therefore, choice D is the best answer.

8. **B is the best answer.** The organization of social movements tends to have a characteristic sequence. First, emergence is the period of discontent before any organizing power arises. Next, during coalescence, dissatisfaction becomes more focused through an understanding of how the factors causing discontent can be overcome. In this step, leaders come forward and specific strategies for the social movement are developed. Choice A, emergence, is therefore not the best answer because choice B, coalescence, is when these leaders the researchers noticed would have emerged, and thus B is the strongest answer. If the movement achieves success and grows, a period of bureaucratization begins to meet the organization's need for coordinating procedures. Choice C, bureaucratization, does not describe the strategy development noted in the question stem, and can thus be eliminated. Finally, after either successfully or unsuccessfully working toward the movements' goals, there is a stage of decline. The development of strategy would not occur in the last step of organization of a social movement, so choice D can be eliminated.

9. **A is the best answer.** With regard to countries of origin, the largest groups of immigrants to the United States are from Mexico, Caribbean nations, and India. Overall, an important pattern of immigration to remember is that immigration is increasing. The PedNSS subject group is representative of the general population, and should contain a proportion of immigrants. Out of these US residents, the immigrants are likely from these three popular countries of origin. With this information, choices A and B are strong answer candidates, while choices C and D are weak, as they list countries of origin that are also popular, but not the most likely. Figure 1 shows that American children have greater incidence of obesity than refugee children, and thus experience overnutrition to a greater extent. Therefore, choices B and D can be eliminated. Choice A is the only answer which identifies the most popular countries of origin for US immigrants, and correctly interprets the data in Figure 1.

10. **B is the best answer.** Urbanization is the increase in the proportion of people living in specified urban areas. Historically there has been a strong relationship between industrialization and urban growth. Although it is likely refugees may concentrate with others of similar ethnic and racial background in urban areas, it is incorrect to describe their pattern of settlement as industrialization. Industrialization describes the development of industry, which generates rapid growth, increases trade with and travel to centralized locations, which leads to urbanization. Therefore, choice A is not a strong answer. Suburbanization refers to the process of large-scale movement from cities to suburbs, which are communities located just beyond an official city boundary. Immigrants, including refugees, are likely to follow this pattern which is widespread in America—first settling in urban locales, then once wealth is accumulated, moving families out into the suburbs. Thus, choice B is a strong answer. There is an analogous relationship between suburbanization and urban decline. Suburbanization leads to a decline in the standard of living in urban areas. As families leave and property values in urban areas fall, less property tax can be collected. The subsequent decline in commerce in the city leads to higher unemployment and crime. This procession of events does not best describe what the refugees would experience, so choice C is not the best answer. Lastly, urban renewal refers to attempts to improve urban conditions through the restoration of buildings and public infrastructure. This term describes attempts made by the government or community to achieve a specific goal, and does not best describe what the immigrant population would experience. Furthermore, gentrification is a specific urban renewal pattern in which middle- and upper-class people move to areas of a city with cheap buildings that are in need of restoration. Gentrification also does not describe what would likely be experienced by the new immigrants, so choice D can be eliminated.

Stand-alones (Questions 11-14)

11. **C is the best answer.** Gender is best described as an intersection of sex, gender identity, and gender expression. Sex is biological and is based on genitalia at birth, while gender identity and expression are based on an individual's internal feelings. Choice A is not the best answer as it is a true statement; gender identity is not necessarily dependent on biological sex. Choice B is not the best answer as it provides the definition of gender identity. Choice C is the best answer as it is a false statement. While society traditionally defines gender as male or female, an individual can identity as both or neither genders. Choice D is a true statement as some cultures may see a non-binary gender identity as taboo.

12. **C is the best answer.** When given a strictly longitudinal study, questions will often test cohort effect, especially in regards to age. Although the students were not randomly assigned to the experimental and control classrooms, distribution of sexes is likely similar, socioeconomic status and previous academic achievement are likely similar given the young age and same schooling, and age is likely closely similar within the same grade. These make choice A a weak choice. Reduced sample size (choice D) may make it difficult to establish significance difference in academic performance between groups. The drop-out rate of students will again affect sample size. When two choices are functionally the same, it is rare that either is the best answer, so choices B and D should be eliminated. Choice C describes an age cohort effect, in that participants in the study will use and respond to technology differently than the population the conclusions will be used to benefit. This makes choice C the best choice, as it specifically addresses a disjunction between the research design and the applicability of the results as intended.

13. **C is the best answer.** Relative deprivation refers to the feeling of disadvantage that arises when individuals compare themselves to others of similar status and feel that they possess relatively fewer resources and privileges. Demonstrations and confrontations are not examples of relative deprivation, so choice A is not a strong answer. A strategy is a general plan describing the goals of a social movement. There is a difference between strategy and tactics. Tactics describe how the movement implements a strategy. Given these definitions, mass demonstrations and physical confrontations are examples of tactics—the actions a group takes to implement their plan, or strategy, to achieve their goals. Other tactics could include advertising or forming official organizations. Thus, choice B can be eliminated, and choice C is the best answer. A proactive social movement is one that promotes change. In contrast, a reactive social movement is one that resists change. The tactics presented in the question stem are not themselves either a proactive or reactive social movement, so choice D can be eliminated.

14. **C is the best answer.** This question requires knowledge of the basic structure of a population pyramid. The pyramid consists of horizontal bars, each representing different age groups within society. The youngest age group within society is placed at the bottom, and age groups ascend up the pyramid, with the oldest age group being placed at the top. The pyramid is vertically bisected by a line that divides the population into the two genders, each placed on a different side of this line. The magnitude of the length of a bar denotes the population size of this age group. Choice A is not the best answer. A widening base indicates an increasing birth rate. While it is possible that the young population may increase due to lower infant mortality rates, this is not expected to be the most pronounced effect of improvements in health care. Choice B is not the best answer because this translates to a decrease in the number of older members of the population, which is the opposite of the expected effect of improvements in healthcare. Choice C is the best answer, and the most pronounced effect of improved healthcare is decreased mortality and possibly an increase in life expectancy. The decreased mortality rates from presumably preventable diseases and the possible increased life expectancy would cause the number of living adults to increase, making the pyramid more "top heavy". The general trajectory that population pyramids follow as a society develops is the transition from a "bottom heavy" pyramid to a more "top heavy" pyramid. Choice D is not the best answer, because this would be indicative of a decreased birth rate, which typically does not occur until much later stages of a society's demographic transition.

Passage 3 (Questions 15-18)

15. **D is the best answer.** The question asks for a concept that differentiates sexual behavior on the basis of gender norms. Remember that norms are expectations that govern acceptable behavior within a group, in this case men versus women. Conflict theory views society in terms of groups competing for a limited number of resources. A conflict theorist would likely describe differences in norms of sexual behavior as the results of men and women competing with each other. Choice A could be a possibility. However, differences in gender norms are not explicitly related to competition, so this choice is a bit out of scope. Social construction of gender is the theory that the development of gender is subject to cultural influences and social interactions. This idea could possibly be extrapolated to say that differences between gender norms are based on the same thing: cultural influences and social interactions. Choice B is also a possibility. However, this choice is again somewhat imperfect because it involves the application of the social construction of gender in a very broad sense. Gender identity is an individual's internal sense of self. Do they view themselves as male, female, both, or neither? This concept doesn't account for differences between genders, so choice C is a weak answer. Gender segregation refers to separation of people based on gender. This can happen formally through rules, laws, and policies or informally through societal norms and pressures. Separation of the genders based on sexual behavior is an example of the latter. There is no doubt that society places different expectation on men and women in terms of sexual behavior. Choice D is a strong answer. Since gender segregation is much more easily applied to the topic of gender differences than either conflict theory or the social construction of gender, choice D the best answer.

16. **C is the best answer.** Figure 1 shows that different counties of California have different levels of HIV-infected women. The results of study 2 showed a correlation between higher levels of HIV-infected people and higher levels of poverty in certain counties. The best answer choice should be based on these findings. Environmental justice refers to the equal treatment of all people with regard to prevention and relief from health hazards. The results contradict this idea because they show that HIV is not distributed evenly. This means that choice A is not the best answer. This choice would be much more ideal if it said something along the lines of "a lack of environment justice." Patterns of social mobility show how individuals move between social strata in society. The idea of social stratification was not referenced in the passage, so choice B is a weak answer. Global inequalities are disparities between regions or countries. The studies found that there are different levels of HIV-infected individuals and low-income individuals in different counties. This is evidence of inequality between these counties, so choice C is a strong answer. Migration is the relocation of people from one area to another. Though the study does differentiate people based on where they live, it does not take movement into account. This means choice D is not the best answer.

17. **A is the best answer.** Sexual orientation is an individual's self identity based on the gender to which they are attracted. Sexual orientation is not dependent on the sex or gender of the individual. For instance, any self-identifying male could be attracted to men, women, both, or neither. This makes choice A a strong answer. There actually can be a difference between who a person is attracted to and who they have sex with. These choices regarding sexual behavior are often influenced by societal pressure. It is not uncommon for people to maintain heterosexual behaviors because they perceive it to be normal. Choice B is not the best answer. Sexual orientation is not binary. Individuals can be attracted to men, women, both, or neither. Choice C is a weak answer choice. In general, it is better to think of categories as spectra rather than simple binaries. Sex is determined at birth based on the infant's genitalia. This is not true about sexual orientation, which is most likely determined by a complex interplay of genes, hormones, and the environment. This makes choice D a weak answer. It is often good test-taking strategy to attribute any cause to a combination of genes and environment.

18. **D is the best answer.** Demographics are statistics used to examine a population by quantifying subsets of that population. Sexual orientation, race, and ethnicity were all mentioned in the very first sentence of the passage. This makes choices A and B weak answers. Socioeconomic status was mentioned as part of study 2, so choice C is also a weak answer choice. Migration status has to do with the relocation of people from one country to another. This passage did analyze the location of HIV-infected individuals, but it did not mention movement. As a result, choice D is the best answer.

Passage 4 (Questions 19-22)

19. **A is the best answer.** Environmental justice is equal treatment and equal access to resources for all people regardless of race, socioeconomic status, or other social grouping. Based on the definition provided by the passage, it can be assumed that the higher the hazard ratio, the higher the risk of dying from breast cancer. Choice A is appealing at first glance because the step-wise adjustment of each model leads to lower and lower risk of dying from breast cancer. Adjustment for stage at diagnosis, treatment, race and rural/urban residence eliminates survival disparities associated with lower SES, which suggests that if all people were treated equally regardless of race and area of residence, then the survival disparities could be reduced or eliminated. Before selecting choice A, it is important to ensure that any other answer choice is not the best answer. Choice B can be eliminated because Table 1 never assumes that these factors are affecting survival disparities. Table 1 is instead drawing a possible correlation between these factors and survival disparities. Correlation does not mean causation. Choice B also makes no mention of environmental justice, a key part of this question. Choice C is not the best answer because it contradicts the findings of Table 1, and it contradicts the reasoning used to explain choice A. Choice C would be tempting if there was confusion regarding the definition of environmental justice. Choice D may be tempting because it mentions socioeconomic status and environmental justice, and Table 1 shows that the p-value of each model becomes less and less significant, but this has nothing to do with the hazard ratio, or with environmental justice, but rather with the demographic factors adjusted for by each model. The hazard ratio simply is a means to measure the risk of dying of breast cancer in each of the models. The best answer can therefore be determined to be choice A after reasoning through each answer choice.

20. **C is the best answer.** Spatial inequality is unequal access to resources within a geographical area. Choice A is not the best answer because the study focused on the relationship between *socioeconomic status* and risk of dying from breast cancer. Race was not a large focus of the study, so it is impossible to generalize findings to make a specific conclusion regarding minority women. Choice B is also not the best answer for the same reason- it is impossible to make a specific conclusion regarding minority women based on the study findings. Choice B also makes no mention of spatial inequality, which is an important part of the question stem. Choice C seems like a good answer because it makes a broad conclusion regarding cancer screening and low socioeconomic status patients. The passage states in the second paragraph that "the proportions of women from the two lowest SES areas who received the first course treatment were lower than that of the highest SES areas." Based on this finding, it can be assumed that low SES patients may not be receiving adequate treatment and/or screening due to spatial inequality. Choice C specifically mentions increasing cancer screening in low SES *neighborhoods*, which would reduce the apparent spatial inequality. After glancing at choice D, it can be determined that choice C is in fact the best answer. Choice D is not the best answer because the findings of this study make no mention of cost. Also, choice D contradicts the finding that low SES patients have a higher risk of dying from cancer and are less likely to have received treatment.

21. **A is the best answer.** This question requires an understanding of the results of table 1 as well as an understanding of demographics. Table 1 shows that adjustment for each demographic qualifier (i.e. race and rural/urban residence) results in the equalization of hazard ratio across socioeconomic status groups. Adjustment for patient age, socioeconomic status, and race all help to equalize the hazard ratio, but model 5 has made adjustments for all of these things, not just one. The concept of demographic parameters encompasses all of these qualifiers- socioeconomic status, race, and age. Demographics can be defined as statistical data about subsets of populations. Common demographic parameters are race, sexual orientation, education level, age, and socioeconomic status. Choice A is the best answer because choices B, C, and D are all examples of different demographic parameters adjusted for in model 5 of the study.

22. **B is the best answer.** This question requires an understanding of experimental design. The fact that there is a large sample population from a wide range of demographic backgrounds makes the findings of the studies generalizable, or applicable to the entire population of women. Based on this logic, it can be inferred that choice B is the best answer. Choice A can be eliminated because the variability of the findings is unrelated to the sample population. The sample population also is not related to whether the findings are inconclusive or conclusive, so choice C is not the best answer. Choice D is also not the best answer. This choice may be tempting if there is confusion regarding the definition of validity. A study is valid if it measures what it was set out to measure. This question stem mentions nothing about whether the findings are reflective of what the study intended to measure, so no conclusion can be made about the validity of the study, as it does not truly relate to the size of the sample population.

Passage 5 (Questions 23-26)

23. **D is the best answer.** This question is best answered through process of elimination. Vertical mobility involves upward or downward movement along the class hierarchy, and because the father moves up the class hierarchy through his financial success, choice A can be eliminated. Social reproduction occurs when social inequality is inherited from one generation to the next, and because the children inherited their father's wealth, choice B can be eliminated. Choice C can be eliminated for the same reason that choice A was eliminated, as upward mobility is simply a subset of vertical mobility. That leaves choice D, which is the best answer. Intergenerational mobility involves movement along the social hierarchy that occurs between several generations, and there is no suggestion that intergenerational mobility has occurred based on the information given in the question. If the children had moved up or down the social hierarchy relative to their father, then intergenerational mobility would apply. However, because there is no indication of that in the question, we cannot conclude that intergenerational mobility actually occurred.

24. **A is the best answer.** The age-specific mortality data reports that "mortality was higher among AAs than among non-Arab and non-Hispanic Whites among all age groups except males aged 25–44 years and females aged 5–44 years." This indicates that AAs have higher mortality rates for males under the age of 25, females under the age of 5, and both males and females over the age of 44. Choice A provides an excellent interpretation of this information because infectious disease disproportionately contributes to child and adolescent mortality (due to underdeveloped immune systems), while chronic disease mainly contributes to mortality among the elderly. Choice B states the opposite of choice A, so it can be eliminated. While choice C does present an actual finding of the study, it does not answer the question because the finding is not based on age-specific mortality, so it can be eliminated as well. Choice D is not the best answer because the passage does establish a relationship between age and mortality rate, which is best explained through choice A.

25. **C is the best answer.** The two main examples of social changes in globalization are international terrorism and civil unrest. Globalization involves human connectivity on an international scale. While it has many advantages, such as the exchange of ideas and international trade, globalization also has contributed terrorism and civil unrest. International terrorism involves violence against another country in order to achieve political or religious goals. Civil unrest and greater incidences of uprisings may arise in nations with authoritarian governments due to the international exchange of democratic values. Terrorism and civil unrest correspond to options I and II. Option III involves a social movement, but does not relate to globalization. Given that options I and II answer the question, choice C is the best answer.

26. **D is the best answer.** Racial formation theory suggests that race is a dynamic social construct that is shaped by social forces. Any representation of race as static or unchanging based solely on phenotypic traits or place of origin is not consistent with racial formation theory. Choices A, B, and C involve using phenotypic traits or place of origin to assign a static definition of race to people of Arab descent, so they can all be eliminated. Given this information, choice D is the best answer.

Stand-alones (Questions 27-30)

27. **B is the best answer.** Choice A is not likely to be the best answer as suburbanization does not necessarily result in improved health access due to geographic considerations—transportation may limit access to urban areas in which healthcare is provided. Choice B is accurate—globalization refers to the spread of technologies throughout the world. Because the internet was first used by the general public in North America and Europe, Brazil would experience cultural lag, but recent data would reflect increasing internet usage. Choice C is inaccurate, as urbanization results in many people living in densely populated areas, conducive to the increased spread of infectious disease. There is no evidence to support choice D; it may be a tempting answer because if there are fewer internet users, self rated health is likely more accurate. However, this answer asks if the proportion of internet users is reflected accurately, not the health of those users. This makes choice D minimally relevant to the question and an unlikely answer.

28. **B is the best answer.** Racial stereotypes are created by society and attributed to individuals of a particular race. A race can include individuals from all different backgrounds and is mostly determined by the outward appearance of an individual. A third-generation Mexican American and newly immigrated Mexican would probably have a very similar appearance and most likely be grouped into the same race by society. This means they are likely to experience similar stereotypes, making option I a strong choice. A person's identity is dependent on the culture with which that person associates. A third-generation Mexican American is likely to be assimilated into American culture and not likely to share as much culture as a traditional Mexican. For this reason, option II is a weaker choice. As mentioned previously, race is determined more on the physical appearance of an individual, so it is likely that these two individuals will have a similar race, which makes option III a strong choice. Choice B the best answer because it includes options I and III without including option II.

29. **A is the best answer.** The question stem describes two patient populations being measured over a period of time (both before and after an intervention, in this case). A cohort study is defined as a study that examines a sample group over a period of time, and the question stem presents two groups meeting this description (one group in Japan, and one in the United States). That makes the situation presented in the question stem that of two cohort studies. Globalization is the proper term to use to classify this example, because it describes the international exchange of ideas and information. Choice B is not the best answer because the assigned study type is inaccurate, and multiculturalism is not the best way to describe what is happening in the question stem. Cross-sectional studies examine a sample group at a single point in time, and the question stem describes the study as being one where quality of life measures are collected before *and* after the intervention (the surgery). Multiculturalism refers to the preservation of and respect for different cultures within a society. The physicians in the question stem are operating in two separate societies, and are taking this opportunity to exchange medical information and insight rather than celebrate their distinct cultures. Choice C is not the best answer because it would not be accurate to explain the study design as being cross-sectional, since results are collected at multiple time points. Additionally, it is not necessarily possible to assert that the physicians are sharing technological advancements; they may just be discussing the use of existing technologies. This answer choice also fails to account for the transnational nature of their exchange. Choice D is not the best answer, because to simply call this an observational study would not be as appropriate and specific as referring to it as a cohort study. Healthcare equity is not necessarily at play here. The United States and Japan are both considered to be developed countries, but this is not required knowledge for the MCAT®. The lack of specific indicators that one population was disadvantaged means that this answer choice cannot be the best answer.

30. **D is the best answer.** 'Push' factors in migration are factors that make an individual or group feel compelled to leave an area in which they once resided. They are typically qualities of that place itself that make it an undesirable place to stay. 'Pull' factors in migration are factors that may make a particular place attractive to migrants, and draw migrants to relocate to that place. Choice D is the best answer, because it correctly associates the 'push' and 'pull' definitions with the particular factors affecting the individuals in the case described in the question stem. Greater economic opportunity in the United States would be an alluring quality that would draw the couple to that area, making them pull factors, while poor economic conditions in their home country would compel them to leave, making them push factors. Choice A states the exact opposite of this, so this would not be the best answer. Choice B is not the best answer because it defines what is actually a push factor as both a push and pull factor. Choice C is not a good answer choice because it incorrectly defines a pull factor. A pull factor is something that draws people to migrate to a new place, not a factor that 'pulls' people to stay in what has historically been their home.

Passage 6 (Questions 31-34)

31. **A is the best answer.** The question is hinting at Malthusian theory of population growth. Eventually, any rapidly growing population is expected to run out of resources, such as access to healthcare, causing a rapid decline in population. Choice A is the best answer. Karl Marx began a political ideology that eventually evolved into communism. This is not relevant to population growth, so choice B is not the best answer. Olduvai theory is not tested by the MCAT®. Be very wary of words that are not familiar. The Examkrackers materials are comprehensive, so an unfamiliar word on the MCAT® is probably a wrong answer. Regardless, the Olduvai theory is also known as the transient pulse theory of civilization and discusses per capita energy production. It is not relevant to healthcare, so choice C is not the best answer. There is no specific theory known as demographic theory, so choice D is not the best answer.

32. **C is the best answer.** Absolute poverty is poverty so severe that the needs of an individual are not met. People living in countries where medical care is not a right may experience absolute poverty, but the question is asking about people where medical care is a right. Choice A can be eliminated. For choice B, mortality is not more likely in a person whom has access to medical care. Choice B can be eliminated. Relative deprivation is the lack of resources to maintain a certain lifestyle. This is applicable to the question, so choice C is a strong answer. Choice D is a trick. Individuals with access to medical care may have improved *mortality* but not improved *morality*. Choice D can be eliminated.

33. **B is the best answer.** First, decide if profits will go up if the income of citizens goes up. Most certainly the answer is yes. So, pick the answer that describes an improvement in the class of surrounding areas. Urbanization is the process of immigration to an urban center. There is likely little change in the average income level in urbanization since, although there is more income, there are also more citizens. Choice A can be eliminated. Gentrification is the process of revamping a lower socioeconomic (SES) area to fit with middle class or even upper class preferences. Think of this as what a real estate agent would call and "up and coming" neighborhood. Choice B is a strong answer. Globalization is increased communication among different countries. This would not change the local population dramatically, so choice C is not the best answer. Industrialization may increase income, but factory workers are not typically paid highly and end up having a low SES. More than likely, average income would decline. Choice D can be eliminated, meaning choice B is the best answer.

186   Examkrackers MCAT® – 101 Passages: Chemistry

34. **C is the best answer.** Race is a social construct. A multiracial individual usually identifies primarily with a certain race but may identify with multiple races equally. More than likely, the person would not consider genetic makeup when self-identifying as a particular race, so choice A can be ruled out. The person may choose the race that is most socially accepted. The first part of choice B is possible. Likewise, the person may choose the race that he or she most identifies with. So, choices C and D are both possible. External validity is the application of the results of a study to a population. Internal validity is whether a measure avoids confounding and is truly accurate. For example, a scale at the supermarket may good internal validity if it accurately measures fruits and vegetables. However, it may have weak external validity if it does not measure body weight well because it is not usable for weights over 10 pounds. A survey that forces individuals to choose a race may not have strong internal validity because it is not accurately measuring what it intends to measure. Strong internal validity would give participants the option to identify as multiracial, and even possibly specify which races. Choices B and D reference external validity and can be eliminated. Choice C is the best answer.

Passage 7 (Questions 35-38)

35. **A is the best answer.** Hidden curriculum can be thought of as the lessons about society that are not explicitly taught in school, but are learned and understood by members of society. Social inequities are often internalized by students through the hidden curriculum. For example, the differences in the way a teacher treats male and female students can be internalized, and eventually propagated as a social norm. Because the concept of "hidden curriculum" contributes to the differing status of men and women, choice A is a good answer. Religion may be the second best answer; after all, many religions promote the unequal treatment of men and women. However, this term is too broad to make such a generalization; many religions promote gender equality. Furthermore, it is rare for all members of a society to belong to a single religion, at least in modern day. Choice B is not the best answer. Class consciousness is a term generally mentioned in the context of conflict theory. Class consciousness can be defined as the awareness of the social standing of one's class, especially as it relates to the struggle over power. Conflict theory generally does not focus on the inequity between men and women, instead opting to focus on the struggle between economic classes. Class consciousness does not explain the difference between men and women, so choice C is not the best answer. Urbanization is transition of an area from a rural to an urban/industrial area. Urbanization does not result in a difference in the treatment of men and women, so choice D is not the best answer.

36. **B is the best answer.** Study 1, using gender as a proxy of social status, found that individuals with lower social status were more affected by stereotype threat. Because income is a common indicator of socioeconomic status and class, it is reasonable that the effect of stereotype threat would decrease with increasing income, of any given individual. Choice A is not the best answer, because the graph indicates individuals with higher income and social status would experience a higher degree of stereotype threat. The opposite is expected, so choice B is the best answer. Choice C indicates that, with increasing status, the effect of stereotype threat decreases initially, which is correct. However, the graph shows the effect of stereotype threat growing at a certain income level, which is not indicated by the results of Study 1. Choice C is not the best answer. Choice D is similar to choice A, but displays an exponential increase in stereotype threat with increasing income. Because the opposite is expected, choice D is not the best answer.

37. **C is the best answer.** Racial formation is the process of socially defining a category of people based on a set of characteristics, forming the concept of "race". A common criteria used to define a race are physical characteristics, such as skin or hair color. Choice A is not the best answer. Contributors the formation of the notion of race are stereotypes. Stereotypes are misconceptions that everyone in a social group behaves identically. Choice B is not the best answer. Conditioning is the formation of new behaviors, usually divided into two categories: operant and classical conditioning. Race, as a social concept, is not really formed from conditioning, which is more of a psychological concept that deals with individual behaviors. Because of this reasoning, choice C is the best answer. Choice D is not the best answer; culture normally does play a role in the formation of race. For example, hair color is used in other cultures as determinants as race, whereas skin color is more important in other cultures.

38. **A is the best answer.** From the first study in the passage, one can conclude that class and social status play a factor in an individual's susceptibility to stereotype threat. So, one possible explanation for the finding is that members of the same family are in similar classes. Social reproduction is the transmission of social inequality from one generation to the next. This concept does explain why family members tend to be in the same class, so choice A is a good answer. In the passage, there is no mention of how culture can affect stereotype threat. Although it may be possible, without further information one can conclude that choice B is not the best answer. Cultural diffusion, or the spread of cultural ideals, does not adequately explain why members of the same family would be similarly affected by stereotype threat. The spread of culture does not address the similarities individuals in the same family share, so choice C is not the best answer. Finally, choice D is not the best answer. Intergenerational mobility refers to the movement between class systems of one's children or grandchildren. A change in social class would likely result in a difference in the effect of stereotype threat, so this answer is not the best choice.

Passage 8 (Questions 39-44)

39. C is the best answer. Socioeconomic status (SES) is a person's social and economic standing in a community. The question refers to income and occupation, but education level is also involved in determining SES. Age, gender, and race can all be involved, but SES is primarily determined by education, occupation, and income. Choice C is the best answer.

40. A is the best answer. Social exclusion is the process by which a person is systematically blocked from basic human rights including adequate healthcare. Choice A is a possible answer. Social inequality describes how different opportunities are available depending on social status. This includes the process of social exclusion. Choice B is not incorrect, but choice A is more specific. Spatial inequality and spatial exclusion describe how certain neighborhoods are discriminated against. Neighborhoods can depend on class and social status, but since the passage focused more on social status than location, choices C and D are not the best answers.

41. B is the best answer. A democracy is a political system that is run by the people. This is not clearly related to poverty or education, so choice A is not the best answer. A meritocracy is a political system where more power is given to those with greater achievements. In some countries, education is a meritocracy where more resources are given to students whom are brighter at a younger age. The No Child Left Behind Act ensures that equal opportunities and resources are given to all children, so choice B is a possible answer. A theocracy is a political system where a deity rules. It does not relate to poverty or education, so choice C is not the best answer. A federacy is a political system where a central body rules, but there is independence for groups to govern themselves. Again, this is not related to school or social class, so choice D is not the best answer.

42. C is the best answer. Puberty does occur in childhood, but it is not clear how it would cause poverty or health problems. Choice A is not the best answer. Horizontal mobility is moving within a social class. There is no change is status. Choice B is probably not the best answer. Vertical mobility is moving up or down a social class. If the child was mostly rich but had a period of extreme poverty, this period of poverty may have biased the results. Choice C is a strong answer. Intergenerational mobility is a change in social class between generations. This could not occur during childhood, but it could occur over a lifetime. Choice D is not the best answer.

43. D is the best answer. The passage states that participants whom experienced material poverty had gait (walking) disturbances, impairments in memory, and depression. The correct answer should include one or more of these. Choice A refers to impairments in memory, so it is a possible answer. Choice B refers to impairments in movement, so choice B is a possible answer. Choice C refers to impairments in personality, choice C is not the best answer. Huntington's disease also causes impairments in movement, but this disease is not tested by the MCAT®. Do not use outside knowledge on the MCAT®. Choice D refers to trouble walking, as well as cognitive and mood changes. This comprises every symptom mentioned in the passage, so choice D is the best answer.

44. B is the best answer. Material poverty as described in the passage would be considered absolute poverty, because it is the absence of water, heat, and bathrooms. Relative poverty describes when a person is less wealthy than those around him or her. For example, not being able to afford to buy a car, but having enough money for necessities, could be seen in relative poverty. Choices C and D can be eliminated. The passage does not refer to clothing, so choice A is not as strong as choice B.

Stand-alones (Questions 45-48)

45. A is the best answer. Residential segregation is a form of spatial inequality. Poor neighborhoods tend to have bad schools, a high crime rate, poor healthcare, and cheap housing. In contrast, wealthy neighborhoods have good schools, a low crime rate, a good healthcare system, and expensive housing. Segregation occurs because relocation is difficult both ways, as poor people can not afford to relocate, and the rich do not want to relocate. Thus, choice A is the best answer because having less segregation would result in an increase in movement between neighborhoods. Less segregation would result in an increase in outdoor exercise activity. Neighborhood safety and violence specifically refers to how poor neighborhoods have high crime rates. This can have both acute and chronic impacts on health—such as residents experiencing fear of crime—which prompts them to avoid outdoor activities such as exercise, which eventually bears negative consequences on their health. Thus, choice B is a weak answer. In general, wealthy neighborhoods have more expensive housing. If there were less segregation, the city would see a decrease in expensive housing in those specific neighborhoods, making choice C not the best answer. Finally, having less segregation would reverse the effects due to fear of crime seen normally on residents' stress levels. Thus, choice D is not a strong answer for the same reasons outlined for choice B.

46. **B is the best answer.** Power is the ability to influence ones community through resources, including all forms of capital. Choice D may be an attractive choice, given the economic value of oil, but the manager is restricted by the wishes of the company in distribution. Doctors carry much prestige, which contributes to credibility when attempting to influence and audience. In this case, however, the individual is retired and now elderly, which means he is unlikely to have any power. Gang leaders can influence community through social capital and threat of violence, but incarceration serves as a harsh barrier to accessing these resources, making choice C weak. Choice B indicates that the woman is currently the leader of members of the community. Not only does this show direct influence of these members, but the respect as well as social and human capital to influence the entire community, making B the best answer.

47. **B is the best answer.** One way that social inequality manifests in society is through the development of spatial inequality. Choice A is an example of inequality due to age, but not spatial inequality. Spatial inequality is the unequal access to resources and variable quality of life due to the geographical distribution of a population and its resources. Thus, choice A is not the best answer. Choice B states that the Western portion of that city would have unequal access to health centers, which is an example of spatial inequality, making it the best answer. Choice C refers to public spaces, but that does not mean the Jim Crow laws are an example of spatial inequality, because it is not a geographical distribution of resources that leads to inequality. This is a better example of social inequality due to demographic categories, which can exist through racial discrimination. Therefore, choice C is a weak answer. Choice D is another example of inequality due to age, and thus is not the correct answer.

48. **B is the best answer.** The poor neighborhood within New York City described in the question is an example of residential segregation. Residential segregation is a type of social inequality that describes a disparity on a local scale that often is a product of race or income. Choices C and D can be eliminated because although Anna's situation prior to becoming a lawyer was due to a social inequality, this social inequality can be more specifically described as residential segregation. By overcoming her prior situation and becoming a lawyer, Anna has experienced intragenerational mobility, which occurs when an individual with limited resources rises to a new social class. Choice A is not the best answer because intergenerational mobility occurs when the children or grandchildren of a person with limited resources rises to a new social class.

Passage 9 (Questions 49-52)

49. **A is the best answer.** There are two important aspects of this question. The best answer must apply to Julia and only Julia. Because each answer choice consists of a vocabulary word followed by a description, the best answer must also have a description that adequately describes the vocabulary word. Any choice that does not satisfy both of these is a weaker choice. Julia experiences a cost barrier to education and health care that Heather does not. This inequality in access to affordable health care coverage and education prevents Julia from upward social mobility. Because she is forced to remain in the working class with insufficient coverage, her experience qualifies as social reproduction. Both criteria for a strong answer choice have been met, making choice A the best answer. Choice B describes relative poverty, in that economic status is compared to that of another group, but proposes absolute poverty as the applicable vocabulary word. Absolute poverty compares income to the determined poverty line. This choice fails to meet the second criteria of a strong answer choice. The passage does not mention societal or personal expectations of Julia or how these expectations influenced the outcome, making self-fulfilling prophecy inapplicable to Julia's experience. Choice C is therefore weaker. Choice D refers to power, which is the influence an individual has on their community. The passage does not mention Julia's ability to influence her community, making D a weak choice.

50. **D is the best answer.** The question is disguised as a generalizability question, but the true difference between answer choices is the relationship between the variables. The best answer must incorporate a relationship explicitly examined by the research in the passage. Choice A is tempting because the passage mentions that "negative health outcomes are related to... economic factors" immediately after introducing CVD. However, the relationship of these variables is never explicitly investigated in the research. Choice B is tempting because pre-medical students are likely aware of the high comorbidity of GAD and MDD, but this relationship is never investigated in the research. Choice C is tempting because HRV is the measure by which CVD is operationally defined, but again there is no mention of the measurement of this relationship in the research. The passage does indicate that "levels of depression were negatively correlated to...social cohesion", making choice D the best answer.

51. **C is the best answer.** Remember the question asks for the LEAST supported statement. The passage states that "[social determinants of health] should be addressed…also by intersectoral policy action and government". Because the passage states that SDH are the "causes of the causes", increasing the economic status of a population should decrease prevalence of mental illness. Choice A is therefore supported by the passage, and can be eliminated. Choice B suggests that increasing social cohesion will decrease negative health outcomes (a negative correlation), which is stated in the passage. Because this statement is supported, choice B can be eliminated. Choice D is tempting because it attempts to link socioeconomic status to CVD through psychiatric illness, a risky leap in inductive reasoning. The passage does imply, though, that social determinants of health are not restricted to psychiatric illness alone, they are related to mental health which is related to CVD, and the statement uses the moderating language "may reduce". Overall, this statement generally supported by the passage and can be eliminated. Choice C illustrates the correct relationship between psychiatric illness and socioeconomic status as indicated in the passage, but applies the information to children. The passage indicates that data were collected by surveying only those 18 years of age or older, making it less appropriate to use the findings to make predictions about a child demographic. This statement is less supported by the passage, making choice C the best answer.

52. **C is the best answer.** Because a specific group (the lower-class) is systematically pushed into a specific neighborhood, the example qualifies as residential segregation. The question also mentions "close proximity to [waste] disposal facilities", which brings to mind unsanitary living conditions and air quality, qualifying as environmental injustice. Neither the passage nor the question stem make reference to division of labor, allowing choice D to be eliminated. Choices A and B do not include both inequities, making choice C the best answer.

Passage 10 (Questions 53-56)

53. **D is the best answer.** Outside of group-specific interactions, people are also connected into large social networks through webs of weaker social interactions, such as friends of friends. Characteristics of individuals' social networks (embedded in place) may increase the risk of experiencing a negative life event. For example, older adults are particularly likely to experience the death of social contacts, simply because many of the people they know are also older adults. Choices A and C are not strong answers because a collection of individuals joining together to coordinate their interactions toward a specific purpose is known as an organization. Being part of an organization contributes to an individual's network, but it is not the best answer to this question. The individuals' networks are not themselves a source of error, because it is not a part of the experimental design (systematic error) or mistakes made by the researchers (random error). Thus, choice B is not a strong answer. A confounding variable is a variable that correlates (directly or inversely) with both the dependent variable and an independent variable, in a way that "explains away" some or all of the correlation between the two. Therefore, choice D is the best answer.

54. **A is the best answer.** Anomie assesses the extent to which residents report a disconnect from basic societal rules (e.g. agreeing with "Laws are made to be broken"). According to strain theory, deviance arises when there is a conflict between societal expectations and the socially condoned methods of achieving those expectations. Strain theory is commonly used to explain the motivation for crime. An individual who feels pressure because he is unable to achieve the societal expectation of economic success may decide to deviate from the socially acceptable way of gaining wealth. The experience of strain can lead to anomie, in which individuals lose their moral guidance due to the pressures of pursuing societal expectations. The subjects in poor neighborhoods, which have higher poverty rates, are not only more likely to live in a high crime area, but because of their environment (those in poverty have an insufficiency of material goods, monetary wealth, and access to resources), they experience strain and develop anomie. This makes choice A the best answer because both crime and anomie are elevated compared to the levels of crime and anomie indicated in the wealthy neighborhoods. Choices B, C, and D can thus be eliminated because either one or both crime and anomie are low compared to wealthy neighborhoods.

55. **B is the best answer.** There are many different types of discrimination, including discrimination based on sex, gender, culture, and race. Intersectionality is the compounding of disadvantage seen in individuals whom belong to more than one oppressed group. These disadvantages can lead to residence in a poorer neighborhood. According to the study findings, someone in a worse neighborhood is likely to experience more negative life events. Some of these life events will lead to health conditions. The researchers would expect a subject who belongs to less minority groups, the female, to be in better overall health, which makes choice A a weak answer. The male belongs to three minority groups: the elderly, the LGBT community, and people of African-American origin, making choice B a strong answer. Although the female may indeed belong to a higher socioeconomic status, as in choices C and D, that conclusion can not be drawn from the given information. So, choices C and D can be eliminated.

56. **B is the best answer.** The study described in the passage takes place in the United States, which is a class system. A class system includes fluidity, and it is possible for individuals of all classes to move up and down the hierarchy, known as vertical mobility. Moving up the class system is as upward mobility and is achieved through education, marriage, career, or financial success. In contrast, a caste system, in which the hierarchy of society is strictly defined, position is inherited, and movement or marriage between castes is prohibited. Downward drift hypothesis refers to the socioeconomic status of those with schizophrenia. It states that schizophrenia causes a decline in socioeconomic status, which leads to worse symptoms because people of lower socioeconomic status have less access to high quality healthcare, which sets up a downward spiral for the patient toward poverty and psychosis. This concept is not relevant to the question, which makes choice A a weak answer. Additionally, although the statement in choice A is true in a class system, it is not true for a caste system. In a caste system, life events of any type, negative or positive, would not have an effect on the residents' social status. Therefore, choice B is the best answer. Life events would not have an effect on social mobility in the given situation, which makes choice C a weak answer. Finally, it is not possible to gauge the effects of life events on horizontal social mobility using the findings of the study. Horizontal social mobility is movement between two equally ranked social positions, and so choice D can be eliminated as an answer.

Stand-alones (Questions 57-59)

57. **D is the best answer.** This question requires drawing a connection between a real world situation and a concept related to inequality and health disparities. The unequal access of resources such as breast cancer screening and treatment is most related to social exclusion, which is defined as lack of access to things that are normally available to those with greater financial resources. Choice D is therefore the best answer. Choice A can be eliminated because social capital refers to social networks that provide personal benefits. Choice B is not the best answer because cultural capital refers to non-monetary things that contribute to social mobility. In the question stem, the situation is not related to social mobility or to personal benefit, but rather to an inequality or disparity. Choice C can also be eliminated because social reproduction refers to the spread of social inequality from one generation to the next, and this question does not mention the transmission of this inequality to the next generation.

58. **B is the best answer.** The collective awareness described in the question stem is the definition of a class consciousness – making Choice A not the best answer. Choice B, a false consciousness, is the best answer because this is the failure to recognize the source of poverty, according to Marx. Choice C, absolute poverty, is a lack of essential resources such as food, shelter, clothing, and hygiene, and is not the correct answer. Choice D can also be eliminated because relative poverty describes social inequality in which people are relatively poor compared to other members of the society in which they live.

59. **C is the best answer.** Horizontal mobility describes a change in position within the same social stratum; for instance, a nurse who accepts a new position at a different hospital. Vertical mobility describes a change in position that involves an upward or downward shift in social status; one example is factory employee who is promoted to an executive position. Intragenerational mobility refers to a change in mobility that occurs within a person's own lifetime, while intergenerational mobility denotes a change in mobility over the course of two or more generations (for instance, children in relation to their parents). The answer stem describes a doctor who maintains the same professional occupation, therefore he undergoes intergenerational horizontal mobility. Though he does move from an urban to a rural setting, such a geographical change does not typically indicate a change in vertical mobility unless it is accompanied by a significant change in profession, education level, or income, so choices B and D can be eliminated. The question stem includes numerous distractors that could mislead the reader. Though the question stem mentions the Doctor's mother, it does not provide any information about a difference in status between mother and son, so any answer choice that includes intergenerational mobility can be eliminated (choice D is confirmed not to be the best answer). Although the Doctor's clientele changes, his occupation does not, eliminating answer choice B and confirming choice C to be the best answer.

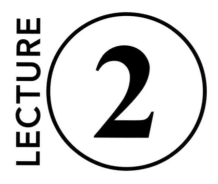

LECTURE

2

Relationships and Behavior

TEST 2A

ANSWERS & EXPLANATIONS
Questions 1–59

LECTURE 2 ANSWER KEY

TEST 2A		TEST 2B	
1. B	31. D	1. D	31. D
2. A	32. A	2. A	32. B
3. C	33. C	3. C	33. C
4. D	34. C	4. D	34. B
5. C	35. A	5. B	35. B
6. B	36. C	6. A	36. C
7. B	37. B	7. C	37. D
8. C	38. C	8. C	38. A
9. A	39. B	9. B	39. A
10. A	40. C	10. A	40. D
11. B	41. C	11. B	41. D
12. C	42. A	12. A	42. C
13. A	43. D	13. B	43. A
14. A	44. B	14. C	44. C
15. C	45. B	15. A	45. D
16. C	46. C	16. B	46. A
17. B	47. A	17. C	47. C
18. C	48. A	18. C	48. B
19. A	49. A	19. D	49. B
20. C	50. C	20. A	50. A
21. A	51. A	21. B	51. D
22. D	52. B	22. D	52. A
23. D	53. B	23. A	53. A
24. C	54. B	24. D	54. B
25. D	55. C	25. C	55. C
26. C	56. B	26. C	56. D
27. B	57. D	27. B	57. C
28. C	58. A	28. B	58. B
29. A	59. B	29. B	59. D
30. B		30. B	

EXPLANATIONS FOR LECTURE 2

Passage 1 (Questions 1-5)

1. **B is the best answer.** Classical conditioning includes an unconditioned stimulus, unconditioned response, conditioned stimulus, and conditioned response. In the study, the unconditioned stimulus was a woman vomiting. The conditioned stimulus is pea soup and a sausage roll. The unconditioned response is disgust to vomiting, and the conditioned response is disgust to pea soup and sausage roll. Choices C and D are both stimuli, not responses, so they can be ruled out. Prior to conditioning (before exposure to the conditioned stimulus), the conditioned response is not present. So, the response would not be disgust but rather no response at all. So, choice B is the best answer.

2. **A is the best answer.** Extinction is in contrast to shaping in the theory of associative learning. Associative learning involves pairing two stimuli or a stimulus and a response. It includes classical and operant conditioning. Observational learning is learning that occurs by watching and imitating. Modeling occurs in observational learning, not associative learning, so choice C and D can be ruled out. Modeling is demonstrating a behavior, whereas shaping occurs by repeated exposure. Choice B incorrectly defines shaping, so choice A is the best answer.

3. **C is the best answer.** Decreasing the frequency of a behavior occurs by punishment. Reinforcement is meant to increase a behavior. Positive and negative reinforcement refer to whether something was given or taken away, respectively. Choices A, B, and D all include option I, which is positive reinforcement that increases a behavior by giving a reward. The correct answer must be a form of punishment, so options II and IV are true, and choice C is the best answer.

4. **D is the best answer.** It is not clear what this question is asking, so deal with the answers one at a time. Eating moldy bread may be difficult for some participants, but everyone would be capable, although not willing. Choice A is probably not the best answer. Pairing the behavior to a non-aversive stimulus like sugar may help achieve the response, so choice B is probably not the best answer. The MCAT® rarely tests ethics, and choice C is too absolute with the use of the word "never." Instinctual drift is the gradual loss of a conditioned response to behaviors that are evolutionarily advantageous. Although conditioning a person to eat moldy bread is possible, the response would likely decrease over time, so choice D is the best answer.

5. **C is the best answer.** Modeling is used in observational learning, not associative learning, so choices A and B can be ruled out. In terms of research design, it is important to keep all conditions constant, so there is no bias in the research design. Using the same "model" would be the best research design, and choice C is the best answer.

Passage 2 (Questions 6-9)

6. **B is the best answer.** Mirror neurons fire both when a person is completing an action and when an individual is observing someone else complete the same action. Therefore, the death of mirror neurons would result in a lack of firing while doing an activity and watching the same activity. Option I states that there would be a lack of mirror neuron firing when an ALS patient is lifting a cup. Since mirror neurons are known to fire while the person is completing an action, option I is true. At this point, it is a good idea to look at the answer choices and eliminate answers that do not include option I; choice A can be eliminated. Option II states that if there was mirror neuron damage, the individual would not experience neuronal firing while watching someone else lift a cup. This effect would be consistent with a loss of mirror neurons. Since option II is true, choice C can be eliminated. Option III states that the individual with ALS would be able to plan a movement, and fail to execute it. Planning motor movements and carrying them out to fruition is an important central nervous system activity, but it is not one of the functions of mirror neurons. Because option III is untrue, choice D can be eliminated, leaving choice B as the best answer.

7. **B is the best answer.** It is possible to condition behaviors using continuous or partial reinforcement. In continuous reinforcement, the subject is rewarded every time the behavior is performed whereas in partial reinforcement, the reward is only given some of the time. The question stem states that the subjects only receive a reward "sometimes", which means that they are on a partial reinforcement schedule, so choices C and D can be eliminated. Within partial reinforcement there are a variety of schedules one can use. Variable-interval partial reinforcement is a schedule in which the reward is presented after an unpredictable time period has passed. Because the question stem does not indicate that the reward is administered based on timing, choice A is not the best answer. Variable-ratio partial reinforcement is a schedule in which a reward is presented after an unpredictable amount of responses, or in this case an unpredictable amount of tasks. The description of this schedule is consistent with the arrangement described in the question stem, so choice B is the best answer.

8. **C is the best answer.** Operant conditioning relies heavily on the administration of reinforcement and punishment. Reinforcement describes a consequence that increases the likelihood of a behavior, while punishment describes a consequence that decreases the likelihood of a behavior. Within these two categories, there are both positive and negative subcategories. It is important to keep in mind that the terms positive and negative have nothing to do with whether the stimulus is pleasant or unpleasant. In the passage, the behavior is patients with FTD putting themselves in social situations and the consequence is ridicule by others. The correct answer choice should therefore describe a situation in which the outcome of an action decreases a behavior. Positive reinforcement is the addition of some stimulus to increase a behavior, which is inconsistent with the information presented in the passage, and choice A can be eliminated. Negative reinforcement describes the removal of an unpleasant stimulus when the desired action is performed. The passage states that when these individuals are in social situations, they receive ridicule from others, so this would be inconsistent with negative reinforcement, and choice B can be eliminated. Positive punishment describes the administration of a negative consequence when a behavior is performed. This is consistent with the information provided in the passage because when the individuals go out (perform a behavior) they are met with ridicule (a negative consequence). Negative punishment describes the removal of a stimulus when an action is performed with the aim of reducing the likelihood of the person doing the action in the future. When the individuals are in social situations, a stimulus is added, not removed, so choice D can be eliminated, and choice C is the best answer.

9. **A is the best answer.** Providing a stimulus that will change the likelihood of future behavior is one of the central tenants of operant conditioning. Depending on the type and frequency of the reward, there are different implications for long-term behaviors. The question stem states that a reinforcement is being provided constantly with every appropriate social interaction, so it is describing continuous reinforcement. Therefore, the choice that will best answer this question is one that does not properly describe continuous reinforcement. When providing a reinforcement, it has been shown that providing partial reinforcement makes a behavior hardest to extinguish. This is because the unpredictability of the rewarding stimulus causes individuals to engage in the behavior for a longer period of time with the hopes of obtaining that reward. Choice A suggests that continuous reinforcement will be most resistant to extinction, which is untrue. So, choice A is a strong answer. A continuous reinforcement scheme has been shown to be the fastest way to elicit a change in behavior due to the predictability of the rewarding stimulus. This is consistent with choice B, so this answer can eliminated. Continuous reinforcement relies on a stimulus that makes the behavior more likely to occur. This can be positive or negative reinforcement, in the form of giving a reward or taking away something unpleasant. Choice C can be eliminated. As stated above, the concept of providing a stimulus that increases or decreases the likelihood of a future behavior is central to operant conditioning, so choice D can be eliminated. This leaves choice A is the best answer.

Stand-alones (Questions 10-13)

10. **A is the best answer.** In classical conditioning, a conditioned stimulus is a previously neutral stimulus that becomes associated with a response- an unconditioned response that turns into a conditioned response in the presence of the conditioned stimulus. Choice A is the best answer because the needle used to be a neutral stimulus eliciting no response/pain relief, but after the chronic pain patient received more injections to relieve his pain, he began to associate the needle with pain relief. The needle became the conditioned stimulus and pain relief upon seeing the needle became the conditioned response. Choice B may be tempting because the needle used to be a neutral stimulus, but it has since become conditioned. Choice C is not the best answer because an unconditioned stimulus is something that causes an innate response without conditioning. The needle cannot cause pain relief by itself with no conditioning. A better example of an unconditioned stimulus in this case may be the actual medication in the syringe rather than the needle itself because the medication is what causes the unconditioned/intrinsic pain relief. Choice D can be eliminated because both the needle and the pain relief have been conditioned at this point.

11. **B is the best answer.** Punishment is something done to decrease a behavior, while reinforcement is something done to increase a behavior. When using the words "positive" and "negative" as qualifiers in this context, they mean adding something in and taking something away, respectively. Choice A is not the best answer because negative refers to taking something away. Choice B is the best answer because in this case, Kelly's parents want to decrease the behavior of sneaking out, so they chose to punish Kelly. The punishment is positive because the parents added something- taking out the trash. Choices C and D can be eliminated because reinforcement refers to something that is done to increase a behavior. Kelly's parents want to decrease not increase the sneaking out.

12. **C is the best answer.** The patient in this question seems to be associating Caucasian physicians with a negative experience. This associative type of learning is operant conditioning. The avoidance response occurs because of a type of operant conditioning called avoidance conditioning. The negative experience is a secondary punisher that causes the patient to respond by avoiding Caucasian physicians. Choice B can be eliminated because classical conditioning is a type of learning in which a previously neutral stimulus becomes associated with an unconditioned stimulus that causes some type of innate behavioral response. In this scenario, there is no unconditioned stimulus or unconditioned/innate response. Choices A and D are also not the best answers because stimulus generalization and stimulus discrimination are part of classical conditioning. Stimulus generalization occurs when a conditioned response is elicited after a stimulus that is similar but not the same as the conditioned stimulus. Stimulus discrimination is a lack of response to a stimulus similar to the conditioned stimulus due to the ability to discriminate between the similar stimuli. Neither of these is related to the question since there the question does not mention the ability or inability to discriminate between stimuli.

13. **A is the best answer.** This question is testing the concept of indistinctive drift and innate behaviors. It is extremely difficult, perhaps impossible, to change the innate behaviors that allows an organism to thrive over the centuries. For instance, an animal may run away based on seeing a certain predictive stimulus. The stimulus could have been indicative of a predator in the wild and overtime became part of the species' biology. Due to this, choices B, C and D serve primarily as distractors from the primary concept behind the question.

Passage 3 (Questions 14-16)

14. **A is the best answer.** Look at Figure 1. The y-axis is learning index, meaning a taller bar would be improved learning and a shorter bar would be diminished learning. CT8 is always higher than CT2, so choice A is the best answer. At 5 minutes, CT14 learning is better than CT8, so choice B is not the best answer. At 5 minutes, CT20 is also higher than CT8, so choice C is not the best answer. Additionally, choice C references observational learning. The experiment is an operant conditioning experiment, which is associative learning, not observational learning, so choice C is not the best answer. Because CT8 is more likely to learn than CT2, choice D can be eliminated.

15. **C is the best answer.** In Figure 1, "5 min" is immediately following training, according to the figure title. The time when learning occurs is called acquisition in classical conditioning. This is not a classical conditioning experiment, so choice A is possible but probably not the best answer. Extinction is the time when learning is lost in classical conditioning. Choice B refers to the absence of learning and the wrong type of conditioning, so it is not the best answer. Shaping is the process of learning in operant conditioning. Choice C is stronger than choice A. Motivation is a stage of observational learning. The experiment is an example of operant conditioning, not observational learning, so choice D is not the best answer.

16. **C is the best answer.** The answer choices all touch on types of reinforcement schedules. Continuous reinforcement is essentially the absence of a reinforcement schedule. It results in rapid learning but also rapid extinction when the reinforcement stops. Choice A is a true statement and not the best answer. The function of reinforcement schedules is to modify the rate of learning and extinction, so choice B is also a true statement and not the best answer. Fixed-interval reinforcement is a very ineffective reinforcement schedule. Fixed-interval means reinforcement is given at fixed intervals of time. For example, if a person is training a dog to "sit" using treats, the dog will only be given a treat for sitting if a predetermined interval of time has passed, e.g. 2 minutes. This would be very frustrating for the dog because any attempts to "sit" prior to 2 minutes would not be rewarded. Choice C is a false statement and likely the best answer. Variable-ratio reinforcement is when a reward is given after a variable number of responses. Using the dog example, the dog may be rewarded for sitting back-to-back but then may not be rewarded for sitting until he sits three more times then four more times then two more times. This schedule delays learning but is very resistant to extinction because the dog learns that sitting will eventually lead to a reward, even if he cannot predict when. Choice D is a true statement and not the best answer.

Passage 4 (Questions 17-20)

17. **B is the best answer.** The smoking studies mentioned in paragraph 2 examine how the association between an auditory tone (neutral stimulus) and cigarettes (unconditioned stimulus) can be trained. The studies are focused on acquisition, the stage of learning over which a conditioned response to a new stimulus is learned, so therefore choice B is the best answer. Extinction refers to the loss of a conditioned response, so choice A is not the best answer. Spontaneous recovery refers to the reappearance of a conditioned response after a period of extinction, so choice C is not the best answer. The passage does not discuss the generalization of the conditioned responses to differentiated stimuli, i.e. differently-pitched variations of a tone, so choice D is not the best answer.

18. **C is the best answer.** An unconditioned stimulus (US) refers to a stimulus that can elicit an innate physical or behavioral effect without learning. The cue was not an US because in this experiment, associative learning was necessary for the audio-visual cue to elicit a response, so choice A is not the best answer. The US in this study would be methamphetamine. A conditioned stimulus is the result of a classical conditioning learning process, so that does not describe the audio-visual cue at the beginning of the experiment. Therefore choice B is not the best answer. At the beginning of the experiment, the audio-visual cue can be classified as a neutral stimulus because it should not produce an innate response from the participants. During the course of the experiment, after multiple pairings with methamphetamine (US), the audio-visual cue was also able to elicit a similar response, so choice C is the strongest answer. As mentioned, the audio-visual cue is at no point an unconditioned stimulus because it cannot elicit these observed responses without learning. Therefore, choice D is not the best answer.

19. **A is the best answer.** This question refers to the following hypothesis in the passage: drug-associated cues can elicit a variety of responses believed to facilitate drug-seeking behavior and elicit relapse in recently abstinent individuals.. Choice A is the only example that implies a conditioned response and provides a situation parallel to the drug-seeking hypothesis: after seeing the logos of familiar food chains (a cue associated with unhealthy food), the individuals experienced a conditioned desire to consume the food. In the smoking cessation example, the graphic ad campaigns condition an aversion to the drug. Though this program involves learning an association between the negative images and the use of cigarettes, it does not support the idea that conditioning can strengthen drug-seeking behavior. In fact, it shows the opposite effect. Therefore, choice B is not the best answer. Choice C reflects the importance of peer pressure and norms, which are sociological concepts that do not directly involve associative learning. The hypothesis in question focuses on the process of associative learning, so choice C is not the best answer. Choice D is an example of an unconditioned physical response to abstinence from alcohol, not a conditioned response. Therefore, choice D is not the best answer, and choice A is the strongest answer.

20. **C is the best answer.** When the researchers choose to use healthy young adults instead of participants with a history of drug use, they are eliminating factors other than the independent variable of interest that could confound the results. External validity refers to the ability for a result to be generalized to other contexts. By using blank-slate participants, researchers actually increase the generalizability of the observed UR by eliminating confounding factors such as drug tolerance. In addition, choice A lists the unconditioned response (UR) as the subject of study, but these experiments are studying the conditioned addiction response (CR). Therefore, choice A is not the best answer. Stimulus generalization is the appearance of CR to stimuli that are similar to the conditioned stimuli (CS). In this case, an experiment to test stimulus generalization would look a bit different from the experiment in paragraph 3, using a number of similar audio-visual cues to observe the CR. Internal validity is the study's ability to meaningfully measure results of interest, and, because this research design is not intended to observe stimulus generalization, internal validity has not decreased. In fact, it has increased due to the decrease in confounding variables involved in the conditioned response. Therefore, choice B is not the best answer. Previous cycles of acquisition, extinction and spontaneous recovery weaken the conditioned response, so a history of drug use confounds the relationship between the independent variable of interest (number of trials) and the dependent variable (level of CR.) By choosing healthy participants with no previous associations with drugs, the studies are trying to minimize confounding variables. So, choice C is the best answer. Stimulus discrimination refers to the gradual ability of participants to differentiate between two or more similar neutral stimuli (NS) that have or have not been paired with an US. Using *de novo* subjects does increase the controlled variables, but the increase in controlled variables does not help with studying stimulus discrimination. The study mentions only one type of audio-visual cue, so stimulus discrimination is not being tested with this research design. Therefore choice D is not the most relevant answer, and choice C is the stronger answer.

Passage 5 (Questions 21-25)

21. **A is the best answer.** The first paragraph refers to how smoking urges can be paired to certain situations. This is most suggestive of associative learning via classical conditioning or operant conditioning. This likely makes choice A the best answer. Kinesthetic learning would be learning to perform a task such as riding a bike. The mice were not performing a task, so choice B is not the best answer. Observational learning would be more relevant to smoking urges being triggered by seeing someone else smoke, so choice C is not the best answer. Classical conditioning and operant conditioning are both types of associative learning. Between the two, classical conditioning is the best answer because smoking has been paired to a stimulus, making smoking the conditioned response and the location the conditioned stimulus. Operant conditioning occurs with reward and punishment. Smoking does activate the reward centers in the brain, but this concept does not explain why smoking is paired to a certain location. Choice A is the best answer.

22. **D is the best answer.** Recall that CPP is conditioned place preference. A neutral stimulus would be one that does not trigger the urge to smoke. Smokers often smoke in and around bars, so choice A is not a strong answer. The passage specifically mentions smoking in the car, so choice B is not a strong answer. A smokers' lounge would certainly be associated with the urge to smoke, so choice C is not a strong answer. It would be fairly difficult to smoke in the shower, since the water would probably extinguish the cigarette. Choice D would not be associated with the urge to smoke and is a neutral stimulus.

23. **D is the best answer.** The unconditioned stimulus is one that naturally leads to the unconditioned response. In the experiment, the unconditioned stimulus is the light chamber and the unconditioned response is avoidance. The knockout mice experience both, so choices A and C can be ruled out. The conditioned stimulus is nicotine exposure, and the conditioned response is preference to the light chamber. The nicotine exposure occurs in the knockout mice, so choice B is not the best answer. According to Figure 1, the knockout mice did not prefer the light chamber because they spent ~30% of their time in that chamber (the non-preferred chamber). The mice were not conditioned, and choice D is the best answer.

24. **C is the best answer.** Nausea would probably result in avoiding nicotine. Addiction would cease, so choice A is not the best answer. Acquisition is the process of learning a behavior. This occurred in the experiment in the passage and in the question stem. However, the question stem is asking about the reversal of acquisition, so choice B is not the best answer. Extinction is the term used for the reversal of acquisition, so choice C is a strong answer. Recovery is when acquisition occurs again after extinction. Choice D is not the best answer.

25. **D is the best answer.** Internal validity is the degree to which a study generates a causal relationship by minimizing bias. This concept is relevant to the question stem, but check that the rest of the answer fits as well. The study not being applicable to humans is a problem for external validity. Choice A does not pair the correct definition to internal validity, so it is not the best answer. As stated, external validity is the degree to which a study can be generalized to a population. The ethics of euthanasia are not relevant to external validity, so choice B is not the best answer. Publication bias is present when performing meta-analyses. Studies that show statistically significant results are much more likely to be published. When a meta-analysis is performed, the studies that show no correlation are rarely included, as they were never published. This idea is unrelated to the mice being genetically identical, so choice C is not the best answer. Confirmation bias is the bias toward rejecting the null hypothesis when there is not enough evidence. If the mice are not genetically identical, genes other than *NR1* may have biased the results, so the causal relationship between *NR1* and nicotine CPP cannot be determined. Choice D is the best answer.

Stand-alones (Questions 26-29)

26. **C is the best answer.** Vicarious emotions are the feelings of another individual as one's own. Even though the woman is not actually experiencing something sad, she feels the characters' emotions onscreen, so choice C is the best answer. Observational learning is not occurring because there is no reason to assume the woman is learning anything from watching the character cry, so choice A can be eliminated. An innate behavior is developmentally fixed in a species, and not every individual may cry while watching the same scene, so choice B is not the strongest answer. Depression is a psychological disorder that involves prolonged periods of feeling sad or disinterested in life. Since the woman is only crying during a short movie scene, her behavior is not characteristic of depression, so choice D can also be eliminated.

27. **B is the best answer.** The decreased perception of a stimulus on repeated exposure is known as habituation. Sensitization is the exact opposite of the process, so choice A is not the best answer. Dishabituation is very similar to sensitization except dishabituation is a recurrence to baseline. Choice C is not the best answer. Learning is the process of obtaining knowledge. The child did not learn about the sweater, so choice D is not the best answer.

28. **C is the best answer.** Aggression is an advantageous trait to a certain extent, after which it would harm survival because of increased risk of death. This concept is most similar to the graph in choice C. Choice A shows a direct relationship between aggression and survival. This would not be the case because aggression would eventually result in an increased probability of death. Choice B shows an inverse relationship between aggression and survival. This is also inaccurate because an animal with very low aggression would likely be killed by a more aggressive animal. Choice D shows a parabolic relationship between aggression, which is the opposite of choice C and is not the best answer.

29. **A is the best answer.** Grooming does not require a social group and our ancestors were not particularly concerned with hygiene. The mental image of apes taking bugs out of each others' hair was not for the purpose of grooming but for food. Choice A is a possible answer. Mating requires at least one other person and preferably a larger group of people so the next generation is not forced to inbreed. Choice B is not the best answer. Defense requires a large group of people with some serving as lookouts and others protecting the home, so choice C is not the best answer. Foraging was an activity that was important in the formation of early social groups. Having more people forage increased the likelihood of finding food and sustaining the needs of the group. Choice D is not the best answer.

Passage 6 (Questions 30-34)

30. **B is the best answer.** The last paragraph provides information that helps answer this question. It describes studies that show males from LMICs may have discriminatory practices that enhance gender discrimination. Aggression towards women may be one such discriminatory practice, eliminating choice A. Altruism consists of behaviors that are disadvantageous towards the individual acting, but confers benefits to other members of the social group, which could include girls. Males that enhance gender discrimination are unlikely to display altruistic behavior towards women, making choice B the best answer. Mate choice is the process by which individuals attempt to judge genetic qualities, overall health, and potential parenting skills when choosing a partner. It is likely that males are still choosing particular spouses via this process, eliminating choice C. Attachment consists of forming relationships between people. Males in LMICs are forming relationships, though these relationships may not always be built on equality. Choice D can be eliminated.

31. **D is the best answer.** All of the answers are examples of communication that might occur between two people that express attraction. However, the question specifically refers to which of the following are unlikely to be nonverbal. Choices A, B, and C all involve actions that do not use words, eliminating them as possible answer choices, as they are nonverbal communications. Choice D specifically references words, making it a verbal, not nonverbal communication.

32. **A is the best answer.** Observational learning occurs when one witnesses another person's actions, retains information on that person's behavior, and later re-enacts what was learned through that observation in one's own behavior. In addition, male members of older generations are likely to have the respect of the younger generations, leading to greater rates of observational learning. If older generations teach responsible and respectful interactions between men and women, it is likely that these behaviors would be emulated by those watching. Choice A is likely the best answer. Telling someone, but not modeling the behavior, might be a way to reduce gender discriminatory practices, but would be less effective than demonstrating the behavior. Choice B is less likely than choice A to be the best answer. Mandating the behavior by requiring a certain proportion of jobs be filled by female applicants, or laws banning certain behaviors are less likely than observational learning to change behavior. Choices C and D can be eliminated.

33. **C is the best answer.** The question stem suggests that each month, boys will receive monetary compensation for not using drugs. A fixed-ratio reward is given after each specific number of responses, such as the number of times the boy would turn down drugs. This is not a time-specified interval, eliminating choice A. The payment is not made after an unpredictable number of responses, decided by the person enforcing the reinforcement, eliminating choice B. A fixed-interval reward is given after a set amount of time, which, in this case, is one month. Choice C is most likely to be the best answer. A variable-interval reinforcement would reward a response after an unpredictable time interval. The time interval is set to one month in the question stem, eliminating choice D.

34. **C is the best answer.** This question asks about designing a study that would help researchers identify some societal influences that might highlight reasons for gender discrimination. A longitudinal survey may help identify some reasons that might change over time, but notice only a few men and no women are included in choice A. This study would be unlikely to find a majority of influences, as only one gender and few members of that gender participate. Choice A is unlikely to be the best answer. While more individuals are included in the study in choice B, the question stem does not ask about designing a trial that would highlight the effect of a particular intervention. Choice B does not answer the question, eliminating it as a possible answer. A cross-sectional survey of many men and women at one time-point would be able to help identify causes in both personal and professional life that might impact achieving gender equality. Choice C is most likely the best answer. While 300 women are included in the study in choice D, no men are included, and the women are only asked specifically about child-rearing activities. The exclusion of one gender from the study and specificity of the questions asked would not allow this longitudinal questionnaire to address the purpose of the study suggested by the question stem. Choice D can be eliminated.

Passage 7 (Questions 35-38)

35. **A is the best answer.** Inclusive fitness is the ability for one's genetic information to pass to the next generation, especially though non-offspring relatives. This study does not relate to the passing on of genetic material. The fact that more money is earned is possibly relevant to inclusive fitness, since money is a resource and more money would allow greater likelihood of passing on genetic information. Occasionally, the MCAT® makes very loose connections like this, but the question can usually be answered another way. The best way to tackle this question is to rule out answer choices that are inaccurate. In the study, the fair choice grants more money overall, so choice A is true and choice B can be ruled out. For choices C and D, there is no reason to believe one group is more evolutionarily prone to a certain behavior. Choice A is the only possible answer.

36. **C is the best answer.** Capitalism is a system where industry has private owners and is profit oriented. Sharing is more associated with socialism, so choice A is not the best answer. Choice B refers to socialism but does not quite fit because the question stem is not an example of socialism. Sharing is merely a term associated with socialism. Choice B is possible but may not be the best answer. Informal social control is a means by which a government controls its citizens through social norms. This is applicable to the question where the norm is sharing. Choice C is a strong answer and a better fit than choice B. Free will is the ability to choose a course of action. This is not applicable to the question, so choice D is not the best answer.

37. **B is the best answer.** The dramaturgical approach encompasses the back-stage and front-stage self, so choices A and B are on the right track. Choices C and D do not relate to the dramaturgical approach, so these can be eliminated. The front-stage self is the one that a person presents to others, whereas the back-stage self is the true self. Under this definition, choice B is the best answer, because a person would not present his back-stage self to the researchers.

38. **C is the best answer.** All of the biases listed are potential issues for any research study. The acquiescence bias is the "yes man" bias where, in a survey, respondents are much more likely to answer "yes" than "no." This study was not a yes or no survey, so choice A is not the best answer. Confirmation bias is the tendency to reject the null hypothesis when there may not be evidence to do so. The research presented was not statistically significant, so the null hypothesis was not rejected and confirmation bias could not occur. Choice B is not the best answer. Social desirability bias is the tendency to behave in the way that is considered socially acceptable. In this study, it would favor the fair choice. This certainly could have been an issue in this study and would mean one cannot generalize the results to other situations, so choice C is a strong answer. The sponsor bias is the tendency for respondents to favor the sponsor of a survey when asked about the sponsor's products. Choice D is not relevant.

Passage 8 (Questions 39-43)

39. **B is the best answer.** The question stem associates a particular behavior, drinking, with a particular action, vomiting. In Pavlov's conditioning, the unconditioned stimulus is paired with an unconditioned response. In this scenario, the unconditioned stimulus would be disulfiram, the conditioned stimulus would be the alcohol and the response would be vomiting. Choice A is a possible answer but a major problem is that the disulfiram is not paired with the alcohol ingestion. Disulfiram is taken prior to ingestion of alcohol and only causes vomiting if alcohol is ingested. The unconditioned stimulus should elicit a response on its own but disulfiram does not, so choice A is probably not the best answer. Operant conditioning is a type of associative learning, where an individual is aware of the consequences of an action and modulates behavior based on the frequency of the consequences of the action. The person taking disulfiram would likely be aware of the consequences, making choice B a strong answer. Extinction is the loss of learning following conditioning, so choice C is not the best answer. Spontaneous recovery is the reemergence of a behavior after extinction, so choice D is not the best answer.

40. **C is the best answer.** The question stem notes that individuals that do not smoke receive monetary compensation from their insurance companies for maintaining better health behaviors. This is an example of a reward but be sure to double check the remaining answers for the best answer. A punishment would negatively affect a behavior. It is unlikely that receiving compensation would be a negative, eliminating choice B. A secondary reinforcement is a reward that does not necessarily harness physiological needs and the drive for survival like primary reinforcers, but they can become equally effective at reinforcing behavior once the response becomes conditioned. Choice C is a more specific reward applicable to the question stem, compared to choice A, making it more likely to be the best answer. Primary reinforcement is a physiological need, of which money is not. Some examples of physiological needs include food and water, but not necessarily abstract ideas like money. Choice D can be eliminated.

41. **C is the best answer.** Modeling is part of observational behavior. By reviewing the results of a survey, the student is not directly interacting with the participants, so he or she is unlikely to directly observe their behavior directly. Choice A can be eliminated. Observational learning can involve direct and indirect interactions. The student may be learning from the results of the survey via an indirect manner, but the remaining answer choices should be considered. Vicarious emotions encompass feeling the emotions of others as though they are one's own. A student that also feels lonely and hopeless when reviewing the study questionnaires may be trying to learn from the successes and mistakes of others through an indirect observational approach. Choice C is a more specific descriptor of the observational learning that is occurring in the question stem, making it more likely to be the best answer than choice B. Nonverbal communication involves the conveyance of thoughts without the use of language. The survey would likely use written forms of language, eliminating choice D.

42. **A is the best answer.** It is not entirely clear what this question is asking, as it presents multiple forms of official organization. The iron law of oligarchy criticizes the hierarchical nature of bureaucracy, stating that the people at the top of the hierarchy come to value their power over the purpose of the organization. Officials that may illegally import cigarettes, even though it is against the law of the country, would be exerting their influence to obtain contraband items above the law. Choice A may be the best answer. Formal organization describes specific rules and guidelines, but is not specific to any form of government, making choice B less likely than choice A to be the best answer. Perspectives on bureaucracy is the general category that encompasses oligarchy, collective thinking, McDonaldization, among others. Choice C is too general compared to choice A to be the best answer. An ideal bureaucracy would not involve government members attempting to subvert the laws of their own government for personal gain or desires. Choice D can be eliminated.

43. **D is the best answer.** A cross-sectional study involves a portion of the population that is hopefully representative of the population as a whole. A study that identifies individuals that may use drugs that are normally illicit may help identify people that have strong addictive behaviors, but the other answer choices should be considered. Tracking alcohol use over time may not necessarily illuminate individuals that have substance abuse challenges, eliminating choice B. Testing a drug may help show individuals that have substance abuse issues, but would not be specific to this population, eliminating choice C. Smoking is highly correlated with self-esteem, weight, and body image issues. Choice D is the best answer, as it would overlap with the similar population.

Stand-alones (Questions 44-47)

44. **B is the best answer.** A collection of individuals joining together to coordinate their interactions toward a specific purpose is known as an organization. Organizations that have specific rules and guidelines are referred to as formal organizations. A bureaucracy is a specific type of formal organization with a particular focus on efficiency and effectiveness. The requirements of an organization do not specify a number of group members. Thus, choice A can be eliminated. All members of an organization, by definition, are working towards a common goal. Thus, choice B is a strong answer. Although organizations could perhaps be registered with governmental organizations, this is not a requirement of organizations. Thus, choice C can be eliminated. Placing an emphasis on workplace efficiency may indicate that the workplace is a bureaucracy, which is a type of formal organization. However, choice B more explicitly lists the fundamental quality of organizations: sharing a common purpose; thus, choice D can be eliminated and choice B is the best answer.

45. **B is the best answer.** A formal organization is an official organization with specific rules and guidelines. Bureaucracies are a specific type of formal organization with a particular focus on achieving the organization's main goals through efficiency and effectiveness. Ideal bureaucracies are typically highly-specialized and organized in a clear hierarchical manner. The Iron Law of Oligarchy criticizes the hierarchical nature of bureaucracies by suggesting that, with due time, the leadership will focus on maintaining their power more than achieving the organization's goals. If the methods to remove these "higher-ups" are excessively difficult, this would be consistent with the Iron Law of Oligarchy, and as such once could expect this to occur in a bureaucracy. Thus, choice A can be eliminated. A hierarchical structure is typically an integral part of a bureaucracy, and it is very unlikely that this structure would be removed. Thus, choice B is unlikely to occur, making it a strong answer choice. Bureaucracies are typically impersonal and impartial in order to prevent distractions from getting in the way of the organization's goals. Thus, it would make sense that employee training would emphasize leaving emotion out of decisions, allowing for choice C to be eliminated. Because efficiency is a crucial aspect to the definition of a bureaucracy, it is very likely that employees would rank this as their number one priority, allowing for choice D to be eliminated. As the only remaining answer choice, choice B is the best answer.

46. **C is the best answer.** A bureaucracy is a type of formal organization which has a focus on efficiency. Purchasing plants to increase morale is an example of increasing efficiency and is consistent with becoming a more ideal bureaucracy, eliminating choice A. Preventing store managers from making decisions on bathrooms is an example of increasing the emphasis on specialization. Specialization is a trait of ideal bureaucracies, eliminating choice B. Bureaucracies have clear hierarchies. By consolidating levels of control through the promotion of regional managers, the hierarchy and extent of specialization is minimized, bringing the company farther away from being an ideal bureaucracy and making choice C the best answer. Redirecting sponsorship money could be in the name of optimization. While the question does not explain this in terms of efficiency, it does not bring the company away from being a more ideal bureaucracy, like choice C, eliminating choice D.

47. **A is the best answer.** Showing teeth has a very different meaning in animals and humans. In humans, it is a sign of happiness, in animals it is a sign of aggression. Choice A is a very strong answer. Ovulatory pheromones are important for reproduction in the animal kingdom and are thought to exist in humans as well. These pheromones always have the same meaning, so choice B is not the best answer. Head tilts are behaviors that indicate confusion or curiosity in both animals and humans, so choice C is not the best answer. Playing fetch is an activity that is not performed by humans, so choice D is not the best answer.

Passage 9 (Questions 48-51)

48. A is the best answer. Microsociology is defined as the study of direct human social interactions, while macrosociology is more focused on bigger picture interactions. Both choices A and B are strong answers as they are both concerned with microsociological measurements. Primary groups consist of an individual's close friends and family. Secondary groups tend to consist of more distant social relationships. As primary social groups include an individual's closest friendships, choice A is the most correct answer. Choice B is tempting, but the question stem better reflects a primary social group friendship. Choices C and D can be eliminated as the study was primarily based on microsociology.

49. A is the best answer. Individuals tend to act in accordance to certain behavioral principles when attempting to impress those within a given social network. Choice A is the best answer as impression management is defined as "the process of consciously making behavioral changes to create a specific impression in the minds of others. The dramaturgical approach and use of a backstage self are closely related processes that refer to how an individual acts differently to satisfy certain individuals. While choice B could be correct, it is not specific enough to directly answer the question. Choice C, while tempting, is not the best answer as an individual would likely use an "on stage" self to enhance their perceived rating from another individual. Group polarization refers to a process that effects the decision making of groups. Choice D refers to another aspect of group interactions that is not being tested in the question stem and therefore can be eliminated.

50. C is the best answer. A group is defined as two or more individuals interacting with one another in a social setting. Smaller groups are labeled as dyads if contain two members or triads if they contain three members. Scientific investigations are also impacted by error which can influence the accuracy of the results. Accuracy is a measurement of how well the collected data matches the true nature of the subject being investigated. To answer this question, it is important to realize that self report data is typically influenced by biases present in the participants. As the data is being recorded by the participants, choice A can be eliminated. Choice B, while tempting, is incorrect as groups of two members would be defined as a dyad. Choice C is the best answer as it correctly defines the group categorization and influence self report would have on the investigation. Choice D is the antithesis of choice C and can be eliminated as self report would have a final impact on the data collected.

51. A is the best answer. The trend shown in Figure 1 is a directly proportional relationship. As mutuality increases amongst participants, the chance of two individuals rating one another similarly on the survey also increases. However, the question is asking to identify where an outlier might occur along the curve. As these two individuals have few mutual friends but rated one another similarly, the point would have a low value on the X axis but a high value on the Y axis. This makes choice A the best answer, as the point shown best fits this criteria. Choice B shows a point with both a low X and Y value and can therefore be eliminated. Choices C and D both occur along the curve and can be eliminated.

Passage 10 (Questions 52-55)

52. B is the best answer. The final paragraph describes the experiments that occurred. They showed that, when surrounded by peers, students were less likely to cheat unless many peers were cheating. The best answer must have both principles apply to the experiments. Social facilitation is the tendency for individuals to perform better when in a group than when alone. This seems relevant to the experiment, except that the experiment focused more on moral ethics of test taking, not actual test taking performance. Obedience is the tendency to follow the rules, or more specifically, to obey another person. The students did eventually cheat, so obedience did not occur. Choice A is a possibility but there is likely a better answer. Stigma is the shame associated with a particular behavior. It is likely stigma that prevents cheating when in a peer group. So, choice B is at least partly accurate. De-individualization is the tendency to behave differently in a group than when alone. De-individualization explains why a student would cheat when surrounded by students whom are cheating. Choice B is stronger than choice A. The bystander effect is the tendency to not offer help when in a large group due to the assumption that someone else will help. This is not relevant to the experiment, so choice C can be eliminated. Social loafing is the tendency to "slack off" in a group. This is also not relevant, so choice D can be ruled out, and choice B is the best answer.

53. B is the best answer. Each answer choice is a type of status. Embodied status is the status that is guided by physical appearance. Lower class people do not all have one particular appearance, so choice A is not the best answer. Ascribed status is the status in society that is inherited by a person. Embodied status is a subtype of ascribed status, but ascribed status also includes ethnicity, socioeconomic status, and other factors. Choice B is a strong answer. Achieved status is the earned status. This is not determined by his upbringing, but rather his work ethic and education. Choice C is not the best answer. Master status is that status that is most important for an individual at a given time. The master status is almost always the achieved status, as it would be for this student. Choice D is not the best answer.

54. **B is the best answer.** Role conflict is when a person is expected to maintain two incompatible roles. The student in the question stem is only expected to maintain one role—that of a student—so choice A is not a strong answer. Role strain is when a behavior is incompatible with a role. This is the case with the student whose role as a student is incompatible with his or her poor grades. Choice B is a strong answer. Role exit is the process of leaving a role. The student is not dropping out of school, so choice C is not a strong answer. Role clarity is when a person clearly knows what is expected in a role and achieves those expectations. It can be thought of the opposite of role strain, so choice D is not the best answer.

55. **C is the best answer.** Emotional support is empathy, concern, and caring. It is often provided by a parent or spouse. This type of support may be provided by a mentor. Choice A is a possible answer. Tangible support involves provision of needs, such as money or shelter. This would not be provided by a mentor, so choice B is not a strong answer. Informational support is support through advice and mentorship. This is exactly the support provided by a mentor, so choice C is a strong answer. Companionship support is support from a family or group of friends that helps a person feel a sense of belonging. This would not be provided by a mentor, so choice D is not the best answer.

Stand-alones (Questions 56-59)

56. **B is the best answer.** Pregnancy and parturition (the act of giving birth) are both only performed by women. It is hypothesized the change occurs so that women can ignore social cues in order to care for their child, e.g. a mother will not be bothered by scowls and sighs from fellow passengers on an airplane with her and her crying infant. The change is believed to be hormonal, so the use of exogenous hormones may confound study results and choice B is the best answer. Education level should not be relevant to a study on recognition of social cues although it is a common confounding variable. Choice A is not a bad answer, it just is not as strong as choice B. Likewise, age is a common confounder, but choice C is not as strong as choice B. The score on a measure of expression interpretation would be the dependent variable in the experiment and is not a confounder, so choice D is not the best answer.

57. **D is the best answer.** Status is usually based on socioeconomic status. The best answer should improve her wealth or apparent wealth. Baking cookies is a nice gesture, but it does not improve her wealth, so her status is likely unchanged. Choice A can be eliminated. Planning a trip to the Caribbean may increase her apparent wealth, so choice B is a possible answer. Getting married could certainly increase her wealth, but the question does not indicate that she is marrying a rich man. So, choice C is not the best answer. Having a pool installed is a sign of wealth, and her friends would likely want to visit to use the pool. Unlike the vacation, this would be a sustained improvement in her status in the group, so choice D is the best answer.

58. **A is the best answer.** Casey increases her fitness, or ability to pass on genes to future generations, by raising her nephew because they share some genetic makeup. One way to remember this concept is that *including* family members increases one's own *fitness*. Social support involves finding help through social connections and Casey is not necessarily finding help by adopting her nephew. Choice B is not as strong as choice A. Because Casey is not the individual mating or reproducing, but rather raising her sibling's child, choices C and D can be eliminated.

59. **B is the best answer.** Altruism, by definition, consists of behaviors that are not advantageous to the individual performing them, but helpful to the social group. Choice B is the best answer then. Aggression, on the other hand, could prove beneficial to an individual if he/she wins a competition or reward. Choice D is not as strong as choice B. Attraction and attachment involve drawing members of a species together, which would be advantageous to the individual because he/she receives help from other individuals. By forming more bonds with other members of the species, the individual has the best chance of surviving and thriving. Choices A and C can be eliminated.

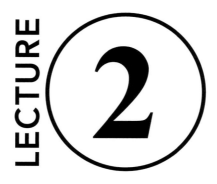

LECTURE

2

Relationships and Behavior

TEST 2B

ANSWERS & EXPLANATIONS
Questions 1–59

Passage 1 (Questions 1-4)

1. **D is the best answer.** The study is attempting to identify how social behavior influences obesity within groups. The passage notes that previous research has shown this social contagion to be particularly strong within married couples, and as such, the researchers sought to conduct this study on these individuals. The researchers looked at two potential mechanisms for how this social-spreading of obesity could work: (1) respondents are influenced by their partners' obesity-related behaviors (tested in paragraph 2), and (2) respondents are acting in ways to mirror their partners' body sizes, which was called the normative body size hypothesis (tested in paragraph 3). The researchers found much more support for the former mechanism, given the significant correlations discussed in paragraph 2 compared to the non- or less-significant correlations found in paragraph 3. Although there was correlation between the married couples' obesity-related behaviors, choice A is far too black-and-white. Moreover, this wording implies causation by noting that these identical obesity-related behaviors are the cause of the body congruence amongst couple. These analyses described in the passage only note correlations, and as such, a causative conclusion cannot be drawn. Thus, choice A can be eliminated. Choice B states the findings found in paragraph 2 very well, except for the fact that it mentions that the body congruence "is due to" behavioral influences. Again, this answer is a far too definite conclusion and infers causation that cannot be drawn from the analyses. Thus, choice B can be eliminated. Choice C represents information that was already known prior to the study. The researchers knew about the social contagion, and they were attempting to find a mechanism for it by conducting this study. Thus, choice C can be eliminated. Choice D mentions a potential behavior modelling mechanism. Behavior modelling is a type of observational learning wherein a person (a respondent) witnesses another person's (their partner's) actions, retains these actions, and later re-enacts what he/she has learned through observation via their own behaviors. This effectively describes the findings in paragraph 2. Additionally, by using "may," choice D does not imply a definitive causation. Thus, choice D is the best answer. As a test-taking tip, because choice D uses "may," it is less absolute than the other choices, potentially making it a more favorable answer choice. As a broad rule-of-thumb, when stuck between two answer choices, looking the less absolute (or more general) answer choice is an effective strategy.

2. **A is the best answer.** A group is a set of individuals who interact with each other and share some elements of identity. The two smallest groups are dyads and triads. A dyad is a two-person group, whereas a triad is a three-person group. It is important to note that dyads and triads are typically both examples of a primary group, which is characterized by relatively permanent relationships that are particularly intimate. A friend of both the respondent and the partner could potentially create a triadic group if the respondent and the partner have remained in close contact with the friend since they met. At this point, choice A is a potentially strong answer. The respondent's father is likely to have a relatively permanent relationship with the respondent, but it is less likely that the father holds a permanently intimate relationship with the partner. Thus, choice B can be eliminated. It is possible that a long-time neighbor could make up a relatively permanent and intimate relationship, but it is more likely that this is true of a childhood friend than of a neighbor. Thus, choice C requires more inference than choice A, and as such, choice C can be eliminated. A co-worker would likely not represent an intimate relationship, but it would portray a more goal-oriented relationship. Thus, choice D can be eliminated. As the only remaining answer, choice A is the best answer.

3. **C is the best answer.** Mating behavior is a type of social behavior surrounding the propagation of a species through reproduction. Mating behavior theory encompasses the motives underlying how an individual of a species choose their mates, and it posits that mate choice is determined by a number of factors, including attempts to judge the genetic qualities, overall health, and potential parenting skills of the potential mate. The study describes married partners, and because it is likely that married partners will reproduce, one could apply mating behavior theory to explain why a respondent would choose a particular partner. Looking attractive could potentially indicate favorable genetic qualities, but choice A is not explicit in mentioning this and requires some inference. Thus, choice A is a weak answer. Perceiving a prospective mate as being able to protect both oneself and offspring would certainly fall in line with the notion of mate choice. At this point, choice B requires less inference than choice A, allowing for the elimination of choice A. Choice B will remain as a potential answer. Assessing the genetic makeup and prospective parenting ability of the partner are two key components to mate choice theory. Because choice B only references one of these components (parenting ability), while choice C references two components (genetic makeup and parenting ability), choice C is a stronger answer than choice B, and as such, choice B can be eliminated. Mate choice theory makes no indication of the social influences of mass media. Thus, choice D can be eliminated. As the only remaining choice, choice C is the best answer.

4. **D is the best answer.** Social norms are expectations that govern what behavior is acceptable within a group. Sanctions are expressions of approval for conforming to these norms or, conversely, expressions of disapproval for not conforming to these norms. It is important to recognize that, although the everyday usage of "sanction" carries a negative connotation similar to that of a "punishment," sanctions can be both signs of approval or disapproval. Refusing to speak to a partner could indicate disapproval for failing to conform to a norm, but choice A gives no definitive indication as to what this norm may be. Thus, choice A can be eliminated, as it requires too much inference past what is provided in the question stem to be true. By purposely choosing to not work out with the partner, the respondent is certainly showing some negative emotions towards the partner, but again there is no indication that this behavior is due to failure to comply to a social norm. Thus, as with choice A, choice B requires too much inference past what is provided to be true, and as such, choice B can be eliminated. By choosing to exercise every time the partner does, the respondent is more-or-less copying the behavior of the partner. Copying a behavior is not indicative of approving/disapproving a social norm; thus, choice C can be eliminated. By smiling at his/her partner in recognition that they returned from the gym, the respondent is conveying a sign of approval to the partner. Although one must infer that it is a social norm within the relationship to exercise in order to read this gesture as a positive sanction, this requires far less inference than would be required for choices A and B to be true. Thus, choice D is the best answer.

Passage 2 (Questions 5-8)

5. **B is the best answer.** A primary group is a specific type of group that involves relatively permanent relationships that are not formed with a particular goal in mind, such as relationships with close friends or family members. This does not describe members of a sports organization, thus choice A can be eliminated. Secondary groups are another specific type of group, except members of a secondary group form relationships that are more goal-oriented and probably would not have formed in the first place if the individuals did not originally meet in the secondary group. Members of the same sports organization would likely fit this explanation, making choice B a strong answer. Networks are larger webs of social interactions, such as friends of friends. A person does not need to have physical interaction with someone in their network; they just need to be connected to them in some way through someone they know. Members of a sports organization are too "close-knit" to be accurately described as a social network, thus choice C can be eliminated. A group is defined as a set of individuals who interact with each other and share some elements of identity. A group is a broader classification than both a primary group and a secondary group. Thus, although choice D is not incorrect, choice B is more specific, and as such, choice D can be eliminated , making choice B is the best answer.

6. **A is the best answer.** First note that besides separating the subjects into groups as described in paragraph 3 of the passage, there is no mention that the researchers attempted to control for level of exercise amongst the subjects. Thus, if it is true that members of the EA group exercised significantly more than members of the AP group, it is likely that the EA group could be experiencing extra health benefits relative to the AP group. These extra health benefits would translate to a lower risk for functional disability, thus a lower HR. However, if the level of exercise was in fact controlled for, the aforementioned relative health benefits of the EA group would decrease, translating to a higher HR than reported in paragraph 5. Thus, choice A appears to be a strong answer. Significant variations in the numbers of subjects within experimental groups could potentially limit one's ability to draw reliable conclusions from a study. While there were more subjects in the EA group than the AP group, there is no indication from the passage that this would affect the HR level of the EA group. Moreover, there is also no indication that this variation affected the significance of the results. Thus, choice B can be eliminated. If the subjects of the EA group were in fact predisposed to incident functional disability, one would expect the EA group to have a lower HR than was reported in paragraph 5, not higher. Thus, choice C can be eliminated. Ideally, in order to assess the health benefits of organization participation, the only difference between the EA group and the AP group should be participation in a sports organization. If the EA group and the AP groups were in fact performing different exercises, then this presents a failure in an experimental control. This could lead one to conclude that the HR levels indicated in paragraph 5 are not 100% accurate, but it gives no indication as to which direction the actual HR of the EA group is relative to the reported value. This answer choice is less specific than choice A, which does imply a specific direction. Thus, choice D can be eliminated due to its lack of specificity in relation to choice A, and choice A, as the only answer remaining, is the best answer.

7. **C is the best answer.** A fad is an example of collective behavior that organizations often display. A fad by definition must rise and fall in popularity relatively quickly. The last sentence of paragraph 4 describes sports organization members reporting wearing some aspect of a uniform, indicating that the group members are participating in a type of collective behavior. Although knowing the length of time that the group members wore the uniform would be useful in classifying this collective behavior as a fad, this information would give no indication to the rise-and-fall nature that is required by the behavior to be classified as a fad. Thus, choice A can be eliminated. It does not matter what aspects of an organization uniform were worn in order to classify the behavior as a fad. In other words, members of the AP and PP groups could report collectively wearing socks, hats, jerseys, or even a full uniform, but without any knowledge of the rise-and-fall nature of the collective behavior, it cannot be known if it is defined as a fad. Thus, choice B can be eliminated. Knowing when the members started and stopped wearing a uniform could in fact allow the researchers to elucidate a rise-and-fall nature in the collective behavior. After collecting responses, if researchers see a strong temporal pattern in uniform wearing that rises and falls relatively quickly, perhaps then researchers could classify this behavior as a fad. Choice C is a strong answer even though it only references the PP group, which reported wearing aspects of a uniform to a lesser degree than that of the AP group. Understanding why members of a group wore a uniform gives little insight into whether the collective behavior is a fad. Thus, choice D can be eliminated, making choice C the best answer.

8. **C is the best answer.** Role exit is when an individual stops identifying with a particular role. This can happen due to role strain and/or role conflict. Role conflict occurs when two or more roles that an individual plays have conflicting requirements. The coach's role as a coach requires him/her to play the players with the best athletic ability, but the coach's role as a friend requires him/her to not hurt the friend's feelings. By choosing not to play the friend, the coach is experiencing conflicting requirements within his/her two aforementioned roles. Thus, option I describes a scenario consistent with role conflict. This could potentially lead to role exit, making option I a component of the best answer. Role strain is when the demands of a single role become overwhelming. The coach is likely to be overwhelmed by the persistent pressure, straining his ability to maintain his role as a coach. Option II thus describes a scenario consistent with role strain. This could potentially lead to role exit, making option II true. At this point, because options I and II are true, choices A and B can be eliminated. If the coach were to accept the lucrative offer to coach for a different team, the coach would still be in his/her role as a coach and no role exit would occur. Thus, option III is not true, and choice D can be eliminated. As the only choice not eliminated, choice C is the best answer.

Stand-alones (Questions 9-12)

9. **B is the best answer.** The iron law of oligarchy states an inevitable outcome of a hierarchical organization is that the people at the top of the hierarchy will eventually focus more on maintaining their power than attaining the organization's goals. If organization owners were to enforce rules more strictly, then perhaps this could make it more difficult for organization members to remove the owners from power. This makes choice A a potential answer. If it became excessively burdensome to replace upper management, the people at the top of the hierarchy would with almost certainly have an easier time maintaining their power. This is consistent with the prediction of the iron law of oligarchy, making choice B a strong answer. At this point, choice B is a stronger answer than choice A, as choice A requires more guesswork in order to ascertain that upper management is having an easier time maintaining their power. Thus, choice A can be eliminated. Having members of an organization quit due to disagreements with the owners does not directly imply that the owners are focusing more on maintaining their power than attaining the organization goals. Thus, choice C can be eliminated. Likewise, a fact about merging with two other sports organizations does not imply anything about the intentions of the organization's top-hierarchy members, allowing for the elimination of choice D. As the only remaining choice and as a strong answer, choice B is the best answer.

10. **A is the best answer.** Football games are usually full of spectators, so this performance can be attributed to social facilitation, which occurs when people perform better while being watched. Choice B can be eliminated because social loafing relates to decreased performance in a group setting. Choice C is not the best answer because group polarization relates to attitudes of groups becoming stronger than those of individual members. The question stem does not mention attitudes of football players, nor does it mention the distinction between the individual and the group. While it is possible that teammates would push each other to perform better via peer pressure, choice D is not as strong as choice A because the question stem does not imply that the players are pushing each other to perform better. The question stem implies that the enhanced performance is related to being in a game where more people are watching versus being at practice where there are less people.

11. **B is the best answer.** The question is asking about which term applies to the "mob mentality". The correct term is deindividuation. The bystander effect is the tendency for onlookers to not act if other onlookers are present- seemingly assuming "someone else will handle this". This is a possibility in riots, but the question asks about those participating in the riots- not onlookers, so choice A is not the best answer. Deindividuation is the process of losing oneself in a group and acting in a way that one wouldn't outside the group. This is a major component of mobs and riots, so choice B is a strong answer. Inclusive fitness is a distractor that in no way relates to the question. It describes the evolutionary fitness of a group of animals that is achieved by adults caring for young that are not their own. Choice C can be ruled out. Self-presentation is how a human presents himself to a group. This is not as applicable to a mob as choice B, so choice D is not the best answer.

12. **A is the best answer.** A folkway is an unwritten rule in society that governs behavior in casual social situations. It can be paralleled to "manners". The scenario in choice A violates the idea of personal space, an unwritten but socially agreed upon behavioral rule. Choice B is an example of a taboo, a behavior that is considered prohibited by society. Taboos carry far greater social consequences than folkways and cannot be explained away by circumstances. For instance, cannibalism, even in the face of starvation, is considered an unacceptable behavior. Choice C is weaker because recycling would not be considered a social behavior and therefore would not be governed by folkways. Choice D is tempting because tardiness is often understood to be an inappropriate behavior regardless of whether or not timeliness is an official rule. This scenario is complicated by the idea of "fashionable lateness", which could make this behavior acceptable or even expected, making choice D weaker.

Passage 3 (Questions 13-16)

13. **B is the best answer.** Study 2 found that patients in a support group were more likely to adhere to treatment than those not in a support group. The researchers' interpretation of this is that being in a support group causes patients to modify their behavior to impress other group members. Choice A is not the best answer because groupthink relates to the idea that group members will agree in order to avoid group discordance. This does not relate to modification of behavior to impress others. Choice B is the best answer because impression management can be defined as consciously changing a behavior in order to make a specific impression on another person or persons. Choice C may be tempting because social facilitation relates to the tendency of an individual to perform better when others are watching; however, social facilitation is not a *conscious* changing of behavior for the purpose of impressing someone. Social loafing relates to the tendency of an individual to decrease performance in a group setting because he/she feels that other group members will do the bulk of the work. This is unrelated to the question stem, so choice D can be eliminated.

14. **C is the best answer.** When a person has anxiety or concern about a negative stereotype, this is called stereotype threat. In the question stem, the diabetic patients who expressed concern about stereotypes are experiencing stereotype threat. Choice A is not the best answer because individual discrimination occurs when one person acts negatively toward another person because of his/her membership in a certain group. The question stem never mentions the act of active discrimination, only the fear of stereotypes. Choice B can also be eliminated because individual discrimination is not caused by nor directly causes a stereotype threat. Choice C is the best answer because stereotype threats can lead to self-fulfilling prophecies if someone makes the negative stereotype a reality. This is exactly what happens in the question stem- the diabetic patients experiencing a stereotype threat made the stereotype a reality by being more overweight on average than those patients not experiencing stereotype threat. Choice D is not the best answer because stereotype threats lead to self-fulfilling prophecies, not the other way around.

15. **A is the best answer.** Study 2 found that diabetic patients who are part of support groups are more likely to be compliant with their treatments than diabetic patients not part of a support group. New members of diabetic support groups are likely modeling their behavior (treatment adherence) after the existing members who are compliant to medications. This is most consistent with choice A. Choice B can be eliminated because operant conditioning is based on positive or negative consequences that occur after a behavior. Support groups do not necessarily provide direct consequences for behaviors. Choice C is also not the best answer because classical conditioning involves developing a behavioral response to a previously neutral stimulus. This is unrelated to the concept of support groups. Spontaneous recovery is related to classical conditioning, so choice D can also be eliminated.

16. **B is the best answer.** This question requires going back to the passage and looking for definitions of the different tests used. For choices A and B, the Morisky Test was used to measure medication treatment adherence. For choices C and D, the Diabetes Self-care Activities Questionnaire was used to measure adherence to diet and exercise recommendations. The question stem asks about medication treatment adherence only, so choices C and D can be eliminated. Choice A can be eliminated based on the respective definitions of conformity versus obedience. Conformity refers to changing behaviors to match group behaviors. Obedience refers to changing behavior due to being commanded by someone in authority. Choice A mentions a scenario of obedience—adhering to treatment after being commanded by a physician—before a scenario of conformity—adhering to treatment because the that it the norm in a support group. This is the opposite order required by the question stem. Choice B is the best answer because it mentions conformity then obedience just as the question stem asks.

17. **C is the best answer.** A stereotype is a concept about a group or category of people that includes the belief that all members of that group share certain characteristics. The question stem indicates that a stereotype of chronically-diseased individuals is that they have difficultly performing strenuous exercise. The participants from the follow-up study have long-term conditions, and thus would likely be included in this stereotype if they were to join a group exercise class. A role is a person's expected set of behaviors in a social setting. A person can have multiple roles, and when the expected behaviors of these roles interfere with each other, a person is said to experience role conflict. The passage does not state the expected behaviors of the participants in relation to exercise, and as such, the roles, and subsequently any role conflicts, of the participants cannot be ascertained from the passage. Thus, choice A can be eliminated. Peer pressure is the social influence exerted by one's peers to act in a way that is acceptable or similar to their own behaviors. The question stem does not indicate whether the other individuals within the group exercise classes are attempting to influence the behaviors of the participants. Thus, choice B can be eliminated. Stereotypes can be positive, negative, or neutral. Negative stereotypes about a group in which a person belongs to can induce anxiety and can subsequently impair performance. It is possible that the participants feel threatened by the negative stereotype of chronically-diseased individuals and are experiencing anxiety due to this stereotype. This anxiety could potentially result in lowered emotional well-being scores. Thus, choice C is a strong answer. Socialization is the process by which people learn customs and values of their culture. The various modes by which socialization can occur are referred to as agents of socialization. The question stem does not indicate that individuals within the group exercise classes are learning customs or values, and as such, agents of socialization are not present. Thus, choice D can be eliminated, allowing for choice C to be the best answer.

18. **C is the best answer.** Note that the question is more-or-less asking for knowledge of what makes up a formal organization. A collection of individuals that join together to coordinate their interactions toward a specific purpose is called an organization. Official organizations with specific rules and guidelines governing behavior are known as formal organizations. The definition of a formal organization does not specify a number of required individuals. Moreover, choice A does not mention if the organizations cited have specific rules and guidelines. Thus, choice A can be eliminated. The workplace could constitute a formal organization, but there are many other formal organizations that participants could possibly be a part of. Only including the workplace involvement could misrepresent the intended independent variable: formal organization involvement. Thus, choice B can be eliminated. Network members from goal-oriented groups with clear rules governing behavior are certainly network members within formal organizations. This designation would better represent formal organization involvement. Thus, choice C is a strong answer. While organizations registered with the government could represent formal organizations, there are many other potential formal organizations that the participants could be a part of. Thus, choice D can be eliminated, allowing for choice C to remain as the best answer.

19. **D is the best answer.** Game theory is the use of mathematical models to represent complex decision making in which the actions of other group members are taken into account. An individual applying game theory would first consider the actions (or "moves") of other people (or "players"), and then act in a way that maximizes his/her reward in lieu of the other players actions. Participants that always take medication on time would be maximizing their health but would not be taking into consideration the actions of other people. Thus, this does not represent an application of game theory, and as such, choice A can be eliminated. Although maximizing "reward/move ratio" is indicative of maximizing reward, this does not indicate whether or not the actions of others were taken into consideration. Thus, choice B can be eliminated. Note that choice B uses common terminology used in the context of games (namely, the word "move") as a distractor. Although applying game theory is an attempt to optimize one's decisions, optimizing between cost and emotional well-being does not imply that the actions of others have been considered. Thus, choice C can be eliminated. Participants that first determine the likelihood of others providing care before caring for themselves would be applying the game theoretic approach, as these participants are considering the actions of other group members before deciding upon their own actions. Thus, choice D is the best answer.

20. **A is the best answer.** Social loafing occurs when members of a group decrease the pace or intensity of their own work with the intention of letting other group members work harder. Social loafing could result in less total work being done if other group members do not compensate for the individual that decreased his/her workload. If a positive relationship was discovered between illness work and emotional well-being, it follows that, if the magnitude of illness work were to decrease, then participant emotional well-being is likely to decrease as well. Social loafing in participant social circles would result in less illness work being done, since members of the social circles would decrease their quantity of illness work and expect other group members to compensate. Thus, reported emotional well-being is likely to decrease. At this point, choices C and D can be eliminated, as they indicate that emotion well-being will increase. Group members expecting others to fully care for the participant could decrease their illness work via social loafing. Thus, choice A is a strong answer. The concept of social loafing does not indicate whether or not group members expect anything in return. Thus, choice B can be eliminated, and choice A is the best answer.

21. **B is the best answer.** A group is defined as a set of individuals who interact with each other and share some elements of identity. Primary groups are a specific type of group characterized by relatively permanent relationships among a small number of people, such as families and close friends. Secondary groups are characterized by impersonal relationships among larger groups that are typically more goal-oriented and less permanent than primary groups. A co-worker could potentially have a relatively permanent relationship with a participant, but this requires one to infer past the information that is provided. Thus, choice A remains as a weak answer. A co-worker is, however, very likely to represent a more goal-oriented relationship that is less permanent than a relationship with a family member. Thus, a co-worker is likely part of a participant's secondary group, allowing for choice B to be a strong answer. At this point, choice A can be eliminated because choice B is a stronger answer. Social networks are weaker webs of social interactions outside of the individual's day-to-day interactions, such as friends of friends. Co-workers are likely seen regularly by participants at the workplace, and as such, describing a co-worker as part of a social network would underrepresent how often the participant does in fact interact with the co-worker. Moreover, describing the co-worker as part of a secondary group is far more specific than that of a social network. Thus, choice C can be eliminated. Bureaucracies are a specific type of formal organization particularly focused on efficiency and effectiveness. A participant could be employed by a bureaucracy, but this requires a good deal of inference. The participant could just as likely work at a local pizzeria, ice cream shop, or other non-bureaucratic entities. Thus, due to its lack of specificity, choice D can be eliminated, allowing for choice B to remain as the best answer.

22. **D is the best answer.** Figure 1 displays a positive relationship between the number of relationship types that a participant has and the participant emotional well-being score. This positive relationship is visible across both age groups and long-term disease groups. It is important to note that this figure is displaying the number of different relationship types and not the quantity of individuals within a particular individual's network. Choice A correctly indicates the positive relationship, but it does not indicate the number of different relationship types as the driver of this positive relationship. Thus, choice A can be eliminated. In order to determine which age group experienced a greater effect from increased number of relationship types, one would have to determine the difference between the peaks of the colored bars and the peaks of the white bars. It is not obvious that this difference is greater for the older participant group, nor is it explicitly mentioned in the figure. Thus, choice B can be eliminated. Figure 1 is measuring emotional well-being. While one could easily infer that greater emotional well-being would benefit CHD and diabetes patients, it is important to appreciate that the results of this figure are not making this inference. The results are just reporting emotional well-being. Thus, choice C can be eliminated. A participant's "network" includes all of the individuals he/she may be connected to via webs of social interactions. The first paragraph of the passage indicates that the relationship types indicated in this question are within the participants' networks. Thus, diversity in webs of social interaction is analogous to saying diversity in a participant's network, which would indicate a greater number of relationship types. Figure 1 indicates that number of relationship types is positively correlated with emotional well-being. Although choice D only mentions a correlation and not a positive correlation, choice D is not incorrect, and the other answer choices have been eliminated. Thus, choice D is the best answer.

Passage 5 (Questions 23-26)

23. **A is the best answer.** Impression management is a socialization process in which an individual attempts to influence others' perceptions of the individual. An individual who is purposefully changing his test results in order to appear "exceptional", such as the one in choice A, would be demonstrating a form of impression management. Choice B is referring to Yerkes-Dodson law, which details the relationship between arousal and performance. This relationship is unconscious, and thus probably not applicable to impression management. Choice C is the application of the concept of group polarization, which states that decisions made in a group, compared to individual decisions, are more extreme. This choice is more related to decision making, which is not an aspect that was tested in this experiment. Choice D applies to the concept of conformity, which is the decision to act in accordance with a social group or attitude. This is possibly the second best answer, as an individual might conform as a form of impression management, in order to fit in with a group. However, conformity is not necessarily always a form of impression management, so choice D is not the best answer.

24. **D is the best answer.** This question is asking about the details of classical conditioning vs. operant conditioning. The experiment detailed in the passage is most likely operant conditioning, as there is no reflexive movement involved; additionally, there is only one stimulus involved. Choices A and B are both terms related to classical conditioning, and can be excluded from consideration. Choice C is not the strongest answer , as positive punishment would be the addition of something undesired by the subject. Therefore, choice D is the best answer. Removal of something painful would be considered as negative reinforcement, reinforcing the behavior of pressing a switch.

25. **C is the best answer.** This question tests the reader's thorough understanding of conformity. Conformity can be defined as acting in accordance with the attitudes and opinions of a larger group. In general, conformity can be thought of as acting and thinking the same. Choice A is tied the concept of conformity; peer pressure is a common social phenomenon that causes people to give in to a group's specific behaviors and norms. Choice B is a psychological phenomenon, in which a group's opinions become uniform, due to a desire for group harmony. Choice C, on the other hand, refers to the improvement of one's performance due to the presence of others. While this concept does involve grouping, individuals do not end up thinking or acting the same due to social facilitation. Because of this, choice C is the best choice. Choice D, deindividuation, is when individuals lose their individual identity and mindset when placed in a large group. Choices A, B, and D are all related to people acting or thinking the same, and are related to the concept of conformity.

26. **C is the best answer.** Cultural relativism can be defined as the practice of trying to understand a culture on its own terms, and to judge a culture by its own standards. Choice C is the best answer, as it takes into account other culture's values and cultural norms. For instance, imagine if having hairy arms were normal and encouraged in a different culture. If a person from this culture were being tested, the fake hairy arm would not have the desired effect of making the participant feel uncomfortable. Changing other factors, such as skin tone, would be additional ways of utilizing cultural relativism to improve the study. Choice A might seem like a tempting subject, as it involves focusing on one culture alone. However, cultural relativism generally involves more than just isolating a culture and studying it in a vacuum; it often deals with how a culture should be understood through its own lens, rather than the lens of another culture. Choice B, while accounting for cultural differences in pain perception and the effect of the rubber hand illusion, does not really integrate the concept of cultural relativism. Choice D would be an action taken if researchers doubted the construct validity of using temperature as a measure of overall pain threshold. This option is minimally related to culture and is not the best answer.

Stand-alones (Questions 27-30)

27. **B is the best answer.** In this scenario, the individual faces two separate power dynamics: as a patient, they are expected to defer to the knowledge of a physician. As a payer, they are a client and expect a service to be carried out. Because the physician and patient perceive the role of the patient differently in this scenario, the patient faces role strain or conflict, two synonymous concepts. Choice A is not the best answer because while the physician is in two different roles, it is the patient who faces psychological harm from this dichotomy. Choice B is a strong answer because the patient is experiencing role strain. Choice C is not the best answer because the patient does not lose a role; instead he gains an additional role. Choice D is also not accurate, because the physician does not change their treatment of the patient due to their preconceived notion of illness.

28. **B is the best answer.** The scenario in the question stem describes a situation where an individual is changing his behavior due to the command of an authority figure. Conformity does not best describe this situation because conformity describes a change in behavior to fit in with social norms. Jason does not enroll in these classes to fit social norms, he does so because his boss has commanded him to by threatening his job, eliminating choice A. Obedience is a behavior change that is the result of a command from someone in a position of authority. Therefore, choice B accurately describes the scenario in the question stem. Socialization is the phenomenon of learning social norms and expectations through others. Since Jason failed to learn social norms of the workplace through others in this scenario, choice C can be eliminated. A punishment is a stimulus that decreases the likelihood of a behavior. Although Jason's boss issued him a warning about his behavior, he did not give Jason a punishment, eliminating choice D and leaving choice B as the best answer.

29. **B is the best answer.** Groupthink is the phenomenon in which the options a group considers are limited because members do not express as many "outside-the-box" perspectives for the sake of maintaining group solidarity and conformity. The illusion of unanimity in decision can lead the group to settle on a less desirable conclusion. Choice A refers to power dynamics. Although unequal power distribution may lead group members to hold back opinions that are different than those of the most powerful group member, it represents the influence authoritative members have on behavior, whereas groupthink refers to the effect of group membership itself. Choice C refers to in-group and out-group biases. This phenomenon is observed in group dynamics, but it is an observation specifically on how groups consider other groups. Groupthink deals with group thought and problem solving more generally, and is not limited to perceptions of other groups. Choice D is tempting because it is similar in appearance to choice B, but remember groupthink occurs when members do not express dissenting opinions in favor of maintaining solidarity, making choice D a weaker answer. Choice B is the best answer because it appropriately names a circumstance that will lead to the phenomenon defined while reading the question stem.

30. **B is the best answer.** The question stem describes a situation in which individuals each have vague ideas that become stronger beliefs following an interaction with a group. Groupthink describes a phenomenon where members of a group tend to think alike and agree for the sake of harmony. The question stem does not directly indicate that members thought alike or agreed in order to maintain accord within the group, so choice A is not the best answer. Group polarization occurs when, through the interactions and discussions of the group, the attitude of the group as a whole toward a particular issue becomes stronger than the attitudes of its individual members. This is consistent with the description provided in the question stem as each individual came in with vague ideas and the result was a list of policies that were more rigid than the ideas of any of the individual members. Peer pressure is the social influence exerted by one's peers to act in a way that is acceptable or similar to their own behaviors. There is no indication in the question stem that peer pressure occurred, so choice C can be eliminated. The bystander effect describes a phenomenon that occurs in a large group when members fail to offer assistance because they assume someone else will do it. This does not best describe the situation in the question stem, so choice D can be eliminated, leaving choice B as the best answer.

Passage 6 (Questions 31-34)

31. **D is the best answer.** The passage states that "Figure 1 displays data obtained from analysis of the entire sample." Choices A and B only draw a conclusion about either low or high risk-takers alone, so they can both be eliminated. Next, the difference between peer pressure and conformity is tested. Peer pressure refers to the influence that others have that encourages a change in behavior, beliefs, and attitudes. Conformity is the act of conforming to the norms of that other group or person. The best answer involves recognizing that it is the influence and presence of peer pressure that causes an increase in the subjective value of Passing, which is the successful outcome , making choice C a weak answer. The best answer will include the entire sample (both high and low risk-takers) and also correctly attribute an increase in the subjective value of the desired outcome to peer pressure, and not conformity. Thus, choice D is the best answer.

32. **B is the best answer.** A sample is a subset of people, items, or events from a larger population that you collect and analyze to make inferences. The complete sample includes both the high and low risk-taking 18-19 year old male adolescents whom took part in the study. Choice A excludes low risk-takers from the sample, which makes it a weak answer. The developmental stage the subjects are experiencing is the Formal Operational stage. The third and fourth stages in Piaget's Stages of Cognitive Development are the Concrete Operational stage and Formal Operational stage. The Concrete Operational stage lasts from about 7 to 11 years of age. In this stage, children can engage in logical thought as long as they are working with concrete objects. The subjects are all at least 18 years old, and so would have progressed into the Formal Operational stage. This stage is marked by the ability to think logically about abstract ideas. Choice B identifies the correct sample and stage, making it the best answer. A population is a collection of people, items, or events about which you want to make inferences. The population being studied is 18-19 year old male adolescents in the U.S. Choices C and D switch the definitions of sample and population, so they can be eliminated.

33. **C is the best answer.** Groupthink is the concept that individuals stifle their ideas in a group to achieve consensus, which can lead to poor decision-making as a group, making choice A is a weak answer. Group polarization is the tendency to make more extreme decisions when in a group. Choice B does not describe what occurred in the question stem, so it is not a strong answer. The situation presented in the question stem describes conformity. Conformity is the phenomenon of adjusting behavior or thinking based on the behavior or thinking of others. This is what happened once the subjects observed the behavior of the confederates (people pretending to be subjects but actually have their behavior pre-determined by those conducting the study). Therefore, choice C is the strongest answer. Lastly, a social more is a social norm that is widely observed and is considered to have greater moral significance than other norms, which is not applicable to the question. Thus, choice D is a weak answer.

34. **B is the best answer.** Under social pressure, the adult experiences equal brain activation (and thus satisfaction) given both a Pass and Crash outcome. Even though adults are less affected than adolescents, we would still expect some effect that favors Passing due to peer competition, making choice A a weak answer. The graph in choice B most closely mimics the adolescent's brain activation when manipulated by the social factor, but the Pass outcome under peer competition results in less activation in the adults, and presumably, less satisfaction due to a favorable outcome. This answer best fits the findings of the study on adolescents, and correctly applies the additional information revealed in the question stem about the effect of peer pressure on adults. The Pass outcome in choice C results in higher activation without social pressure applied, and this does not fit the broad findings of the study, so choice C can be eliminated. The Pass outcome under social pressure in choice D results in higher activation in the adult than in adolescents, the opposite of what the researchers found in the question stem, making choice D a weak answer.

Passage 7 (Questions 35-38)

35. **B is the best answer.** Although this question sounds like it does not rely on the passage, using the information in the passage is the key to answering this question. The amygdala is part of the limbic system and is involved in emotion. There is no information in the passage about emotion, so choice A is not the answer. Mirror neurons are involved in observational learning and are activated when a behavior is observing and performing a certain learned behavior. In the passage, participants have to sync their movements with another person. This may activate mirror neurons, so choice B is a strong answer. Broca's area is involved in speech. The passage focuses on nonverbal interactions. Like choice A, choice C is not clearly related to any information in the passage, so choice C is not the best answer. The brainstem is involved in alertness and other automatic functions. If the brainstem was damaged in people with schizophrenia, they would have extensive problems and may be in a coma. Choice D is not specific to the deficits seen in patients with schizophrenia. Choice B is the best answer.

36. **C is the best answer.** Schizophrenia has a strong biological basis. The greatest evidence that a disease is biological is that monozygotic twins share the disease more frequently than do dizygotic twins. However, dizygotic twins should also share the disease more frequently than complete strangers. Option I correctly states that monozygotic twins have the greatest concordance and applies a finding of the study. Option I is correct, so choice B can be ruled out. Option II states that dizygotic twins have a high rate of concordance and applies a finding of the study. Option II is also true, so choice A can be ruled out. Non-twin siblings should still have an increased risk of schizophrenia in a biological model. Remember, non-twin siblings and dizygotic twins, statistically speaking, share the same amount of DNA, but dizygotic twins have a more similar environment. So, option III is incorrect, and choice C is the best answer.

37. **D is the best answer.** This question is really testing the definition of a control group. In general, a control group is a group that lacks the independent variable and thus should not show any result in the dependent variable. In this study, the control group does not have schizophrenia and thus should not have impaired social behavior. Choices A, B, and C all describe types of social behavior, but none of them should be impaired in the control group, so choice D is the best answer.

38. **A is the best answer.** Only one of the answer choices correctly defines a group process. Group polarization is when the attitudes of the group become more extreme, or polarized, than the attitudes of the individuals alone. Choice A is the best answer. The bystander effect is when onlookers in a crowd fail to help a person in need, likely because they assume someone else will help. Choice B incorrectly defines the bystander effect and is thus not the best answer. De-individualization is when people forget their individuality and become immersed in the attitudes and behaviors of the group. Choice C incorrectly defines de-individualization, so it is not the best answer. Social loafing is when members of a group work less than they would on their own. Choice D incorrectly defines social loafing, so it is not the best answer.

Passage 8 (Questions 39-42)

39. **A is the best answer.** Choice A is a good choice because the experimental size of 52 participants is a relatively small sample size and makes it hard to generalize about how the whole population would respond to the study. Also, the participants in the study are all university students which also makes it difficult to generalize to the demographics of a broader population. CRT is a task used to measure aggressive behavior. This is one of the things that the study is looking at relating to BP and ingroup/outgroup variance, therefore, choice B can be eliminated because the use of the CRT task was not ineffective. Experimenters are looking at how the blood pressure changes for various groups of participants. Because they are looking at this change, the SBP as a dependent variable is unavoidable. This is not a problem in the experimental design and therefore does not pose a threat to external validity. Choice C, therefore, can be eliminated. Personal accounts are not a useful way to collect or review data in a scientific study, therefore, Choice D can be ruled out.

40. **D is the best answer.** The group that had the highest SBP level is the ingroup with least reaction to the deviant. This can be seen on the Y axis of Figure 2 with the solid, declining line starting at 118 SBP. The SBP level here is higher than all other levels, this group had the largest margin of change in their blood pressure. The pattern is the same in outgroup non-deviates, as seen on the Y axis of Figure 2 with the dashed, declining line starting at 112 SBP, but there was a less dramatic difference in the SBP levels. A is not the best answer because it is hard to determine whether BSE did, indeed, directly affect the blood pressure. While blood pressure was a correlating factor, it is impossible to say from the information given if the blood pressure directly affected the BSE. It is important not to confuse correlation with causation. Choice B can be ruled out because the graph shows that the ingroup deviants in fact have a lower SBP than the non-deviants. Notice that the third point on the ingroup (solid) line shows that those with a higher than normal reaction to the deviant had lower SBP levels. Choice C can be ruled out because the graph shows\ that the outgroup deviants also have a lower SBP than the non-deviants. Observe this by looking at the third point at the outgroup (dotted) line and noticing that those with a higher than normal reaction to the deviant had lower SBP levels.

41. **D is the best answer.** The question is asking about SBP on an individual level and also addresses the psychological and physiological relationship of stress and blood pressure in the answer choices. On an individual level one cannot generalize about blood pressure comparisons, the question asks about specific participants and not the averages of participant scores. Therefore, the best answer will address what you can assert from an individual not the whole group. In Choice A while it is true that SBP was higher in participants who did not deviate this does not mean that on the individual level all non-deviates will always have higher SBP levels. Additionally, while it is true blood pressure is usually known to have a complementary relationship with stress (more stress, higher blood pressure), the first part of the answer means choice A can be eliminated. Choice B can be eliminated because it misinterprets group SBP levels as individual SBP levels. While it is true that has a whole SBP was always higher in participants who did not deviate, the individual SBP levels are not presented so this assertion cannot me made. The biological phenomena in the second part of this answer is correct but choice B is not the best answer because of the error in the first part of the answer. Choice C states that non-deviates have higher SBP levels which is not supported by the data. Again, it is true that increased blood pressure is linked to stressful behavior but the first part of this answer causes the entirety to not be the best choice. Choice D is the best answer because it explains that blood pressure is individual and these individual values cannot be determined by the averages supplied, therefore it is not reasonable to assume that any participant who does not deviate will always have higher blood pressure. The physiological truth that is present in the three other answers is not present in this answer but it is still the best choice because it addresses the issue of individual vs. averaged data.

42. **C is the best answer.** Group polarization occurs when, through the interactions and discussions of the group the attitude of the group as a whole toward a particular issue becomes stronger than the attitudes of particular members. This does not address whether interactions with divergent members or non-members therefore choice A is not the best answer. Deindividuation occurs when people lose awareness of their individuality and instead immerse themselves in the mood or activities of a crowd. While this is related to the actions of a whole group, it addresses when an individual becomes completely immersed in the group and not interactions with divergent members or non-members therefore choice B is not the best answer. Ethnocentrism is the belief that one's group is of central importance and includes the tendency to judge the practices of other groups by one's own cultural standards. If ingroup members are worried about their cultural identity they are more likely to judge their members more harshly, therefore, they care more about divergent ingroup members than outgroup members. Choice C is a strong answer. Socialization refers to the process which people learn customs and values of their cultures not how they treat divergent members, therefore, choice D can be eliminated.

Stand-alones (Questions 43-46)

43. **A is the best answer.** This question is vague and difficult to answer but process of elimination is helpful. The first sentence is actually just meant to distract, no knowledge of this test is required to answer the question. Subconscious bias is very difficult to overcome but cognitive skills can be used to overcome it. Choice A is possible. Prejudice is often race or gender specific so choice B is not a strong answer. Racial bias is probably age specific so choice C is a possible answer. Racial bias is certainly a problem in present society so choice D can be ruled out. Between choice A and choice C, choice A is a stronger answer. Choice C is too absolute, with use of the word "always".

44. **C is the best answer.** Remember that a stereotype is the belief that all members of a group share certain characteristics. This belief can be positive, negative, or neutral—no matter what, it is always a generalization. This belief about one nationality is not particularly good, because positive qualities are not attributed to the group. Choice A can be eliminated. Similarly, the generalization is not negative because there are not negative connotations associated with enjoying the taste of rice. Choice B can also be eliminated. This is an example of a neutral stereotype so choice C is the best answer. Stereotype threat refers to the anxiety caused when an individual feels a negative stereotype directed towards him/her. Since this situation does not apply to Ashley, choice D is not the best answer.

45. **D is the best answer.** Choice A is an agent of socialization, something that helps develop an individual's personal beliefs, attitudes, and behaviors. Likewise, choice B, radio, is another agent that helps inform individuals on specific aspects of society, and help shape individual's social persona. Religion, choice C, is social institution that can be a heavy influencer on an individual's set of personal beliefs. Emotion is not an agent of socialization, so choice D is the best answer.

46. **A is the best answer.** Deviance is defined as the choice to not follow social norms, and that is exactly what the student in the question stem is doing. While it may not be an explicitly stated rule that people are forbidden from tearing pages out of library books, people generally recognize that this behavior is inappropriate. This trust that people will stick to socially acceptable behaviors is how many public institutions such as libraries are able to operate. Thus, choice A is the best answer. Choice B is not the most fitting answer because Antisocial Personality Disorder is a bit too specific of a definition for this example. While it is true that someone with Antisocial Personality Disorder may engage in behavior that violates social norms, the broader term of deviance encompasses all non-normative behavior, regardless of whether or not it is pathological. Choice C is not the best answer because the back stage self has little to do with non-normative behavior. The back stage self is a version of the self that does not follow specific conventions that may be necessary to convey a certain impression to a literal or figurative 'audience'. Lastly, Choice D is simply a distracting answer that has no relevance to social norms. Foraging behavior is the term for the behavior that animals engage in when they are finding and acquiring food.

Passage 9 (Questions 47-52)

47. **C is the best answer.** The study looks at a group of individuals from the HRS population and assesses their weight status relative to various types of discrimination. Although the study focuses on weight discrimination, Table 2 shows that age, sex, and race discrimination are more prevalent among the HRS population, so choice A can be eliminated. The passage states that the only type of discrimination that was associated with increased risk of becoming obese is weight discrimination, so choice B is not the best answer and can be eliminated. The finding that weight discrimination is associated with future obesity suggests that the lowered expectations and stress that accompany the negative stereotype associated with being overweight may actually be contributing to the problem; more people are becoming obese after being discriminated against due to their weight. Choice C is therefore supported by the passage, because weight discrimination may lead to a self-fulfilling prophecy of more weight gain. It is important to note here that even though choice C is the best answer, with any research study, there is always the possibility that a 3rd, confounding variable is actually responsible for the outcome. Be cautious of these hidden variables when determining causal relationships in research. This study design did a good job exploring other potentially confounding variables like race, age, and gender. In-group and out-group mentality can be a major contributor to bias. In-group describes a group to which a person belongs and feels loyalty, while out-group describes a group to which the individual does not belong. Although this can lead to bias and stereotypes, there is no direct evidence to suggest that weight discrimination is due to in-group mentality. While this may be true, because there is no direct evidence, choice D is not the best answer, and choice C should be selected.

48. **B is the best answer.** It has been shown that power, prestige, and class can be the sources of significant biases and prejudice. It is stated in the passage that individuals in the study had an average of 12.83 years of education. Choice A states that individuals on the study team had an average of 20 years of education. Since higher education can be a reflection of power, prestige, and social class, it would be important to consider the large difference in education level when screening for potential biases within the study design, and choice A can be eliminated. Certain biases arise based on gender, so it is ideal to have a study team made up of equal members male and female. Since this study team has a nearly even gender divide with 5 males and 4 females, this would minimize any overarching gender biases, making choice B a strong answer when considering study design and analytic bias. Because this study focuses on measures related to weight and weight discrimination, controlling for weight bias within the study team is essential to the research design. Choice C states that the research team has an average BMI that is overweight, while choice D states that the research team has an average BMI that is underweight. Both of these answers show that the research team is homogenously over or underweight, which can lead to implicit and explicit biases. These would be particularly relevant to this research due to the fact that weight is the main focus of the study, so both choices C and D should be eliminated. Although gender may cause bias in the study design, choice B is the best answer because in this scenario it would be expected that a study team of 5 males and 4 females would contribute the least to study bias relative to the other answer choices.

49. **B is the best answer.** The question stem states that individuals who discriminate based on weight possess certain beliefs about people who are obese. A stereotype is a concept about a group or category of people that includes the belief that all members of that group share certain characteristics. This is consistent with the description in the question stem, and choice A can be eliminated. Discrimination describes the unfair treatment of others based on their membership in a specific social group. The question stem does not describe how these individuals act or behave, only that they share a set of ideas about people who are obese, so choice B is inconsistent with the question stem. Stigma describes a negative social label that changes a person's social identity by classifying them as abnormal. People who are obese are stigmatized when they are characterized by negative social labels like lazy, unsuccessful, and weak-willed based on the beliefs of others, so choice C is true and can be eliminated. Prejudices can be described as strict generalizations about certain groups of people that can lead to feelings of hostility or antagonism. This is consistent with what is described in the question stem, so choice D can be eliminated, leaving choice B as the best answer.

50. **A is the best answer.** The question stem describes a situation in which a large group of people fail to defend an individual in need in a crowded in public setting, whereas in a small and less populous setting, someone will reliably come to their defense. The bystander effect describes a phenomenon that occurs when members of a large group fail to offer assistance because they assume someone else will do it. The phenomenon at play here is diffusion of responsibility. This occurs in the bystander effect because the presence of others makes people feel that their individual action is not as critical as it otherwise would be because there are others present to carry out necessary tasks. People will also tend to excuse their inaction because other people in the same situation did not take action either. This is not observed in a more intimate or private setting because the assumption does not exist that someone else will come to the aid of the individual in need. The absence of others prevents people from diffusing the responsibility and excusing their inaction. This phenomenon is consistent with the description provided in the question stem, so choice A should be selected as the best answer. Social loafing describes a phenomenon in which people in a group will work less diligently with the expectation that other members of the group will work harder. This does not apply to the scenario in the question stem because there is a not a particular goal that needs to be achieved by this group of people. Social loafing would also fail to explain the differences in behavior of these individuals in large group versus intimate settings when it comes to defending someone in need, so choice B can be eliminated. Social facilitation describes the tendency to perform better when an individual is being watched. The question stem does not describe a scenario in which the individual's performance is being measured, so choice C can be eliminated. Groupthink describes a phenomenon where group members think alike and tend to agree to promote harmony. Since the group of bystanders watching the altercation in a public place do not represent a group of people working together that need to come to an agreement to reach a common goal, groupthink is not the best answer. Therefore, choice D can be eliminated, and choice A is the best answer.

51. **D is the best answer.** This question is testing the difference between prejudice and discrimination and then the level on which they occur, individual or institutional. Prejudice describes a set of beliefs or ideas about a group of people, while discrimination describes actions or behaviors taken against a group based on those beliefs. The question stem states that individuals are not allowed to be admitted to the emergency room if they are obese. This is an action that is founded on a specific set of beliefs, so this is an example of discrimination, and choices A and B can be eliminated. Individual discrimination occurs when one person behaves negatively toward another because of that person's membership in a specific social group or category. The question stem describes the actions of an entire hospital system, so choice C is not the best answer and can be eliminated. Institutional discrimination takes place at the level of social institutions when they employ policies that differentiate between people based on social grouping. This is consistent with what is described in the question stem, so choice D is the best answer.

52. **A is the best answer.** The question stem states that individuals who are overweight will tend to socialize more with individuals who are like them in this way, irrespective of where they are from. In-group describes a social grouping in which the individual identifies and feels loyalty. A sense of belonging and feeling of loyalty could explain why individuals with like weights tend to group together and socialize. Out-group describes a group with whom the individual does not identify and may feel hostility towards. Out-group mentality would fail to explicitly explain why individuals who are overweight would group together, so choice B can be eliminated. While social facilitation may sound tempting, the phenomenon described by the term social facilitation is not relevant to this question stem. Social facilitation describes the tendency to perform better when an individual is being observed by others, so choice C should be eliminated. Ethnocentrism is the belief that one's group is of central importance and includes the tendency to judge the practices of other groups by one's own cultural standards. Ethnocentrism is what often leads to the formation of an in-group and out-group. Since the question stem does not address how this group of people judges groups with other practices and beliefs, ethnocentrism is not the best answer, eliminating choice D and leaving choice A as the best answer.

Passage 10 Questions 53-56)

53. **A is the best answer.** Diagnosis based on symptomatology is highly dependent on what is considered "abnormal" in a given culture. Clearly, norms are important, so choice A is a possible answer, but the other choices must be definitively ruled out. Anomie is the lack of social norms. This is the opposite of choice A, so choice B can be ruled out. A taboo is a prohibited behavior, thus outside of social norms. Symptoms may be taboo, but they do not have to be, so choice A is stronger than choice C. A fad is short-lived norm. Some diseases are fads, as was the diagnosis of hysteria in the nineteenth century. However, autism is a pervasive disorder and the diagnosis is not likely to disappear. Choice D is not the best answer.

54. **B is the best answer.** Western cultures focus on individuals, whereas Eastern cultures focus on groups. Choices A and D reverse this, so they can be eliminated. Between choices B and C, choice B is more relevant to the passage, which directly references ability to display emotions. Mood was never referenced in the passage, so choice C is not the best answer.

55. **C is the best answer.** Only autistic individuals were biased by the reference group on the SRS. An autistic individual would consider autistic people as the in-group. It is very uncommon to have prejudice against or discriminate against one's in-group. Choices A and B can be ruled out. The passage mentions that individuals with autism may have difficulty displaying emotion. Furthermore, emotion plays a huge role in prejudice. Although capable of prejudice, an individual with autism may not be able to display those feelings, so choice C is a possible answer. It is a misconception that people with autism have low intelligence. They have social impairment but do not always have intellectual impairment. Choice D can be ruled out.

56. **D is the best answer.** The question is asking which researcher studied attachment, which is the relationship formed between a child and parent. John Watson performed the famous Little Albert experiment on classical conditioning. He studied a child but did not study attachment relationships, so choice A is not the best answer. Carl Rogers began the humanistic approach to psychological disease. He did not study attachment, so choice B is not the best answer. Sigmund Freud made many contributions to psychology, but he did not study attachment, so choice C is not the best answer. Mary Ainsworth did study attachment in the "strange situation" experiment. The experiment includes observing the child with and without the parent to determine the attachment type. Choice D is the best answer.

Stand-alones (Questions 57-59)

57. **C is the best answer.** Power, prestige, and class are all directly related to each other. When one increases, so do the others. The graphs are 3D and may be difficult to interpret at first. Choice A shows a scenario where class and prestige (z axis and y axis respectively) are high when power (x axis) is low, so choice A is not the best answer. Choice B shows all three variables increasing together, so choice B is a strong answer. Choices C and D both show parabolic curves. In choice C, when power is moderate, prestige and class are both low. When power is low, prestige and class are high. For the same reason as choice A, choice C is not the best answer. Choice D has the opposite problem and shows low class and prestige at when power is high, so choice D is not the best answer.

58. **B is the best answer.** Prejudice is a preconceived notion about a particular person or group. The medical student is likely prejudiced towards patients with addiction, but the question does not indicate what that prejudice is, so choice A might not be the best answer. Stigma is the dislike and avoidance of a certain group based on assumptions about that group. Stigma and prejudice are closely related, but, in this instance, choice B is the better answer. If the question described how the student assumes all addicts are liars, that would be a better example of prejudice. Discrimination is the change in behavior that is a result of prejudice. The student did not change her behavior- the question only mentions dislike, so choice C is not the best answer. A stereotype is an oversimplified belief about a certain group of people. Stereotypes often lead to prejudice and discrimination. The question does not mention a belief, so for the same reasons as choice A, choice D is not the best answer.

59. **D is the best answer.** Prejudice is a preconceived notion about a particular group, whereas discrimination is differential behavior based on prejudice. Since the question describes a behavior (following minority women), choices A and B can be eliminated. Between choices C and D, choice D is the best answer. The discrimination is based on class, not power. Workers assume minority women do not have enough money (are lower class) and may shoplift. They do not assume that minority women lack the power to purchase clothing or retaliate against discrimination. Choice C is eliminated, and choice D is the best answer.

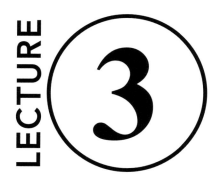

LECTURE 3

Identity and the Individual

TEST 3A

ANSWERS & EXPLANATIONS
Questions 1–59

LECTURE 3 ANSWER KEY

TEST 3A		TEST 3B	
1. A	31. A	1. A	31. C
2. A	32. C	2. C	32. A
3. B	33. B	3. C	33. D
4. D	34. A	4. A	34. D
5. D	35. B	5. B	35. A
6. C	36. A	6. C	36. A
7. B	37. A	7. D	37. B
8. A	38. B	8. D	38. D
9. D	39. B	9. B	39. C
10. C	40. C	10. D	40. A
11. A	41. C	11. D	41. A
12. B	42. D	12. A	42. D
13. C	43. B	13. C	43. B
14. A	44. A	14. B	44. A
15. C	45. B	15. B	45. C
16. C	46. C	16. A	46. A
17. D	47. B	17. C	47. B
18. C	48. D	18. A	48. A
19. C	49. C	19. A	49. D
20. A	50. C	20. B	50. A
21. A	51. D	21. D	51. A
22. B	52. A	22. B	52. D
23. B	53. C	23. C	53. B
24. C	54. C	24. C	54. D
25. A	55. D	25. D	55. C
26. B	56. D	26. A	56. A
27. B	57. B	27. C	57. C
28. B	58. A	28. C	58. D
29. B	59. A	29. D	59. C
30. C		30. A	

EXPLANATIONS FOR LECTURE 3

Passage 1 (Questions 1-5)

1. **A is the best answer.** A trait is a characteristic that varies between people but is stable over the course of a lifetime, regardless of environmental factors. Being hard-working is likely a character trait that persists over time, despite the individual circumstances of the situation. Choice A is a possible answer choice. A personality is a set of traits and lasting characteristics that make a person unique. Being hard-working may be a component of a student's personality, but it is unlikely to define their personality, making choice B less likely to be the best answer. A hereditary factor typically refers to a genetic change that is passed from generation to generation. Diseases that transmit within families are often defined as hereditary, but traits are not usually considered to pass between generations. Choice C is less likely than choice A to be the best answer. A behavior is similar to a trait, but is considered to be more transient than permanent. Being hard-working is likely a characteristic that applies long-term rather than situational. Choice D can be eliminated.

2. **A is the best answer.** The question stem suggests that the more similar the student and the teacher are, the better the student may perform in his or her classes. A student that identifies with the same group as his or her teacher may be more motivated to study harder or be more engaged in the material. The teacher and the student would likely belong to the same in-group. Choice A is a reasonable answer choice. While individuals in the same in-group likely have shared experiences, this does not mean that they will have all the same experiences, making choice B less likely to be the best answer. Neither the passage nor the question stem imply that there is racial hostility between the teacher and the student, eliminating choice C. Role stain involves the feeling of stress to meet a pre-conceived notion of the action or job. The question stem does not imply that the teacher feels undue stress, making choice D less likely than choice A to be the best answer.

3. **B is the best answer.** The question stem eludes to teasing out the environment-only effect on socioemotional development. It is conceivable that genetics could also contribute to development, so the question stem asks for how to distinguish between these two. A heredity study would help determine how a particular trait, such as socioemotional development, was influenced by genetic inheritance, eliminating choice A. A twin study is particularly useful in helping elucidate the environmental component of a trait, as the genetic make-up is shared between identical twins. Choice B is a strong answer. A temperament study would suggest the baseline pattern of social and emotional interactions, but it would not specifically describe the environment-only effect. Choice C can be eliminated. An IQ test would also not show the environmental component, as IQ is likely a mix of both genetics and environment. Choice D can be eliminated.

4. **D is the best answer.** The question stem hints at the popular five-factor theory of personality, which distills possible personality traits down into five main categories. These five categories include openness to experience, making option I part of the best answer, conscientiousness, making option II part of the best answer, extraversion, agreeableness, and neuroticism, making option III part of the best answer. The five-factor model is often helpful in examining health-related behaviors and traits.

5. **D is the best answer.** Gender and racial/ethnic inequalities within classes are either not very pronounced or show a trend in the opposite direction of the one suggested in the passage, meaning that racial/ethnic and gender minorities outperform white males. Choices A and B can likely be eliminated, as the variations within a class are not stark. However, when looking across classes, it is apparent that variations in any of the traits listed are the greatest in disadvantaged racial/ethnic groups, with little variation due to gender. Two useful columns to compare are the ones for "intellectually and contextually disadvantaged" and "intellectually and contextually wealthy," as these represent opposites of one another in terms of available resources. This indicates that choice D is the best answer.

Passage 2 (Questions 6-9)

6. **C is the best answer.** This question is pure memorization. Marcia expanded on Erikson's identity vs. role confusion stage, which is the fifth stage. The first stage is trust vs. mistrust. The third stage is initiative vs. guilt. The seventh stage is generativity vs. stagnation. Choice C is the best answer.

7. **B is the best answer.** The IC and NIC groups occurred only with imaginary agents. The IC children had more "yes" responses when answering the questions. The questions are all about internal attributions of the imaginary agent. Internal attributions relate to a person's disposition, whereas external attributions relate to a person's situation. The study did not ask about external attributions, so choices A and C are not the best answer. The IC group, not the NIC group, gave more positive responses, which is indicated by the higher bar in Figure 1. Choice B is the best answer.

8. **A is the best answer.** In Africa, there is a focus on the group rather than the individual. However, it is not clear that this question is testing that fact, so deal with the answers systematically. Collectivist feelings, or those related to the group, are important in African cultures, so choice A is a strong answer. Sampling more children is a great idea, but it is not clear why this is a change related to sampling children in Africa. Choice B is a great idea for research design but does not relate to the reference to Africa, so choice B is not as strong as choice A. In research design, it is always important to sample participant in their native language, so choice C is not the best answer. Sampling children over many time points is a nice idea, but, like choice B, choice D does not relate to Africa, so it is not the best answer.

9. **D is the best answer.** Locus of control refers to who controls an individual's fate. Choice D is the best answer; the others choices are just distractors. Ironically, the children would be probably unable to answer this question, because they do not understand abstract concepts like fate, but the question does not consider this. A tip for the MCAT® is to just answer the question at hand, do not overthink the answer choices!

Passage 3 (Questions 10-13)

10. **C is the best answer.** The last paragraph of the passage mentions that the results may reflect the desire of patients with cancer to establish positive relationships with others and suppress their fear for the purposes of self-betterment. This sounds most like the humanistic theory of personality, which states that people pursue situations that make them more fulfilled. Based on this reasoning, choice C is the best answer. While choice A still describes a theory of personality, the psychoanalytic theory attributes personality to the flow of energy between the id, ego, and superego. The id strives for instant gratification while the superego strives to uphold morality established by society. There is no mention of instant gratification or the moral rules of society in this passage, so choice A is unlikely to be the best answer. Choice B is inconsistent with the passage because behaviorist theory attributes personality to learning experiences that occur throughout the lifetime of the person rather than the experiences that the person makes for him/herself for self-betterment. The researchers state in the last paragraph that the results are likely due to the patients' desire to better their lives, so choice B can be eliminated. The biological theory states that personality is a result of genetics. The passage never relates the results to genetics, so choice D is not the best answer.

11. **A is the best answer.** Recognize that researchers attributed the positive personality traits of patients with malignant tumors to their desire to lead a normal and positive life without fear of their cancer. These patients are establishing control over their behaviors and the circumstances in their lives in order to eliminate fear from their lives. Choice A is the best answer because people with an internal locus of control believe that they have control over their behaviors and that these internal factors will shape their lives, or in this situation, eliminate fear from their lives. Choice B is weaker than choice A because it is not descriptive. A locus of control only refers to the extent to which a person believes internal or external factors play a role in shaping their life. Choice C can be eliminated because people with an external locus of control believe that their life is shaped by external factors (i.e. cancer) without internal control. The passage and the question make no reference to the idea that patients are modeling their views or behaviors after a reference group, so choice D is inconsistent with the passage.

12. **B is best answer.** This question requires an understanding of both the results of the study and the interpretation of the study provided in the last paragraph of the passage. The study found that patients with malignant tumors are more extroverted and less neurotic than patients with nonmalignant tumors. Researchers attributed these results to the idea that patients with malignant tumors have more positive behaviors in order to fulfill their desire to obtain a higher quality of life. This best corresponds to choice B. Choice A is inconsistent with the passage because the study did find a possible relationship between behavior and the existence of a malignant tumor, as stated in the last paragraph of the passage. Choice C may be tempting because it uses wording found in the passage, but it can be eliminated because these results are opposite of those found in the study. Choice D is not the best answer because patients with malignant tumors were found to be *less* neurotic, not more neurotic.

13. **C is the best answer.** Attribution theory states that people consciously and unconsciously attribute the observed behaviors of others to certain things. Since this question is related to the attribution theory, it may be tempting to select choice A, but this is not the *best* answer because choice C more specifically describes the idea to which researchers attributed the personalities of patients with malignant tumors. Choice C is most consistent with the passage because researchers attribute the behavior of the patients to an inherent desire. This means of attributing is otherwise known as dispositional attribution. Choice B can be eliminated automatically because personality attribution is not a real term. Choice D is weaker than choice C because situational attribution relates to attributing a behavior to an external factor. This choice may be tempting because cancer could be considered an external factor; however, the question stem mentions attributing the behavior to the *desire* to obtain a better quality of life rather than the *situation* of having cancer.

Stand-alones (Questions 14-16)

14. A is the best answer. The biological theory of personality emphasizes that any differences in traits are due to hereditary, or genetic inheritance, rather than environmental factors. Monozygotic twins have the same genome, so any differences in their personality should be due to environmental factors. If they are raised apart, then the study can focus on how much the separate environments affected personality traits, so choice A is the best answer. Monozygotic twins raised in the same household will likely have similar environments, so it would be difficult to determine the cause of different personality traits, so choice B can be eliminated. Dizygotic twins have separate genomes and are no more related than normal siblings, so the genome could not a fixed variable in that study, and choices C and D can be ruled out.

15. C is the best answer. The behaviorist theory emphasizes that personality is shaped by the environment and learning experiences. For this reason, choices A and D can be eliminated. These events will lead individuals to act in predictable ways and produce observable behaviors. Choice B is also not the best answer. This theory is very externally-driven, as it does not consider psychological drives or biological factors. For this reason, choice C is the best answer. Remember this characteristic of the behaviorist theory because it is unique.

16. C is the best answer. The influence of individuals on childhood identity formation is strongest from interactions with individuals most immediately available to them. This is often close family members or parents. Remember this by thinking the children must interact with the individual a lot to imitate them, not simply observe them from afar. For this reason, choice C is the best answer. The children are not as likely to imitate one another because they do not usually spend as much time with friends as family. Choice A is not the strongest answer. Since the children do not actually interact or talk with television characters or strangers in public, they are not as likely to imitate them when forming their identities. Choices B and D can be eliminated.

Passage 4 (Questions 17-20)

17. D is the best answer. Under the trait perspective of personality, traits should be present very early on in life and constant over a lifetime. These are both statements described by choices A and B, so these are not the best answers. According to the passage, perfectionism may be associated with anxiety, so it may not be desirable. Traits are not always positive attributes, so choice C is probably not the best answer, although the trait theory does not specifically discuss the desirability of traits. Choice D is directly contradictory to choice A and the trait perspective of personality. The passage suggests that perfectionism is only found in the fifth grade, but the question does not ask about the study, it asks about the trait theory, so choice D is the best answer.

18. C is the best answer. The authors explain a psychosocial approach to disease. They discuss social factors like interpersonal relations and psychological disorders like anxiety. They never mention any biological factors like genes or heredity. The best answer should not refer to biology. So, choice A and choice D can be ruled out. Physiology is the study of biological processes in the body. So, choice B can also be ruled out. This leaves choice C as the best answer.

19. C is the best answer. There are three clusters of personality disorders. Cluster D does not exist, so choice D can be eliminated. Cluster A is thought of as "odd" and includes paranoid, schizoid, and schizotypal personality disorder. Cluster B is thought of as "emotional" and includes histrionic, narcissistic, borderline, and antisocial personality disorder. Cluster C is thought of as "anxious" and includes avoidant, dependent, and obsessive-compulsive personality disorder. The passage indicated that gifted children were more likely to be anxious and perfectionistic. Perfectionism is associated with obsessive-compulsive personality disorder, and cluster C is considered "anxious," so choice C is the best answer.

20. A is the best answer. The passage indicated that 5th graders whom were gifted had more anxiety. If the results are bidirectional, decreasing anxiety may also decrease giftedness. Anxiety can be thought of as an overactive brain state. The best answer should be a drug that depresses or calms the brain. Serotonin is a calming, "feel-good" neurotransmitter. Blocking reuptake of serotonin would increase the activity of serotonin, so choice A is a strong answer. Choice B is not specific enough. A GABA analogue could block GABA receptors or over-activate them. Gabapentin is sometimes used as a treatment for anxiety, but that knowledge is outside the MCAT®. It is very important to not use outside knowledge on test day. Choice B can be eliminated. Choice C and choice D would increase the activity of dopamine, which is an excitatory neurotransmitter. Furthermore, choice C and choice D are saying the same thing, so it is impossible to choose between the two. Choice C and D should be ruled out.

Passage 5 (Questions 21-25)

21. **A is the best answer.** The final sentence of the passage describes the conclusions from the two-year follow-up study: decreased persistence across the two-year time interval was correlated with higher BMI levels. Note that the previous passage sentence describes that BMI levels could be mediated by changes in personality traits over time. It can be concluded that "persistence" is the personality trait mediating BMI levels. Trait theory posits that personality consists of a set of traits, which are stable over the course of a lifetime, regardless of environmental influences. A trait theorist is likely to question the results of the two-year follow-up study, as it cites changes in a personality trait over time. Thus, choice A is a strong answer. Psychoanalytic theory suggests that personality is determined largely at the subconscious level by the interplay between three systems: the id, the superego, and the ego. Psychoanalytic theory also posits that early experiences can have lasting effects on the individual throughout life. The two-year follow-up study does not disagree with the above tenants of psychoanalytic theory, and as such, a psychoanalyst is less likely to question these results than would a trait theorist. Choice B can be eliminated. Humanist theory suggests that humans are consciously seeking experiences that will allow them to live a better and more fulfilling life. The two-year follow-up study does not mention the notion of self-fulfillment, and as such, it does not disagree with this notion. A humanistic psychologist is unlikely to question with these results, and, choice C can be eliminated. Although, as implied by the name, an attribute-constancy psychologist would likely question the notion of changing personality traits over time, there is no such thing as an attribute-constancy psychologist. Choice D can be eliminated, and choice A is the best answer. As a test-taking tip, do not be tempted by answer choices that sound correct but are not familiar. This is a common tactic employed by the MCAT® that attempts to trick students who do not trust themselves and assume they do not have the knowledge required to select the correct answer.

22. **B is the best answer.** Social cognitive theory posits that personality develops due to a reciprocal causation between learning experiences with the environment, observable behaviors, and personal factors, such as an individual's mental life and personal choices. Central to social cognitive theory is the idea that personality can be shaped via observational learning, in which people observe the experiences of others and then apply these lessons to new situations in their own lives. A humanist would most likely suggest that attempting to attain self-actualization would influence personality, as the concept of self-actualization, or achieving one's full potential in life, is central to humanistic theory. Choice A can be eliminated. Learned experiences of others applied in novel situations describes the process of observational learning, which is central to social cognitive theory. Choice B is a strong answer. Although social cognitive theory does include a triadic reciprocal causation, this causation does not include latent biases. Choice C can be eliminated. Although behavior, the environment, and genetic influences are all aspects of social cognitive theory, this theory does not suggest a one-way "causative" relationship between the aspects, but instead suggests a triadic reciprocal causation between the aspects. Choice D can be eliminated, allowing for choice B to remain as the best answer.

23. **B is the best answer.** Note that, for a child, residence in metropolitan cities and accessibility to physical activity centers are largely out of the child's control. Studies linking this residence to obesity-related behaviors would thus be suggesting that child body fat accumulation is largely out of the child's control. Role-taking is adopting the role of another person, either by imitating behaviors associated with specific roles or by taking the other persons' point of view in a social interaction. The question stem does not indicate that the children are imitating behaviors or taking other points of view; choice A can be eliminated. Attribution is the process of assigning a cause to other peoples' behaviors. Situational attribution suggests that the cause of a behavior is due to environmental influences. The question stem cites that the cause of a behavior (obesity-related behaviors) is due to environmental influences (living in metropolitan cities); choice B is a strong answer. Locus of control is a person's belief about the extent to which internal and external factors play a role in shaping his or her life. An external locus of control indicates that the person believes that external factors, such as the environment and luck, determine outcomes. It is important to note that an external locus of control focuses on how the individual explains his or her own behavior, whereas situational attribution focuses on how people explain the behavior of others. The studies described in the question stem indicate the latter and not the former; namely, the studies are attempting to explain the behaviors of others through the environment (situational attribution), not determine the extent to which the individuals feel the environment is controlling their life (external locus of control). Choice C can be eliminated in favor of choice B. Fundamental attribution error is the process by which people tend to automatically favor dispositional attributions over situational attributions in attempting to explain others' behaviors. The studies referenced in the question stem are attempting to explain obesity-related behaviors through a situational lens. Choice D can be eliminated, and choice B is the best answer.

24. **C is the best answer.** The results at the end of paragraph 4 indicate that parental personality characteristics are a mediating variable between a child's personality characteristics and that child's adult BMI levels. The results suggest a genetic inheritance of personality characteristics. Variables that would hinder the ability to suggest a genetic link would be good control variables. If these variables were not controlled for, they would be considered confounding variables. Adult BMI level is the dependent variable described in the study, and as such, adult BMI is changing and not being controlled. Choice A can be eliminated. Children personality traits are the independent variable in this study, and controlling for this variable would compromise the findings of the study by disrupting the study design. Choice B can be eliminated. An individual's reference group is a group that provides him or her with a model for appropriate actions, values, and world views. A child's reference group can heavily influence that child's behaviors, which could include obesity-related behaviors. While this study is attempting to isolate a potential genetic influence of BMI, variations in a child's reference group could also potentially affect BMI through influencing the child's behaviors. Controlling for aspects of a child's reference group would ensure that these other influences are minimized, making choice C is a strong answer. Self-concept can be thought of as a person's view of his or her own personality. While a person's view of his or her own personality could potentially affect BMI levels, a person's reference group is far more likely to affect this, as a reference group by definition provides the child with a model of appropriate actions. Choice D can be eliminated in favor of choice C.

25. **A is the best answer.** The question stem is asking what would Carl Rogers suggest causes psychological distress. It is important to note that Carl Rogers is a famous humanistic psychologist, which is a branch of psychology that suggests a healthy personality results from an overlap between the actual self, ideal self, and the perceived self (or self-concept). Psychological distress results when these three aforementioned qualities do not overlap, an instance known as "incongruence." A difference between child's view of their own personality (self-concept) and what the child wants to be (ideal self) represents an incongruence consistent with what humanistic theory would suggest causes psychological distress. Although this answer would have been stronger if it also mentioned the actual self, choice A will still remain as a potentially strong answer. An in-group is the collection of individuals that a person identifies with. In-group expectations would indicate the behaviors a person expects his/her in-group to display. In-group expectations are not part of the concept of incongruence, and choice B can be eliminated. An overlap between self-concept, actual self, and ideal self would be indicative of a healthy personality, not psychological distress. Choice C can be eliminated. Humanistic theory posits that individuals have complete personal control over the development of their personality, and as such, Carl Rogers (a humanist) would not suggest inheritance of parental personality characteristics as a determinant of psychological distress. Choice D can be eliminated, and choice A is the best answer.

Stand-alones (Questions 26-29)

26. **B is the best answer.** Remember to differentiate between these terms, since they are often confused with one another. Self-efficacy refers to one's ability to complete a task. Self-esteem refers to one's overall judgment of him/herself. Because Danielle is doubting her ability to play volleyball well, and not her overall personality or contributions, choice B is stronger than choice A. Self-concept refers to a person's views of his/her own personality, and usually relates to an individual's self-esteem. Choice C can be eliminated. If Danielle was struggling with locus of control, she might be wavering between an individual locus of control, or feeling as if she has complete control over her actions, versus an external locus of control, in which the environmental factors would determine her actions. This scenario does not apply to Danielle's situation, since she is concerned only internally, so choice D can be eliminated.

27. **B is the best answer.** In psychoanalytic theory personality is determined by the flow of psychic energy between three systems that reside in different levels of consciousness: the id, the super ego, and the ego. This does not really have to do with a mother and her daughter having similar personality traits. Choice A can be eliminated. Biological theory focuses on the biological contributions of certain traits. This theory assumes that a person's genome contributes to the formation of personality. Maria has been separated from her mother since birth, in a different environment, but she shares many of the same personality traits; therefore, there is a strong genetic component to her personality. Choice B is a strong answer. Behaviorist theory states that personality is constructed by a series of learning experiences that occur through interactions between the individual and their environment. For this theory, it is the environment that shapes personality rather than biological factors, therefore choice C is not the best answer and can be eliminated. Social cognitive theory also focuses on learning experiences and observable behaviors, thus choice D can also be eliminated.

28. **B is the best answer.** Imitation is indeed what these children are doing; however, it is not the most specific answer, thus choice A is not the best answer. Role-taking means adopting the role of another person, either by imitating behaviors associated with specific social roles or by taking the other person's point of view in a social interaction. It seems that the children are taking the roles of their parents in this example, thus choice B is a strong answer. Social comparison is evaluating oneself by contrast with others. This helps facilitate the development of a distinct sense of self, but this is not what occurred in this study, and thus choice C can be eliminated. While imitating their parents my cause them to become part of the in-group, this is not necessarily true. For example, if the parent does not identify as part of the in-group, the child may also not identify as part of the in-group. Therefore, choice D is not the strongest answer.

29. **B is best answer.** This question requires the understanding of social influences on identity and personality. The question stem implies that cancer patients participating in support groups are positively influenced by being able to identify with a group of people in a similar situation. This is most related to the idea of an in-group, which is a reference group in which a person identifies with its members. Choice B is therefore the best answer. An out-group is the opposite of an in-group because an individual does not identify with its members. This would not be the situation in a cancer support group, so choice A can be eliminated. Choice C may be tempting because it could be assumed that positive self-esteem is a behavior that members of the group are imitating; however, it cannot be assumed that members are imitating the positive self-esteem of other members of the group. The question stem only implies that participation in the support group itself allows for improvement of self-esteem. Choice C can be eliminated. Choice D is unrelated because the question never implies that support group members are adopting the role of another person, which is defined as role-taking.

Passage 6 (Questions 30-34)

30. **C is the best answer.** According to the last paragraph, TCIs experience a disruption in identity development, possibly as a result of having to integrate multiple facets of both the heritage and host cultures. Erikson's theory of development has eight stages. Stage 2 concerns autonomy vs. shame and doubt, centering on whether an individual is able to carry out self-care. The passage does not suggest TCIs are not able to provide for themselves, eliminating choice A. Stage 4 involves industry vs. inferiority, where the person views him- or herself as capable of mastering skills that are societally valued. TCIs, according to paragraph two, see themselves as excelling at moving between cultures, so they are unlikely to doubt their skills. This eliminates choice B. Stage 5 is explicitly concerned with identify formation and is the stage of identity vs. role confusion. TCIs may struggle to find their role in society, given they do not completely belong to one culture or another. Choice C is most likely to be the best answer. Stage 7 involves generativity vs. stagnation, which deals with how individuals determine the extent to which they wish to put energy into family, work, community, or simply care for their own needs. The passage does not provide information related to how TCIs would think about these choices, making choice D a weaker answer choice than choice C.

31. **A is the best answer.** Vygotsky believed that learning takes place through interactions with others, leading to the development of culturally shared values and beliefs. This approach is known as the sociocultural approach. Choice A closely matches this answer choice, so it is most likely the best answer. Identity versus role confusion is Stage 5 of Erik Erikson's theory of development. While the passage does suggest that TCIs never fully resolve this stage, the question pertains to Vygotsky, not Erikson, eliminating choice B. The return of sexual urges in late adolescence defines the final stage of Freud's theory of development, but does not relate to Vygotsky's sociocultural approach directly. Choice C can be eliminated. An additional stage, Stage 7, of Erikson's theory of development is described in choice D. In the generativity vs. stagnation stage, individuals must balance contributing to their community versus sustaining themselves. Because the question pertains to Vygotsky, not Erikson, choice D can also be eliminated.

32. **C is the best answer.** Kohlberg's theory of moral development is alluded to in the question stem, which mentions postconventional morality. Postconventional morality is defined by Stages 5 and 6, which involve developing a sense of social contract and universal ethics. The development of these ideas would require a full understanding of how the individual fit into the current culture, as well as understanding the expectations the culture has for each person. Because the individual did not grow up fully in one culture, he or she may be unaware of the nuances and norms of either the heritage culture or host culture, and may have difficulty figuring out exactly how he or she fits into the larger society. This likely means that the individual would not display greater postconventional morality, eliminating choices A and B. Notice choice D is an extreme answer, as it suggests that the individual would only be aware of the norms of one culture but not the other. It is likely that TCIs will learn some, but not all, of the cultural values of both cultures, making choice D less likely than choice C to be the best answer.

33. **B is the best answer.** Dispositional attribution assigns the cause of a situation to internal qualities, such as the personality of the individual. Notice that the question stem instead suggests that it is an environmental reason that TCIs do not fully integrate into the host community. Choice A can be eliminated. Situational attribution suggests environmental factors are behind a certain situation, which resembles the information provided in the question stem. Choice B is most likely to be the best answer. The fundamental attribution error favors dispositional attribution over situational attribution to explain a behavior or situation, which is the opposite of the question stem. Choice C can be eliminated. Self-serving bias is the tendency to attribute success to one's internal qualities rather than environmental factors. In the question stem, environmental factors, not personal factors, play a larger role in hampering the success of TCIs to integrate, eliminating choice D.

34. **A is the best answer.** The answer choices refer to the stages of identity exploration and identity commitment described by James Marcia, whom furthered Erik Erikson's work by proposing four types of identity status that describe an individual's progress through Erikson's Stage 5, identity vs. role confusion. The first stage is identity diffusion, which describes a state in which a person has no sense of identity or motivation to engage in identity exploration. Both individuals would begin their journey towards self-identity at this stage, meaning neither should enter the stage earlier than another. Choice A may be the best answer, but consider the other answers first. Identity moratorium describes an individual in the midst of an identity crisis, actively attempting to develop a unique set of values and an understanding of self in society. There is no information to suggest that TCIs and monocultural children would enter this stage at different time points, as it is possible they would begin to care about their self-identity at similar times. As suggested by the passage, TCIs never fully finish their identity formation, meaning they are unlikely to enter identity foreclosure or identity achievement stages before monocultural children. Choices C and D can be eliminated.

Passage 7 (Questions 35-38)

35. **B is the best answer.** The findings of the study relate to the idea that emotional, physical, and sexual abuse across developmental periods could play a role in shaping the personalities and behaviors of adults. This most relates to choice B. Behaviorist theory states that personality is shaped by interactions between the individual and the environment. In this case, the environment is the abuse endured by the individual. This question could be difficult if there is confusion regarding the differences between personality theories. Biological theory relates to the genetic effects on personality. Based on this definition and the ruling out of genetics in the question stem, choice A would not be the best answer. Choice C is not the best answer because psychoanalytic theory states that personality is attributed to the balance of id, ego, and superego. The passage does not mention any desire for instant gratification, which is controlled by the id; therefore, this theory does not best describe the findings of the study. Choice D is also not the best answer because the humanistic theory states that personality develops from the desire for betterment of self, which was not mentioned in the passage findings.

36. **A is the best answer.** The passage findings suggest that negative experiences across developmental disorders play a role in identity and personality development. It is also important to understand Freud's psychosexual stages of development- oral, anal, phallic, latent, and genital. Choices C and D are stages in Erikson's psychosocial model of development, so these choices can be ruled out. Choice A is the best answer because the latent stage is the Freudian developmental stage that occurs from ages 7-11 and that is characterized by social development. Since negative experiences likely shape identity and personality according to the results, the latent stage is the stage that most correlates with this. Choice B may be tempting because this is also one of Freud's psychosexual stages; however, the genital stage relates to the return of sexual urges and the development of mature sexuality. Development of sexuality was not mentioned in the passage even though sexual abuse was mentioned. The passage was more focused on the social development and personality development.

37. **A is best answer.** Since emotional neglect and abuse were most common in adolescence, the study suggests that adolescence is the most sensitive period to negative experiences. This understanding allows for the ruling out of choices C and D. The best answer is choice A because it labels adolescence as the most sensitive period, and it names a crisis in a stage of Erikson's psychosocial developmental model that Erikson characterizes to be part of adolescence. The *identity* vs. *role confusion* stage is the point at which adolescents explore their role in society and form their identity. Choice B may be tempting because it names adolescence as the most sensitive period; however, choice B does not name the stage that is most closely related to adolescence. The *integrity* vs. *despair* stage occurs in late adulthood when people are evaluating their lifetimes. Choice C is not the best answer because it names adolescence as the least sensitive period, and it states that it is because it is characterized by a psychosexual developmental stage, which relates to Freud's stages of development, not Erikson's.

38. **B is the best answer.** While it may seem that this question is referring to the passage, it can actually be answered without looking at the passage. This question requires drawing a conclusion based on the idea that some patients attribute their personalities to negative experiences during development. This idea most correlates with the idea that patients have an external locus of control, meaning that they believe that their negative experiences shaped their lives and influenced their identity. Choice B is the best answer based on this reasoning. Choice C is not the best answer because a person with an internal locus of control does not believe he/she can be influenced by external factors but is rather completely in control of his/her behaviors. Choice A is not the best answer because self-efficacy refers to the person's belief in his/her ability to carry out an action successfully. This is unrelated to the question. For this reason choice D is also not the best answer even though the word "negative" in choice D may be tempting.

Passage 8 (Questions 39-43)

39. **B is the best answer.** In Erikson's stages of psychosocial development, there are eight stages. It is worthwhile to develop a way to remember these as well as the time frame over which they occur. The final stage is ego integrity vs. despair and occurs over the age of 65. The stage prior to that is generativity vs. stagnation and occurs from age 40-64. So, choice B is the best answer. Autonomy vs. shame is the second stage. Initiative vs. guilt is third stage, and intimacy vs. isolation is sixth stage.

40. **C is the best answer.** The environment has a strong influence on perceptions and behavior. Subconsciously, humans are more fearful in the dark and gloomier on overcast days. Choice A is a true statement, but it does not answer the question of *how* the environment biases the study. There is likely a better answer. Choice B refers to a reference group, which is the main group of individuals one is likely to identify with. This is not an environmental effect, so choice B is not the best answer. As stated, an overcast day may make a person gloomy and a dark environment may make a person fearful. The passage refers to despair, not fear, so choice C would have a greater effect on the study than choice D.

41. **C is the best answer.** This is a question about research design. The best answer must refer to sampling a social network. Sampling an entire family would be partially on track, but a social network usually includes friends as well, so choice A is a possible answer. Differentiating which members of a social network have low or high NEIS scores would be helpful, but it is not clear how this would show the effect of a social network on one person's NEIS score in particular. Choice B is stronger than choice A but probably not the best answer. First sampling participants then sampling friends and family could show if participants with low NEIS are surrounded by others with low NEIS as well. Choice C is a strong answer. Choice D does not refer to sampling social networks, so choice D is not the best answer.

42. **D is the best answer.** The question sounds like it is asking about experimental design, but really it is asking about different types of identities. Every demographic category can have an associated identity so the three options listed are all possible. Other types of identities include age and occupational identity.

43. **B is the best answer.** The MCAT® requires knowledge about Parkinson's disease, although this is not a psychological disorder. One component of the illness is the unusual emotional affect called, "masked facies." People with Parkinson's disease often show restricted facial expression and may be interpreted as being sad since they smile infrequently. This may bias the results to show more participants with despair than ego integrity, so choice B is a strong answer. Depression is a psychological illness that is not necessarily associated with Parkinson's disease. Although they appear less happy, patients with Parkinson's disease are not at greater risk for mental illness, so choices C and D are not the best answer.

Stand-alones (Questions 44-47)

44. **A is the best answer.** The DSM-5 does list common symptoms, but it is not used simply as a checklist without interpretation. Choice A is likely the best answer. Psychological factors identified by both the clinician and described by the patient can be extremely helpful in reaching a diagnosis, so choices B and C can be eliminated. Similarly, cultural ideas factor into DSM-5 criteria, as it changes over the years according to cultural beliefs. In some societies, hallucinations are accepted as normal occurrences and not a pathological symptom. That is not the case in America, where hallucinations are used to diagnose many psychological disorders. For this reason, choice D is not the best answer.

45. **B is the best answer.** The question stem is describing bipolar disorder, which is a mood disorder characterized by two extremes of emotional experience: extreme sadness (depression) versus excitement so intense that it is detrimental to well-being (mania). Therefore, the best answer would be the one that does not accurately characterize bipolar disorder. As stated above, bipolar disorder is a mood disorder, so choice A can be eliminated. Bipolar disorder is a singular diagnosis with two extremes of symptom manifestation, so choice B is false and fails to properly describe her condition. For a patient with bipolar disorder, a single diagnosis of depressive disorder would be incorrect, and choice C can be eliminated. It has been shown in the literature that there is a strong genetic component that correlates with bipolar disorder. Therefore, choice D can be eliminated, leaving choice B as the best answer.

46. **C is the best answer.** Choice A, Erik Erikson, proposed that identity and personality develop through discrete stages, which is a structure that his theories and Freud's theories share. However, Erikson's theory lacks psychosexual stages, and instead focuses on how the individual interacts and exists within a greater society. Erikson never theorized that persistent fixations or neuroses can develop due to dysfunction during any of these stages, so choice A can be eliminated. Choice B is not the best answer because Vygotsky theorized on the development of identity as it is shaped by culture and social interactions. In fact, Vygotsky can be thought of as the originator of the sociocultural approach to identity. The question mentioned neither societal nor cultural interactions nor influences. Sigmund Freud proposed that children go through a series of psychosexual stages of development starting from birth, many of which have to do with children's relationships with their parents. According to Freud, if a child's urges are either unmet or overindulged during a certain stage, a *fixation* will persist into adulthood and become a part of that individual's personality. This best fits the question stem, which is why choice C is the best answer. Lastly, choice D is not the best answer, because Piaget's work was focused on cognitive development rather than personality development.

47. **B is the best answer.** The five-factor model is best remembered by the acronym OCEAN. The letters stand for Openness to experience, conscientiousness, extraversion, agreeableness, and neuroticism. Thus, choices A, C, and D can be ruled out. Narcissism may have been a tempting answer, particularly because it is likely to come up elsewhere in the study of personality, particularly disorders. Remember that the OCEAN traits are thought to be extremely broad categories under which many different personality traits can fall, and that all of the OCEAN traits contain their own continuum on which there are many different places for individuals to fall. Narcissism refers to a more specific and infrequent trait, without a great deal of space on a continuum. In fact, it is more often associated with psychological disorders.

Passage 9 (Questions 48-51)

48. **D is the best answer.** The passage states childhood adversity is associated with reduced adjustment, increased distress, and somatoform complaints. Somatoform complaints refer to complaints of physical symptoms without a physical cause. Resilience was a variable measured by the researchers, but it was not correlated to childhood adversity. In fact, resilience was a moderator on the outcomes listed above. Choice A is not the best answer. Psychological stress would be expected following adversity, but this is not necessarily a "symptom" as requested by the question stem, so choice B is probably not the best answer. Psychological stress has been long-accused of reducing the immune response and putting individuals at risk for infections. This has not been completely proven by science. Additionally, infections have a physical cause for symptoms whereas the passage mentions somatoform complaints. Choice C is just not quite right. Headaches are common, with almost everyone experiencing one at some point during life. Headaches are a very common somatoform complaint because there is not an identifiable cause most of the time. Choice D is the best answer.

49. **C is the best answer.** For the MCAT®, it is worth knowing a few key facts about psychological disorders, particularly some of the main diseases covered in the Diagnostic and Statistical Manual of Mental Disorders (DSM). Conversion disorder is when a neurological symptom (such as blindness, numbness, or weakness) has a psychological cause. It is relatively common and has not been debunked, so choice A is not the best answer. Somatization disorder includes conversion disorder but also refers to non-neurological symptoms like pain and gastrointestinal disturbance. It is also common and not debunked, so choice B is not the best answer. Dissociative identity disorder is also known as multiple personality disorder. It has been removed from the DSM V because many of the popularized cases have since reported that they were feigning their illness. Choice C is a strong answer. Major depressive disorder is one of the most common mental illnesses and is certainly still in the DSM, so choice D is not the best answer.

50. **C is the best answer.** Freud's defense mechanisms are not specifically tested by the MCAT®, but the MCAT® often asks questions that seem to test specific content but can be answered with reasoning and past experience. The participants experienced childhood adversity, so the answer should be something a child would do to respond to stress. Passive aggression is a fairly advanced way to respond to an event. Children often just throw temper tantrums rather than plan a subtle way to "get back" at someone. Choice A is probably not the best answer. Humor is also a very advanced way to deal with an event. Children are barely capable of making jokes, so choice B is probably not the best answer. Displacement would be possible. It is easy to imagine an upset child taking his feelings out on a toy or a sibling, so choice C is a possible answer. Intellectualization is very unlikely, because children do not have the mental capacity to do this. Choice D is not the best answer.

51. **D is the best answer.** The MCAT® rarely asks about treatment for mental disorders, but there is one thing that is important to know—DBT (dialectical behavioral therapy) is typically used to treat borderline personality disorder. It has been used to treat other mental illnesses but with limited success. Anti-depressants and anti-anxiety medicines are effective in most psychological disorders, especially PTSD, which shares features of depression and anxiety disorders. Choices A and B are not the best answer. CBT (cognitive behavioral therapy) is also effective for just about every mental disorder, so choice C is not the best answer. For test day, know that antidepressants, anxiolytics (anti-anxiety medications), and CBT are all effective treatments for mental illness.

Passage 10 (Questions 52-55)

52. **A is the best answer.** In order to determine whether the schizophrenia patients were more likely to smoke, first look at the results in Table 1. There are three rows that relate to smoking, these can be found in the first column: Ever smoker, Current smoker, and Ex-smoker. By looking at the numbers in Sample A, Sample B, and healthy controls it can be determined that Sample A and Sample B are much more likely in all categories to smoke. Sample A and a Sample B are the two categories of schizophrenia patients, therefore, the answer is Yes, schizophrenia patients were more likely to smoke. Thus, choices C and D can be eliminated because they state the opposite. The passage states that this association *may* be due to reduced side effects of antipsychotics. However results to this effect are not presented. Antipsychotics are drugs that block the receptors for dopamine. While it is possible that an ingredient in the cigarettes has this effect, this is not supported by evidence, therefore choice A is the best answer, and choice B can be eliminated.

53. **C is the best answer.** The patient is exhibiting a lack of motivation. Positive symptoms are disturbances that add to or modify the individual's normal psychological function such as perception, belief, or communication. A lack of motivation is not an added disturbance to the patients' normal psychological function, but rather something the patient is lacking. Therefore, choice A is not the best answer. It is true that depression often causes individuals to withdraw from activities they used to enjoy. However because the question asks about a patient with schizophrenia choice B is not the best answer. Negative symptoms, in contrast to positive symptoms, are characterized by absence. Negative symptoms often consist of lack of emotion, motivation, and enjoyment of activities, this is exactly what the patient in the question is experiencing, thus, choice C is a strong answer. While it is true that schizophrenia has been linked to genetics, this is not a good explanation for the symptoms the patient is experiencing. Therefore, choice C is better than choice D.

54. **C is the best answer.** Choice A is very vague and does not answer the question, and therefore cannot be the best answer. Antipsychotics act by blocking dopamine receptors and can trigger various side effects including extrapyramidal side effects (EPS). The passage explains that EPS has to do with involuntary movements. Therefore, it makes sense that the nicotine could help induce dopamine release in the pre-frontal cortex. However, it does not make sense that this would then decrease the hepatic clearance of antipsychotics thus choice B is not a good answer. It is true that this dopamine release could also increase the hepatic clearance of antipsychotics and thus help EPS be alleviated by smoking. Therefore, choice C is a strong answer. It is true that the passage does not give evidence that smoking will provide these benefits, this does not mean there is no way that smoking would reduce the side-effects of antipsychotics, and the question asks the reader to hypothesize, therefore, choice D can be eliminated.

55. **D is the best answer.** The results of the study do not show that cigarettes help schizophrenics, the study does not show conclusive evidence either way. Therefore choice A can be eliminated. While it makes sense that nicotine could act as a dopamine inducer and thus decrease symptoms from anti-psychotic medication there is not enough evidence to support this theory and justify any type of prescribing smoking. Therefore choice B can also be eliminated. The passage did not present evidence either way as to whether cigarettes were more harmful or beneficial. Therefore, this is not the reason a doctor should encourage a patient not to smoke. Choice C is not the best answer. It is true that the negative effects of cigarettes such as addiction and cancer are known while the positive effects are unknown and only hypotheses, therefore choice D is the best answer.

Stand-alones (Questions 56-59)

56. **D is the best answer.** Jane is afraid of only one specific situation, heights, so she is suffering from a specific phobia. Generalized anxiety disorder involves persistent anxiety triggered by multiple stimuli, so choice A can be eliminated. Social phobia would be a specific phobia to be in social settings, but because Jane's fear is caused by another stimulus, choice B is not as strong as choice D. Panic disorder involves short, intense panic attacks with stimulation of the sympathetic nervous system. This symptom is not described in the question stem, so choice C can be eliminated. Jane's fear of heights is a specific phobia, likely making choice D the best answer.

57. **B is the best answer.** The question stem is describing a medication that benefits both psychological symptoms and physical symptoms (pain). It is also stated that the medication is an antidepressant. Although this medication undoubtedly has uses for individuals with depression, choice A is not the best answer because it fails to address the fact that this medication was found to relieve the bodily manifestation of pain. Choice B is a strong answer because an individual with a somatoform disorder would have bodily manifestations and psychological symptoms. Choice C can be eliminated because, similar to a depressive disorder, using this medication for a mood disorder would address the psychological use of the drug but not its use for pain. Post-traumatic stress disorder could be caused by the motor vehicle accident described in the question stem, but again, using the drug to treat this disorder would fail to address its functionality as a pain medication. Therefore, choice D can be eliminated, leaving choice B as the best answer.

58. **A is the best answer.** The important thing to keep in mind is that all humans exhibit emotional variation from time to time, and extreme emotions in response to certain circumstances. In addition, what constitutes a psychological disorder depends greatly on cultural and societal definitions of what is "abnormal." A hallmark that all psychological disorders share, however, is that they are *maladaptive* to the individual. Choice A is the best answer, because it describes a situation in which an individual experiences an extreme level of sympathetic nervous system activation in response to circumstances that do not warrant a literal fight-or-flight. In fact, this person's symptoms unnecessarily affect her ability to live a normal life. Choice B is not the best answer. This answer choice may very loosely meet the definition of obsessive compulsive disorder, but there is no evidence that indicates this activity is particularly maladaptive. Perhaps burglary rates are high in this individual's neighborhood. In addition, this activity is likely not particularly time consuming and likely does not affect the individual's abilities to keep employment commitments and the like. Choice C is not the best answer because it describes a behavior that is a reasonable reaction based on circumstances and not necessarily a situation that is pathological. Lastly, choice D is not the best answer because epilepsy and seizure disorders are not classified as psychological disorders.

59. **A is the best answer.** This question requires an understanding of Attribution Theory, which provides an explanation for behaviors of others. Max attributes the behavior of the waitress to her innate qualities, which is dispositional attribution. Choice B is still not the best answer because Max's judgment was incorrect. Choice A is the strongest answer because Max committed the fundamental attribution error, which is the tendency to attribute the behavior of others to disposition rather than to external factors. Choice C can be eliminated because situational attribution occurs when an individual attributes the behavior of others to environmental or external factors. This would have been the case if Max would have assumed that the waitress had other things going on in her life that made her behave the way she did. Choice D can also be eliminated because personality attribution error is not a real term associated with Attribution Theory.

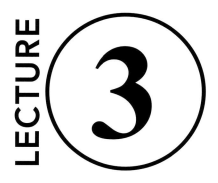

LECTURE

Identity and the Individual

TEST 3B

ANSWERS & EXPLANATIONS
Questions 1–59

Passage 1 (Questions 1-4)

1. **A is the best answer.** Trait theory says that personality consists of a set of traits, which vary between people, but are stable over the course of a lifetime, regardless of environmental factors. Participation in a class aimed at smoking reduction would count as an environmental factor, so, according to trait theory, the traits should not change. Choice A shows that the trait scores are similar between pre-treatment and post-treatment surveys, likely making it the best answer. Choice B shows that some traits increase, while others decrease, over the course of treatment, eliminating it as a possible answer. Choice C shows a global increase, while choice D shows a global decrease in the trait scores over the treatment time, eliminating both as possible answers.

2. **C is the best answer.** The biological perspective states that traits are due to differences in genetic make-up, not environmental attributes. The social relationships of a family unit and their impact on smoking would be more environmental than genetic, making choice A unlikely to be the best answer. The effect of psychotherapy on the relationship between two traits is also not purely biological, eliminating choice B. If a mutation in a gene leads to an increase in aggressive behavior and smoking, this would support the biological perspective. Choice C is most likely the best answer. The hormone T_3 is a thyroid hormone that increases the basal metabolic rate, which helps to eliminate choice D. In addition, environmental factors could modulate the level of the circulating hormone, making its relationship to a trait not necessarily solely reliant on genetics. Choice D is less likely than choice C to be the best answer.

3. **C is the best answer.** According to the last paragraph, extraverts are a group of people that may have a high need for stimulation. Paragraph one also identifies that extraverts have high sociability. This does not necessarily mean that extraverts have a strong sense of themselves as a member of a social group. They may be associating with multiple groups because they do not have a firm understanding of themselves. Choice A can be eliminated. Most individuals identify with one ethnicity, and the passage does not discuss how the personality traits mentioned may relate to one's sense of belonging to a racial or ethnic group. Choice B can be eliminated. Those that need a significant amount of stimulation may be belong to a large social group. This would fit the common definition of extraversion, making choice C likely to be the best answer. Agreeableness, not extraversion, might suggest being more open to variations in sexual orientation. Choice C is a better answer choice than choice D.

4. **A is the best answer.** According to the passage, neuroticism is correlated with high anxiety, of which obsessive-compulsive disorder (OCD) is a manifestation of severe anxiety. OCD involves ritualistic behaviors that are geared as specifically reducing anxiety, likely making choice A the best answer. Post-traumatic stress disorder (PTSD) could manifest itself at a higher incidence in individuals with neuroticism. However, PTSD requires an inciting event, which the passage does not allude to. Choice A is likely a better answer than choice B. Both bipolar disorder and schizophrenia are not commonly classified as pure stress, anxiety, or depressive disorders, but a combination of the three, with additional physical symptoms such as mania or hallucinations. The passage does not refer to individuals with higher levels of neuroticism as being at higher risk for these types of mental disorders, eliminating choices C and D.

Passage 2 (Questions 5-10)

5. **B is the best answer.** The question alludes to a twin study, which is useful for separating the effects of genetics and the environment. Monozygotic twins are identical twins, meaning they share the same DNA but may or may not share the same environment. Choice A can be eliminated, because the twins share both the same genetics and environment. Twins with the same genetics but different environments would be the ideal candidates for a twin study to help determine how genetics would contribute to the predisposition to smoke, likely making choice B the best answer. Dizygotic twins do not share the same genes, eliminating choices C and D.

6. **C is the best answer.** There are multiple theories that describe the development of behavior. Freud's theory, the psychoanalytic theory, relies on the id, ego, and superego, focusing on the internal flow of energy between those three levels of consciousness. It does not explicitly include environmental influences, likely eliminating choice A. The biological theory asserts that the predominant determinant of behavior is genetics. While genetics may contribute, the question stem also implies a social influence, as the parents described their experiences smoking. Choice B can be eliminated. The MCAT® does not favor the biological theory, so the answer is almost always the biopsychosocial model. The biopsychosocial theory integrates the influence of genetic, environmental, and psychological components of behavior, which most closely matches the question stem situation. Choice C is most likely the best answer. The behaviorist theory states that personality is constructed by a series of learning experiences that occur through interactions between the individual and their environment. While the environment would contribute in the case presented in the question stem, genetics may also play a role, as the child is the biological offspring of the parents and would inherit their genes. Choice D is less likely than choice C to be the best answer.

7. **D is the best answer.** According to the passage, cluster 3 students were the ones that were high users of both alcohol and marijuana. These students may feel more pressure to use these substances to cope with increased stressors in college, fit in with peer groups, or may be otherwise genetically or environmentally predisposed. It is common for alcohol, tobacco, and marijuana to serve as "gateway" drugs for other substances, such as prescription drugs. In addition students that use alcohol and/or marijuana to cope with additional stress may turn to other substances for the same numbing effect. Option I is a component of the best answer. The high alcohol and marijuana consumption could be related to increased anxiety and stress, making option II a component of the best answer. Eating disorders are found in a higher percentage of people with anxiety, compared to the general population. Option III may also be plausible, making choice D the best answer.

8. **D is the best answer.** The bystander effect describes diffusion of responsibility, where, in the presence of large groups of people, individuals assume someone else will help. This is not applicable to the scenario presented in the question stem, eliminating choice A. Social loafing occurs when members of a group decrease the pace or intensity of their work with the intention of letting others in the group work harder. This term is also not applicable, eliminating choice B. Social facilitation is the tendency to perform better when a person knows he or she is being watched. This term is also not applicable, eliminating choice C. Peer pressure is the social influence exerted by one's peers to act in a way that is similar to their own behavior. If many members of the party, including the host, smoke, other students may feel pressure to "fit in" with the remaining party-goers. Choice D is the best answer.

9. **B is the best answer.** The question stem hints at the challenge to the trait-based explanation of personality. In addition, the third paragraph of the passage notes that personality traits are one factor in determining whether a student will use alcohol and marijuana or not. The situational approach to explaining behavior says that the concept of enduring personality traits is flawed because of variations in behavior that take place across different situations. The best answer will be the one that shows varying behavior in two circumstances. A student that drinks coffee in the morning both at home and while at college is upholding the same behavior in both environments. Choice A can be eliminated. Drinking while in college but abstaining while at home shows a variation in behavior in two circumstances. Choice B is most likely to be the best answer. Both choices C and D do not provide two situations to compare behavior in, making them less likely to be the best answer.

10. **D is the best answer.** Notice that over the second and third semesters, the GPA values for cluster one and cluster two students are comparable, as their error bars overlap. This stands in contrast to the first semester, where cluster 2 students perform significantly worse than cluster 1 students. If cluster 2 students developed tolerance to higher levels of alcohol, then the effects attributed to alcohol may not affect their academic performance. Choice A can be eliminated. Similarly, if a student only consumes alcohol when there are no upcoming exams, he or she may be lessening the quantitative effect of alcohol on academic performance. If students chose to switch to less rigorous majors, these students may be able to achieve higher grades in these courses compared to more challenging courses. Choice C can be eliminated. Choices A-C would provide an example for why the GPA measurements of cluster 1 and cluster 2 students became equivalent after semester one. If cluster 2 students reported less time studying, then their grades should have continued to decrease, making choice D the best answer.

Stand-alones (Questions 11-14)

11. **D is the best answer.** The behaviorist theory focuses on learned experiences, so it is a possible answer choice. The humanistic theory focuses on choices and the role of the individual, so choice B is also a possible answer. Ideally, the best answer would combine postulates of the behaviorist and humanistic theories. The psychoanalytic theory focuses on the id, ego, and superego. These were not mentioned in the question stem, so choice C is not a strong answer. The social cognitive theory is similar to the behaviorist theory in that it focuses on learning but is also similar to the humanistic theory in that it focuses on choices, so choice D is the best answer.

12. **A is the best answer.** The humanistic theory says that people continually seek experiences that make them better, more fulfilled individuals. This means the best answer will be an experience that was not required, but would help an individual grow for his or her own benefit and the benefit of others. Reading a book that would help explain how a doctor may improve his discussions of end of life care with cancer patients is an example of an experience that would likely improve the doctor and the care of his patients. Choice A is a good candidate for the best answer. A student that does not seek extra enrichment suggests he or she may not be attempting to grow academically. This makes choice B less likely than choice A to be the best answer. A lawyer that prepares for a case at the last minute is also not seeking experiences to enrich him or herself, eliminating choice C. In addition, failure to double check a new article indicates that the journalist is not upholding him or herself to the most stringent standards, making choice D less likely than choice A to be the best answer.

13. **C is the best answer.** The situation presented in the question stem implies that others attend these mortality and morbidity conferences in order to learn from the mistakes of others in the attempt to prevent future patient harm. Self-actualization is the development and realization of one's full potential in life. That is too broad of a definition for attendance at a mortality and morbidity conference to fulfill, though this could be a component. Choice A is unlikely to be the best answer. Social cognitive theory focuses more on how thought and emotion affect the learning process. The conferences described seem to focus on learning from observed behavior rather than emotional exploration. Choice B is unlikely to be the best answer. Observational learning occurs when people learn from the experiences of others, as exemplified by the question stem. Choice C is a strong answer choice. Psychoanalytic theory describes how personality is determined by the flow of psychic energies between the id, superego, and ego. The presented conference is not an example of these energies, making choice D less likely than choice C to be the best answer.

14. **B is the best answer.** The question stem describes two scenarios, where the student displays confidence in one scenario but a lack of confidence in a second scenario. A personality is often considered a fixed set of traits for a particular individual that does not vary with a changing situation. Choice A is unlikely to be the best answer. Differences in situational anxiety could help explain why the student appears confident in one scenario, but not in another. Choice B may be the best answer. Temperament is an innate baseline of personality that includes a tendency towards certain patterns of emotional and social interaction. It is unlikely to change depending on the situation, eliminating choice C. Heredity describes the genetic influence on behavior. The student's genetic make-up would not change between situations, eliminating choice D.

Passage 3 (Questions 15-18)

15. **B is the best answer.** Self-efficacy is defined as a person's perception of being able to accomplish something, in this case work. Choice A only touches on situational attribution, associating illness with the ability to work. Self-efficacy ought to be a more global self-judgment, so choice A is not the best answer. Choice B correctly defines self-efficacy as feeling able and willing to work, making choice B the best answer. Choice C may be tempting because perception of ability to work would correctly be considered self-efficacy, but the perception of self as a whole is defined as self-esteem, which is unrelated to the question stem. Choice D can be eliminated because this also relates to self-esteem and not self-efficacy.

16. **A is the best answer.** This two-part question requires an understanding of personality theories and the experimental design of Study 1. The hypothesis that combining CKD treatment with work will stimulate a positive sense of self is most related to the humanistic theory because this theory states that people seek out experiences—in this case work—that make them more fulfilled. By looking at the answer choices, choices A and C are the only ones that include humanistic theorist as part of the answer choice. Choices B and D can be eliminated because the social cognitive theory is more focused on observational learning and the interaction among personal, behavioral, and environmental factors rather than on personal fulfillment. The second part of the question requires an understanding of the experimental design of Study 1. The answer choices show only slight differences- the use of "independent variable" or "dependent variable". Looking at the remaining choices A and C, choice A is the best answer because it talks about maintaining the same independent variable in the study, which is employment status (employed versus unemployed). This is something that can be manipulated by the researcher. Choice C mentions maintaining same the dependent variables, which in this study are the results of the questionnaire (i.e. job satisfaction, level of fulfillment, etc.). The dependent variable is not changed by the researcher, so choice C can be eliminated because it infers the possibility of changing the dependent variable. This leaves choice A as the best answer.

17. **C is the best answer.** This two-part question requires drawing a connection between the "follow-up study" and the results of Study 2 as it relates to education level of CKD patients. Study 2 states that educated patients had higher self-esteem compared to patients with a low and moderate educational level. Self-esteem can be defined as the way a person judges themselves, so higher educated patients tend to judge themselves more positively than lower educated patients. This corresponds to choices A, C and D, leaving choice B to be eliminated. The follow-up study described in the question stem found that educated patients were more motivated to continue working even in a changing and stressful situation. This is most related to the idea of a positive self-concept. A person with a positive self-concept not only has high self-esteem but also remains constant through variable situations (in this case, dialysis). Choice A can be eliminated because while it does correctly describe lower educated patients as having a more negative self-esteem, it incorrectly describes them as having a positive self-concept. Choice B is not the best answer because it incorrectly states that lower-educated patients have a higher self-esteem. Choice C correctly describes higher educated patients as having high self-esteem and positive self-concept, making choice C the best answer. Choice D cannot be the best answer because it describes higher educated patients as having a negative self-concept.

18. **A is the best answer.** The situational approach to explaining behavior states that a person may behave differently across varying situations. In the case of dialysis, it may be possible that a patient is unemployed not because working is unimportant to them but because they consider working to be impossible due to this situation. Study 1 reveals that unemployed patients ranked the importance of working as a 5.2 out of 7, which is not that different from the score of employed patients (5.8). This affirms the idea that unemployed patients may consider working as important but simply not possible because of their situation, which corresponds to choice A. Choice B is not the best answer because unemployed patients do consider working to be fairly important. Choice C can be eliminated because there was no mention in the study of dialysis being more important than working. Study 1 also does not mention anything about self-efficacy, so choice D can also be eliminated.

Passage 4 (Questions 19-22)

19. **A is the best answer.** Multiple factors contribute to the central part of self-concept, which is how people integrate psychological, sociocultural, and biological factors to define themselves and how they interact with others. Individuals that have a high level of scientific literacy are likely to be familiar with the rigors of scientific research and incorporate data into their decision-making process. The authorities referenced in the passage are likely scientists and physicians, so those with high scientific literacy would likely trust these authorities more and be more affected by their recommendations, likely making choice A the best answer and eliminating choice B. Those participants with high scientific literacy are likely to be aware of the miniscule dangers of vaccination and integrate this into their decision-making, making choice C less likely to be the best answer. Those participants that were able to incorporate data into their decisions would also feel less powerless than other participants, likely eliminating choice D as the best answer.

20. **B is the best answer.** Kohlberg's theory of moral development proposes that children and adults progress through a predictable sequence of stages of moral reasoning. These stages can be divided into three levels of preconventional morality, conventional morality, and postconventional morality. Stage 6, universal ethics, is the final stage of development and belongs in postconventional morality, eliminating choice A, which incorrectly pairs it with preconventional morality. Choosing to vaccinate the child likely plays into an implicit social contract with other parents to also vaccinate their children in order for the population to reach herd immunity vaccination rates. Social contract is a postconventional level, likely making choice B the best answer. Rule following is a conventional morality stage, but parents have the choice to vaccinate or not vaccinate, meaning choice C is less likely to be the best answer. Social disapproval is a conventional morality stage, not a postconventional morality stage, eliminating choice D.

21. **D is the best answer.** The study includes follow-up questions about how four factors determined whether a participant would vaccinate a child. The question stem notes that some participants ranked powerlessness to interpret the medical literature as the greatest reason for avoiding vaccination. This suggests that these participants may feel that they have less control over the decision-making process compared to individuals that would be comfortable interpreting medical literature. These participants can be considered to have a weaker internal locus of control relating to their decision to vaccinate or not. As the individual beliefs do play a role in determining whether a study participant would have vaccinated a child, choice A can be eliminated. Remember that the MCAT® rarely uses all-or-nothing words, like sole, in the best answer choice. Decision-making and locus of control likely incorporate beliefs, as well environmental factors and life experiences. This makes it unlikely that these four beliefs are the only factors the participants considered, making choice B unlikely to be the best answer. The question stem notes that some participants ranked powerlessness to interpret medical literature as the greatest reason for avoiding vaccination. This means that some participants did not weigh each belief equally. Choice C is unlikely to be the best answer. Beliefs and how these beliefs shape the participants locus of control over the vaccine decision-making process likely does affect their ultimate decision to vaccinate or not. However, additional factors, such as cost, medical contraindications, and other factors not specifically mentioned in the last paragraph would likely affect the decision to vaccinate or not. Choice D is the best answer.

22. **B is the best answer.** Freud proposed a theory of developmental stages that were a sequential series of psychosexual stages in early childhood. It is important to know that the MCAT® requires the ages to be memorized for every theory discussed. These theories are tested often, so it is worth spending the time to memorize the correlations between age and stage. During the Anal Developmental Stage, around age 2, children are learning toilet training, eliminating choice A. During the Phallic stage, between ages 3-6, children are learning about gender and sexual identification. This matches the age range of the children presented in the passage, making choice B most likely to be the best answer. Between the ages of 7-12, children are in the Latent stage, where they are exploring social development. This eliminates choice C. The skills necessary to nurse are learned during the first year of life, eliminating choice D.

Passage 5 (Questions 23-26)

23. **C is the best answer.** Behaviorism theory refers to the belief that behaviors are developed through conditioning, without thought or feeling. Behaviorism focuses on the environment, not genetics, so choice A is not the best answer. Behaviorism does suggest personality is dynamic, but there is not a major focus on evolution. Choice B is possible, but there is likely a better answer. As stated, behaviorism does focus on environmental contributions to behavior as well as learning, which is sometimes used as a synonym for conditioning. Choice C is a very strong answer. Choice D refers to training, which may be used to describe conditioning, but it is not clear what "repeated exposures" means. If anything, this is suggestive of Pavlovian classical conditioning or of the exposure therapy used for individuals with specific anxiety. Choice D is too vague whereas choice C is succinct and accurate.

24. **C is the best answer.** The diagnosis of bipolar disorder requires at least one manic episode. This is a fact worth knowing for the MCAT® but was also mentioned in the passage. The only feature specific to BD was manic emotional response. Anxiety, depression, and suicidality can be seen in bipolar disorder, but they are not specific to BD.

25. **D is the best answer.** Imitation is a mechanism of identity formation. In a patient with BD, the parent should have similar characteristics if imitation occurred. A parent who is dismissive, self-absorbed, and unreliable may produce a child with mental illness, but these are not words used to describe a person with BD in the passage, so choice A is not the best answer. The terms amicable, popular, and formidable are all positive, so these are probably not the best answer. Also, these terms were not mentioned in the passage, so choice B is not the best answer. Ornery, strong-willed, and dependable are mostly positive terms so again, choice C is not the best answer. Impulsive, grandiose, and self-centered are all features that may be present in bipolar disorder. Notice how impulsive and grandiose were specifically mentioned in the passage, and self-centered is suggested by the phrase "poor social skills."

26. **A is the best answer.** The key to this question is to pick the test that is similar to the one used in the passage. Choice A refers to behaviors that are not specific symptoms of OCD but may be expected in a person with OCD. Choice A is a strong answer. Choice B refers specifically to obsessive thoughts, these are diagnostic of OCD, but notice how the test in the passage focused on "composing items not related to symptoms themselves, but rather to behavioral tendencies." Choice B focuses too heavily on symptoms, so it is not a strong answer. Choice C references checklists. It is not clear if the authors used a checklist (yes or no) or scales (1-10). Choice C is possible but very vague and not as strong as choice A. Choice D makes the same error as choice B, as it refers to a symptom of OCD, not a behavior that may predispose a person to OCD. Choice D is not the best answer, and choice A should be selected.

Stand-alones (Questions 27-30)

27. **C is the best answer.** The question stem implies that the student both improves herself by asking for continued feedback and gains increased trust from her mentors as a result of her asking for feedback. Social cognitive theory describes how thought and emotion direct the learning experience, with interactions with others taking a less prominent role. The student's request for feedback does match social cognitive theory, but the other answer choices should be considered as well. The student is not observing others' behavior, but rather asking about her own. This is not observational learning, eliminating choice B. Reciprocal causation is a key tenant of social cognitive theory and states that behavior, personal factors, and environmental factors continually interact with one another. This is a prime example of what is occurring in the situation described in the question stem. The student initiates an action and a reciprocal reaction from the mentor is to trust the student's work more. Reciprocal causation is a more specific example of what is occurring, compared to social cognitive theory, likely making choice C a better answer choice than choice A. Self-actualization describes fulfilling one's life goals, which seems too broad of an answer for the situation described in the question stem. Choice D is unlikely to be the best answer.

28. **C is the best answer.** The question stem notes that the patients are only able to correctly administer insulin injections with the doctor's help, implying that they cannot correctly administer the shots alone. Thus, the correct psychological classification would involve some sort of classification that takes into account a patient's ability to only complete a task with the guidance of others. An individual's reference group is a group that provides him or her with a model for appropriate actions, values, and world views. While a patient is likely to model some behaviors after the pediatrician (such as administering medication), the patient's interactions with the pediatrician are likely too limited in quantity to be considered part of the reference group. Thus, choice A can be eliminated. Freud's latent stage of psychosocial development describes a period during which sexual impulsivities are suppressed and children are able to focus on other developmental tasks. This does not have to do with completing a task with the guidance of someone else, nor does the question stem indicate suppressed sexual impulsivity, and as such, choice B can be eliminated. Vygotsky proposed that the development of a child can be defined in terms of the child's current and potential levels of achievement. The current developmental level consists of tasks that the child can do alone. The potential developmental level represents the most advanced tasks that a child can do with guidance from more knowledgeable people. The range of activities in-between these two levels are considered within the zone of proximal development, and these activities are all of the tasks that can be accomplished successfully with help. The zone of proximal development thus describes patients that can only accomplish a task (administering insulin shots) with the help of others (the doctor), and as such, choice C is a strong answer. Erikson's developmental stage of autonomy vs. shame and doubt describes a stage of development in which the child develops a growing sense of whether he or she is competent to carry out self-care. While the patients described in the question could potentially fall in this grouping, the question stem does not indicate the thoughts of the patients, which are crucial to classifying these patients within Erikson's developmental stages. Thus, choice D can be eliminated, and choice C can be selected as the best answer.

29. **D is the best answer.** Different demographics are used to develop a person's identity. These include race/ethnicity, age, gender, socioeconomic status, and education level. Choices A, B and C are all types of identity. Although choice D, personal identity, sounds like a strong answer choice, it does not refer to a specific type of identity, so choice D is the best answer.

30. **A is the best answer.** Kohlberg's theory of moral development suggests that children progress through a predictable sequence of stages of moral reasoning: the preconventional level, then the conventional level, and finally the postconventional level. At this point, because trust vs. mistrust and obedience vs. disobedience are not stages of Kohlberg's theory of moral development, choices C and D, respectively, can be eliminated. The preconventional level describes moral judgments that are based solely on consideration of the anticipated consequences of behavior. The question stem indicates that the patients are taking their medications due to the anticipated consequences of not taking them (namely, from their parents). This is consistent with the preconventional level, and as such, choice A is a strong answer. The conventional level takes into account social judgments, and it describes behaviors as a result of gaining approval from social groups and society in general. The question stem does not indicate that the patients are taking medication to gain favorable social judgments, and as such, choice B can be eliminated, allowing for choice A to remain as the best answer.

Passage 6 (Questions 31-34)

31. **C is the best answer.** There are multiple theories to explain personality. The humanistic theory focuses on how the individual can shape there own personality. The behaviorist theory believes that personality is shaped by learned experiences and behaviors. Neither of these quite fit with the passage, which focuses on traits, so choice A and B are not the best answer. The trait theory is also known as the dispositional theory because it states that certain traits can be used to explain personality, and these traits are inherent and stable over time. Choice C is a strong answer. The psychoanalytic perspective was developed by Freud and utilizes the id, ego, and superego constructs to describe personality. These were not mentioned in the passage, so choice D is not the best answer.

32. **A is the best answer.** The passage focuses on the trait perspective of personality, which states that personality traits are stable over time. According to the passage, empathetic concern is predicted by agreeableness, so choice A is true and likely the best answer. Because it is correlated to agreeableness and agreeableness is stable over a lifetime, according to the trait perspective, empathetic concern should be stable too. Choice B is not as strong, because it states that empathetic concern is not stable over a lifetime. Choices C and D are both inaccurate in that empathetic concern was not predicted by conscientiousness. Conscientiousness predicted perspective taking only.

33. **D is the best answer.** There is no information in the passage that is useful for this question. In fact, this question is a pseudo-standalone question. Freud's psychoanalytic theory of personality has three parts—the id, the ego, and the superego. His psychoanalytic theory of psychopathology focuses extensively on the unconscious, but this is not a part of his theory of personality. Choice A can be ruled out. The id is the part of personality that can be thought of as being fueled by all the animalistic drives. The superego is the opposite of the id; it relies on moral reasoning to control the id. The ego is the result of the id and superego competing to produce an organized and realistic behavior. Empathy is not a trait developed by the id, so choice B can be ruled out. It is now necessary to choose between the ego and the superego. The ego is not always moral; at times it favors the id and may not exhibit empathy. Between choices C and D, the best answer is choice D.

34. **D is the best answer.** An in-group is the group which a person identifies with. The passage indicates empathy is related to agreeableness, neuroticism, openness, and conscientiousness. This means that an empathetic student is likely to have an in-group that possesses those traits. Choice A is true and not the best answer. A reference group is the group that provides the model for appropriate actions. A student's reference group should be empathetic and thus will have the traits mentioned above. Choice B is true and not the best answer. Imitation is a way of mimicking desirable behavior. Again, an empathetic student would be likely to relate to other empathetic students. Because empathy is related to agreeableness, choice C is true and not the best answer. The locus of control is the extent to which a person believes he or she has control over his or her life. This is very important in identity formation, but not related to the passage at all. Choice D is the best answer.

Passage 7 (Questions 35-38)

35. **A is the best answer.** There are two ways to answer this question—knowledge of the features of each type of personality disorder or knowledge of which personality disorders fall under "Cluster B." Antisocial personality disorder is in Cluster B and is associated with cynicism and manipulation. Choice A is a strong answer. Obsessive-compulsive personality disorder (OCD) is considered Cluster C, which is characterized by anxious behaviors. Neither OCD nor anxiety is associated with Machiavellian traits, so choice B is not the best answer. Paranoid and schizotypal personality disorders are both Cluster A, which encompasses odd and eccentric behaviors. These disorders are not associated with Machiavellian traits, so choices C and D are not the best answers.

36. **A is the best answer.** Under trait theory, a personality trait should be constant over a life span and present in varying amounts from person to person. This means a trait can be measured on a continuum. This is most consistent with choice A. Choice B states traits are dichotomous variables when they are not. Choices C and D state traits vary over a life time which they do not according to the trait perspective.

37. **B is the best answer.** The self is comprised of the id, ego, and superego under Freud's psychoanalytic perspective of personality. Choice A is too vague, so it is not likely the best answer. The id is responsible for instincts and is often thought of as the devil on one's shoulder. On the contrary, the superego is the angel on one's shoulder and considers morals and ethics. The ego melds these two competing perspectives to produce behavior. Drug use would be more result of the id than the ego or superego, so choice B is the best answer.

38. **D is the best answer.** In the passage, drug use was associated with Machiavellianism, low cooperativeness, and low self-directedness. There is no mention of self-esteem, although it is likely drug users do not have very high self-esteem, so choice A is not the best answer. Self-efficacy is the extent to which one believes he or she can accomplish his or her goals. Since there was low self-directedness, self-efficacy is likely low as well. Choice B is not the best answer. The locus of control can be either internal or external, where internal locus of control is the belief that one can control his or her life, whereas the external locus of control is the belief in "fate" or a power outside oneself that is controlling his or her life. The low self-directedness is probably associated with an external locus of control, so choice D is the best answer.

Passage 8 (Questions 39-44)

39. **C is the best answer.** An in-group is the social group to which an individual belongs to, while an out-group is a group to which an individual does not belong to. The 120 individuals are all part of a group of participants and do belong in the same group. However, in-group dynamics, such as preferable treatment or favoritism, are not a major factor in this experiment, so choice A is not the best answer. There are no divisions amongst the participants to create separate groups, so it is unlikely that out-group dynamics are in effect in this experiment. Therefore, choice B is not the best answer. A reference group is a group to which an individual looks to for information or comparison. Because the individual is shown the average rating of the group, the individual can use that information as a reference of the overall opinion of the group. While the rest of the participants are also members of an in-group, their primary role in this experiment is as a reference group. This reasoning is why choice C is a better answer than choice A. A primary group is an intimate group that interacts on a day-to-day basis, such as a family or close friend circles. The 120 participants do not interact with each other on a daily basis and are not members of a primary group. Therefore, choice D is not the best answer.

40. **A is the best answer.** The trait theory of personality theorizes that personality consists of a set of traits that vary from person to person. These traits are stable over the course of a lifetime, which is an important factor in answering this question. Because the study found that food preferences change minimally over a lifetime, this study offers support for the trait theory. The psychoanalytic theory proposes that personality is determined by the flow of psychic energy between three systems: the id, the superego, and the ego. There is no mention of these three systems in the passage or the question. Additionally, a central premise of psychoanalytic theory is the transition of an individual through different stages of life; this tenet runs counter to the idea that food preferences stay stagnant through a lifetime. Choice B is not the best answer. The behaviorist theory postulates that personality is constructed from differential learning experiences over the course of a person's life. Again, this theory focuses on how people change their personality and behavior over time; choice C is not the best answer. The humanistic theory postulates that people continually seek experiences that make them better, more fulfilled individuals. This has a tenuous application to an individual's food preferences; generally, this theory focuses on achievements in life, and maximizing one's potential. Choice D is not the best answer.

41. **A is the best answer.** The study in the passage revealed that a person's food preferences can be altered by shifting the social norms the person is exposed to. However, the second study revealed that although a person's preference for healthy foods can be changed through social interaction, their actual eating habits do not vary. This suggests that eating behavior is more influenced by a person's disposition, rather than the situation or social influences. Choice A focuses on attempting to alter an individual's eating behavior through one-on-one interaction. While there is no guarantee that this strategy will be effective, this answer choice is the strategy that focuses the most on changing an individual's disposition, rather than attempting to influence them socially. This strategy best incorporates the results of the studies, which was the original goal of the nutritionist. Therefore, choice A is a strong answer. Choices B and C both involve trying to influence a person's eating behavior through altering their social environment. The results of the studies in the passage suggest that these methods would be ineffectual in actually changing eating behavior, so choices B and C are not the best answers. Choice D is a restatement of the experimental procedure. The act of rating food items, without the exposure to either a healthy or unhealthy social norm, is unlikely to change a participant's food preferences. Additionally, a change in food preferences does not even equate to a change in eating behavior. Choice D is not the best answer.

42. **D is the best answer.** Because the experimenters want to study the effect of mood disorders, it is reasonable to assume that only participants with mood disorders should be allowed to participate in the study (excluding the control population). Choice A is a symptom of depression. Because depression is a mood disorder, patients with these symptoms would be allowed in the hypothetical study. Choice B is a symptom of bipolar disorder, which is a mood disorder. There are no psychological disorders that can be diagnosed based on serum levels of monoamines. The serum is a component of the blood and neurotransmitters are rarely found in the serum in concentrations high enough to measure. If diagnosing mood disorders was as simple as checking serum levels, there would be no purpose for using the DSM. Choice C is not the best answer. Choice D includes symptoms of various personality disorders, which are NOT considered in the same category as mood disorders. Choice D is the best answer.

43. **B is the best answer.** Erikson's stages of psychosocial development are a high-yield topic in the MCAT®, and should be generally memorized in order to answer this question. It is safe to assume university students are generally between the ages of 18-25. Choices A, C, and D have age ranges of 65+, 5-12, and 4-5, respectively. These age ranges are not strict, but choice B, intimacy vs. isolation, has the closest age range to that of university students, at 19-39. Most university students would fall into this range, making B the best answer. Additionally, this is an age range where romantic relationships often become priorities for individuals, giving additional evidence that choice B might be the best answer.

44. **A is the best answer.** The biomedical approach attributes disease to biological causes, without regard to psychological or sociological effects. Choice A is an example of the biomedical approach, which emphasizes that genes are the sole cause of eating behavior, likely making it the best answer. Choice B is an example of the application of the biopsychosocial model, which does integrate concepts of biology, psychology, and sociology when attempting to explain a disease or behavior. Choice B is not the best answer. Choices C and D are both criticisms of the experimental design, rather than interpretations of the results. Neither make mention of key biomedical concepts, such as genetics, pathophysiology, or neurological functioning. Therefore, neither of these choices are the best answer.

Stand-alones (Questions 45-48)

45. **C is the best answer.** Stem cells can be either pluripotent or totipotent. The answer choices are all pluripotent, so it is necessary to choose the cell line that can produce neurons. Neurons are derived from ectoderm, so these stem cells would be most effective. The endoderm gives rise to the gut, so choice A is not the best answer. The mesoderm gives rise to the muscles, bones, and vascular system, so choice B is not the best answer. Ectoderm gives rise to neurons and skin, so choice C is the best answer. Mesenchyme tissue from the mesoderm, so choice D is not the best answer.

46. **A is the best answer.** β-amyloid plaques and neurofibrillary tangles are associated with Alzheimer's disease, likely making choice A the best answer. Amyotrophic lateral sclerosis (ALS) is a complex degeneration of motor neurons leading to paralysis and is not tested by the MCAT®. It is also not associated with β-amyloid plaques and neurofibrillary tangles, so choice B can be eliminated. Korsakoff's syndrome is usually seen in chronic alcoholics and has similar symptoms as Alzheimer's disease but lacks the characteristic β-amyloid plaques and neurofibrillary tangles, so choice C can be eliminated. Parkinson's disease is a progressive motor disease that is associated with Lewy bodies but not β-amyloid plaques and neurofibrillary tangles, so choice D can be eliminated.

47. **B is the best answer.** While these are all symptoms of schizophrenia, choice B is the only term that describes the symptom in question. A hallucination is a sensory perception that does not correspond with reality. If John hears a voice in his head that is not actually there, then he is experiencing an auditory hallucination, so choice B is the best answer. A delusion is an unrealistic or unreasonable belief without an associated stimulus, so choice A is not the best answer. Disorganized thought describes cognition and how John thinks through something, which does not characterize this stimulus, so choice C is also not the best answer. A negative symptom is the absence of normal behavior, while a positive symptom is the addition of abnormal behavior. Because this would be classified as a positive symptom, choice D can be eliminated.

48. **A is the best answer.** Anxiety disorders are the most common psychological disorders. Bipolar disorder is a mood disorder that is relatively rare, so choice B is not the best answer. Depression is also very common but considerably less so than anxiety, so choice C is not the best answer. Schizophrenia is a rare psychotic disorder, so choice D is not the best answer.

Passage 9 (Questions 49-52)

49. **D is the best answer.** The table shows under the "diagnosed depression" category that there are fewer patients with breast cancer diagnosed with depression, 355 vs. 579. Therefore patients with breast cancer were less likely to be diagnosed with depression, so choices A and B can be eliminated. There is no evidence to suggest that the patients with breast cancer are less likely to be depressed than other patients, therefore choice C can be eliminated. Because of the rigor and regimented nature of breast cancer treatment it is true that an oncologist might fail to consult a mental health professional even if their patient was showing signs of depression. Out of these options, choice D is the most probable, thus it is the best answer.

50. **A is the best answer.** Anxiety disorders are defined by the experience of unwarranted fear and anxiety, physiological tension, and behaviors associated with the emotional and physical experience of anxiety. Anxiety can manifested physically as excessive sympathetic nervous system activation, so choice A is a strong answer. Depression is defined by pervasive feelings of sadness and hopelessness and/or the loss of interest in activities that an individual usually enjoys. Excessive sympathetic nervous system activation has to do more with the body's preparation for "fight or flight" responses. The symptoms for depression are not listed for the patient in the question and the symptoms associated with excessive sympathetic nervous system activation are not associated with depression, therefore, choice B can be eliminated. Because depression does not seem to be correlated with the symptoms described choice C can also be eliminated. Anxiety does fit the symptoms listed in the question, thus choice D can be eliminated.

51. **A is the best answer.** The categories that the study used to match participants were age at admission, race/ethnicity, length of stay, insurance type, residential income, and discharge disposition. Matching participants is important because it attempts to control for confounds that might make the results insignificant or falsely significant. Genetic predisposition to depression was not controlled in the experiment yet is an extremely important factor as to the likelihood that a patient will develop depression. This would be very hard for experimenters to control for yet would have a big effect on the reliability of the results, choice A is very strong. Personality is the collection of lasting characteristics that make a person unique. This is extremely imprecise and hard to quantify or categorize and thus would not be a good tool for researchers to use to match participants. Choice B is not the best choice. Residential income was looked at by researchers, this is similar to the category of financial situation, thus, comparing this would not make as big of an impact on the results as choice A. Choice C can be eliminated. Temperament is a component of personality, thus for the same reasons as choice B, choice D can be eliminated and choice A is still the strongest option.

52. **D is the best answer.** The biomedical model assumes that all illness can be fully explained through biological processes alone. The biopsychosocial model was developed by George Engel as a response to the biomedical model and states that biology alone cannot account for the intricacies of disease progression in an individual patient, even in cases where biology underlies the development of psychological condition. This model is much better suited for discussion of psychological conditions that likely have environmental factors. Thus, choices A and B can be eliminated. Choice C offers the correct model, biopsychosocial, but offers the wrong reason for it being the best answer. While it is true that biological processes are extremely important this does not tell the whole story, thus, choice D is better than choice C because it offers both biological and external factors to weigh in.

Passage 10 (Questions 53-56)

53. **B is the best answer.** The PGC is a morale measure where a low score means low morale. This is associated with depression, according to the first paragraph. Depression is a mood disorder, so choice B is the best answer. Other mental disorders including anxiety disorders, personality disorders, and trauma-related disorders can coexist with mood disorders, but a mood disorder was mentioned specifically in the passage, so choices A, C, and D are not the best answer.

54. **D is the best answer.** The researchers have focused their model on social factors that influence morale and depression. The best answer should be a perspective that focuses on situations and experiences that shape behavior. The biological theory focuses on genetic causes for personality. The researchers do not take this approach to depression, so they would not favor this view. Choice A can be eliminated. The psychoanalytic theory of personality is unique. It is Freud's theory and has the id, ego, and superego. It is not a behavioral perspective, so choice B can be eliminated. The trait theory is similar to the biological theory in that it focuses on innate aspects of personality, called traits. It does not suggest that experiences shape personality, so choice C can be ruled out. This leaves choice D as the best answer. The social cognitive theory of personality focuses on how experiences and choices can shape behaviors. It is very similar to the approach taken by the researchers to explain depression in the passage.

55. **C is the best answer.** The first paragraph refers to depression. Under a biological framework, depression is thought to be caused by a relative depletion of neurotransmitters called monoamines, which include epinephrine, dopamine, and serotonin. Epinephrine, also known as adrenaline, would be depleted, so choice A is a possible answer. GABA is an inhibitory neurotransmitter. It is not a monoamine, and it is not thought to be depleted in depression, so choice B can be eliminated. As stated, the biological theory of depression focuses on monoamine depletion. Choice C is broader than choice A and thus a better answer. Orexin is involved in appetite and sleep cues. It is not a monoamine and not typically cited as being depleted in depression, so choice D is not the best answer.

56. **A is the best answer.** The MCAT® requires knowledge of prevalence of psychiatric disorders. Anxiety disorders are most common, with a prevalence of about 20%. Depression and other mood disorders have a prevalence of about 10%, so choice B is not the best answer. Dissociative disorders and schizophrenia are both rare with a prevalence of about 1%, so choices C and D are not the best answer.

Stand-alones (Questions 57-59)

57. **C is the best answer.** Parkinson's disease is characterized by slow movement, tremors, and a flat affect. The researchers seem to be monitoring the mood, or affect, of patients over the course of their disease. A confounding variable would be anything other than the disease that affects mood. SSRIs are used to treat depression and likely have a positive impact on mood, so option I is a component of the best answer. Option II is not a confounding variable; it is the dependent variable, or the one being measured by researchers. Presence of a mood disorder would be a confounding variable, so option III is a component of the best answer, which makes choice C the best answer.

58. **D is the best answer.** Choices A, B, and C are all commonly believe to have a genetic component. Choice D, post traumatic stress disorder, is a rare condition that is usually caused by an intensely stressful situation experienced by an individual earlier in his or her life. It is unlikely that genetics play a large role in PTSD, compared to choices A, B, or C, so choice D is the best answer.

59. **C is the best answer.** The fundamental attribution error is a concept that is closely related to the situation described in the question stem, but describes something slightly different, so choice A is not the best answer. The fundamental attribution error is the tendency to attribute the actions of others to dispositional rather than situational causes. The question stem does not present a situation in which one person judges another's actions. Choice B is not the best answer because dispositional attribution is the process by which a person concludes that the cause of a certain action is due to an intrinsic quality of the person. This describes the individual in the question stem when she attributed her promotion to the good qualities she possesses, but does not account for her conclusion that her failure was due to a reason that was out of her control. Choice C is the best answer because self-serving bias is defined as the tendency for an individual to attribute success to inherent qualities but attribute failures to situational factors. This accurately describes the situation explained in the question stem. Choice D is not the best answer because reciprocation theory is a term not tested by the MCAT®.

LECTURE

4

Thought and Emotion

TEST 4A

LECTURE 4 ANSWER KEY

TEST 4A		TEST 4B	
1. B	31. D	1. A	31. D
2. D	32. A	2. B	32. A
3. D	33. B	3. C	33. A
4. A	34. C	4. D	34. A
5. A	35. B	5. B	35. C
6. C	36. D	6. D	36. B
7. D	37. B	7. C	37. D
8. C	38. C	8. C	38. A
9. B	39. D	9. A	39. B
10. C	40. A	10. D	40. D
11. B	41. C	11. A	41. A
12. D	42. B	12. C	42. C
13. B	43. D	13. A	43. B
14. C	44. A	14. A	44. A
15. C	45. D	15. A	45. D
16. B	46. A	16. A	46. C
17. B	47. B	17. A	47. C
18. C	48. D	18. C	48. C
19. A	49. C	19. C	49. C
20. C	50. B	20. A	50. B
21. B	51. C	21. C	51. D
22. D	52. A	22. A	52. C
23. A	53. A	23. C	53. D
24. D	54. C	24. A	54. C
25. D	55. C	25. C	55. C
26. A	56. D	26. D	56. B
27. D	57. D	27. C	57. D
28. A	58. A	28. B	58. D
29. C	59. D	29. A	59. C
30. B		30. B	

EXPLANATIONS FOR LECTURE 4

Passage 1 (Questions 1-4)

1. **B is the best answer.** The passage focuses on cognition and language coevolution. The "skills" in the question stem refer to cognition. The question asks about the brain area that coevolved with the cognitive areas. So the question is asking which area of the brain is involved with language. The frontal lobes function primarily in planning and personality and also include Broca's area, which is responsible for productive speech. The insula is a deep cortical structure that has a role in cognitive function, emotion, and awareness. The frontal lobes, but not necessarily the insula are involved in language, so choice A is a possible answer but probably not the best answer. The temporal lobes are involved in the sensation of hearing and include Wernicke's area, which controls language fluency. Choice B is stronger than choice A because it only includes a part of the brain that controls language and does not list any structures involved in other processes. The amygdala is involved in emotion, and the entorhinal cortex is important in memory. Neither of these relate to language directly, so choice C is not the best answer. The occipital lobes are involved in vision, so choice D is not the best answer. This question seems very hard but is easier with this tip: the MCAT® will rarely have correct answers including terms that are unfamiliar. That rules out choice A and choice C. Between choices B and D, the occipital lobes really only function in vision. So, choice B is the best answer.

2. **D is the best answer.** This question is really about practicality. The brains and vocal cord specimens for humans prior to the evolution of language and cognition would be long decayed. So, choices A and B are not the best answer. Choice C refers to designing an experiment. Usually that is a very strong choice, but in this instance, it would take thousands of years for cognition and language to evolve fully in primates so choice C is not the best answer. Comparing the timing of tool usage and hieroglyphics would reveal more about cognition and language respectively. Choice D is the best answer.

3. **D is the best answer.** In order, Piaget's stages are sensorimotor, preoperational, concrete operation, formal operational. The sensorimotor stage is from 0-2 years old. This is prior to language development. Presumably, prior to the cognitive and language evolution in the passage, individuals remained in the sensorimotor stage. So, choice D is the best answer. Choices A, B, and C require more advanced cognitive abilities.

4. **A is the best answer.** Personality is mainly controlled by the frontal lobes. The popular example is that of Phineas Gage who had his frontal lobes damaged in an accident and had no symptoms except for wild changes in his personality. Executive function describes the ability to plan and execute tasks. This is also controlled by the frontal lobes. So, choice A is a very strong answer. The parietal lobes and temporal lobes are both involved in sensation, so choices B and C are not the best answer. The occipital lobes are involved in vision, so choice D is not the best answer.

Passage 2 (Questions 5-8)

5. **A is the best answer.** The student incorrectly summarized the results of the study. The study only proves correlation, not causation. The correct answer likely incorporates a technique that is prone to error. Heuristics are mental shortcuts. They are quick ways of solving a problem but are prone to error. Choice A is a possible answer. Trial and error, as its name suggests is prone to error. This method requires multiple attempts to achieve a correct answer. The student only made one statement, so choice B is a possible answer. An algorithm is a stepwise method for solving a problem. It is a very accurate problem solving approach. Choice C is not the best answer. Intuition is solving a problem by going with ones "gut." It is prone to error. Choice D is a possible answer. Between choices A, B and D, choice A is the best answer because of the "shortcut" implied by heuristics. The student made a shortcut in reasoning by equating correlation to causation. For this reason, choice A is the best answer.

6. **C is the best answer.** IQ is constant over a lifetime in the absence of neurological decline. The study revealed that the participants who volunteered had less dementia. It is safe to assume that the question refers to a participant who does not have dementia. Since IQ is constant over a lifetime, the best answer is the value nearest to 124, which is choice C, 125. Any test has a standard error of measurement. A participant who takes an IQ test on Monday and scores a 110 may score a 112 on Friday. This is likely within the standard error. The increase from 124 to 125 is not because the participant got smarter, but because the test has intrinsic error in measurement.

7. **D is the best answer.** Culture has a huge impact on cognition and aging. There are no cultures that expect the elderly to volunteer, so choices A and B are not the best answer. Between choice C and D, cognitive decline is more common in developed countries. In underdeveloped countries, healthcare is subpar. Individuals have a much shorter life expectancy due to death from infection and other treatable disease. Often, individuals do not live long enough to develop dementia, which rarely occurs before the age of 60. So, between choices C and D, choice D is the best answer.

8. **C is the best answer.** Dementia is a disease that affects memory in the elderly population. Forgetting names is a normal part of life; it is not specific to older age or to dementia. Choice A is not the best answer. Not recognizing loved ones is one of the challenging symptoms of dementia. Choice B is not the best answer. Delayed reaction time is a normal part of aging and is not a symptom of dementia, so choice C is a possible answer. Forgetting to eat is another symptom of dementia and is the mechanism by which dementia can be lethal. Choice D is not the best answer.

Stand-alones (Questions 9-12)

9. **B is the best answer.** There are two theories of language development: the nativist and the interactionist. These theories are not obvious from their names. The nativist theory states that language is an innate ability and implies that language could develop in isolation from other humans. Choice A provides the definition for the interactionist theory and is not the best answer. Choice B provides a partial definition of the nativist theory and is a strong answer. The interactionist theory states that language is learned through interacting with a fluent human. It does not refer to the interaction between biology and psychology, so choice C is not the best answer. It also does not rely on other theories, so choice D is not the best answer. This leaves choice B as the best answer.

10. **C is the best answer.** The information processing model compares the human brain to a computer and states that information enters the brain and is then processed so it can be stored and retrieved later. Choice A correctly describes the information processing model but does not explain the relationship to dementia. Choice A is a possible answer but is probably not the best answer. Choice B is a true statement but does not relate to the information processing model, so choice B is not the best answer. Choice C correctly describes the information processing model and provides an explanation for its relation to dementia. Choice C is a strong answer. Choice D has the same problem as choice B. It is a true statement, but it does not relate to the information processing model, so choice D is not the best answer.

11. **B is the best answer.** The therapist is trying to increase the child's interactions with other children. Interactionist theory proposes that the human brain develops to better socialize and become more receptive to new language inputs. It proposes that a child's motivation to expand their language capacity is increased when they interact more with other children. This makes choice B a strong answer. Nativist theory asserts that our brains have innate language acquisition mechanisms, which allow humans to learn syntax and grammar without significant environmental assistance. This theory is not being used as support for the recommendation of increasing the child's opportunities for social interactions, so choice A can be eliminated. Learning theory suggests that language is learned through the application of punishments and rewards, such as excitement or attention from parents. There is no reason to suspect that these parents are not creating an environment that utilizes this form of learning, so choice C can be eliminated. Relational theory does not exist and is included as an answer choice to sound tempting since it sounds like it might deal with relationships. Choice D can be eliminated.

12. **D is the best answer.** Broca's area, in the frontal lobe, contributes to speech production. Wernicke's area, located in the temporal lobe, contributes to the understanding of language. Since the patient can produce normal speech sounds but not comprehensible phrases, the damage is most likely in Wernicke's area. Remember that if two answer choices say the same thing but in different words, as is the case with choices A and C, then neither answer can be the correct answer. Choice B is unrelated to language and is not the best answer.

Passage 3 (Questions 13-16)

13. **B is the best answer.** The answer choices may seem intimidating, but the question can be answered with one key fact. The navigation task is a verbal task. Language is controlled by Broca's area and Wernicke's area in the frontal and temporal lobes, respectively. The occipital notch is likely in the occipital lobe. The occipital lobe is involved in vision, which is important when driving. The question refers specifically to the navigation task, which is a verbal task, so choice A is probably not the best answer. The left inferior frontal gyrus is the location of Broca's area. It is not necessary to memorize this fact. Notice that the answer choice includes the word "frontal" so it is safe to assume it is in the frontal lobe. Choice B is a strong answer choice. The subthalamic nucleus is a deep brain structure, just below ("sub-") the thalamus. It is not relevant what the function of the subthalamic nucleus is because it is not a brain region that is tested by the MCAT®. In fact, the function of the subthalamic nucleus is largely unknown. The superior parietal lobule is in the parietal lobe, which is not involved in language. So, choice D can be ruled out, and choice B is the best answer.

14. **C is the best answer.** Numerous factors would affect performance on a driving task. Caffeine is a stimulant that can increase focus and attention, so choice A is not the best answer. Alcohol is a depressant that can decrease focus and attention, so choice B is not the best answer. High IQ would probably not effect a participant's performance on the task since IQ is not clearly related to the task. This makes choice C a strong answer. Low IQ may impair a participant's ability to understand the directions for the task, so choice D is not the best answer.

15. **C is the best answer.** The MCAT® requires knowledge of certain psychological tests. The word association test is one in which participants are told a word and asked to say the first thing that comes to mind. This test is not related to driving or divided attention, so choice A is not the best answer. The Stroop test is very popular. It requires participants to look at colored text and state the color. The difficult part is that the words are all colors. For instance, if shown the word "red" in black font, participants would have to say "black" because the text is black. This is related to attention but more closely selective attention than divided attention, so choice B is possible but may not be the best answer. Field sobriety testing is conducted by law enforcement agents for DUI screening. The primary goal of the testing is to assess divided attention. The infamous heel-to-toe walk down a line is a test of balance but also of divided attention. A person has to remember the instructions, "take 9 steps down the line, turn around, and take 9 steps back. Count aloud and each step should connect the stepping heel with the standing toe". Remembering to count, turn around, and walk back requires divided attention, so choice C is a strong answer. Operational span testing tests a person's working memory. Working memory relies on divided attention to an extent, but choice C is stronger than choice D.

16. **B is the best answer.** The radio tuning task must be performed in a certain order every time—much like an algorithm. Analogies, intuition, and heuristics are all effective means of problem solving. Analogies compare the current problem to a previous problem. The participants likely have tuned a radio while driving before, so this is a possible answer. An algorithm is a step-wise method for completing a task. The radio tuning task and navigation task both have certain steps to follow, so choice B is better than choice A. Intuition is a form of problem solving based on instinct. Since the task has specific steps, choice C is not the best answer. Heuristics are mental shortcuts that can be used to solve a problem quickly. The tasks both need to be solved quickly, but shortcuts cannot be taken, so choice C is not the best answer.

Passage 4 (Questions 17-22)

17. **B is the best answer.** The question is asking about barriers to problem solving. The four answer choices are common barriers and should be known for the MCAT®. Confirmation bias occurs when a person seeks information that conforms to his or her preconceived idea. This is not clearly applicable to the passage, so choice A is not a strong answer. Fixation is the failure to see a situation from a new perspective. Fixation often results in the inability to make a decision. This loosely applies to the passage because this phenomenon was observed in the patients with schizophrenia. Choice B is better than choice A. Heuristics are mental shortcuts used to make quick decisions. The schizophrenia patients were unable to make a decision about the "regret" item, so choice C is not as strong as choice B. Belief bias is the tendency to judge an argument based on the plausibility of the conclusion, not the strength of the argument. This does not clearly apply to the passage, so choice D is not the best answer.

18. **C is the best answer.** Handle this question by process of elimination. The first part of choice A and B is true: there is a theory of intelligence that states there are eight types of intelligence. This is also known as Gardner's theory of multiple intelligences. They include musical, visual-spatial, verbal-linguistic, logical-mathematical, bodily-kinesthetic, interpersonal, intrapersonal, and naturalistic. It is likely that some of these intelligences are impaired in patients with schizophrenia but not all or none of them. Choices A and B are too absolute and likely not the best answers. Between choices C and D, choice D does not answer the question. If an IQ test was biased by psychiatric disorders, the average IQ would be different between the groups. So, choice C is the best answer.

19. **A is the best answer.** A case control study starts with a group of people with a known illness and compares them to a group without that illness. Choice A is a strong answer. A cohort study compares people with certain traits or risk factors to determine if that predisposes them to an illness. Since the schizophrenia group has a known disease, not a known trait or risk factor, choice B is not as strong as choice A. Unlike observational studies like case-control and cohort studies, experimental studies, including randomized control trials, do not describe existing phenomena. There was no intervention performed, so choices C and D are not the best answers.

20. **C is the best answer.** Algorithms, analogies, intuition, and trial and error are all ways to solve problems. An algorithm utilizes process oriented stepwise problem solving. Analogies rely on comparing the current situation to a previous one. Algorithms and analogies are both cognitively challenging and thus not easy, so choices A and B are not the best answer. The method that is considered the easiest is intuition because there is no reasoning involved, but rather just relying on a "gut" reaction. So, choice C is a strong answer. Trial and error requires multiple attempts and would take significant time, so it is not easy, and choice D is not the best answer.

21. **B is the best answer.** In the passage, the authors describe how patients with schizophrenia may not display normative behavior, especially in situations of regret and rumination. There is no discussion of verbal interactions, so choice A is not the best answer. Choice B closely summarizes the article. It is a strong answer, but it is important to check the other answers. The passage only discusses schizophrenia, no other psychological disorders, so choice C is not the best answer. Choice D is very similar to choice B and is therefore a strong answer. Comparing the two, choice D is weaker because it says the authors checked the progression of schizophrenia. That did not occur, so choice B is the best answer.

22. **D is the best answer.** The MCAT® often tests Piaget's stages. It is important to memorize them, the time frame in which they occur, and a buzzword associated with each. The sensorimotor and pre-operational stages include basic cognitive development. Object permanence is a buzzword associated with the sensorimotor stage. Egocentrism is a buzzword associated with the pre-operational stage. Inductive reason occurs in the concrete operational stage, so choice C is not the best answer. Deductive reasoning occurs in the formal operational stage. This is considered high-level cognitive reasoning and thus is last to develop. Choice D is the best answer.

Passage 5 (Questions 23-26)

23. **A is the best answer.** Information processing takes place in the cerebral cortex, which is divided up into four lobes. The frontal lobe is associated with decision-making and long-term memory storage, which would likely contribute to the development of personality traits. Choice A is likely to be the best answer. The occipital lobe processes visual information, not decision-making, eliminating choice B. The temporal lobe processes auditory and olfactory information and may play a role in processing emotion. Adaptation to a particular stressful setting is more likely to be a frontal lobe characteristic rather than a temporal lobe characteristic, eliminating choice C. The parietal lobe processes tactile information, eliminating choice D.

24. **D is the best answer.** The average IQ is defined as 100, with every 15 points above or below this value representing one standard deviation above or below the mean, respectively. IQ scores of 92 and 102 both fall within one standard deviation, eliminating choices A and B. A score of 128 falls within two standard deviations, eliminating choice C. The question stem indicates that individuals that have IQ scores over two standard deviations above the mean, or 30 points over the mean, are more likely to experience resilience. Choice D is the best answer.

25. **D is the best answer.** According to paragraph four, those individuals that experience resilience are likely to take a task-oriented approach to solving a problem and believe that persistence will enable them to overcome the particular obstacle. An algorithm is a step-by-step procedure that leads to a definite solution. While not the most efficient, it is likely to lead to a productive result. Choice A can be eliminated. Analogies allow a new problem to be simplified based on a previously known problem. They are often an effective and time-efficient manner of solving a challenge, eliminating choice B. Heuristics are mental shortcuts that often lead to a solution and can be helpful and timesaving. Choice C can be eliminated. The passage notes that individuals that experience resilience take a task-oriented approach to solving a problem. Intuition relies on a "gut" feeling, rather than a logic-based approach. Choice D is most likely the best answer.

26. **A is the best answer.** Cognitive biases are various tendencies to think in particular ways, which can be helpful but also inhibit problem solving skills. Some biases include belief perseverance, where people hold on to their initial beliefs, even when rational arguments would suggest that they are incorrect. Overconfidence, fundamental attribution error, and self-serving bias are other examples. A longitudinal survey of both genders should be able to identify biases, as these biases would prevent individuals from incorporating new information into problem-solving. Choice A is likely the best answer. A short study of only men would be less likely than choice A to elucidate various cognitive biases. Notice that choice B at first appears appealing, as it directly uses two biases in the answer choice. Be certain that these are not distractor answers before selecting a similar answer choice in other questions. The impact of financial stability on emotional well-being does not directly relate to problem-solving and cognitive biases. Choice C is less likely than choice A to be the best answer. Attribution of failure to internal versus external factors describes the thought process behind self-serving bias. A survey about this particular topic could identify whether self-serving bias played into burnout, but not identify the various other types of bias. Choice D is less likely than choice A to be the best answer.

Stand-alones (Questions 27-30)

27. **D is the best answer.** An IQ test is constant over a lifetime because it is normalized against age matched controls, so choices A, B, and C are all true and thus not the best answer. An IQ test can be biased or confounded by learning disabilities, such as dyslexia. People with learning disabilities can be very intelligent, but slowed down by the disability, which biases the test result. So, choice D is the best answer.

28. **A is the best answer.** Twin studies are a great way to determine the effects of genes and the environment on particular traits, including cognitive abilities. Monozygotic twins share the same DNA, so manipulation of the environment in which they are raised is a great way to study the effect of the environment. Dizygotic twins have different DNA, so these studies are not has helpful, and choice B is not as strong as choice A. Children raised in the same household may not actually be raised in the same environment because they have different DNA, which means they will appear differently and be treated differently by others. So, choice C does not provide enough control and is not as strong as choice A. Comparing the genes of children raised in different environments is unlikely to yield any data that can be used to draw a conclusion of significance since the results will be affected by both differences in both the genetics of the children and the environment in which they were raised.

29. **C is the best answer.** Under than Cannon-Bard theory, physiological response and psychological response occur simultaneously. This is stated in choice C. No theory of emotion claims that perception occurs simultaneously with a response; perception is always first. So choices A, B and D are not the best answers.

30. **B is the best answer.** The table indicates that children from low income households have lower IQs than children from high income households. When exposed to the program, both groups show improvement in IQ, but the effect is greatest in the low income group. This means that intelligence can be potentiated (increased) by cultural influences, and choice B is the best answer. Choice A states that intelligence is mostly genetic. This choice can be eliminated because the data in the table shows a cultural influence on intelligence, and there is no reason to assume that low income is synonymous with low IQ. Choice C can be eliminated because high income children are shown to benefit from the program, although not as much as low income children. Choice D can be eliminated because, even with the program, low income children do not completely catch up with high income children.

Passage 6 (Questions 31-34)

31. **D is the best answer.** Choice A, lead exposure, is an environmental factor that can have a dramatic impact on cognitive function. The question, however, states that environmental factors are controlled for, so choice A is not the best answer. Choice B, a genetic disorder, accurately describes an inherited factor, but mistakes viral disease as a hereditary illness, making it a weaker answer. Drug and alcohol abuse during gestation can have devastating effects on cognitive development, but they are considered environmental hazards, not inherited disorders. Because the question is testing genetic influences on cognitive function, choice C is not the best answer. Choice D addresses the question stem by proposing a genetic factor and then identifies a heritable condition, phenylketonuria, which could lead to poor cognitive performance. This makes choice D the best answer.

32. **A is the best answer.** Choice A is looking at cultural determinants of cognition. Language is a powerful cultural tool that allows people to share ideas and values. Choice A is a strong answer. Choice B addresses the biological factors that are related to language. Language is processed differently in native speakers and non-native speakers, but this would not affect the validity of this study. Choice B is not the best answer. Choice C addresses the environmental determinants of cognitive development. While the study seeks to better understand the role of environmental factors in cognitive development, language is not an environmental factor, so choice C is a weaker answer. Lastly, choice D is addressing the psychological determinants of cognitive development. Psychological factors may affect cognition, but this choice does not address the language component of the question stem, so it is not the best answer. Choice A is the best answer because it identifies that language is a potential confounding variable stemming from the cultural determinants of cognitive development that would affect the generalizability of this study.

33. **B is the best answer.** The follow-up study is looking to identify environmental factors that can mediate the effects of poverty on cognitive development, to supplement the conclusions drawn from the initial study. In picking the sample to test, the researchers want a group that is representative of the society and does not have confounding factors that could impact the validity of the test. A child with no signs of gastrointestinal health is not necessarily going to be excluded because a lack of diarrhea does not mean he or she belongs to a wealthy family, so choice A can be eliminated. Choice B states that a child with Down syndrome would be excluded from the study. This choice is better than choice A because a child with an inherited condition like Down syndrome would likely experience a difference in cognitive development that is independent of socioeconomic status. Choice C presents a situation that would not have any influence on cognitive development in children, regardless of economic status, so these children would likely be included. Choice D is tempting because the researchers conclude that maternal education can affect cognitive development, but in order to make to this conclusion, the researchers needed to have included these participants. In this case, choice B is the best answer because it identifies a factor that is inherited and likely affects cognition.

34. **C is the best answer.** Choice A is not the best answer because it undermines the role of stress in cognitive development. Keep in mind that people can "choke" under pressure, which would affect their cognitive development. Choice B can also be eliminated because the physiology of stress is the same in humans, regardless of socioeconomic status. Choice C accurately identifies the consequences of stress and how stress might affect the results of the follow-up study, which uses a standardized test to measure cognitive development. This makes it the best answer. Choice D is not the best answer for the same reasons as choice B—the physiology of stress is the same regardless of socioeconomic status or age.

Passage 7 (Questions 35-38)

35. **B is the best answer.** This question requires interpretation of the figure in tandem with an understanding of the major parts of the brain. The first step is to understand what part of the figure the question addresses. The biggest change in z-score, and therefore the biggest effect between PCE users and the control group, is in the executive functions category on the figure. This can be found by looking to the far right of the figure and noticing that with the control group on the axis, executive function has the greatest difference in z-scores for the PCE group. The next step in answering the question is understanding what the category executive functions means. Executive functions are usually associated with reasoning, memory storage, and problem solving. Consider the answer choices to determine which part of the brain is most closely associated with reasoning and problem solving. The parietal lobe is associated with the processing of tactile information, so choice A is not the best answer. The frontal lobe is associated with motor control, decision making, and long term memory. Choice B is a strong choice. The temporal lobe is associated with auditory and olfactory information. Because these do not directly relate to executive functions, choice C can be eliminated. The cerebral cortex contains the parietal lobe, frontal lobe, temporal lobe, and occipital lobe. Though it is associated with executive functions, the frontal lobe is a more specific answer, so choice D can be eliminated. Choice B is the best answer.

36. **D is the best answer.** This question is testing comprehension of the findings of the study and an understanding of related concepts. The question is asking about characteristics of a PCE user, which can be found in the last paragraph of the passage. Emotional intelligence requires talents such as perceiving emotions, using and reasoning with emotions, understanding emotions, and managing emotions. PCE users were said to show less cognitive empathy. Cognitive empathy is the drive to understand another's emotional state—a form of emotional intelligence. Because they demonstrate less cognitive empathy, the PCE user is likely to have lower emotional intelligence than a non-PCE user, so choice A can be eliminated. The use of intuition in problem solving is based on personal perception or feelings rather than logic, this involves cognitive empathy and social interaction skills, which PCE users are less likely to possess, so choice B can be eliminated. PCE does not play a role in intelligence enhancement, and while it is true that a PCE user may have a high IQ, that does not mean that they always do. Choice C is not the best answer. There was a negligible effect in regards to actual cognitive enhancement for PCE users, but PCE users tend to believe that the PCE assists them in achieving their goals in a large way. This could lead to overconfidence because users feel they are much more powerful on the drug than off the drug although their capabilities are very similar. Choice D is the best answer.

37. **B is the best answer.** The last paragraph of the passage details traits associated with PCE users. The question is testing your ability to apply this information to vocabulary. The sensorimotor stage of development occurs from birth to age two. Here, children recognize their ability to act on and affect the outside world. These are not specific enough abilities to associate with the traits of PCE users, nor are they underdeveloped in PCE users. Choice A is not the best choice. The formal operational stage is the learning stage from age eleven into adulthood. In this stage, the abilities children develop include deductive reasoning skills and post-conventional moral reasoning, which is the ability to help others and act morally. Deductive reasoning skills are well developed in PCE users, but their social skills, which are developed in the formal operational stage, tend to be underdeveloped. Choice B, therefore, is a strong answer. The concrete operational stage is from ages seven to eleven where the child becomes more logical in concrete thinking, and they develop inductive reasoning skills. These traits are also present for PCE users, making choice C a weaker answer. The preoperational stage occurs from age two to seven. During this stage, children learn to use language while they continue to think very literally. They maintain an egocentric world-view and have trouble taking the perspective of others. PCE users tend to have weaker social skills, and many social skills are not yet developed in the preoperational stage, so the PCE users do not seem to differ from the norm in this stage. Choice D is not the best answer.

38. **C is the best answer.** According to incentive theory, people are motivated by external rewards, for example, studying hard to receive an A on a test. While it is true that PCE medication may lead to external changes such as improved focus, it is not implicit that these changes will come with rewards. Choice A is not the best answer. Negative feedback systems have to do with balancing drives and arousals in order to remain at a level of homeostasis. This process is not directly involved in patient response to PCE, so choice B can be eliminated. Drive reduction theory focuses on internal factors in motivation. PCE causes internal changes to a patient, causing them to act a certain way. This process may play a role in patients who respond well to PCE, so choice C is a strong answer. Environmental influences, while important in determining whether or not a patient should use PCE, are not the whole picture when it comes to how they will respond. Therefore, choice C is better than choice D.

Passage 8 (Questions 39-43)

39. **D is the best answer.** Figure 2 shows that men with schizophrenia have lower testosterone levels than men without schizophrenia. This suggests that there is a correlation between testosterone levels and schizophrenia. The relationship may be caused by many things including mechanisms behind schizophrenia, the production of testosterone, or direct effects of testosterone on schizophrenia symptoms. The passage mentions emotional regulation as a process disrupted by schizophrenia. If testosterone improves emotional regulation, then it would make sense for people with schizophrenia to have lower testosterone levels, so choice A is not the best answer. It is also possible that having schizophrenia reduces the production of testosterone, which would result in males with schizophrenia having lower testosterone levels. Choice B is not the best answer. Recall that gene promoters are regions of the genome that regulate transcription. Multiple genes can be downstream of the same promoter. If the genes for testosterone production and schizophrenia share a promoter, promoter dysfunction could cause decreased levels of testosterone as well as schizophrenia. Choice C agrees with Figure 1, so it is not the best answer. If testosterone directly contributes to the onset of schizophrenia, then it makes sense that higher testosterone levels would be linked to schizophrenia. This is not the case according to Figure 1, so choice D is a false statement and does not answer the question.

40. **A is the best answer.** This question asks about the effect of emotional stress on psychological wellness. Recall that stress can be caused by physiological as well as emotional changes and can be experienced acutely or chronically. A tough break up would be an example of acute an emotional stressor because it is an event that occurs only once in a while. Stress negatively impacts psychological functions even in people who do not have diseases like schizophrenia. It makes sense that a person with schizophrenia could expect to experience worsening symptoms as a result of this emotional stress. This eliminates choices C and D. The effects of acute stress last for shorter periods of time than the effects of chronic stress. It makes sense that the stress of the break up would be worse in the immediate days following the break up than it would be months after the break up, so choice A is the best answer.

41. **C is the best answer.** This question asks specifically about an interventional study. An interventional study is one in which an experimental treatment is performed and the outcomes of that treatment are studied. Giving males with schizophrenia extra testosterone would be an example of such an experimental treatment. This is also a reasonable line of questioning based on Figure 1, which shows males with schizophrenia have less testosterone than healthy males. Measuring and recording testosterone levels of patients with schizophrenia is not an example of an interventional study because no intervention is performed, so choices A, B, and D are not the best answer.

42. **B is the best answer.** Figure 2 shows that in males with schizophrenia, higher levels of testosterone are linked to higher levels of brain activation in three different areas of the brain that process emotions. Studies have shown that emotional processing leaves distinct patterns of neural activity in the brain, so that the same areas of the brain are activated for everyone when processing the same emotions. This "fingerprint" of brain activity means that males without schizophrenia would show brain activation in the same regions of the brain as males with schizophrenia if they were given the same experimental task. Choice B is the best answer. It is unlikely for testosterone to enhance emotional processing in males with schizophrenia but have no effect or a negative effect on the emotional processing in males without schizophrenia. If males without schizophrenia showed no correlation between testosterone and brain activity, this would indicate testosterone has no effect on emotional processing. If they showed a negative correlation, it would suggest that testosterone might be hindering emotional regulation. Choices C and D can be eliminated.

43. **D is the best answer.** Their inclusion in the study in the passage suggests that the frontal gyrus, insula, and precuneus are areas of the brain involved with the processing of emotions. The MCAT® would not expect the test taker to known what these parts of the brain are, but it would expect the test taker to infer from the context provided in the passage what these regions do. Recall that the limbic system of the brain is where most emotional processing occurs. The hypothalamus, amygdala, and prefrontal cortex are all parts of the limbic system, so it makes sense that researchers studying emotional processing would be interested in these areas of the brain. Since the question is asking for the exception, choices A, B, and C can be eliminated. The cerebral cortex is the outer layer of brain tissue largely associated with memory, learning, and consciousness. It does not have a major known role in the processing of emotions, so choice D is the best answer.

Stand-alones (Questions 44-47)

44. **A is the best answer.** Choice A best describes the relationship between heredity and the environment in cognitive development. While it can be difficult to determine which plays a larger role, it is clear that cognitive development is driven by some combination of inherited and environmental factors. Choice B overstates the role of genetics in cognitive development and dismisses the environmental role, which goes against the information presented in the passage. For this reason, choice B is not the best answer. Choice C uses the passage to present an idea that is not the best answer. The environment plays a role in development, and the passage seeks to better understand that role, but it does not go so far as to say that inherited factors do not affect cognitive development. This is a common distractor, be mindful of answers that look like the passage but do not answer the question. Choice D states that the roles of genetic and environmental factors work against one another. Both genetic and environmental factors play a role in driving development, rather than acting as opposing forces. This makes choice A the best answer because it accurately describes the relationship between genetics and the environment in development.

45. **D is the best answer.** IQ scores are best at predicting academic success, so it could be used to predict which students will perform the best and earn the highest class rank. IQ scores reveal nothing about future career choice or success, so choices A and B can be eliminated. While IQ scores can be used to predict if an individual is more adept at math or verbal reasoning, they do not predict artistic or designing ability, so they could not provide enough information to determine an individual's class schedule. Choice C is not the best answer. While the likelihood of a greater level of career advancement is likely for those with higher IQ, there are many other factors that are important in a person's career path. Since choice D is more likely to be directly reflective of the differences in IQ, it is the best answer.

46. **A is the best answer.** The James-Lange theory states that emotion is physiologically based and that the emotional response is secondary to the initial physiological response. So, choice A is the best answer. The Cannon-Bard theory suggests that emotional and physiological responses are experienced simultaneously, not sequentially, so choice B can be eliminated. The Schachter-Singer theory is similar to the James-Lange theory, but it requires a cognitive appraisal. So, choice C is not incorrect but it is not the best answer. The opponent process theory focuses on the theory that when one emotion is experienced, another emotion is suppressed. This is not similar to the question stem, which only mentions one emotion, so choice D is not the best answer. Also, the opponent process theory is not tested by the MCAT®.

47. **B is the best answer.** The quest stem states TORCH infections can cause cognitive delay, which is most related to impaired intelligence. These infections are considered environmental factors, so choice B is the best answer. While infections might not be the first thing that comes to mind when considering environmental factors, by using process of elimination for this question, it is the better option when compared to a hereditary explanation. The term hereditary is difficult in this question since the infection is technically passed from the mother to the fetus. It is important to remember, however, that hereditary causes are the result of genetic material, not infections, being passed down from parents to their offspring. Choices A and C are not the best answers. In general, it is not believed that infections cause psychological disease. Although there may be some data that certain infections are correlated with psychological disease, the TORCH infections are most associated with cognitive delay, so choice D can be eliminated, and choice B is the best answer.

Passage 9 (Questions 48-51)

48. **D is the best answer.** The temporal lobe is associated with hearing, language, memory, and emotion. Damage to the temporal lobe could result in a variety of problems, but the only two things mentioned in the answer choices relate to fear and ANS functioning. During the MCAT®, it is important to read the choices before wasting time trying to think through possible answers to questions with multiple answers that could be true. The amygdala is an integral part of the limbic system, chiefly responsible for the emotional processing of anger and fear. Damage to this structure would compromise the ability of the participants to experience and process fearful stimuli. Since participants would not be able to identify and process fear, they would not be best described as fearful nor would they experience more freezing episodes, eliminating choice A. ANS functioning is largely governed by the hypothalamus. The hypothalamus is located in the midbrain, and would not be directly affected by temporal lobe damage, so choices B and C can be eliminated. Without the ability to process fear, participants would be expected to have a decreased number of freezing episodes and episodes of shorter duration due to fearlessness, making choice D the best answer.

49. **C is the best answer.** In the last paragraph, the emotional perception of an anxiety producing situation is accompanied by the physiological response of panic attacks or heart rate increases. The Schachter-Singer theory states that physiological arousal comes first, and then cognition is necessary to evaluate the situation. Since the last paragraph does not address a cognitive process, choice A is not the best answer. It is also important to note that answer choices A and D are two different names for the same theory. The MCAT® will often provide two answers that are saying the same thing, and since two answers cannot both be correct, they can both be eliminated. Similar to the Schachter-Singer (two-factor) theory, the James-Lange theory also suggests that the physiological arousal comes first. The passage states that the emotional and physiological components come together, so choice B is not the best answer. The Cannon-Bard theory of emotion states that emotions and physiological reactions to stimuli are experienced simultaneously. This is consistent with the information given in the passage, and choice C is the best answer.

50. **B is the best answer.** This question is asking about the involvement of the autonomic nervous system in the stress response. It is important to remember that fear can be a source of both acute and prolonged stress, which is why there can be physiological symptoms associated with fear. Based on the graph, the HIGH environment is associated with increased fear. Increases in fear are positively correlated with increased cortisol release from the adrenal glands. Therefore, choice A is true and can be eliminated. Increased cortisol levels lead to an increased heart rate and blood pressure. Choice B suggests that in the high fear environment, participants would have a lower blood pressure, which is not expected. When moving from an environment of high fear to low fear, the heart rate should decrease as a function of decreasing norepinephrine and cortisol concentration, so the finding in choice C is likely and can be eliminated. Patients who experience more fear and release more cortisol are likely at risk for some of the long-term effects of cortisol release like weight gain, sleep disturbances, and immune system suppression. Non-freezers experience less fear in both conditions and therefore would be less subject to the long-term effects of cortisol, making choice D true. Based on this analysis, choice B is the most inconsistent answer, making it the best choice.

51. **C is the best answer.** This question is testing the concept of serial versus parallel processing. The answers require the reader to use the study findings to decide whether serial or parallel processing is being used and to determine which answer correctly describes the processing schema indicated. Serial processing describes a schema in which each input is processed one at a time. A parallel processing schema would be one in which multiple inputs are processed simultaneously. Choice A incorrectly pairs the label of serial processing with a description of a parallel processing schema, and can be eliminated. Although choice B accurately describes a serial processing schema, it suggests that patients are processing inputs one by one, which is the opposite of what the results of the study state, eliminating choice B. Choice C correctly describes parallel processing, and it is consistent with the study findings that inputs are processed simultaneously. Choice D incorrectly pairs the label of parallel processing with a description of a serial processing schema and can be eliminated, leaving choice C as the best answer.

Passage 10 (Questions 52-56)

52. **A is the best answer.** Emotion is adaptive because it allows humans to avoid danger. Recognizing emotion of another human is also adaptive because it allows rapid understanding of a situation. Choice A is a strong answer. Choice B is correct in that emotion is adaptive, but it does not answer the question. This answer choice simply uses buzzwords from the study to distract from the fact that it is not providing a useful reason for why interpreting emotion is important. So, choice B can be ruled out. Choices C and D are both not strong answers because emotion is adaptive.

53. **A is the best answer.** The 20-month-olds were able to interpret emotion whereas the 12-month-old could not. Emotions are controlled by the amygdala, hippocampus, and hypothalamus, which comprise the limbic system. Choice A is a strong answer. The cortex is the surface of the brain and has many functions. This is about as specific as saying "the whole brain", so choice B is very vague and not as strong as choice A. As stated, the hypothalamus is involved in emotion. It is also very important in homeostasis, so it is functioning in 12-month-olds at least in a homeostatic capacity. So, choice C is not as strong as choice A. The thalamus is not a part of the limbic system and is the relay center of the brain. It most certainly is functioning in 20-month-olds and 12-month-olds, so choice D can be ruled out.

54. **C is the best answer.** The study focuses on the difference between 12-month-olds and 20-month-olds in terms of recognizing facial emotions and auditory stimuli. There is no reason to believe that prior to 20-months of age, infants cannot hear, so choice A can be ruled out. The passage never mentions specific emotions, so choice B is likely not the best answer. Choice C is appropriately vague about the findings of the study and is a strong answer choice. Choice D is directly contradicted by the last paragraph, which states parental estimation of language and communication was not related to child sensitivity to emotion. So, choice D can be eliminated.

55. **C is the best answer.** This question is tricky because it is not clear what is being asked. First, consider the differences between the theories of emotion. There is no three factor theory of emotion. The Schachter-Singer is a two factor theory, so choice D can be eliminated. The James-Lange theory is physiologically based where changes are experienced and emotion follows. The Cannon-Bard theory suggests physiology and emotion occur simultaneously. The Schachter-Singer model focuses on a cognitive appraisal. The study is looking at infants' interpretation of emotion-not vicarious emotions in infants, so neither term fits perfectly. However, the passage mentions cognition, and the consideration of congruent or incongruent emotions suggests a cognitive component. For this reason, when forced to pick the theory that is most applicable, choice C, the Schachter-Singer theory is the best answer.

56. **D is the best answer.** There is no such thing as a personal component of emotion, so choice A can be eliminated. This question is difficult to answer because the infants are not experiencing vicarious emotions. The physiological component of emotion is the change in the autonomic nervous system that occurs during an emotion. There is no reason to believe that the infants have a physiological response, so choice B is not the best answer. The behavioral component of emotion describes the actions that occur in response to emotion. This is stronger than choice B but may not be the best answer. The cognitive component of emotion is the subjective assessment of an emotion. The infants are certainly assessing emotional states, so choice D is the best answer.

Stand-alones (Questions 57-59)

57. **D is the best answer.** Fear induces the fight or flight response which is associated with a discharge of adrenaline (epinephrine) by the sympathetic nervous system. Choice D is the best answer. The other neurotransmitters mentioned may be released as well but the buzzword for this question is that fear = fight or flight = sympathetic nervous system = epinephrine.

58. **A is the best answer.** The James-Lange theory is a physiologic theory that is not known as the two factor theory. The two factor theory is actually the Schachter-Singer theory, so choice A is a strong answer. The Cannon-Bard theory is a theory that states that emotional feelings and physiological reactions to stimuli are experienced simultaneously, so choice B is accurate and can be eliminated. The Schachter-Singer theory focuses on a cognitive appraisal of a physiologic response, so choice C is accurate. The facial-feedback theory suggests that facial expressions are triggered and, in turn, lead to the experience of a certain emotion, so choice D is accurate. Choice A is the best answer.

59. **D is the best answer.** Avoidance is way of coping by avoiding a stressor. This may relate to the question stem in that smokers use avoidance to not think about how bad smoking is to their health. Choice A is a possible answer, but the other choices should be evaluated before selecting it.. Classical conditioning is the pairing of a stimulus to a response. This is involved in initiation and perpetuation of smoking but does not relate to attitudes, so choice B is not the best answer. Denial is the refusal to believe in something that may be too difficult for your ego to accept to be true. It is possible that the 10% of smokers who indicated that smoking was not bad for their health may truly believe that or they may be in denial about the possible negative health effects that smoking can cause. Since this survey is discussing a large group that seem to understand the risks of smoking, choice C is not the best answer. Cognitive dissonance describes a conflict between internal attitudes and external behaviors. Most smokers know smoking is bad for their health, but they continue to smoke anyway. Choice D is a stronger answer than choice A.

LECTURE

4

Thought and Emotion

TEST 4B

ANSWERS & EXPLANATIONS
Questions 1–59

Passage 1 (Questions 1-6)

1. **A is the best answer.** In this question, it is necessary to understand how self-determination theory (SDT) relates to the other theories of motivation. The best answer is choice A because incentive theory is about motivation related to external rewards. The psychological needs described in SDT are all internal, so incentive theory is not applicable. Drive reduction theory says that motivation comes from drives to address physiological needs. While psychological and physiological needs are not necessarily the same, the drive reduction theory is more applicable to the SDT of motivation than incentive theory is, so choice B can be eliminated. Cognitive theory, choice C, addresses both internal and external awards in motivation, which is also referred to as intrinsic and extrinsic motivation. While this study does not address extrinsic motivation, it does specifically focus on intrinsic motivation. Need-based theory is applicable to the study because it states that motivation is based on the desire to fulfill unmet needs. The passage specifically cites that in SDT, motivation comes from the desire to fulfill psychological needs. Therefore, aspects of the theories in choices B, C, and D are all in the study, and choice A is the least relevant to the study, so it is the best answer.

2. **B is the best answer.** The good differentiators in the study are one of the groups created based on the independent variable, emotional differentiation. Choice B is a better answer than choice A because there is not evidence that good differentiators are the control version of poor differentiators in the study. The level of emotional differentiation is the independent variable that the researchers are manipulating. A control group would be people who have average levels of emotional differentiation to which the poor and good differentiators can be compared. However, the level of emotional differentiation is how the researchers divide their two study groups, so they are studying the impact of different emotional differentiation capabilities on motivation. While choice C is true, including two groups with differing levels of emotional differentiators more accurately reflects the general population variability, this is not the research driven reason for including them in the study. Furthermore, two groups do not effectively reflect the true variability of the population. Choice D can be eliminated because there is no indication that good differentiators do not use the cognitive aspect of emotion. The cognitive aspect of emotion is when an individual has emotion related to their personal assessment of a situation. Most likely, in fact, the cognitive aspect of emotion is necessary for the good differentiators' ability to discern different emotions and be variably motivated.

3. **C is the best answer.** The hypothesis and results of the study indicate that poor differentiators are equally motivated by all positive and negative emotions, while good differentiators are less motivated by certain positive or negative emotions than others. Choice A would more likely be true of a poor differentiator than a good differentiator because they are two different positive emotions. Choice B can be eliminated because the hypothesis states that poor differentiators are more motivated by negative emotions than good differentiators are. Choice C is the best answer because it addresses the core of the researchers' hypothesis. A good differentiator needs a specific positive emotion, not a generic positive emotion for motivation. This is exemplified by being more motivated by enthusiasm than cheerfulness. Universal emotions are the most basic emotions and are recognized as distinct in all cultures, so it is very likely that a good differentiator would be able to distinguish between them and be differentially motivated. Choice D can be eliminated.

4. **D is the best answer.** A very important point to remember is that correlation does not equal causation. This is often a drawback of research designs, and it is necessary to keep in mind when thinking about the implications of research findings. Therefore, choice A can be eliminated. Choice B is not the best answer because the independent variable that the researchers are studying is level of emotional differentiation. While they include two groups, good and poor differentiators, they do not include a control group representative of the average level of emotional differentiation in the population. This third group would help provide insights into the study that might be missed by just comparing good and poor differentiators. Self-reporting in any kind of study can lead to variability that cannot be controlled, and is often a drawback of studies, eliminating choice C. Choice D is the best answer because the adaptive nature of emotions is not relevant to the study design. The adaptive nature of emotions refers to the fact that emotions help individuals and communities thrive. While this highlights the importance of understanding emotion in motivation, it is not a variable that needs to be controlled.

5. **B is the best answer.** The Schachter-Singer theory of emotion and the Cannon-Bard theory of emotion both posit that physiological responses as well as emotional feeling are necessary to appraise an emotion. However, choice B is a better answer than choice A because the Cannon-Bard theory states that the emotional feeling and physiological occur simultaneously, while the Schachter-Singer theory, or the two-factor theory of emotion, states that the physiological response occurs before the emotional feeling. Choice C can be eliminated because while the James-Lange theory of emotions states that the physiological experience of emotion precedes emotional feeling, the theory only includes the influence of the physiological response and not the emotional response on the perception of the emotion. Choice D can be ruled out because the theory that emotions are adaptive, or promote the ability to thrive, does not address how emotions are perceived.

6. **D is the best answer.** Each of the answer choices presented represents an aspect of the role of biological processes in perceiving emotion, but choice D is the best answer because it is the only statement that is supported by the study findings. Biological processes play important roles in the perception of emotion. The amygdala is involved in unconscious emotional processing, which may be occurring when emotion is regulating the motivation of the participants in the study. Choice A is a true statement in that the hippocampus and amygdala allow recollection of emotional memories when a similar emotion occurs; however, this is not demonstrated in the study. A broad spectrum of emotions were studied in this experimental design and the role of the hypothalamus in the physiologic response to emotions, such as sweating or increased heart rate, is an important biological process in perceiving emotion. However, the study does not mention any investigation of such physiological responses, so choice B can be eliminated. Finally, choice C can be ruled out because while it is important to know that the prefrontal cortex plays a central role in temperament and decision making, this was not investigated in this study.

Passage 2 (Questions 7-10)

7. **C is the best answer.** The passage stated that fearful eyes were detected better than neutral or happy eyes. The signal did not change. So signal/detection will be decreased for fearful eyes because the denominator is larger. Always check the axes on graphs on the MCAT®! Choice C is the only option where the condition of fearful eyes is lower than neutral and happy eyes, so choice C is the best answer.

8. **C is the best answer.** Universal emotions include sadness, happiness, fear, disgust, surprise, and anger. The passage mentions fear and happiness, so the emotions are universal. Emotions are always adaptive unless associated with a psychological disorder. The passage does not mention a psychological disorder. So, options I and II should be components of the best answer. This narrows the answers down to choice C. Emotions are not required, there are disorders like Autism Spectrum Disorder where emotions are not expressed and are likely not felt. So option III is not a component of the best answer, and choice C should be selected.

9. **A is the best answer.** Epinephrine, norepinephrine and cortisol are all released in the stress response. Epinephrine and norepinephrine are somewhat immediate whereas cortisol has a slow controlled action. It is a misconception that norepinephrine counteracts epinephrine in the stress response; both are stress hormones with slightly different physiological effects. During the stress response, hormones cause blood sugar to surge so the muscles can metabolize glucose for energy. Insulin lowers blood glucose, which would starve the muscle of energy and prevent a successful "fight or flight" response. Insulin may be released towards the end of the stress response in order to normalize blood sugar levels. However, the question stem asks about the early stress response, so choice A is the best answer.

10. **D is the best answer.** Emotions are adaptive and have evolved over many years. The question states that perceptions of faces enter a less evolved part of the brain prior to being interpreted by the cortex. Choices A, B and C all refer to a theory of emotion with either the psychological or physiological component not occurring. All of these theories include both the psychological and physiological components but differ in the timing of each. Choices A, B and C are inaccurate statements, which leave choice D as the best answer.

Stand-alones (Questions 11-14)

11. **A is the best answer.** The drive reduction theory focuses on internal factors of motivation, such as hunger, thirst, and sex. Another component of the drive reduction theory is the need for a drug in animals that are addicted. This need is physiological and intrinsic. So, choice A is the best answer. In contrast to intrinsic motivation is extrinsic motivation, in which a reward elicits a task. In choice B, the toy would be the reward, so this is not an intrinsic factor and can be eliminated. Choice C is not clearly related to the question stem. It is not obvious how administering a sedative would relate specifically to the drive-reduction theory of motivation, so this is not the best answer. Choice D references a drive but not a reduction. The drive to urinate is powerful, but since there is no reference to the rats reducing the drive, choice D is not the best answer.

12. **C is the best answer.** The nervous system is an integrated system, and most processes require multiple branches. The somatic nervous system is the motor component of the nervous system and likely has little to do with emotional processing but rather the subsequent behavioral component of emotion. Choice A can be eliminated. Choice B is a tempting answer because the enteric nervous system is the nervous system of the gut, which may bring to mind the idea of "gut feelings," but it can be eliminated as it is not one of the key players in emotional processing. Choice C is the best choice because the autonomic nervous system is one of the key players in emotional processing along with the limbic system. It is helpful to remember that the autonomic nervous system is involved in unconscious processing and actions of the body. Choice D is not the best answer choice because the peripheral nervous system is not involved in mental processing. Mental processing instead lies in the domain of the central nervous system.

13. **A is the best answer.** Appraisal of stress is important in responding to dangerous stimuli. Between choices A and B, a dog will interpret the situation as dangerous more so than safe, so choice B should be eliminated. There is no reason to jump to the conclusion that a dog will mirror his owner's body language or defend his owner. The fight or flight response dictates that fighting is not always required—fleeing is also an option. Choices C and D are too extreme, so choice A is the best answer. This question is related to the discussion of facial cues in the passage but actually requires no information from the passage. Questions like this are common on the MCAT®. Do not be tempted to look back at the passage for hints because there are not any!

14. **A is the best answer.** The elaboration likelihood model and social cognitive model are both theories of attitude and behavior change. The elaboration likelihood model relies on two routes for attitude formation. The peripheral route relies on intuition and heuristics, whereas the central route relies on logic and reason. The peripheral route occurs rapidly when a person does not fully evaluate a situation, and the central route includes deep thinking and reasoning. The question stem describes a rapid and incomplete type of attitude formation. This is most similar to the peripheral route of the elaboration likelihood model, and choice A is a strong answer. The central route is more complete, so choice B can be eliminated. Choices C and D are weaker answers because the social-cognitive model does not describe central and peripheral routes. The social-cognitive model is in contrast to the elaboration likelihood model and suggests that behavior changes through reciprocal causation with many factors contributing.

Passage 3 (Questions 15-18)

15. **A is the best answer.** This question does not require information from the passage although it would be easy to waste time trying to find a hint in the passage. Assuming that the group with probable PTSD patients has PTSD, individuals in that group tend to appraise normal stressors as though they are cataclysmic events. A cataclysmic event is one that is caused by a catastrophe and may cause death. Personal events are not a threat to a person's life but can be very stressful and include divorce or death of a loved one. Choice A is the best answer. A failure to appraise the stressor as a cataclysmic event would occur in the non-PTSD group, so choice B is not the best answer. Personal events can be stressful but the key feature of PTSD is appraising non life-threatening stimuli as life-threatening, so choices C and D are not the best answer.

16. **A is the best answer.** A drive is a sensation that is uncomfortable and causes an action, e.g. thirst, hunger. A drive cannot be consciously controlled. The feelings of discomfort associated with PTSD result in abnormal responses that are outside of a person's control. Choice A is a strong answer. A need is something required for a fulfilled life. Needs include simple things such as food and water as well as higher level concepts like self-actualization. Drives are considered primitive and needs are considered evolved. The sensation associated with PTSD is more primitive than a need, so choice B is not the best answer. Emotions are feelings resulting from certain situations. Emotions are natural and predictable. Discomfort is not an emotion. Had the questions said "fear" instead of "discomfort", choice C would be the best answer. An attitude is a set belief about something. Attitudes are much more evolved than the primitive feeling described in the question, so choice D is not the best answer.

17. **A is the best answer.** Exercise, relaxation and spirituality have all shown benefit by providing stress relief. Diets often contribute to stress because hunger can cause the release of stress hormones. Choice A is the best answer because it would increase stress hormone levels.

18. **C is the best answer.** Participants with normal activation of the SFG were part of the non-PTSD group. They would be expected to have normal brain anatomy. An increase in the connections between the amygdala and hypothalamus is abnormal. It is hard to know what result this would have on an individual. Choice A is not the best answer. A hippocampus with increased gyri may be specially equipped to store more memories. This would not necessarily be expected in the non-PTSD group. An amygdala with normal size and shape would be expected in the non-PTSD group. Choice C is a strong answer. The parasympathetic nervous system is the "rest and digest" portion of the peripheral nervous system. The probable-PTSD group would likely have increased sympathetic activity, but the non PTSD group should not have excess sympathetic or parasympathetic signaling since there is no reason for one to predominate. Choice D is not the best answer.

Passage 4 (Questions 19-22)

19. **C is the best answer.** This question is challenging. Using Figure 1, there are only three types of sounds present—non-linguistic human sounds, musical sounds and environmental sounds. Choice A can be eliminated because it was not assessed by the passage. The affective component of a response is the emotional component. Of the types of sounds used in the experiment, musical sounds are the most likely to elicit an emotional response. Non-linguistic sounds, such as coughing, and environmental sounds, such as bird chirping are not associated with affective responses. Music has been shown to elicit emotional responses, so choice C is the best answer.

20. **A is the best answer.** Two of the answer choices describe methods of influencing behavior by changing attitudes. The foot-in-the-door technique is a slow way of achieving a behavior where a person is convinced to perform a series of increasingly desirable behaviors. For example, if a child wants a puppy, he may first ask for a hamster. Choice A is a possible answer. The door-in-the-face technique is the opposite, a person makes an absurdly large request followed by a smaller more reasonable one. So, in the previous example, the child may first ask for a horse. The door-in-the-face technique can be equally effective and is usually quicker than the foot-in-the-door. The question refers to a slow technique, so choice A is better than choice B. Role-playing is a way that behavior influences attitudes, not visa versa. It is not particularly slow and does not fit as well as choice A, so choice C can be eliminated. Cognitive dissonance is a state of disagreement between attitudes and behaviors. It is not a technique to influence attitudes or behaviors, so choice D is not the best answer.

21. **C is the best answer.** Role-playing is a way of putting oneself in another person's shoes. It includes "make pretend" play that is common in childhood. In fact, the frequency of role-play is largely decreased by adulthood. Choice A is a true statement but does not explain how role-play may have confounded the results. Choice A is possible, but there is probably a better answer. Role-play is more common in children than adults, so choice B can be eliminated, and choice C is a strong answer. Since choice C could provide an example of potential bias, choice D is not the best answer. A general tip, bias and confounding variables are very common, especially in psychological research. It is unwise to pick an answer choice that says a variable could not have biased the results.

22. **A is the best answer.** The final paragraph states that children listened to the sounds more times and created more categories. Children have less exposure to the sounds and seem to struggle with the Gestalt principles of grouping. Choice A makes sense and may be the best answer. Choice B is too extreme—children were able to categorize sounds, but it took them longer, and they used more categories. Choice B can be eliminated. Choices C and D both refer to specific Gestalt principles of grouping. Although the passage suggests children struggle with grouping, it is not clear which principle is lacking. Furthermore, these principles typically refer to visual perception, not auditory perception, so choices C and D are not the best answers.

Passage 5 (Questions 23-26)

23. **C is the best answer.** The SSH is not well explained in the passage, but there is enough information to answer the question. There is apparently a component that requires approach actions (the "sword") and avoidance actions (the "shield"). The handedness of the approach seems to always favor the dominant hand whereas the avoidance actions occur with the non-dominant hand. A need is something that is required for life. The handedness of the SSH is not a need because it is not a true life-or-death situation, so choice A is not the best answer. A want is a reward that is desired but not required. There does not seem to be a reward in the SSH, so choice B is not the best answer. An instinct is an unlearned behavior. The passage suggests the SSH shows an unlearned favoritism for the dominant hand as the approach hand, so choice C is a possible answer. A drive is a sense of urgency to perform a behavior to fill a need. As discussed, the SSH is not relevant to needs, so choice D is not the best answer.

24. **A is the best answer.** Drives are strong desires to perform a behavior that satisfies a need. According to Maslow's hierarchy, physiological needs include water and food. The only need listed is choice A. Socialization is necessary and is even a need identified by Maslow. However, water is a physiological need and socialization is not, so choice A is a stronger answer, and choice B can be eliminated. Money is a want, not a need, so choice C is not the best answer. The mention of conditioning is a complete distractor and was designed to waste time. The passage in no way relates to conditioning. When presented with an answer choice like this that does not relate to the passage, do not waste time considering it, just move on!

25. **C is the best answer.** Needs are things require for life including food and water, so choices A and B are not the best answer. Money is generally not classified as a need because it itself is not required for vitality. Choice C is the best answer. Self-actualization is the peak of Maslow's hierarchy of needs. It is a need, so choice D is not the best answer.

26. **D is the best answer.** Sociocultural motivators are those that motivate individuals to "fit in." Peer pressure can be a sociocultural motivator, but it does not really make sense that peers would pressure an individual to modify handedness. Choice A is possible but probably not the best answer. Left-handedness was previously frowned upon and teachers would force children to switch hands. This was occurring earlier in the 20th century and is not relevant to participants in a study published in 2012. Choice B is not the best answer. A left-handed batter does have an advantage against right-handed pitchers but switching handedness to play baseball would be very difficult because playing the sport would not begin until well after handedness was established. Choice C is probably not the best answer. Scissors and doorknobs do favor right-handers. This has led many young children to naturally switch from being left-handed to right-handed because it is simply easier to navigate the world. Choice D is the best answer.

Stand-alones (Questions 27-30)

27. **C is the best answer.** Caffeine is a stimulant used to induce arousal, so choice A is not the best answer. Simulation of an attack would trigger a fight or flight response, which causes a surge of epinephrine. This would promote arousal, so choice B is not the best answer. Meditation is very soothing and can help with stress relief and sleep. It does not promote arousal, so choice C is a strong answer. A new environment is known to enhance arousal. This is likely evolutionary because our ancestors needed to be on guard in unfamiliar settings. Choice D is not the best answer.

28. **B is the best answer.** The foot-in-the-door technique is a process by which attitudes influence behavior. It involves making a series of increasingly larger requests until the desired behavior is achieved. Choice A does not refer to an initial smaller request, so choice A is not the best answer. Choice B perfectly describes the foot-in-the-door technique, so choice B is probably the best answer. The foot-in-the-door technique is more associated with tricky behavior than truly working one's way up at a company, so choice C is not the best answer. Choice D is nearly an example of the foot-in-the-door technique, but there is no small initial task. If choice D said, "Obtaining a job interview by first obtaining a phone interview," it may have been the best answer, but as written, choice D is not the best answer.

29. **A is the best answer.** Drive-reduction theory says people are motivated to do things in order to reduce internal arousal in response to a physiological need. Incentive theory suggests people are motivated by external rewards. Cognitive theory says that people behave in a way that will yield the best outcome. Need-based theory says motivation is caused by a desire to fulfill unmet needs. Stress can be thought of as an example of psychological arousal. When someone is moderately stressed, they are motivated to relieve this feeling of stress. With academic stress, this would mean studying more or doing homework, which are behaviors that increase academic performance. Motivation that is caused by a desire to relieve tension is best supported by the drive-reduction theory. Stress also causes physiological arousal through the production of stress hormones, so choice A is the best answer. Moderate stress levels do not create an external reward, so choice B is not the best answer. The cognitive theory of motivation would say people study in order to do well academically. It doesn't explain how stress creates conditions that promote academic behavior, so choice C is not the best answer. Studying under moderate stress does not fulfill an unmet need, so choice D is not the best answer.

30. **B is the best answer.** The theory of emotion that refers to cognitive appraisal is the Schachter-Singer theory. In this theory, an event triggers a physiologic response that is cognitively appraised before an emotion is developed. Neither the James-Lange nor the Cannon-Bard theories refer to a cognitive appraisal, so choices A and C are not the best answers. Cognitive behavioral theory would likely focus on cognition and cognitive appraisals, but it is not a theory of emotion, so choice D is not the best answer.

Passage 6 (Questions 31-36)

31. **D is the best answer.** Recall that Maslow's hierarchy of needs is a need-based theory of motivation. Maslow organized five human needs into a pyramid, and said that upper levels of need can only be attained if lower needs are met. The five needs, in order from lowest to highest, are: physiological, safety, belongingness, esteem, and self-actualization. Academic achievements are an example of an esteem need because good performance increases self-esteem and gains the respect of teachers and peers. According to Maslow, a student would not be motivated to seek out academic achievements if he or she did not adequately meet physiological, safety, and belongingness needs. Supportive friends and family is an example of a belongingness need because they provide social connections and support for emotional health, so choice A is not the best answer. Stable housing is a safety need because a good home should provide a feeling of security and safety, so choice B is not the best answer. Food and water are physiological needs that the body requires to survive, so choice C is not the best answer. Self-fulfillment describes an individual's ability to attain whatever it is that makes him or herself feel totally satisfied with life. This could be anything from pursuing higher education to painting or writing. Self-fulfillment is an example of self-actualization, which is the highest level in Maslow's pyramid. This level is above esteem, so choice D is the best answer.

32. **A is the best answer.** Recall that instinct is based on physiological need, arousal is physiological or psychological tension, drive is the urge to perform behaviors in order to decrease arousal, and a need can be physiological or psychological. The passage says that academic self-concept is a subjective measure of academic ability, so it is likely influenced by psychological needs, such as the need for approval. A desire for academic achievement can cause psychological arousal, which feeds the urge to study and do homework. Choices B, C, and D are not the best answer. Choice D includes physiological needs, but is not limited to them and is thus too broad to be the best answer. Since academics do not influence a person's physiological need to survive, it makes sense that instinct does not play a major role in motivating academic behavior. Choice A is the best answer.

33. **A is the best answer.** Recall that in the appraisal view of stress, the amount of stress a person feels is caused by the presence of a threat (primary appraisal), and the person's ability to cope with that threat (secondary appraisal). When discussing academic stress, a high-stakes exam is an example of a threat. The stress felt in reaction to the exam is related more to a person's confidence in their ability to do well on the exam, and less to the existence of the exam itself. The passage says that academic self-concept is a personal judgment of one's own academic ability. People with high academic self-concept are more confident in their academic abilities, so high academic self-concept is likely correlated to lower stress levels. The figures in the answer choices measure stress by cortisol level. Recall that cortisol is a stress hormone, so more cortisol means higher stress. Choice A shows an inverse relationship between stress and academic self-concept, so it is the best answer. Choice B also shows an overall negative relationship between stress and academic self-concept, but it also shows a pattern of deviation from this relationship for mid-range academic self-concepts that is not based on any passage or content information, so choice B is not the best answer. Choice C shows that those with lower self-concept are less stressed while those with higher self-concept are more stressed. This goes against the explanation presented above, so choice C is not the best answer. Someone with very low academic self-concept would not be expected to have the same stress levels as someone with very high academic self-concept, so choice D is not the best answer.

34. **A is the best answer.** This question asks about intrinsic and extrinsic motivators as defined by the cognitive theory of motivation. Recall that intrinsic motivators are internal, such as the feeling of satisfaction that comes with success. Extrinsic motivators are external, such as pressure by others to perform a certain behavior. Allen's motivation is intrinsic because it stems from a personal interest in the subject. Richard is motivated by external factors like money and stability, so his motivators are extrinsic. This eliminates choice B and C. The passage says that male students who have high internal motivation fare better in their STEM classes than those with high external motivation. This eliminates choices D. The question stem says both boys have high academic self-concept, but only Allen has high internal motivation, so he would be expected to get better grades. Choice A is the best answer.

35. **C is the best answer.** The passage describes academic self-concept as a subjective judgment on one's own academic abilities. It is a measurement of self-confidence. The finding that female STEM students scored lower than male STEM students on academic self-concept is a reflection of societal expectations of women in STEM. There is a longstanding stereotype that women lack the natural ability for STEM fields. It is common for women in STEM fields to devalue their own abilities because they have been influenced by the doubts of others. With these doubts in mind, it is likely that women in STEM would be less likely to seek out positions of high power because this behavior requires confidence that they are qualified for the job. This is best described by the scenario in choice C, which is the best answer. The other scenarios do not describe behaviors that require self-confidence to perform. Choices A, B, and D describe the behavior of journal editors, project leaders, and patients, respectively. The question refers to a behavior by women in STEM themselves, so choices A, B and D are not the best answer.

36. **B is the best answer.** The conclusion of the study in the passage can be found in the last paragraph. The study found a positive correlation between internal motivation and academic performance, but the existence of such a relationship does not equate causation. In general it is very difficult for scientific studies to prove causation beyond correlation because of confounding factors that could exist in the relationships studied. The wording in choice A implies causation by saying that increasing internal motivation makes the students do better. The study's conclusions do not support this strong of a statement, so choice A is not the best answer. The study also found a positive correlation between high academic self-concept and academic success in STEM. Choice B supports this finding without making an assertive claim that high academic self-concept is the cause of academic success, so it is the best answer. An incentive rewards system such as the one in choice C is an example of an external motivator. The study concluded that internal motivation was associated with better performance than external motivation. Choice C does not agree with the study's findings, so it is not the best answer. The study in the passage was focused only on students in STEM fields, so its findings can only be applied to other STEM students. It would be inappropriate to generalize these results to other types of students, so choice D is not the best answer.

Passage 7 (Questions 37-40)

37. **D is the best answer.** Figure 1 shows an elevation in stress hormones during and after the stress task. This suggests that a stress response occurred, so choice A is not the best answer. The experiment illustrated in Figure 1 was performed to determine if the first experiment was flawed. Since the first experiment did not have statistically significant findings, the authors sought to determine whether these results were due to an inadequate stress response. If so, the experiment would need to be repeated with a different stressful task that was sufficient to invoke a stress response. Based on the findings in Figure 1, there was a stress response. The first experiment may have been inaccurate, but that is not supported by the findings in Figure 1, so choice B is not the best answer. Internal validity refers to how well an experiment was performed. High internal validity avoids confounding variables and uses accurate measures and tests. Since the stressful task produced stress , there is no reason to think the first experiment was flawed by poor internal validity. Choice C is not the best answer. By process of elimination, choice D is the best answer. It may not necessarily be true as an overall statement about the first experiment. However, the question is asking only about conclusions supported by Figure 1. Figure 1 shows a rise in stress hormones which means there was not a procedural error in producing stress. Although this answer choice is uncomfortable, choice D is the best answer to the question.

38. **A is the best answer.** Epinephrine and norepinephrine are both involved in the stress response. Choice A is likely true because these two hormones would be released in response to stress, just as cortisol is. Although epinephrine and norepinephrine have slightly different functions, both are involved in the stress response. There is no reason to believe that norepinephrine and epinephrine would have different shaped curves. So, choices B and C are not the best answers. The key to deciding between choice A and choice D is to determine if the curves for epinephrine or norepinephrine would be similar or different from the curve for cortisol. Although cortisol is considered to be more of a chronic stress hormone, whereas epinephrine and norepinephrine are both acute stress hormones, they are all stress hormones. Based on this fact, the curves are more likely to be similar than they are to be different. So, choice A is a better answer than choice D.

39. **B is the best answer.** Stress has emotional, behavioral, and physiological effects. The first study was investigating decision making, which is a behavioral response. An emotional response to stress would involve measuring the emotions of participants, so choice A is not the best answer. A physiological response to stress would involve measuring cortisol as was done in the second experiment, so choice C is not the best answer. A psychological response to stress would be similar to an emotional response, so choice D is not the best answer.

40. **D is the best answer.** Mindfulness meditation is actually a way to reduce stress, so choice A can be eliminated. Exercise is a type of physical stress and can cause acute elevations in stress hormones but actually reduces stress over time. So, choice B can be eliminated. A written exam is a type of psychological stress but compared to choice D, choice C is not the best answer because it is not clear that the exam would have any effect on the participants' social status or self-worth. The experiment was specifically studying psychosocial stressors. Psychosocial stressors are any threat to a person's social status or self-worth. Only choice D is a type of psychosocial stressor.

Passage 8 (Questions 41-44)

41. **A is the best answer.** Figure 1 shows that acute sexual exposure results in elevation of corticosterone. This corresponds to choice A. Choice B is not the best answer because corticosterone is elevated, not depressed, compared to the control condition ("naive" rats). Choice C is not the best answer because the changes in corticosterone levels between the rats exposed to chronic stress are minimal compared to controls. Although the level appears to be slightly elevated, when choosing between choice C and choice A, choice A is the better answer because the Figure 1 shows greater elevations in the acute stress scenario. Similar to choice B, choice D is an opposite statement and thus is not the best answer.

42. **C is the best answer.** The question is asking how researchers can reduce stress in rats. In humans, exercise and meditation are effective ways of reducing stress. These are options in choice D and choice C, respectively. It would be difficult to force rats to meditate, so choice D is impractical and not the best answer. Choices A and B would not definitively lower corticosterone levels. Exposing rats to a different stress-inducing task may lower corticosterone, but it could also elevate corticosterone depending on the task selected, so choice A is not the best answer. Using an alternative method to measure corticosterone would not lower the true corticosterone levels but could result in artificially lowered or raised corticosterone levels due to potential systematic error, so choice B can be eliminated. This leaves choice C as the best answer. As stated, exercise reduces stress in humans. There is no definitive way to know if a similar effect would occur in rats based on the information provided, but of the answer choices, choice C is the most likely way to decrease the likelihood of increased corticosterone levels.

43. **B is the best answer.** The question is asking about theories of stress and motivation. Stress can be caused by cataclysmic or personal events. Cataclysmic events refer to natural disasters, whereas personal events refer to the death of a loved one or being diagnosed with a terminal illness. Choice A is a weaker answer because it states that cataclysmic events elevate corticosterone (stress hormones) in rats. The rats were not exposed to a cataclysmic event, so this is not a conclusion the researchers would be able to make. Motivation can be described through many theories that focus on either internal or external sources for motivation. Sex is considered a source of internal motivation, which is the primary focus of the drive-reduction theory. For these reasons, choice C is a weaker answer. Since sex is a basic internal source of motivation it falls towards the bottom of Maslow's hierarchy of needs so, choice D can also be eliminated. Choice B is a general statement about primary and secondary appraisals. It is true that these appraisals are used to assess the severity of a stressor. So, choice B is a true statement and by process of elimination, the best answer.

44. **A is the best answer.** First, identify that the amygdala is part of the limbic system. The limbic system is most known for its role in emotion and addiction. Choice A is correct because it references emotion and keeps the rest of the study the same: the independent variable is still stress exposure. In the question stem, the new dependent variable should be changed to the amygdala, so this also lines up with choice A. Choice B is a weaker answer because it changes the independent variable to changes in memory formation. Changes in memory formation is the old dependent variable and is no longer being studied in the experiment proposed in the question stem. Choice C is a weaker answer because it goes out of the scope of the question stem. There is no reason to consider the frontal lobe in this scenario. Choice D describes the question that is being addressed by the original experiment. Since the question stem is proposing a new experiment where the effect of stress on the amygdala, rather than the hippocampus, is being studied, this is not the best answer and can be eliminated.

Stand-alones (Questions 45-48)

45. **D is the best answer.** Many factors contribute to motivation, which is a psychological factor providing impetus for a behavior. All of the answer choices listed can contribute to motivations and can even overlap in some respects. The question asks for the largest contribution to this particular motivation, so it is best to go through and think about how each will contribute. Drives occur as a result of physiological arousal from unsatisfied needs and can be thought of as a combination of need and arousal. Needs refer to the psychological or physiological needs of an organism, such as food and water, which is not part of the question stem, so choice A can be eliminated. Instincts are innate tendencies towards certain behaviors present in all individuals. Since not all individuals are afraid of heights, choice B is a weaker answer. Arousal is physiological and psychological tension, which can be caused by excitement or fear and is variable from individual to individual. The high arousal of being near the edge of the roof motivates the tourist to move away from the edge and return to their baseline arousal levels. Because this motivation is more based on arousal than necessary needs, choice D is a better answer than choice C.

46. **C is the best answer.** The best way to answer this question is to pass each choice through the elaboration likelihood model and consider whether the peripheral or central model route is more likely. The question stem is seeking long lasting change, which is more indicative of the central route. The student is not motivated and more likely to evaluate the lecture based on the quality of the food served rather than the actual presentation, eliminating choice A. A religious extremist is likely to pass harsh judgment on the teachings of a more liberal leader. This eliminates choice B. Choice D is a good, but not great answer. Even though the recovering alcoholic fits well for the profile of the twelve step program, they may or may not be motivated. Since the answer choice only says that he or she was ordered into the program by a judge, there is no way to know. One of the most important factors in attitude change is characteristics of the source. In choice C, the medical journal is described as respected. This means that the physician is likely to internalize and accept its findings, even though it is incompatible with his current protocol. Note that the question describes it as protocol instead of a personal opinion, making it more likely that his actions are already based on previous studies and evidence rather than personal opinion. This makes choice C better than choice D and the best answer.

47. **C is the best answer.** The drive reduction theory is a theory of motivation that focuses on taking an action to reduce a physiological drive, such as hunger. There is no physiological drive to accept the money, so choice A is not the best answer. The foot-in-the-door phenomenon is based on the premise that people are more likely to give in to a large request if they first agree to a smaller on. There is only one request in the question stem, so choice B is not the best answer. Cognitive dissonance is the conflict between inconsistent attitudes and actions. The woman says she is patient, but she does not wait for the larger amount of money, so her attitude is inconsistent with her behavior, and choice C is the best answer. Central route processing is a part of the elaboration likelihood model and occurs when an individual thinks deeply about an argument. There is no reason to believe the woman thought deeply about the offers, so choice D is not the best answer.

48. **C is the best answer.** As stated in the question stem, the publication bias results in publication of only the studies that show statistical significance. A meta-analysis compiles the findings of multiple studies to determine if there is indeed a relationship between two variables. If there are no studies that show no relationship between two variables, the meta-analysis is likely to be biased. The confirmation bias describes how a person values information that supports a belief he or she already holds. This is applicable to meta-analyses because the meta-analysis (new information) supports the studies that have been published (prior belief). So, option I is true and choice B is can be eliminated. The causation bias is the tendency to assume a cause and effect relationship. Meta-analyses can be used to determine cause and effect, so this is applicable to the question stem. So option II is true, and choice A can be eliminated. The self-serving bias is the process of attributing one's own failures to external factors. This is not related to a meta-analysis because it is too personal. So, option III is false, and choice D can be eliminated. This makes choice C the best answer.

Passage 9 (Questions 49-52)

49. C is the best answer. A personal stressor is associated with a life change such as moving, marriage, divorce, or birth of a child. There is no life change in the TSST, so choice A is not the best answer. A cataclysmic stressor is associated with a natural disaster like a hurricane or tsunami. The TSST is unrelated to a natural disaster, so choice B is not the best answer. A daily stressor is something in daily life that is stressful. In daily life, it is common to have to give presentations or do mental math. The TSST is an exaggerated version of these daily stressors. Choice C is possible. A physical stressor is one that physically induces stress on the body, such as a running a marathon. Choice D is unrelated to the TSST, leaving choice C as the best answer.

50. B is the best answer. The last sentence states that the autonomic, endocrine, and psychological components of stress are all being assessed. Choice A corresponds to the endocrine response, which is slow and sustained, so choice A is not the best answer. The component of fear would be the emotional response, which was not assessed by researchers. Choice B is a possible answer. The rapid physiologic response corresponds to the autonomic component that was assessed by researchers, so choice C is not the best answer. Anxiety is a psychological state, which the last sentence says was assessed. Fear and anxiety are closely related, but anxiety is a psychological state, and fear is an emotion. This minor distinction is key to answering the question. Rule out choice D, and choice B is the best answer.

51. D is the best answer. The researchers measured cortisol, amylase, and heart rate. Since cortisol was already measured, choice A is not the best answer. Dopamine is a neurotransmitter that has many functions throughout the nervous system, including in the systems of movement and personality. Dopamine is not released in large quantities during a stress response, but epinephrine is. Outside of the scope of the MCAT®, dopamine can be used by doctors to increase blood pressure similar to a stress response, but this is not physiologic, so choice B is not the best answer. As stated, heart rate was measured, so choice C is not the best answer. Sweating occurs during a stress response and can be very important to maintaining body temperature. The researchers did not measure sweating, so choice D is a strong answer.

52. C is the best answer. Associative learning includes classical conditioning and operant conditioning where a behavior is increased or decreased through training. The student did not change his behavior, so choice A is not the best answer. Blind faith is a distractor and out of the scope of the question. The question does not say the student did not study and is relying on God to help him pass. Choice B should be eliminated. Cognitive dissonance is a discrepancy between a belief and a behavior. The student believes he should listen to music but never actually does so. This is an example of cognitive dissonance, so choice C is a strong answer. Doublethink is a term that was coined in the novel *1984* and is not tested by the MCAT® but could show up as a wrong answer, just as it does here. Doublethink refers to believing in two contradictory statements, and while knowing they contradict, believing both are true. The student only has one belief mentioned in the question stem, so choice D is not the best answer.

Passage 10 (Questions 53-56)

53. D is the best answer. When controlling for variables, the effect of variations among confounding variables that are not being examined is removed. For instance, lacking financial problems may be associated with a higher socioeconomic status , a confounding variable. By controlling for socioeconomic status, the effect of this association on the results is removed. Controlling allows subjects of low socioeconomic status and financial problems to only be compared with subjects of low socioeconomic status without financial problems. Choices A and B, while true do not specify that researchers are modifying the results based on confounding variables and are not elements specific to controlling, so they can be eliminated. The passage does not mention controlling for the emotional state, eliminating choice C. Choice D is the best answer as it describes a modification of the data that the researchers performed.

54. C is the best answer. Showing causation requires changing one variable and seeing a change in the other. The passage describes an observational study and does not involve the researchers controlling any variables, so only correlations can be drawn, eliminating choices B and D. Deciding between choices A and C requires close reading of the passage, which specifies that repeated incidents of problems are being compared to singular or the absence of incidents, eliminating choice A. Choice C is the best answer as it follows the experimental procedure and is supported by Figure 1.

55. C is the best answer. The passage explains that a third of the potential patients were excluded from the study, which could significantly skew the data, eliminating choice A. The patients were given the option to of whether or not to participate, signifying that the subjects are self selected. The explanations given for the lack of participation could be reasonably associated with patients of more serious health conditions or specific lifestyles, skewing the data, which allows choice B to be eliminated. The utilization of questionnaires in acquiring data is risky as patient's may not want to tell the truth, or may not effectively be able to due to the psychological effects of being released from surgery just hours prior to participation, so choice D can be eliminated. As the study seeks to analyze the effects of stressors on cancer progression, a cancer free control group would not show lymph node involvement and would be of no use, making choice C the best answer.

56. B is the best answer. The foot-in-the-door technique is an example of behavior influencing attitudes and involves the requester having the subject initially agree to a small commitment before asking for a larger commitment. Choice B is the only choice which utilizes these steps and is the best answer. Choice A is an example of the door-in-the-face strategy since large request is made before falling back to the desired request, so choice B can be eliminated. Choice C is an example of using cognitive dissonance (being good natured but rejecting the study) to achieve a desired response, and it can be eliminated. Choice D is an example of harassment and can be eliminated.

Stand-alones (Questions 57-59)

57. D is the best answer. All four of the answer choices are factors that influence motivation. However, choice D is a better answer than choice B because it is an instinct of infants to exhibit nipple seeking behavior to feed. While a decrease in the need for a mother's milk could lead to reduced breast feeding, it is unlikely that a deficit that reduces nutrition for a baby would be prevalent or compatible with survival. Choice A is also a tempting answer choice, because a reduced physiological drive for breast milk would lead to decreased breast feeding. Again though, it is very unlikely that the complex systems in the human body that lead to drives for hunger and thirst would be a common problem in infants. Finally, choice C can be ruled out because lack arousal, or the physiological and psychological tension that contributes to the motivation for feeding, is unlikely to lead to just a deficit in breast feeding and would likely present with many other attributes of lack of responsiveness.

58. D is the best answer. The question is asking you to interpret the results of the study and then apply them to concepts. Operant conditioning, while related to the phenomena of heightened responses due to rewards, it only looks at the outcomes of reinforcement and punishment, without attention to the involvement of inner processes such as emotion and motivation. Operant conditioning is also not a formal theory of motivation; therefore, choice A is not the best answer. Drive reduction theory focuses on internal factors in motivation; it posits that people are motivated to take action in order to lessen the state of arousal caused by a physiological need. This theory does not correspond to the findings of the study, so Choice B can be ruled out. Need-based theories propose that people are motivated by the desire to fulfill unmet needs. There is no mention of motivations within this theory so Choice C can be eliminated. Incentive theory people are motivated by external rewards, the participants in this study were given and motivated by external rewards and therefore Choice D is the best answer Choice.

59. C is the best answer. In the described example, the teaching assistant is receiving a mild stressor. Since the lecture he is giving is on his thesis work, he most likely has expertise in the subject matter. This combination of expertise and low levels of stress actually tends to improve performance, making choice C the best answer. The fact that he is nervous despite his expertise means his confidence will most likely not be improved, ruling out choice B. While stress can lead to anxiety and memory impairment, this is more likely when the stress is chronic and the individual is not skilled at the task at hand. Therefore choices A and D can be eliminated.

LECTURE 5

Biological Correlates of Psychology

TEST 5A

ANSWERS & EXPLANATIONS
Questions 1–59

LECTURE 5 ANSWER KEY

TEST 5A		TEST 5B	
1. C	31. A	1. B	31. A
2. B	32. C	2. D	32. A
3. D	33. B	3. B	33. B
4. A	34. B	4. B	34. C
5. A	35. D	5. B	35. A
6. B	36. A	6. C	36. B
7. C	37. C	7. D	37. B
8. C	38. C	8. A	38. B
9. C	39. B	9. B	39. D
10. B	40. A	10. B	40. A
11. A	41. A	11. D	41. D
12. C	42. D	12. B	42. B
13. B	43. D	13. C	43. C
14. A	44. B	14. B	44. C
15. C	45. B	15. D	45. B
16. C	46. C	16. C	46. C
17. C	47. B	17. B	47. C
18. D	48. D	18. C	48. C
19. D	49. D	19. B	49. A
20. D	50. D	20. A	50. C
21. C	51. D	21. C	51. D
22. D	52. B	22. C	52. A
23. A	53. C	23. B	53. D
24. B	54. B	24. B	54. C
25. D	55. A	25. D	55. C
26. C	56. B	26. A	56. B
27. B	57. C	27. D	57. C
28. D	58. C	28. C	58. D
29. A	59. A	29. C	59. C
30. B		30. B	

EXPLANATIONS FOR LECTURE 5

Passage 1 (Questions 1-4)

1. **C is the best answer.** CpG islands are sites of DNA methylation, which decrease the amount of transcription of a gene. The only gene mentioned in the passage that is directly related to the nervous system is *CPLX1*, which functions at the axon terminal to promote exocytosis. The protein may be present in dendrites, but choice A is probably not the best answer as there is no indication that the protein plays a role in dendritic spine maintenance. Likewise, the protein may be present down the axon, but choice B is probably not the best answer. Excitatory post synaptic potentials are signals that cause the postsynaptic neuron to fire an action potential. If the presynaptic neuron does not release enough neurotransmitter, the postsynaptic neuron may not be stimulated enough to initiate a signal. If complexin is not present, exocytosis cannot occur, which would prevent a post synaptic potential from occurring. Choice C is a strong answer. The resting membrane potential is controlled by ion channels. Complexin is not an ion channel, so choice D is not the best answer.

2. **B is the best answer.** The passage shows how DNA can be modified by smoking (the environment). The passage does not claim that smoking is predicted by genetic information, so, choice A is not the best answer. Choice B correctly summarizes the findings in the passage because smoking is correlated to DNA methylation, which alters transcription. Choice C makes a causal claim not supported by the passage. The passage does not prove causation, only correlation, so choice C is not the best answer. The passage does not discuss cancer in the gonads or pancreas, just the modification of a tumor suppressor gene. Choice D draws a conclusion not directly supported by the passage, so choice D is not the best answer.

3. **D is the best answer.** Only one of the answer choices is practical and ethical. Selectively hypomethylating a person's DNA is essentially impossible. Although hypomethylation of the whole genome is possible, there is not yet a way to target specific sites in the clinical setting. So, choice A is not the best answer. Choices B and C both hint at a form of conditioning to achieve the desired change in behavior. Conditioning experiments are ethically questionable because a conditioned child may then feel ill when exposed to a stranger smoking. Choices B and C are probably not the best answer. Decreasing exposure to parental smoking would certainly help decrease the risk of smoking in the next generation. Smoking is often correlated to parental tobacco use. This would be an effective way to prevent smoking, so choice D is the best answer.

4. **A is the best answer.** The passage states *F2RL3* encodes for a G-protein coupled receptor (GPCR). GPCRs are membrane bound, and when activated, they cause lasting changes in the cell usually via phosphorylation of cytosolic proteins. This is consistent with choice A, so choice A is a strong answer. GPCRs are membrane bound and cannot translocate to the nucleus, so choice B is not the best answer. GPCRs themselves are not ion channels although they can be coupled to ion channels. Choice C is not the best answer. Regulatory genes are ones that control transcription of certain DNA sequences. Well-known regulatory genes are those controlling the lac operon. *F2RL3* encodes a GPCR, so choice D is not the best answer.

Passage 2 (Questions 5-9)

5. **A is the best answer.** Built into the hypothesis is the assumption that for the children with ASD, there is some ideal level of stimulation and that they can get that stimulation from their environment or they can create it for themselves if environmental stimulation is not sufficient. To maintain this ideal level of stimulation, if one type of stimulation increases, the other must decrease. If each segment of the study was repeated in a room with music playing, vocalizations should decrease. Music—soft or not—is more stimulating than silence. The creator of this vocal stimulation hypothesis would need to be on guard for evidence that vocalizations were not being made for the reason we normally think of vocalizations being made: communication. If the children were vocalizing right before breakfast, these vocalizations could be the children communicating that they are hungry, rather than be the result of self-stimulating. Two adults per participant should be more stimulating than one, so self-stimulating vocalizations should decrease substantially. If the hypothesis is correct, a still-faced adult should be less stimulating than an adult engaging in either kind of play. Accordingly, self-stimulation behavior should be higher in the still-faced segments than in either play segment.

6. **B is the best answer.** Each of these answer choices plays a role in cognition and behavior, but which principle is *demonstrated* by the fact that children spent more time playing with toys in the second still-faced segment than in the first? The most important change that took place between the two still-faced segments was that the children had more experience with the toys. So the best answer choice will use increased experience with the toys to account for the children's increased playfulness. Bottom-up processing is the means by which sensory information is organized in real time, moment to moment. Top-down processes utilize prior experience to make understanding and interacting with the current environment more efficient. As a result of top-down processing, children would likely be less hesitant to approach and play with toys they had already played with, so choice B is a better answer than choice A. Parallel processing organizes two or more sensory inputs to construct a more nuanced understanding of a stimulus. Vision and touch, for example, would play a role in playing with toys. This is not as strong of an explanation for the changes described in the passage, so choice C can be eliminated. Neural plasticity is the way that life experiences can remodel the actual hardware of the human brain. While experience factors in to the increased amount of time the children play with the toys, neural plasticity is a much slower process that could not meaningfully account for changes in the course of an hour. Choice D can be eliminated.

7. **C is the best answer.** Gestalt principles describe top-down processing of stimuli, such as visual sensory information according to simpler forms. A quick, hand-drawn sketch of a human eye might include a white almond shape with a darker circle in the center. This is far from an eye, or even a photograph of an eye, but the brain may perceive it as an eye according to Gestalt principles. Psychosocial evolution has shaped an important role for eye contact in human communication, but this does not explain the human tendency to perceive geometric shapes as an actual eye nearly as well as Gestalt principles do, so choice A can be eliminated. Interactionist theory is a model for understanding the development of language as a product of both nature and nurture. Since it is not related to visual perception, choice B can be eliminated. Parallel processing would be a part of a real time interaction with another person, but this question addresses purely visual processing, so choice D can be eliminated.

8. **C is the best answer.** Disease models in mice can be created via genetic engineering, but they can also be created using selective breeding. Notice first that to really repeat the study would mean to assess eye contact between two mice, which is probably impossible, and might not be meaningful even if it was successfully measured. The task is to identify which characteristic in mice would be the most useful dependent variable in a study analogous to the one in the passage. The passage does not indicate that either experimental or control subjects in the human study were selected for their serum oxytocin levels—oxytocin, administered by the experimenters, is the independent variable in this study, so choice A can be eliminated. Repetitive behaviors are studied in paragraph 1, not paragraph 2, so choice B can be eliminated. In the passage, eye contact is a stand-in for social engagement, so if particularly unsociable mice could be selected from a population, it would be interesting to see the effect oxytocin may have on them. This makes choice C a strong answer. Each of the traits in choices A, B, and C—behavioral and biochemical alike—would vary in a natural population, and some of that variation may be heritable. Choice D can be eliminated.

9. **C is the best answer.** Neither stimulation nor hypnosis would account for a new sense of enjoyment of social interactions in the long-term, so choices A and D can be eliminated. A stimulant increases activity of the central nervous system, and an increase in CNS activity is expected when two people interact. But stimulants are also associated with feelings of vigilance and alertness, which would be unlikely to increase a person's feelings of enjoyment. This makes choice B a possible answer, but there may be other choices that are better. The reward pathway is often implicated in addiction, but it is also activated in feelings of happiness and pleasure with less nefarious causes, as well. Activation of the reward pathway accounts for pleasant experiences that an organism would therefore strive to repeat, so choice C is a stronger answer than choice B. Long-term reward pathway induction in social interactions would be of significant therapeutic interest to researchers studying ASD.

Passage 3 (Questions 10-13)

10. **B is the best answer.** Table 1 shows that subchronic administration of FLX decreases immobility and number of jumps and increases latency before next jump. This is associated with alleviation of anxiety symptoms, which would support choice B. The table also shows that acute administration of FLX actually increases anxiety symptoms, so choice A would not be the best answer. It may be tempting to choose choice C because it mentions the best drug administration for treatment of anxiety symptoms, but choice C mentions only atrial fibrillation and not anxiety, so the patients of choice C may not have anxiety at all. Choice D is not the best answer because Table 1 shows that acute administration of FLX actually increases jumps and decreases jump latency, and thus it increases anxiety related symptoms.

11. **A is the best answer.** When a neurotransmitter is released into a synapse, its effects on postsynaptic receptors are transient due to mechanisms that remove the neurotransmitter from the synapse. Reuptake is a process that prevents constant stimulation of postsynaptic receptors by allowing neurotransmitters to be taken back up into the presynaptic neuron. Neurotransmitter reuptake inhibitors prevent the reuptake of a neurotransmitter into the presynaptic neuron. It may be tempting to choose any of the other choices because they all seem to perpetuate the effects of the neurotransmitter. However, choice B is the definition of a neurotransmitter agonist, which chemically mimics and binds to the receptors of another neurotransmitter. This can happen in the presence or absence of the neurotransmitter of interest, so it can be eliminated. Choice C also defines a type of neurotransmitter agonist. Choice D defines an enzyme inhibitor, which prevents the breakdown of neurotransmitter by an enzyme. Choice A is the best answer because it provides the definition of a neurotransmitter reuptake inhibitor.

12. **C is the best answer.** By adding another antianxiety medication to the study, researchers would be adding an independent variable that they can change and manipulate. Choice A is not the best answer because a dependent variable is one that the investigators measure and that is affected by the independent variable. In this case, the dependent variables are the behaviors measured, which are affected by the independent variables or antianxiety drugs. Choice B and D are not the best answers because reliability and validity are related to the repeatability and credibility, respectively, of the study, which is unrelated to the question.

13. **B is the best answer.** The beginning of the passage states that there is a link between atrial fibrillation and anxiety and that the use of psychiatric medications may improve outcomes of the treatment of atrial fibrillation by reducing anxiety. The passage then went on to describe the model used for extreme anxiety. This suggests that the model would indeed be an effective way to investigate anxiety disorder and its relationship to atrial fibrillation, so choice A can be eliminated. The study does not suggest that this model will prove anything about the relationship, but rather simply facilitate further investigation. This suggests that choice B is the best answer, and choice C is not the best answer. Choice D can also be eliminated because the study makes no mention of potential scientific failures or the need for improvement.

Stand-alones (Questions 14-16)

14. **A is the best answer.** Consider each answer choice. Aggression is likely genetically encoded especially by genes involved in testosterone-mediated responses. Choice A is a possible answer. Creativity may be genetic, but it is difficult to think of a biological mechanism (as was easier to do in the aggression-testosterone example). So, choice B is not the best answer. Hunger is controlled by a few hormones in the brain and blood, but it is not clear why some individuals are obese and others are not. Choice C is not the best answer as obesity is more likely explained by a multifactorial model. Infidelity may be mediated by testosterone and probably has an evolutionary basis, but the relationship is not as clear as aggression to testosterone, so choice D is not as strong as choice A.

15. **C is the best answer.** This question asks about the adaptive value of behaviors. While the behaviors in the answer choices are not instinct behaviors hardwired into the genome, these types of behaviors can also have adaptive advantages and disadvantages. Recall that different behaviors can increase an individual's chances of survival and producing children, and that evolution selects for these behaviors to be passed on to future generations. Texting while driving a car is a dangerous behavior that increases the chances of mortality, so it would not make sense for this behavior to be passed on. Choice A is not the best answer. Using contraceptives, while considered a positive health behavior, decreases the chances of an individual having children. This works against the principles of natural selection, so choice B is not the best answer. Extreme sports put individuals at higher risk of injury or death. Exercise is a healthy behavior but this increased risk decreases an individual's chances of surviving to pass on his or her genes, so choice D is not the best answer. Working overtime and getting promotions contributes to financial stability, which helps an individual establish a more comfortable lifestyle and increases the chances of starting a stable family. This increases the individual's chance for passing on his or her genes, so choice C is the best answer.

16. **C is the best answer.** When available, using a research design with monozygotic twins allows the researcher to control for genetics since the siblings share identical DNA sequences throughout their genomes. This is relatively simple to achieve, so choice A is not the best answer. Epigenetic changes, like DNA methylation can be controlled for in a similar manner. If a pair of MZ twins has a similar epigenetic landscape as well, that would control for epigenetics. This would be more difficult to control for than genetics, so choice B is a possible answer, but the other choices should still be evaluated. Past environmental exposures are impossible to control because it is nearly impossible to recall every known exposure and control for it. Choice C is a stronger answer than choice B. Controlling a person's behavior is difficult, but it is certainly easier than controlling for past unknown exposures, so choice D is not as strong as choice C.

Passage 4 (Questions 17-20)

17. **C is the best answer.** The question is asking about the relationship between obesity and sleep deficiency that the study explores. While it is true that the fourth stage of sleep is almost entirely delta waves, and it is the deepest stage, the first few sleep cycles of the night are the deepest level of sleep dominated by delta waves, so these would not necessarily be missing for the participants. This choice also does not offer a link to the obesity component present in the participants, so choice A is not the best answer. The circadian rhythm regulates the body's functions on a predictable schedule, such as the daily balance between wakefulness and sleep. These functions also include appetite and the sensation of fullness. Choice B is a plausible answer. The suprachiasmatic nucleus in the hypothalamus is a group of cells that regulates the timing of many of the body's circadian rhythms, including maintaining the drive for wakefulness. This answer is more specific than choice B because it specifies what is regulating the circadian rhythms. Therefore, this is an even stronger answer than choice B. While it is true that less rest can sometimes lead to poor decision-making regarding food, choice D is the least biologically relevant and not as strong or specific as choice C.

18. **D is the best answer.** The label on the y-axis of the graph is "individuals in category of neuropsychological function (%)" therefore, the function that has the highest bar was the most affected. Looking at the bars displayed on the graph the tallest bar belongs to executive functions. Therefore, the highest percent of individuals had their executive functions affected. While motor skills do affect depth perception, motor skills were not the function affected in the highest percentage of participants, thus choice A can be eliminated. Choice B is tempting because circadian rhythm does have to do with sleep deprivation, however, motor skills is still not the most affected function. Choice B is not the best answer. The hypothalamus regulates the timing of many of the body's circadian rhythms, so choice C is very similar to choice D. Choice D is more specific than choice C since the hypothalamus is responsible for maintaining homeostatic control over many variables of the body, other issues would likely be present in obese individuals if the function of the hypothalamus is being altered on a larger scale. Since a disturbance in the sleep patterns is the only issue discussed in the passage, choice D is a better answer. The circadian rhythm releases hormones via a cyclical pattern to allow a person to shift between wakefulness and sleep at predictable intervals. Choice D is the strongest answer.

19. **D is the best answer.** The absolute threshold refers to the lowest intensity of a stimulus that can be sensed. This is not necessarily related to the categories used for measurement in this study. This is also not the paradigm used originally in the study, and researchers should remain as consistent as possible when repeating experiments or performing additional studies. Choice A is not the best answer. Difference threshold describes the smallest difference that is sufficient for a change in a stimulus to be noticed. It measures the sensory system's ability to detect small changes from the perceived stimulus. This is not the paradigm that the researchers used initially to measure participants' skills and it is important to remain consistent; therefore, choice B is not the best. While the control group is important to establish a threshold for baseline scores unaffected by the study, it is better to compare scores of participants with their original scores to see how the study affected them directly. Therefore, choice D is better than choice C.

20. **D is the best answer.** The obesity hypothesis states that obesity is an inherited trait. The question is asking whether the results of the study support this hypothesis. The study does not explicitly look at obesity as an inherited trait, but instead it looks at the correlation and relationship between obesity, sleep patterns and several neurocognitive tests. Choice A, choice B, and choice C all make a stand on the position of whether obesity can be inherited, and this is not directly addressed in the study. Therefore, choice D is the best.

Passage 5 (Questions 21-25)

21. **C is the best answer.** The Gabor patch is alternating hazy white and black lines with a sinusoidal grading. Our minds group the lines and close them into a circle. The Gabor patch does have symmetry, but that principle normally applies to two shapes being mirror images of each other, so choice A is not the best answer. Linearity sounds like a good answer, but it is not a Gestalt principle, so choice B is not the best answer. As stated, a Gabor patch is just lines, but our minds enclose them into a circle, so choice C is a strong answer. Figure-ground applies usually to a black and white image where the black and white form different images, respectively, and a person can switch between the two when deciding what is figure and what is ground. The Gabor patch does not change when thinking about the white versus black, so choice D is not the best answer.

22. **D is the best answer.** Each of the answer choices is a perceptual organization tool that the brain is assessing constantly. Only one was considered by researchers- constancy. The researchers exposed participants to either familiar (constant) or novel (not constant) images, so choice D is the best answer.

23. **A is the best answer.** Each of the choices listed is a legal drug. Caffeine is one of the most addictive legal drugs. It is a stimulant that increases attention. Choice A is a strong answer. Alcohol is a central nervous system depressant and hinders attention so choice B is not the best answer. Marijuana is legal in some states but hinders attention in a similar way as alcohol so choice C is not the best answer. Lidocaine is used as an anesthetic (numbing agent) and antiarrhythmic and is available by prescription only. Cocaine is a powerful and addictive stimulant that could increase attention but is illegal. Interestingly, cocaine is available to doctors and is used to treat nose bleeds. Although they are chemical cousins, lidocaine does not share the same stimulant effects as cocaine so choice D is not the best answer. Remember to not pick answers that are not familiar- they are usually incorrect and serve to trick a test taker who is not confident!

24. **B is the best answer.** The fractals are the images used in the experiment that were either familiar or novel. The brain region should either be related to vision or memory. As it turns out, none of the areas mentioned in the answer choices relate to vision, so this question is testing the areas of the brain involved in memory. The amygdala has a minor role in memory but functions mostly in emotions. Choice A is possible, but there is probably a better answer. The hippocampus is involved in memory storage, especially short term memory, so choice B is a very strong answer. The frontal lobes and temporal lobes are involved in long term memory but not short term memory, so choices C and D are not the best answers.

25. **D is the best answer.** There is no information in Figure 1 about the novel cues becoming boring. The x-axis is not time, it is orientation or contrast, so there is no way to interpret boredom from either cue. Choice A is not the best answer. Choice B compares the two graphs and states that the orientation graph (left) had greater variation between novel and familiar groups than the contrast graph (right). On a graph, variation refers the space between the lines. It looks like the orientation lines are farther apart, but check the scale of the y-axis! Actually, the contrast lines are just as variable. Choice B is possible, but consider the other answers. Choices C and D deal with the graphs individually. Both choices state that the novel (not constant) fractal always makes the Gabor patch easier to identify. This means the novel cue line (solid) should always be above the familiar cue line (dashed). On the contrast graph, the lines cross, so choice C is not the best answer. On the orientation graph, the solid line is always higher, so choice D is a true statement and is the best answer.

Stand-alones (Questions 26-29)

26. **C is the best answer.** Choice A is specifically showing an example of the role of environment on the development of behavior as an adopted child shares no genes with his or her adopted parents. Choice B shows the role of genetics on the development of behavior. In both instances, as in almost all situations, both genes and environment play a role in the behavior of the individual, but the predominant effect described in the answer choice is either genetic or environment. Choice C is a better option because a blind person's genetics determine the wiring of the brain, but the environmental influence of having no visual input also influenced the wiring such that the visual part of the brain further developed the ability to perceive the environment through improved auditory processing. Choice D can be eliminated because it is demonstrating only an environmental impact and no role of genetics.

27. **B is the best answer.** A few examples of Gestalt principles are so common, and so testable, that they are worth memorizing. The "+" sign is an example of continuation because it is perceived as two intersecting lines rather than four lines that meet at a central point. The other answer choices are not incorrect, but they do not apply to a plus sign. Below are example images of similarity, proximity, and closure.

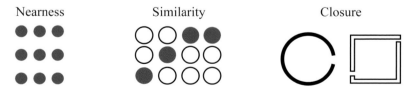

Nearness   Similarity   Closure

Similarity is the principle where similar items are grouped together. Proximity is the principle that states the spacing of objects changes the way they are perceived. In the figure above, the proximity of the dots results in the perception of three rows rather than three columns or nine individual dots. For closure, parts of the brain look for shapes like circles, squares and triangles. The figures above are not actually a circle or square, but the brain uses the principle of closure to perceive these shapes.

28. **D is the best answer.** The question is asking about what processing stage of learning occurs from ages 0-24 months relating to the absorption of language. The Gestate principles describe the top-down processing that organizes sensory information, including the ability to distinguish between figure and background or between objects in a group. While the type of learning described in the question stem is probably top-down, it is not visual; therefore, choice A can be eliminated. Since the process of language acquisition requires auditory as described by the question, rather than visual processing, choice B is not the best answer. Top-down processing and bottom-up processing usually work together in order to learn and create perception. However, top-down processing brings the influence of prior knowledge into play to make perception more efficient. Bottom-up processing involves the construction of perceptions from individual pieces of information provided from sensory processing. Newborns do not have very much stored knowledge and therefore a lot of the processing they use will be bottom-up. Therefore, choice D is better than choice C.

29. **A is the best answer.** Participants in this study are overweight and under-rested. Attention selects sensory information for perceptual processing, so it is responsible for a wide variety of functions. The more sleep deprived a person, is the worse their attention becomes. This is a reasonable answer for something that might be decreased in participants in this study compared to the general population. Choice A is a strong answer. Depth perception, motion perception, and visual processing all can be worsened by lack of sleep; however, all of these faculties also have to do with attention. Since choice A encompasses all three of these faculties, it is the strongest option.

Passage 6 (Questions 30-34)

30. **B is the best answer.** Sensation is the act of converting a physical stimulus into an electrical signal. This requires an intact sensory apparatus. For the eye, there should be an intact retina and optic nerve. Perception is giving attention to a sensation to bring it into consciousness. Perception is generally performed by the cortex. Hemianopia is defined as partial blindness, which is the inability to perceive visual stimuli. This means perception must be impaired, so choices A and C can be eliminated. Next, decide if the problem is in the cortex or in the eye. After auditory stimulation, perception was restored. This suggests that sensation must be intact, so choice B is the best answer. If sensation was not intact, i.e. if the eye was damaged, vision could not be restored via the auditory stimulation. If perception was intact initially, there would be no blindness.

31. **A is the best answer.** The absolute threshold is the minimum amount of a stimulus that can be perceived. The passage describes a change from blindness to an improvement of almost 100%. This is a reduced absolute threshold, so choice A is a strong answer. The difference threshold describes the smallest difference that is sufficient for a change in a stimulus to be noticed. There is no indication that a change in stimulus intensity was used, so choice B can be eliminated. The significance threshold is not a term used in neurology or psychology and is just a distractor, so choice C is a weaker answer. The Weber threshold likely refers to the Weber fraction that is derived from the difference threshold. The Weber fraction is the amount of the originally presented stimulus that must change to meet the difference threshold. So, it is the difference threshold normalized for intensity. For the same reasons above, choice D can be eliminated.

32. **C is the best answer.** The question is asking which concept could explain the findings in the study. The passage indicates that after an auditory stimulus, participants were able to regain vision in areas that were previously blind. The term that applies most to this is neural plasticity. Neural plasticity is the ability of the brain to "re-wire" its electrical connections. In order to regain function, neurons must develop or enhance connections. Choices A and B refer to two types of attention where two stimuli must be presented and either both are given attention, as in divided attention, or only one is given attention, as in selective attention. The auditory stimulus was not presented at the time of visual field testing, so these answer choices can be eliminated. Stem cell activation is a rare phenomenon in the CNS. There is no evidence that stem cell activation is occurring, so choice D is not as strong as choice C. If stem cells show up on the Psychology and Sociology section of the MCAT®, it will likely be in the context of treatment neurological disorders like Parkinson's disease.

33. **B is the best answer.** The question stem states that depth perception requires input from two eyes. Participants have input from both eyes, but some parts of the visual field may not be perceived. In these areas, there would be no depth perception. This is most similar to choice B. Choice A is a weaker answer because there will be no depth perception in the areas of blindness. Choice C is can be eliminated because depth perception is only completely impaired if one eye is completely blind. Choice D is a weaker answer for the reasons above and is a common distractor on the MCAT®. Typically, enough information is provided, and this answer choice is usually not the best answer.

34. **B is the best answer.** This question applies not only to regained vision but to most gained functions of the brain. The brain enhances neural connections through long-term potentiation, which is the increased likelihood a neuron will fire in response to stimulation. The term is usually applied to memory but may also account for other gained functions of the brain. Choice A can be eliminated because GABA is an inhibitory neurotransmitter in the brain. GABA decreases the likelihood of a neuron firing, so choice A is the opposite of choice B. Often when the MCAT® presents two answer choices that are opposites, one of them is true. Neuronal differentiation, choice C, is a very rare event in the central nervous system. Neuronal differentiation is essentially neuronal mitosis or growth from stem cells. Many sources still claim that it does not occur at all, although recent research suggests it may occur in a few locations. For the MCAT®, know that neuronal differentiation is a very rare event and unlikely to account for any neural phenomena. The question stem asks for a "normal" process, which differentiation is not, so choice C is not the best answer. Choice D, regulatory genes, refers to the effect the environment can have on the nervous system by modifying transcription and translation of certain proteins. This is a good answer choice because in general, any change to a cell is likely controlled by a regulatory gene. However, this answer choice is too vague, and compared to choice B, choice D is not the best answer.

Passage 7 (Questions 35-39)

35. **D is the best answer.** This question requires an understanding of the influence of light on the drive for sleep. Sleep and wakefulness are in constant opposition. Throughout the day, the drive for sleep builds, but it is opposed by signals from the suprachiasmatic nucleus (SCN) of the hypothalamus. The SCN sends inhibitory signals to the pineal gland, which blocks melatonin production, suppressing the drive for sleep. Choice A can be eliminated because an overactive SCN would promote wakefulness by strongly inhibiting the pineal gland, and this is inconsistent with the information presented in the question stem. When inputs from the SCN diminish as the day goes on, melatonin production is increased and sleepiness ensues. Light contributes significantly to the regulation of circadian rhythms by stimulating the SCN and increasing the inhibitory effect on melatonin production. Choice B could lead to increased ratings of sleepiness, but it does not explicitly address the effect of light exposure, so choice B is not the best answer. Since there is not enough information in the passage or question stem to suggest that this aneurysm causes a visual impairment, choice C can be eliminated. If the connection between the SCN of the hypothalamus and the pineal gland were severed, there would be no way for the SCN to inhibit the pineal gland. Light exposure is able to affect circadian rhythms by signaling through the SCN to the pineal gland, so without this connection, light would be unable to affect sleepiness. This is consistent with the information provided in the question stem, so choice D is the best answer.

36. **A is the best answer.** This question requires knowledge of how different sleep disorders manifest and when in the sleep cycle they typically occur. The passage states that Equatorial workers rarely enter REM sleep. Sleep terror disorder is characterized by vivid, nightmare-like imagery that occurs in non-REM sleep. This is a major concern because when a patient has a night terror, they have not achieved REM sleep, and the body is not immobilized. This can result in people acting out their dreams. Unlike night terrors, nightmares occur in REM sleep, much like dreaming. They can be disturbing, but patients are not free to move around during this phase of sleep. It was also stated in the passage that this group of workers rarely enters REM sleep, so choice B can be eliminated. Insomnia describes a sleep disorder in which falling asleep is difficult, and the quality of sleep is disrupted. The passage does not state that Equatorial workers had trouble falling asleep nor does it comment on their quality of sleep, so choice C is not the best answer. Narcolepsy describes a sleep disorder in which sleep begins without warning and patients enter directly into REM sleep. Equatorial workers rarely enter REM sleep according to their EEGs, so a condition with rapid ascent into REM sleep would likely not be of greatest concern, so choice D can be eliminated, leaving choice A as the best answer.

37. **C is the best answer.** The phases of sleep serve different functions. While in the deepest stages of sleep, Stage 4, there is recovery from the fatigue of the day. REM sleep, a lighter sleep, is believed to be the time when the brain processes experiences and consolidates memories. Based on the functions assigned to deep sleep versus REM sleep, it would be reasonable to assume that individuals achieving better REM sleep would perform better on memory tests. Choices A and B can be eliminated because while Stage 4 sleep is important for other functions, it is not thought to be directly responsible for memory consolidation. Looking at the passage, it states that Equatorial workers rarely achieve REM sleep. Choice C states that Arctic workers would outperform Equatorial workers because they achieve better REM sleep, which is consistent with the passage and function of REM sleep. Choice D states that Arctic workers would perform more poorly than Equatorial workers because they achieve better REM sleep. This finding is inconsistent because better REM sleep should correlate with better memory consolidation, eliminating choice D can be eliminated and leaving choice C as the best answer.

38. **C is the best answer.** The question tests the function of different stages of sleep. Individuals with inadequate amounts or poor quality of deep sleep would be expected to experience daytime fatigue and problems awakening. It is stated in the passage that Arctic workers experience more sleep problems, which include sleep quality problems, awakening problems, and sleepiness. This indicates that Arctic workers are not achieving adequate deep sleep. Deep sleep is characterized by a delta wave EEG pattern, which is consistent with the information presented in the question stem, although it is not necessary to know this in order to select the best answer. Stage 1 sleep is a light sleep characterized by the presence of alpha waves. This stage of sleep is associated with a form of wakefulness that is more relaxed than full alertness, so choice A can be eliminated because Stage 1 sleep is not considered deep sleep. Stage 2 sleep is characterized by bursts of activity that indicate a full transition into sleep. Although this stage of sleep represents an important transition into what is considered fully sleeping, it is still not a stage of deep sleep, so choice B is not the best answer and can be eliminated. Deep sleep, which consists of Stages 3 and 4, is typically associated with rejuvenation of fatigue and recovery from the day. Delta waves can be observed on the EEG in Stage 3 and 4 of sleep, consistent with the question stem. A lack of stage 3 sleep would lead to feelings of tiredness and problems awakening. REM sleep is characterized by a period of high brain activity. REM sleep is considered important for memory consolidation but not necessarily for relieving the fatigue. Since a lack of REM sleep would not best explain feelings of tiredness and problems awakening, choice D can be eliminated, leaving choice C as the best answer.

39. **B is the best answer.** This question is testing the mechanism of action of stimulants. Stimulants work to increase alertness and energy, usually by increasing the levels of monoamines in the synaptic cleft. Monoamine neurotransmitters include dopamine, norepinephrine, epinephrine, and serotonin. A drug that increases the reuptake of a serotonin would diminish the concentration of monoamine in the synaptic cleft and would not be a good candidate for a stimulant, eliminating choice A. Blocking the reuptake of a monoamine, like norepinephrine, would increase its availability in the synaptic cleft allowing it to bind to receptors and exert its effects over a longer period of time. This would lead to increased feelings of alertness and energy, so choice B is a reasonable mechanism of action. Choice C can be eliminated because acetylcholine is not a monoamine, and drugs that prolong its action are typically not classified as stimulants for this reason. Increasing the reuptake of dopamine would diminish the concentration of monoamine available in the synaptic cleft and would therefore not promote alertness or increased energy, eliminating choice D and leaving choice B as the best answer.

Passage 8 (Questions 40-43)

40. **A is the best answer.** The least restful (or most wakeful) stage of sleep is the most likely stage to have a correlation with poor mental health because the passage states that decreased sleep is correlated with poor mental health. The "lightest" stage of sleep is Stage 1, so choice A is the best answer.

41. **A is the best answer.** The passage states that decreased sleep is associated with mental illness. Insomnia is a disorder where a person is unable to sleep, so choice A is a possible answer. Narcolepsy is associated with falling asleep at inappropriate times, usually resulting in frequent sleep, so choice B is not the best answer. Kleine-Levin syndrome is not tested by the MCAT®, but the answer choice says it is known as sleeping beauty syndrome. Sleeping beauty is a fairy tail character who slept constantly, so choice C is probably not the best answer. Remember, the MCAT® will not test diseases that are unfamiliar, although sometimes incorrect answers will include them as distractors. Non-24-hour sleep-wake disorder is a disorder where the sleep-wake cycle is inappropriately timed but lasts an appropriate interval. So, a person may fall asleep at 5 PM and awake at 3 am. Or he may fall asleep at 3 am and awake at 11 am. Since the amount of sleep is preserved, choice D is not the best answer.

42. **D is the best answer.** The best answer is the one supported by the passage. The passage focuses on the association between decreased sleep and mental illness. Alcohol, marijuana, and heroin are all depressants, meaning they slow the brain and can induce sleep. In contrast, crystal meth is a stimulant that decreases the ability to sleep, so choice D is the best answer.

43. **D is the best answer.** A student with a mental disorder may benefit from psychotherapy or hypnosis, but neither of these are "rest-replacing techniques," so they are probably not the best answer. A "rest-replacing" technique may be one that provides the benefits of sleeping without actually sleeping. A carbohydrate rich diet may be associated with peaks and troughs in energy levels that can make a person more like to get tired during the day. A protein rich diet is associated with slow, sustained energy, so choice C is not the best answer. Meditation is a technique that can produce the positive effects of sleep in much less time. Choice D is the best answer.

Stand-alones (Questions 44-47)

44. **B is the best answer.** The best way to prevent jet lag is to slowly adjust one's circadian rhythm. Sleeping on the plane may prevent jet leg but only if it helps change a circadian rhythm. Choice A is possible but there is probably a better answer. Modifying bedtime prior to travel is very effective in preventing jet lag via its effect on the circadian rhythm. Choice B is a very strong answer. Light therapy is an effective treatment for depression and has been studied extensively as such. Light therapy has not been tested for jet lag, so choice C is not the best answer. Melatonin is a natural sleep aid. Ingesting it upon waking would make a person very sleepy which is not ideal. Choice D is not the best answer.

45. **B is the best answer.** Stimulants are known to raise the level of activity in the central nervous system. This is the opposite of what would be wanted to increase the amount of sleep a participant is getting. Choice A is not the best answer. A depressant causes a decrease of activity in the central nervous system so choice B a better answer than choice A. Hallucinogens offer an alteration in sensory and perceptual experience. This would not be helpful for a patient to get more sleep and can be dangerous; therefore Choice C can be eliminated. Carcinogens are substances capable of causing cancer and do not directly have to do with effects on central nervous system. These do not have to do with sleep, so choice D can be eliminated.

46. **C is the best answer.** The pineal gland releases melatonin, which is a sleep-promoting neurotransmitter. Decreasing wakefulness neurotransmitters and increasing sleep-promoting neurotransmitters would improve sleep, so choices A and B are not the best answers. Deciding between C and D is difficult. Light near the UV range is "cool" blue/violet light. Light near the IR range is "warm" red/yellow light. The sky is blue, and recent evidence suggests humans have evolved to be more awake when surrounded by blue light, so choice C is the best answer.

47. **B is the best answer.** This question requires an understanding of Weber's Law and difference thresholds. A difference threshold is the amount that a stimulus needs to change before that change will be sensed by an individual. Weber's Law states that this change is a certain fraction, or the Weber fraction, of the original stimulus. The question stem provides a theoretical Weber fraction (2/5) and the original stimulus (17.5 mA). To find the difference threshold, multiple 2/5 by 17.5 mA, which results 7 mA or choice B.

Passage 9 (Questions 48-51)

48. **D is the best answer.** Bottom-up processing is using input from sensory information for perception whereas top-down processing uses already stored information to allow for more efficient perception. In this question, it is important to remember that there are usually multiple influences leading to a mental process, and in particular, top-down and bottom-up processing usually work together. With phantom pain after amputation, top-down processing is being used to perceive pain that was perceived previously and stored, but also the neurons that the sensory neurons used to communicate with are conveying sensory signals to the brain. Therefore, choice D is a better option than choice A or B on their own. Another component of this question is distinguishing between perception and sensation. Choice C can be eliminated because sensation is at the level of sensory input, while perception is the integration of this information at a higher level, as is occurring with phantom pain.

49. **D is the best answer.** The key to this question is understanding which type of memory storage is most affected by emotional context. Sensory memory is the first stage of information encoding. It is very brief, and without active attention, is not retained. If active attention is given to that sensory information, the memory is then converted to a short term memory. A component of short term memory is working memory, which utilizes active attention and memory storage. Finally, if emotional meaning is given to a memory, it is then encoded for long-term memory. Due to the chain of memory encoding, it is reasonable to consider all answer choices. However, choice D will be the best answer choice because of the specific role emotional significance plays in the encoding of long-term memory. Additionally, choice D would be a better answer than choices B and C because of the time frame of phantom pain. Choice B and C are based on active attention, which is not necessarily occurring with phantom pain after amputation. The brevity of short-term memory and working memory compared to long-term memory further makes choice D the best option. Choice A is a tempting answer because of the role of sensation in the experience of pain, but the role of emotion and length of memory storage, makes choice D the better answer.

50. **D is the best answer.** While choice A is a correct statement, it does not necessarily limit the conclusions about pain threshold, specifically because of the notation in the passage of previous research showing that BreEStim reduces the affective pain component of phantom pain. It can be concluded that BreEStim conducted on the non-amputated limb resulted in a reduction in pain from the amputated limb, eliminating choice A. Again, choice B is a factual statement, but it is not the best answer because the role of control of pain is not a component of pain threshold. Thresholds just refer to the ability to detect a stimulus, or in the case of pain, the ability to detect pain. Choice C can be eliminated because of the notion that an increase in the threshold for pain in itself is correcting for perceived pain. Individual participants will have different levels of threshold for sensation and for pain, but by having the participants self-identify these points, the differences are controlled for. Choice D is the best choice because it addresses the important point that phantom pain after amputation is affected by the event of the amputation itself. The role of emotions in encoding long-term memory is crucial, and this cannot be reflected in studies of healthy, pain free subjects.

51. **D is the best answer.** Absolute threshold refers specifically to the amount of a specific stimulus necessary before sensation of that sensation is achieved, while difference threshold is the amount of change in a stimulus that is necessary before a change is detected. Therefore, choice D is better than choice C. It is important not to confuse absolute threshold and difference threshold in this situation. In the passage, a pain threshold can also be thought of as an absolute threshold, but for when a subject felt pain rather than sensation. Signal detection is a different sort of detection than threshold that involves differentiating salient signals from background signals. In this experiment, only one signal was given at a time, and no differentiation was necessary, so choice B can be eliminated. Finally, attention is the process of focusing on particular sensory input for processing. While attention was utilized by subjects in detecting their thresholds for the various stimuli, choice D is a better answer than choice A because the researchers were attempting to establish baseline thresholds to assess changes after giving the EStim or BreEStim.

Passage 10 (Questions 52-55)

52. **B is the best answer.** This question is very difficult to answer because synesthetes have different visual perceptions than the controls. The first study indicates that the synesthetes truly have synesthesia. When presented with a black grapheme (a letter or number), the synesthetes consistently paired it with a certain color whereas the controls were inconsistent in pairing it with a color. This suggests that the synesthetes truly interpret certain graphemes as certain colors. The first study is not necessarily a memory study. Controls would have to memorize which grapheme corresponds to which color, but synesthetes are truly perceiving the color, so there is no need to memorize. This makes choice A a weaker answer. The visual cortex is responsible for interpreting visual information. Graphemes and color are both types of visual information, so the visual cortices of synesthetes may be superior to the cortices of control participants. Choice B is a possible answer. The Weber fraction is the change in a stimulus that can be perceived. If the participants were looking at different hues and shades and having to decide if they were different, the Weber fraction would apply. However, the Weber fraction does not clearly apply to this experiment, so choice C is not a strong answer. Likewise, the absolute threshold is the amount of stimulus needed to be perceived as present. This is applicable to a certain decibel of sounds or a certain intensity of light. The graphemes are not truly colored, so the synesthetes do not have any difference in absolute threshold for visualizing the graphemes. Choice can be eliminated, and choice B is the best answer.

53. **C is the best answer.** First, decide who the authors expected to excel at the memory tasks. The first paragraph states that case studies suggest that synesthetes are superior on these tasks, so choice B and D can be eliminated. Between choices A and C, it is necessary to decide whether visual processing or semantic networks are associated with memory. Visual processing was certainly used in the first task, but it is not as clearly applicable as semantic networks to the second task. Semantic networks describe the interconnections between many related points that enhance memory. For example, if trying to remember the term "semantic networks" it may be helpful to think of the following closely related terms: spreading activation, neural plasticity, and hippocampus. Since synesthetes interpret graphemes as colors, they have an extra connection in their semantic network. This may improve memory, so choice C is the best answer.

54. **B is the best answer.** There are several ways to improve memory. Emotionally charged memories are more easily retrieved. However, stress is known to impair memory. Choice A is a possible answer, but there could be a better answer. Stimulants like caffeine and amphetamine have been shown to improve memory in some situations. Choice B is a better answer than choice A since there are instances where choice A is untrue. Alzheimer's disease is a disease that impairs memory. If the controls had Alzheimer's disease, they would have trouble with the memory task. Choice C is a true statement, but it does not answer the question. The question asks which technique could improve memory, not which technique would cause the synesthetes to perform better than controls. So, choices C and D do not answer the question, and choice B is the best answer.

55. **A is the best answer.** In the passage, synesthesia is the interpretation of color when there is no color present. This may occur if the part of the brain that interprets color is cross-wired with other parts of the brain. Choice A describes this cross activation and is a possible explanation for the experience of synesthesia. During neural development, neurons are "pruned", which occurs when extra connections are destroyed. If this does not occur, synesthesia may result. Choice A is a strong answer. Choice B describes the way in which a disease may be inherited. Synesthesia may follow this paradigm, but there is no information in the passage to suggest that synesthesia has a major genetic cause, so choice B is too specific and not the best answer. Choice C describes a physical change to the brain where there are more gyri (peaks) and sulci (troughs). In general, this does not occur. Additionally, it is not clear how more gyri and sulci would lead to synesthesia. Choice C is not as strong as choice A. Choice D is very similar to choice A. Instead it refers to tangled axons. However, diffuse electrical activation in the brain causes epileptic seizures. Choice A is the best answer.

Stand-alones (Questions 56-59)

56. **B is the best answer.** The "default" state of consciousness is alert because most individuals are alert when they are awake and ready to carry out tasks. Remember this by thinking of the tasks an individual must accomplish each day since each of those requires being alert. Being awake is not the same as being alert. Individuals can be awake and not alert. For this reason, choice A is not as strong as choice B. While individuals may be absorbing information from the environment around them, it is not considered a state of consciousness, so choice C can be eliminated. Consciousness is generally associated with awareness, and individuals who are asleep are not aware, so choice D is not the best answer.

57. **C is the best answer.** Jane is trying to access all of the information she has stored while studying over the past few months, so she is utilizing retrieval. When Jane was studying for the test, she was storing the information and encoding it to be accessed later, so choices A and B are not the best answers. Working memory is a form of short-term memory, and since Jane is accessing memories from a long time ago for her cumulative test, choice D can be eliminated.

58. **C is the best answer.** Sleep is regulated by the push and pull of two parts of the brain. The suprachiasmatic nucleus of the hypothalamus maintains wakefulness and the pineal gland of the epithalamus promotes sleep via release of melatonin. The experiment showed that sleep deprivation impaired memory, so the damage must decrease sleep. Damage to the pineal gland would cause relative excess of suprachiasmatic nucleus signals, and a person would sleep very little. So, choice C is the best answer. Damage to the suprachiasmatic nucleus actually increases sleep, which according to the experiment may improve memory. A trick to remember this is that the supra*chias*matic nucleus makes a person awake and alert which makes them *charismatic*. The subthalamic nucleus is involved in movement, and the lateral geniculate nucleus is involved in vision, so choices D and B are can be eliminated.

59. **A is the best answer.** Selective attention refers to the focus of attention on one stimulus while ignoring others. Edward was paying attention to the music playing in his ears rather than looking at the path ahead of him. Divided attention refers to devoting some attention to multiple stimuli, but because Edward was not receiving visual stimulation from the sidewalk at all, choice B is not the strongest answer. Edward is still receiving sensations normally and perceiving the stimuli presented to him. Additionally, sensory imbalance and perception loss are not real concepts and just answer choices trying to distract from the concept being tested. Remain confident in your answer and do not be swayed by a choice that simply sounds good.

Biological Correlates of Psychology

TEST 5B

ANSWERS & EXPLANATIONS
Questions 1–59

Passage 1 (Questions 1-4)

1. **B is the best answer.** Table 1 shows the results of the finger tapping and word pair learning tasks. The results are presented as "relative" percentages. Retention performance is indicated by the percentage of word pairs recalled at retrieval, with performance on the criterion trial during learning set to 100%. The means that performance greater than 100% is the result of better performance on the second day and performance less than 100% results from decreased performance on the second day. Based on the table, the relative learning for the finger tapping task is greater than 100%. This means that performance on the second day was better than performance on the first day, so there was an improvement in memory. Choices A and B are both consistent with this statement. Between choices A and B, the only difference is in the last part of the answer choice. Long term memory can be improved by rehearsal and encoding, so choice B is the best answer. Only short term memory can be improved by attention, and since the task is occurring one day later, choice A is not the best answer. Choices C and D can be eliminated because they state that memory decreased, which is only true for the word pairs task.

2. **D is the best answer.** This question requires interpretation of the table and some knowledge about Alzheimer's disease. Alzheimer's disease is rarely diagnosed before the age of 40, even in cases of early-onset Alzheimer's, so choices A and B are very unlikely. If finger tapping is impaired in Alzheimer's, a person could be misdiagnosed with Alzheimer's if finger tapping is impaired for another reason. According to Table 1, finger tapping is impaired in low sleep, low calorie conditions only. However, the passage states that the low calorie meal was actually 50% of a daily dietary requirement. Since this was only one meal, 50% of the daily calories is actually a relatively normal amount of calories. This means that choice D is the best answer. The other answer choices are possible, but they cannot be concluded based on the findings in Table 1. Choice C only mentions calorie intake and does not mention sleep deprivation. So, choice C is not as complete as choice D and is thus not the best answer.

3. **B is the best answer.** Confounding variables are those that may affect the results of the experiment. The experiment is primarily considering sleep and memory, so an answer choice that would affect these variables in any way would be a confounding variable. Although low IQ may have an effect on memory, and obesity may have an effect on food intake, these variables are not clearly related to the experiment, so choice A is not the best answer. Choice B is the best answer because it references an impairment in sleep, insomnia, and an impairment in memory, Korsakoff's syndrome. Although depression and anxiety can impair sleep and memory, they were not referenced in the passage and are not as clearly related to the experiment as are insomnia and Korsakoff's syndrome, so choice C is a weaker answer. Low income and dyslexia are associated with low IQ and learning disabilities, respectively, but these are not clearly related to the memory tasks in the experiment, so choice D is not the best answer.

4. **B is the best answer.** In general, declarative memory is memory of facts whereas procedural memory is memory of a task. The word pair task requires declarative memory and the finger tapping task relies on procedural memory. For the word-pair task, only sleep deprivation had an effect on memory. So, choice A can be eliminated. Increasing energy intake did not improve memory as it did for the finger tapping task. So choice B is possible, and choice C can be eliminated. According to Table 1, sleep deprivation caused a reduction in learning greater than the standard deviation. The table does not indicate if the results were statistically significant, but since choice B is more specific than choice D, choice B is the best answer.

Passage 2 (Questions 5-8)

5. **B is the best answer.** Events at the beginning of a task or interaction are likely to be remembered due to the primacy effect, so choice A is not a strong answer. During the middle of an interaction, the primacy effect has worn off and the recency effect has not yet begun, so choice B is possible. The recency effect occurs at the end of a task or interaction and makes those events more memorable, so choices C and D are not strong answers, and choice B is the best answer.

6. **C is the best answer.** The question is asking which statement could be an explanation for the findings in Study 2. Study 2 found that in sexual assault victims, seeking medical or police assistance is associated with higher rates of PTSD in the victims. The passage also focused on the creation of false memories soon after an event. Options I and II are very similar, and there is no answer choice that allows both to be true, so it is necessary to determine which is better. One possible explanation for Study 2 is that victims who seek assistance are exposed to questioning that may cause false memory formation. For example, if asked, "Was the attacker tall?" a victim who originally had no memory of the height of the attacker may create a false memory in which the attacker is very tall. This would be an error in encoding where an imagined detail is recorded as fact. So, option I is a strong answer. Option II is not necessarily incorrect, it is just not as strong as option I. The passage focuses on how deception soon after a task can lead to false memories. Encoding occurs at the time a memory is made whereas retrieval occurs when a memory is recalled. Since the error is occurring near the task, the error is more likely to be made during encoding rather than in retrieval. So, choices A and D can be eliminated. Option III has to be true because it is included in both choice B and C. Also, it is a reasonable explanation for the findings of Study 2. If a victim has a very traumatic experience, he or she is more likely to seek help from law enforcement than someone who had a less traumatic experience. Also, people with more traumatic experiences may be more prone to later psychopathology including PTSD. Since both options I and III are true, choice C is the best answer.

7. **D is best answer.** The correct answer must be practical and related to memory formation. Choice A is impractical because there is not an easy way to screen rats for false memories, so choice A is not a strong answer. Choice B does not have to do with memory formation and would only indicate if the drug crosses the blood-brain barrier, so choice B is not a strong answer. Choice C loosely relates to memory because it refers to maze running and relates this activity to the effect of the drug. Maze running may be a memory task but that is not explicitly stated. Choice C is possible, but there may be a better answer. The limbic system is the part of the brain that is responsible for memory. A common way to measure brain activity is through an electroencephalogram (EEG). EEGs are used to look at brain activity during sleep, seizures, and other medical conditions. However, it is not necessary to know what an EEG is to answer this question. Choice D refers to a way to measure activity in the part of the brain that controls memory before and after drug administration. This is the strongest experimental design because it includes causality, so choice D is the best answer.

8. **A is the best answer.** Dreaming occurs during REM sleep, which is a period when the brain is very active even though the body is paralyzed. The graph shown is a common depiction of the sleep cycle where the y-axis is brain activity, and the x-axis is time. REM sleep is associated with the most brain activity, so choice A is the best answer. Choices B, C and D refer to stages 1, 2 & 3, and 4, respectively. Dreaming does not occur during these stages.

Stand-alones (Questions 9-12)

9. **B is the best answer.** Addiction is associated with the reward pathway, which is found in the limbic system. The reward pathway is not in the frontal lobe, although the frontal lobe was mentioned in the passage. So, choice A is not a true statement and can be eliminated. Choice C is a true statement as parallel pathways do synchronously process information about the same stimulus but they are not relevant to the question stem, so choice C is not the best answer. Choice D is a true statement since mirror neurons fire when participants perform or observe a task. There is also some research suggesting that mirror neurons play a role in addiction, but this is not well established. So compared to choice B, choice D is not the best answer to the question.

10. **B is the best answer.** Any technique that can increase real memories would also be expected to increase false memories. The best way to tackle this question is to determine which answer choice would prevent any type of memory formation. Repetition and chunking are common means of increasing memory of facts. There is no way to know if they would enhance false memories, but since they both are memory aids, it is impossible to determine which would be a better answer, so neither choice A nor C is likely to be the best answer. Fatigue is associated with poor memory, so choice B is a strong answer. Spreading activation occurs when one neuron activates a few other neurons that each activate a few other neurons. This creates a network in the mind where information can be accessed more readily. Spreading activation is a cellular means of memory. Since spreading activation is associated with successful memory formation, choice D is not a strong answer, and choice B is the best answer.

11. **D is the best answer.** In the sleep cycle, sleepers move from Stage 1 to Stage 2, Stage 3, and then Stage 4. These stages make up non-Rapid Eye Movement (NREM) sleep. Sleepers then move backwards from Stage 4 into Stage 3, Stage 2, then Stage 1. At this point, they enter Rapid Eye Movement (REM) sleep. After REM sleep is over, they move back into Stage 1 to repeat the cycle again. Every time the cycle repeats itself, the sleeper spends less time in NREM sleep and more time in REM sleep. The entire cycle lasts approximately 90 minutes. The question stem states that the patient can only sleep an hour at a time. This means that the patient is not going through the entire sleep cycle. Because REM sleep is the final stage, REM sleep is likely decreased. In addition, REM sleep starts off shorter than the NREM sleep stages, so the patient is already spending less time in REM sleep compared to the NREM sleep stages. As a result, choice D is the best answer. Choices A, B, and C can be eliminated because the patient is most likely experiencing the normal amount of time in Stages 1, 2, and 3.

12. **B is the best answer.** The information provided about the study in the question stem indicates that the researchers are looking for a link between the content of dreams and the events that have happened to the individual having the dreams. One theory about the purpose of dreams is that they play a role in reviewing events of the previous week and consolidating those memories. This study would investigate that theory, making choice B the best answer. It is true that dreams occur only during REM sleep and not during non-REM sleep, but the information provided about the study gives no evidence that any information about the type of sleep during dreams is being collected. There is no indication that any sort of brain activity is being recorded from the subjects during sleep at all, eliminating choices A and C. It is possible that this study design could be used to investigate a link between stressful events, as measured from the journal entries and number of dreams. Despite this, choice D is not as good of an answer as choice B because there is not much information on a link between stress and the number dreams, while there is information linking dreams and memory consolidation.

Passage 3 (Questions 13-16)

13. **C is the best answer.** The results of the study are displayed in Table 1. Memory is not specifically addressed in the results of the study, but the table shows that mindfulness was significantly improved in meditators, while general cognitive function was not. Sensory memory refers to the temporary storage for incoming sensory stimuli; it is the first stage of declarative memory. Here, encoding is the process of transducing physical stimuli into electrical information that is then accessible to the nervous system. Mindfulness refers to the practitioner's intentional attention to their emotions and sensations relating to a specific moment. While these systems appear closely related, mindfulness is done consciously and the recording of sensory memory is not. There is no evidence in the study that an improvement in mindfulness will lead to an improvement in sensory memory, so choice A is flawed. Working memory refers to a component of short-term memory that combines memory storage and active use. Mindfulness has to do with the amount of conscious attention a meditator is putting towards everyday things. While it seems logical that being more mindful could lead to better memory, this is not demonstrated in the results of the study. Again, there is no evidence in the study that improvement in mindfulness will lead to an improvement in memory, so choice B is also flawed. While it would be interesting to learn whether or not memory is improved in meditators, this study does not provide results related to this hypothesis, thus, choice C is the best answer. There is also no evidence presented in the table that memory is superior in non-meditators or that memory is degraded in meditators. The variables in the table are anxiety, mindfulness, depression, cognitive function, dopamine, glutamate, and months spent meditating. None of these variables directly address memory at all, and therefore there is no evidence that memory is better in meditators or non-meditators. Choice D can be eliminated.

14. **B is the best answer.** Excitatory postsynaptic potential (EPP) is involved in long-term potentiation (LTP). EPP refers to when the presynaptic neuron and the postsynaptic neuron's repeated stimulation leads to an increase in the strength of the potential resulting in LTP. This LTP event, while it does involve the strengthening of a potential is not a lasting change like the change experienced by meditators. Also, this LTP process has to do specifically with memory formation, which is not an area of concern in the study. Thus, choices A and C can be eliminated. Neural plasticity refers to the ability of the brain's networks of neurons and their synapses to change. Researchers in the study did find changes in the meditators' brains as well as outward expressions of those changes. Therefore, choice B is a strong choice. Parallel processing refers to a process using multiple pathways to convey information about the same stimulus. It is usually associated with the visual system and different ways the brain responds to various visual stimuli. While parallel processing certainly occurs in meditators, it is not necessarily something that changes when a person meditates nor is it shown to be different from the parallel processing in non-meditators, so choice D can be eliminated.

15. **D is the best answer.** Other states of consciousness include sleep, hypnosis, under the influence of drugs, and meditation itself. The results of the study found significant results in changes in anxiety, depression, and mindfulness during alert wakefulness. Sleep is a complex but normal state of consciousness, with distinct patterns of brain activity. While sleep is understood to be necessary for physical and psychological functioning, it is not a time when a participant would be able to partake in goal oriented behavior such as mindfulness. Effects of anxiety and depression may affect quality or length of sleep but it is hard to say that these effects would be greater than those in the original study, so choice A is not the best answer. The results of this study were compiled due to the results of neuroimaging techniques MRI, MRS, and DWI as well as various behavioral tests. While it is true that the results of the study appear to be a result of meditation, this does not mean the results would be greater if the study was conducted during meditation. The results are lasting behavioral and physiological changes and should not be affected by the state the participant is in. Additionally, the control group would also be assessed during meditation which might cause a confound in that the control may begin to see some of the meditation benefits they did not exhibit before taking part in meditation. For both of these reasons choice B can be eliminated. There is also no evidence to suggest that the results would be less pronounced in other states, so Choice C can be eliminated. Choice D explains that these are lasting neurological and behavioral changes, thus it is the best choice.

16. **C is the best answer.** Glutamate is the primary excitatory neurotransmitter in the brain; as a result, glutamate-meditated synaptic transmission is critical for brain functions. It is true that glutamate is the primary excitatory neurotransmitter, but this is not necessarily the whole story. Choice A is true but could perhaps contain more information. While it is true that the GABA system does inhibit neuronal activity in the hippocampus, this is not related to glutamate. Glutamate does the opposite; it stimulates neuronal activity through the hippocampus. Choice B can be eliminated. Glutamate's role in the glutamine cycle is indeed important to neural activity, and this neural activity is what is decreased during meditation. This answer is more specific than choice A, so choice C is better than choice A. The hippocampus does have the ability to stimulate or inhibit neuronal activity in other structures, but this is not specific to glutamate's role, so while true, choice D not as good of an answer as choice C.

17. **B is the best answer.** Korsakoff's syndrome is a memory disturbance that is seen in chronic alcoholics. The disease is caused by a dietary deficiency in thiamine, which is also known as vitamin B1. Schizophrenia is a psychological disorder characterized by psychosis and is associated with substance abuse. However, Korsakoff's syndrome is known to be caused by chronic alcohol abuse whereas the association between Schizophrenia and alcoholism is not as clear. Additionally, the passage does not focus on the symptoms of schizophrenia but instead focuses on the symptoms of Korsakoff's syndrome, so choice A is not as strong of an answer as choice B. Alzheimer's disease is a neurological memory disorder that is similar to Korsakoff's syndrome but is not associated with alcohol abuse, so choice C is not the best answer. Stockholm syndrome is a psychological disturbance that is not tested by the MCAT®. It is described as a hostage empathizing with, defending, or falling in love with his or her captor. This is unrelated to the passage or the question stem, so choice D can be eliminated. This syndrome may have sounded familiar but be careful to not pick answer choices that describe diseases not tested on the MCAT®.

18. **C is the best answer.** The question is asking which feature of memory is associated with decreases in memory since an increase in confabulation is actually the result of a decrease in memory. This is because confabulation is the falsification of information. For example, if asked what year it is, a patient may confidently reply that it is 1996. So, more confabulations actually mean worse memory, which can be represented as an inverse relationship. The only choice that lessens memory is decay. Decay describes the gradual loss of memory over time. A gradual loss of memory over time may cause a gradual increase in confabulation because the more memory that is missing gives more opportunity to falsify answers. Choice C is the best answer. Rehearsal is the process of repeating information to keep it in short term memory. Encoding is the process of storing information in long term memory. Since these processes have to do with memory formation rather than the fading of memories over time, choices A and B do not answer the question. Retrieval is the process of recalling information from long term memory. Frequent memory retrieval can actually strengthen the memories that are being retrieved and would be associated with a decrease in confabulation, so choice D is the opposite of the best answer.

19. **B is the best answer.** For this question, it is important to correctly identify the drug class of alcohol and ensure it is correctly paired with effects for that class. Alcohol is a stimulant and depressant since its small structure allows for it to interact with many receptors. As a stimulant, alcohol increases talkativeness and decreases social inhibition. In choice A, the symptoms described are actually hallucinations. Alcohol is not known to cause hallucinations, and stimulants are not often associated with hallucinations, so choice A is not the best answer. As a depressant, alcohol decreases attention, impairs cognition, and can even lead to respiratory failure. This is described in choice B, so choice B is both true and answers the question. As stated above, alcohol is not usually considered a hallucinogen. Common hallucinogens are PCP, LSD, and marijuana. Hallucinogens cause hallucinations that are best defined as distortions in visual perception. Choice C can be eliminated because alcohol is not a hallucinogen, and the effects described are more similar to those seen with stimulants. A popular use of alcohol is as an antiseptic. This is why liquor with high alcohol content can be used to sterilize a wound. However, the question is referring to classes of drugs with neurological effects. Ingestion of alcohol is not known to kill bacteria infecting the nervous system, so choice D does not answer the question.

20. **A is the best answer.** Figure 1 indicates that alcoholic participants have a diminished sense of smell. This could be due to an elevated absolute threshold. The absolute threshold is the lowest intensity of a stimulus that can be sensed. The difference threshold is the lowest amount of change of a stimulus that can be perceived as different. The passage does not suggest that this type of stimulus exposure was being used, so choice B is not the best answer. Likewise, the difference threshold can be used to calculate the Weber fraction. The Weber fraction is the change required to meet the difference threshold. It accounts for the fact that a greater change in intensity is needed when the initial stimulus has a very high intensity. Again, it is not clear that this type of stimulus exposure was performed, so choice C can be eliminated. Remember that answer choices that are too similar are often not correct answers. The signal to noise ratio is an important part of signal detection theory. A signal is something that is perceived whereas noise is ignored. If the signal to noise ratio was elevated, alcoholics would have improved sense of smell, so choice D is a weaker answer.

21. **C is the best answer.** A comorbidity is a co-existing medical condition. Age is not a medical condition, so option I and therefore choices A, B, and D can all be eliminated. Alzheimer's disease is a memory disease similar to Korsakoff's syndrome. It causes impairment in memory, particularly in recent memory. It would be important to control for this comorbidity because if participants in one group had a higher incidence of Alzheimer's disease, that group would have worse memory and thus may have low stop signal and high confabulation scores. Any time a variable other than the independent variable could affect the outcome of a test, it is important to control for it. So, option II is correct. The olfactory nerve is the cranial nerve that transmits information about the sense of smell, so damage to the olfactory nerve is another important comorbidity. Option III should be controlled for as well as option II, so choice C is the best answer.

Passage 5 (Questions 22-25)

22. **C is the best answer.** Neural plasticity describes the brain's ability to form new synaptic connections, usually through development of new axon terminals. Acetylcholinesterase is the enzyme that destroys acetylcholine in the synaptic cleft. Inhibiting this enzyme enhances the activity of acetylcholine resulting in a presynaptic signal that is more likely to induce a postsynaptic effect. Neurons are often in G_0 of the cell phase, so neuronal mitosis is very rare and does not relate to the synaptic drug, donepezil, so choice A is not the best answer. Axonal pruning is the process of destroying axons during development. This is the opposite of the process that occurs for neural plasticity, so choice B is not a strong answer. Synaptic development would occur through growth of new axons and is related to the synaptic drug donepezil, so choice C is a strong answer. Stem cell implantation is a method for treating nervous system disease, but it is unrelated to neural plasticity or donepezil, so choice D is not the best answer.

23. **B is the best answer.** Memory is vital for learning. The research in the passage suggests a child with HIV at birth may have a decreased memory and therefore capacity for learning. This is a health disparity but not a healthcare disparity, so choice A is not the best answer. Choice B is a broad statement that would likely occur if HIV impairs memory, so choice B is a strong answer. Choice C is very vague and not clearly related to a child with HIV. Do not be tempted by answer choices like this as they are almost always wrong. Choice D is not the best answer because the passage indicates that the cognitive decline is not age related and may be an expected progression of the disease.

24. **B is the best answer.** Emotion has been shown to be important in creating powerful memories. Very rarely, emotions can block or hinder memory formation, especially after a traumatic event. This is the exception rather than the rule, so choices A and C can be eliminated because emotion enhances memory formation. If emotion is absent in participants with HIV, this could help explain why memory is also impaired, so choice B is the best answer.

25. **D is the best answer.** The primacy effect is the phenomenon by which items mentioned first in a list are more easily remembered. The recency effect is the phenomenon by which items mentioned last in a list are more easily remembered. These are not techniques that can be utilized to aid in encoding, just tendencies that occur naturally. It would be hard to choose which is the better answer between choice A and B and neither quite answer the question. Weber's law is related to perception, not memory, so choice C can be ruled out. Hierarchies can be used to help with memory formation. It is easiest to remember things in order from smallest to largest. For example, if trying to memorize the following list of months: April, September, August, February; it may be easiest to put them in chronological order. Choice D is an effective memory tool, so choice D is the best answer.

Stand-alones (Questions 26-29)

26. **A is the best answer.** Pay attention to the y-axis which is forgetting, not memory. Over time, forgetting will increase because memory decreases. The question states this relationship is linear so choice A is the best answer.

27. **D is the best answer.** This question refers to the ability to focus on one stimulus (fear-provoking stimulus) at the exclusion of other stimuli (food), which is the definition of selective attention. It may be tempting to select choice A since divided attention is a closely related concept in which multiple stimuli are given attention in a divided fashion, but this question is related to the ability to focus on one stimulus via selective attention. Choice B is related to the formation of long term memories, and choice C represents the first stage of memory formation. Since these concepts are related to memory formation and not to attention, they are not the best answers.

28. **C is the best answer.** Except for very rare circumstances, neurons are unable to undergo mitosis. So, choice A is not likely the best answer. Neurons are never able to undergo meiosis because only germ cells can undergo meiosis. Choice B is impossible. Long term potentiation is the selective enhancement of neuronal signals that increase the likelihood that presynaptic signals will lead to an action potential in the post synaptic neuron. This is one means of memory and learning so choice C is a strong answer. Post-synaptic excitation is the end result of long term potentiation. It is the result, not the cause, of memories, so choice D is not as strong as choice C.

29. **C is the best answer.** Remember that attention is the gatekeeper of consciousness. In this case, the gateway of consciousness has narrowed to the size of a tiny cancerous nodule—everything else is deemed extraneous. This explains why a radiologist that is closely scrutinizing a slide may not notice something that would seem obvious or out of place. Retrieval cues might have aided the radiologist in noticing the cartoon If the radiologist had examined the slide in front of the TV in her childhood living room, but they do not explain this example, so choice A can be eliminated. Outside of the psychological context, we might say that the radiologist's focus interfered with her ability to notice the cartoon, but on the MCAT®, interference is a phenomenon in which one memory is obscured by a similar memory. This eliminates choice B. Constancy of image describes a way in which we can perceive a certain object the same way despite different conditions. For example, if the lighting on the slide had been decreased slightly, the radiologist would still perceive the image the same and be just as likely to overlook the cartoon, so choice D can be eliminated.

Passage 6 (Questions 30-33)

30. **B is the best answer.** Dementia is the gradual loss of cognitive function to the extent that it impairs daily life. Its effects are not usually seen until a person is older, and symptoms worsen as the person ages. It makes sense that researchers studying dementia would be most interested in information that raises the relevance of a study's results to their population of interest. In this case, the results described in the passage would be most interesting if the participants were older, so choice B is the best answer. The number of participants in the study is important to know to ensure that the sample size is large enough to draw valid conclusions, but that information would be of interest to all researchers, not specifically to dementia researchers. Choice B answers the question more specifically than choice A, so choice A is not the best answer. How the study created conditions requiring high demand retrieval processes might be interesting for dementia researchers looking to study how dementia patients perform in those conditions, but that information does not increase the relevance of the study's findings to patients with dementia, so choice C is not the best answer. Knowing how researchers tested verbal and nonverbal memory allows other scientists to judge the quality of the study and the validity of the results, but it does not make the study more relevant to patients with dementia, so choice D is not the best answer.

31. **A is the best answer.** This question is asking about the relationship between sleep and memory. Recall that a sleep-wake disorder describes unusual patterns of sleep in which individuals repeatedly wake up in the middle of the night and are unable to achieve a full night's sleep. Considering that sleep quality affects such a broad range of cognitive functions including concentration, alertness, and mood, it is unsurprising that sleep affects both verbal and nonverbal memory. These two processes are rooted in different areas of the brain, but recall that sleep impacts the whole brain. Sleep deprivation caused by conditions like sleep-wake disorders would decrease performance on verbal and nonverbal memory tests, so choice A is the best answer.

32. **A is the best answer.** This question is asking about different ways memory retrieval is measured. Researchers measure memory retrieval by studying recall, retention, and relearning. Recall refers to the ability to remember information without being prompted. Retention refers to the ability to remember information when prompted with an external cue. Relearning refers to the ability to learn information that had previously been learned but then forgotten. The passage says that bilingualism strengthens the recollection process of memory retrieval, and defines recollection as the ease of access an individual has to a memory. Someone with strong recollection ability and easier access to memories would not need external cues to prompt memory retrieval, so it makes sense that bilinguals would perform better than average on recall tests. Of the test formats in the answer choices, only an essay response tests memory retrieval without external cues, so choice A is the best answer. True/false, multiple choice, and fill in the blank questions all offer external cues in the form of the question stem, so they are all exercises in memory retention. Choices B, C, and D are not the best answer. Essays have a prompt, but that is not the same as a question stem since the essay prompt rarely directs the writer to which pieces of information should be included to correctly answer the essay question. Question stems, on the other hand, usually contain terms or ideas associated with the correct answer.

33. **B is the best answer.** This question is asking about what happens to the brain on a cellular level when someone has good memory. The passage establishes that speaking multiple languages strengths memory abilities, so the brain of a polyglot would reflect structures that support memory abilities. Research shows that memory is related to the strength of synaptic connections, and there is a body of research that suggests long term memory is stored in these synaptic connections, so choice B is the best answer. A polyglot would also likely have a large number of synaptic connections because connections are created when the brain learns new information, and polyglots have a large body of knowledge about language. However, individuals who are monolingual but are experts in other fields would also have learned a large amount of information and would have a large number of synaptic connections as well, so it cannot be said that a polyglot would have more synaptic connections than a monolingual. Choice A is not the best answer. Neurotransmitters are the substances released at the synapse that relay neural signals. So far, there is no evidence linking neurotransmitter concentration to memory function, so choice C is not the best answer. A larger neuron does not necessarily reflect improved cognitive function, as cognitive function has more to do with the relay of signals between neurons. Choice D is not the best answer.

Passage 7 (Questions 34-37)

34. C is the best answer. This question asks about the validity of study design. In any scientific study, it is very important to have control groups, which ensure that the results are not affected by confounding factors that might make the results be misleading. It makes sense that every intervention should have its own control to make the relationship between intervention and results as clear as possible. Since this study has two interventions (retrieving the memory, and learning the new folktale), this study has three control groups. The group of participants who learned the folk tale but did not reactivate memories beforehand controls for the effects of the new learning. This is what is described in choice C, so it is the best answer. The group that reactivated memories but did not learn the Indian folk tale controls for the effects of memory reactivation. The last group that did not learn the folk tale or retrieve memories and represents the status quo behavior. The study is looking at the effect of new learning on memory consolidation, not the other way around, so choice A does not make sense and can be eliminated. Choice B describes what the researchers hope to learn from the study, so it does not answer the question and can be eliminated. Since the researchers are studying the possible interference of new learning on future memory retrieval, choice D is not the best answer.

35. A is the best answer. This question asks about the difference between declarative and non-declarative memories. Recall that declarative memories are those which are consciously known, and include memories of autobiographical events. Since the study in the passage uses autobiographical events, it is a study about declarative memory. Non-declarative memories are memories of how to perform different tasks. Unlike declarative memory, non-declarative memory is unconsciously accessed. The knowledge of how to use a microwave is an example of a non-declarative memory, so choice A is the best answer. Memories about what happened last weekend are autobiographical memories, and thus declarative memories. Choice B is not the best answer. The design of the American flag represents general knowledge about the world and has to be retrieved consciously, so choice C is another example of a declarative memory and is not the best answer. Childhood events and the emotions they carry are examples of autobiographical, and thus, declarative memory. Choice D is not the best answer.

36. B is the best answer. This question asks about the different stages of memory encoding. Recall that the first stage of memory formation is when incoming stimuli are stored very temporarily as sensory memory. Information in the sensory memory that receives attention is further encoded to short term memory. Short term memory can be stored passively or used actively. The memories that are used are known as working memory. The most permanent form of memory storage is long term memory, in which memories are stored unconsciously but can be accessed when needed. When the long term memories are accessed for use, they become part of working memory again. The last paragraph of the passage says that new learning impedes the reconsolidation of neutral autobiographical memories if that memory had prior reactivation. If reactivation describes the conversion of long term memory back to working memory, it makes sense that reconsolidation is the process by which working memory is returned to long term memory. Since working memory is a form of short term memory, choice A is redundant and can be eliminated. Recall that working memory is a form of short term memory, so choice B is a strong answer. The conversion of long term memory to working memory describes reactivation of the memory, so choice C is not the best answer. The conversion of sensory memory to short term memory happens very early in the process of memory formation, so choice A is not the best answer.

37. B is the best answer. The best way to answer this question is to go through each of the statements in the answer choices and evaluate the logic of the statement. It is true that emotions are retrieval cues. This means that feeling certain emotions can lead to the retrieval of memories featuring those same emotions. Though the study makes use of emotional memories, it does not manipulate the emotions of its participants to study memory reconsolidation. Choice A is not the best answer. It makes sense that emotional memories are retrieved more frequently than neutral memories, because emotional memories are often the most significant. There is evidence that frequent accessing of a memory makes that memory stronger because the neural pathways associated with that memory are strengthened with each activation. This is known as long-term potentiation. It makes sense that a stronger memory would be more difficult to interfere with, which would explain the lack of results in the study for emotional memories. Choice B is the best answer. There is no evidence that emotional memories are consolidated differently than neutral memories, so choice C is not the best answer. There is also no evidence that emotional memories are more likely to use semantic networks. Recall that a semantic network is how long term memories are organized by memories that are related to one another. Neutral and emotional memories can both use semantic networks to organize their information, so choice D is not the best answer.

Passage 8 (Questions 38-41)

38. **B is the best answer.** This question describes an altered study investigating semantic networks. Semantic networks are a way of organizing meaningfully related memories. Choice A can be eliminated because while synaptic plasticity is necessary in the formation of memories, studying the efficiency of networks memories are stored in would not reveal the necessity of synaptic plasticity. Choice B is the best answer because spreading activation occurs when related memories are recalled together because they are stored in semantic networks. Choice C is also true. Emotion does play a role in the consolidation of memories, whether it is the role of anxiety in decreasing consolidation or some sort of salient emotion increasing consolidation. This has little to do with studying the efficiency of networks of memory, and consolidation cannot be studied in this experimental design because these memory networks refer to already stored long-term memories. Choice C can be eliminated. Choice D is tempting because an increase in long-term potentiation does increase the strength of a network of synaptic connections, but this network is on a smaller scale than the network to which the proposed study refers. A network of memories would require groups of memories, each having their own set of synaptic connections. Choice D can also be eliminated.

39. **D is the best answer.** This question is asking about retrieval cues. Retrieval cues enhance recall and recognition and would aid in retrieval of memories. They are environmental stimuli that are related to the memory. The stimuli are often things that were present during memory formation. Choices A and B can be eliminated because they are both features that were present during the formation of the memory. Choice C shows the connection between semantic networks and retrieval cues. A related memory helps retrieve the sought memory through the semantic network. Choice D is the best answer choice because it does not represent any sort of retrieval cue. In fact, learning something new similar to a previous memory can serve as interference and prevent the retrieval of the original memory.

40. **A is the best answer.** Encoding of sensory memory is achieved through activation of sensory receptors and dendritic summation. More sensory receptors of a particular type will lead to more signaling and more dendritic summation for the encoding of sensory memory. Choice A is the best answer choice. Choice B can be eliminated because increased numbers of synapses formed would actually increase the encoding of a memory, not worsen it. It is helpful to remember that cells that fire together, wire together. If there are increased synapses connecting neurons, there will be an enhanced network. Choice C can be ruled out because the presence of emotions during the experience of sensory information can affect the strength of encoding. If an animal had a fearful encounter with a predator, it would be more likely to remember the smell of the predator to protect itself in the future. Choice D is a tempting answer choice, but in fact if all sensory receptors are activated, that will improve the encoding of the memory. The more receptors that are activated, the better.

41. **D is the best answer.** This study investigates different levels of synaptic plasticity in memory formation and the different roles highly plastic and less plastic synapses may play. Choices A, B, and C are all factually correct statements. The study does not investigate the concept of semantic networks, so choice A can be eliminated. While long-term potentiation is important in the strengthening of synaptic connections, this study does not address the molecular level of synapse formation, so choice B can be eliminated. Choice C can be eliminated because this computational study does not investigate strength of networks, but instead looks into the plasticity of the connections. The results from the study provide more evidence that synaptic connections are the basis of memory formation because it shows that different levels of synaptic plasticity lead to differences in memory storage capability. Choice D is the best answer choice.

Stand-alones (Questions 42-45)

42. **B is the best answer.** This question requires familiarity with the ways that memory retrieval can go wrong. In this question, the woman has a memory of an event that she believes to be true, but in reality it did not occur. This is known as a constructed memory, and narrows down the answer choices to A or B. Interference refers to how memories from one point in time blocks memories from another point in time. For example, learning a new list of vocabulary terms can make it harder to remember the vocabulary learned a week ago. The situation in the question is not memory interference because the woman does not have trouble remembering her interview because of her dream. Rather, she does not recognize the difference between the two memories. Choice A is a weaker answer for this reason. The woman confuses an experience in her dream with another memory of a real experience. This is known as source confusion, since she misattributes her dream as a real event. Choice B is the best answer. Memory decay is the theory that memories get weaker as people get older and is not pertinent to this question since the woman's memory was of a recent job interview. Errors in memory storage cause the memory to be forgotten because a memory that is not stored cannot be retrieved. The Spanish interview memory is not caused by the woman forgetting the memory of her original interview, so choice D is not the best answer.

43. **C is the best answer.** The relationship between aging and memory is more complicated than previously thought. Depending on the region of the brain affected, the type of memory deficits that may occur with age can be variable. If the prefrontal cortex is affected, there is a decline in source monitoring. Age-related changes in the hippocampus, a key region of the brain in memory formation, can lead to deficits in memory formation. Choice C is the best answer because, while not all aged individuals will have these deficits, there is variability. There is no evidence that gender, race, or ethnicity have a role in the consolidation of memory, so choices A, B, and D can be eliminated.

44. **C is the best answer.** Plasticity, or neuroplasticity, is the ability of the brain to change and build neuronal connections in response to stimuli. These stimuli can come from a variety of sources, ranging from information to experiences and emotions. The question stem proposes that neuroplasticity protects cognitive control functions, and it is asking which of the four listed activities also increases neuroplasticity. It is well established that activities that exercise cognitive processes, such as reading and solving puzzles, increase plasticity, so options I and II are true. Traveling to new places may not seem like it exercises mental capacities, but traveling exposes people to new cultures and experiences, which can also stimulate brain changes. Option III is also true. Regular exercise is important for brain health as it promotes adequate circulation to the brain, but it does not specifically promote the development of new synaptic connections as the others do. Option IV would not increase neuroplasticity. Choice C is the only answer choice that lists only I, II, and III, so it is the best answer.

45. **B is the best answer.** Neurogenesis is the "birth" of neurons from stem cells. Choice C suggests that neurogenesis would be a helpful treatment for neurodegenerative diseases. Another therapeutic option is stem-cell therapy which is tested by the MCAT®. Knowing that stem-cells and neurogenesis share similar therapeutic capabilities suggests that they are similar. In fact, choices A, C, and D all suggest that neurogenesis is the production of new neurons. This is rare in the adult central nervous system but does occur in the hippocampus, so choices A and D are true of neurogenesis. Choice B is the best answer because it does not describe neurogenesis. Neurogenesis is not synonymous with long term potentiation. Long term potentiation describes the strengthening of neural synapses, without the production of new neurons.

Passage 9 (Questions 46-50)

46. **C is the best answer.** The sleep group undergoes the same assessment as the no-sleep group, but the group sleeps in between learning the paired words and being tested for recall. The investigators then compare the average scores on the paired-associate test from each group. The two groups undergo different conditions, so their data cannot be pooled into one group. As a result, choice A can be eliminated. The only way to minimize the effects of confounding variables is by randomly assigning study participants to the different groups in the study. This means choice B may be eliminated. Investigators compared the sleep and no-sleep groups' scores, because the sleep group serves as a comparison group. Their performance on the paired-associate test illustrates how well a group can be expected to perform with sleep. Their scores can be compared to the scores of the no-sleep group to see how a lack of sleep affects performance. This makes choice C the best answer. Source monitoring refers to when a person attributes a memory to a specific source. The paired-associate test does not test the sources of memories, so choice D can be eliminated.

47. **C is the best answer.** Interference occurs when one memory prevents the remembrance of another memory. The paired words are not interfering with the learning of new material, because the paired-associate test evaluates memory, not learning. As a result, choices A and B can be eliminated. Retroactive interference occurs when a newer memory prevents the remembrance of an older memory. The no-sleep group formed new memories throughout the day, and these memories may interfere with the older memories of the paired words. This is the definition of retroactive interference. In comparison, the sleep group did not form many new memories that could retroactively interfere with their remembrances of the paired words because they are asleep for most of the time between learning and testing. For this reason, choice C is the best answer. Proactive interference occurs when an older memory prevents the remembrance of a newer memory. Choice D can be eliminated because patients are trying to remember an older memory, not a newer memory.

48. **C is the best answer.** The first experiment is a survey of class IV heart failure patients. Source monitoring occurs when a memory is attributed to a particular source. The neuropsychological evaluation of these patients assesses memory, but it is not stated that source monitoring is specifically being evaluated. In addition, it is unclear why source monitoring would specifically need to be evaluated in this study. As a result, choice A is a weaker answer. The passage states that the investigators are interested in creating a "cognitive profile" of patients with class IV heart failure. They are not using the study to investigate the link between cognitive deficits and adherence to treatment regimens post-transplantations, so choice B can be eliminated. Choice C refers to a control group, which is a group with the same demographics as the experimental group except that the independent variable is held constant. In this study, a control group could have been formed by using healthy people of the same age as the participants. Since the investigators only study patients with stage IV heart failure, it is unclear whether or not the observed cognitive deficiencies in the patients are typical for healthy people of their age. As a result, it is difficult to determine whether or not the patients in the study have a higher or lower rate of neuropsychological impairment. Because of this, choice C is the best answer. Accuracy of a measurement refers to whether the measurement is close to the true value, while the precision of a measurement refers to whether repeated measurements are close together. The passage gives no indication on the accuracy and precision of the measurements the investigators make, so choice D can be eliminated.

49. **A is the best answer.** Recall and recognition are two distinct processes in the brain. Recall involves remembering information, while recognition involves realizing that something is in memory already. The paired-associate test used in the second study only assesses recall. As a result, the statement in choice A is false, so choice A is the best answer. In an experiment, the experimental and control groups are treated in nearly identical manners, except in regard to the independent variable. This means that choice B is a true statement, and can be eliminated. Declarative memory is memory of facts, ideas, and events. The paired-associate test evaluates memory of words, which is a form of declarative memory. As a result, choice C is a true statement and can be crossed out. Confounding variables are variables that are in some way linked to the dependent variable, and can lead to incorrect conclusions. Intelligence may be a confounder in this study because those who are more intelligent are more likely to have a better memory and perform better on the paired-associate test. Choice D is a true statement, so it can be eliminated.

50. **C is the best answer.** Spreading activation occurs when one memory leads to the remembrance of other memories in the same semantic network. Related word pairs are likely to be in the same semantic network, so option I is a component of the best answer. This eliminates choice B. Mnemonics are any type of memory tool. Mnemonics may be used for remembering both related and unrelated word pairs, so option II is not a component of the best answer. This removes choice D. Priming occurs when a word cues retrieval of a semantically related word, similar to spreading activation. This would only help in remembering related word pairs. As a result, option III is a component of the best answer. This eliminates choice A. Since choices I and III are the only components of the best answer, choice C must be the best answer.

Passage 10 (Questions 51-56)

51. **D is the best answer.** This question focuses on cognitive decline associated with aging. The control population in this study is comprised of 20 age- and education-matched individuals. Therefore, the data collected from these participants represents the performance of a sampling of elderly individuals, and choice A can be eliminated. Although age related cognitive decline is normal amongst the elderly population, the severe memory loss in patients with Alzheimer's disease is abnormal. The data from AD patients cannot generalize to older individuals in the population for this reason, so choice B is a true statement and can be eliminated. Since the control group is comprised of 20 elderly individuals, their performance could generalize to individuals with age related cognitive decline because this would be expected even in otherwise healthy elderly people, and choice C can be eliminated. As stated above, the cognitive decline associated with AD is more severe than what would be observed in the average elderly patient. Therefore, choice D is not a true statement and should be selected as the best answer.

52. **A is the best answer.** There are various types of memory storage through which new information progresses in order to potentially become a long term memory. Moving through this process requires encoding along the way. The first phase is sensory memory, which is simply the memory storage for incoming sensory stimuli, so choice A is the best answer. The second phase is working memory, in which items are held in conscious awareness. Because this is the second phase, choice B can be eliminated. The last phase is long-term memory, in which memories are held outside of conscious awareness and can be called upon when needed, so choice C can be eliminated. Encoding is the process where information is transformed into the type of representation that is used by that particular form of memory storage. Encoding occurs through all stages of this process, and although it is the first step to memory formation, it is not the first phase, eliminating choice D.

53. **D is the best answer.** A confounding variable is one that threatens the internal validity of the study because it is correlated with the independent variable and has a causal effect on the dependent variable. In this study, a confounder might be a variable or trait that occurs within some participants that would also lead to a direct impact on memory performance. Patient recruitment can be a place where research teams can confound their results. For example, if all patients were recruited from the same doctor, and this particular doctor previously gave all of these patients a drug that inhibits memory formation, this would confound the data. In this particular instance, there is no indication that all patients being recruited from the same physician would pose a problem for this experiment, and choice A can be eliminated. Neuroimaging can be a useful tool for mapping CNS anatomy and functioning. The existence of previous neuroimaging would not be a confounder unless there was direct evidence that neuroimaging has an effect on memory formation and storage. The passage does not suggest that neuroimaging has a causal effect on the dependent variable, memory, so choice B is not the best answer and can be eliminated. Parkinson's disease is a neurodegenerative disorder that is associated with motor deficits. Choice C states that 2 of the control patients have a family history of Parkinson's disease, but not the disease itself. While a neurodegenerative disorder might be a tempting choice as the biggest confounder, a movement disorder would likely not impact the findings of this study, eliminating choice C. Severe alcoholism can lead to vitamin deficiencies, particularly a deficiency in vitamin B1. This deficiency can lead to Korsakoff's syndrome, which presents like AD in that it hinders patients' abilities to form new memories. If control patients were suffering from this syndrome, they would perform more poorly and cause the memory ability of the control group to be reported as closer to the ability of the AD group. This would be a major confounder of this study, so choice D should be selected as the best answer.

54. **C is the best answer.** The question stem states that the learning of new information (new toys) caused the participants to forget the information they had already learned through completing the navigation task. Based on this information, the best answer would be one that is a process related to forgetting. Source monitoring occurs when a person attributes a memory to a particular individual or source. This would not explain the learning and subsequent forgetting described. The process occurring in the question stem has more to do with the observation that learning a series of new toys impedes the participants' ability to remember the old set of toys than it does with the particular source of the information, so choice A can be eliminated. Interference is a process that prevents successful memory retrieval and can happen in two ways. Proactive interference occurs when previously held knowledge prevents successful retrieval of more newly learned information. This sequence of events is the opposite of that described in the question stem, so choice B is not the best answer. Retroactive interference occurs when newly learned material prevents successful retrieval of related, older memories. This concept appropriately describes the scenario in the question stem. Relearning describes the process of learning previously encoded material again, often faster since the individual has already been exposed to the information. Since relearning does not apply to the scenario in the question stem, choice D can be eliminated, leaving choice C as the best answer.

55. **C is the best answer.** The question tests the idea that emotions contribute to successful memory retrieval. Studies have shown that emotions can be used as retrieval cues just as much as any other cue that might help one conjure up a previously learned memory, making choice A a tempting answer. However, it has also been shown that certain emotions hamper one's ability to retrieve memories. For example, if an individual is experiencing high levels of anxiety during an exam, this can actually be maladaptive and cause forgetting of previously learned and remembered information. This rationale could make choice B a tempting answer. Since there is evidence to suggest that emotions may help or hurt the process of memory retrieval, the statement made in choice C that there is no way to tell how his memory for this object will compare is true. There is no evidence to suggest that his emotional response is a result of his age, so choice D can be eliminated, leaving choice C as the best answer.

56. **B is the best answer.** The question is testing the concepts related to source monitoring. Source monitoring occurs when a person attributes a memory to a particular source. They can do this either correctly or incorrectly. It has been shown that with age, the ability to correctly attribute a memory to a particular source declines, so choice A is true and can be eliminated. Studies suggest that individuals who source monitor and attribute the memory to an inaccurate source often do not know that what they believe is not true. Choice B states that attributing a memory to the wrong source is always an act of deceit or a misrepresentation, which is not true. It is also very important to be wary of answer choices that include extremes like "always" or "never", because it is rare on the MCAT® that a correct answer will state that something is "always" or "never" true without exceptions. The process of source monitoring is a function of declarative memory, so choice C is true and can be eliminated. Because source monitoring may also lead to the construction of memories of events that never actually occurred, choice D is true and should be eliminated. This leaves choice B as the answer that is least likely to be true.

Stand-alones (Questions 57-59)

57. **C is the best answer.** This question asks about the role of emotion in memory retrieval. Recall that emotion is a retrieval cue. Memories containing strong emotions are easily accessed when the individual feels that same emotion in present day. It makes sense that patients with PTSD would relive the traumatic event when they are in a situation that makes them feel the same emotions they felt during the trauma. There are different types of trauma that can lead to PTSD, from war to sexual assault, but it makes sense that fear would be an emotion felt in most of the situations severe enough to cause PTSD. When individuals with PTSD feel fear in their current environment, fear can act as a retrieval cue to the memory of their trauma, making choice C the best answer.

58. **D is the best answer.** To do well in a busy work environment George must be able to narrow his focus to only his work and be able to ignore any surrounding distractions. While it is true that George must be conscious in order to focus on his work, this answer is not very specific. Choice A is therefore lacking weaker answer. Divided attention is when perceptual resources are split between multiple stimuli or behaviors. This is the opposite of what George should do, so choice B can be eliminated. Meditation is a very focused, relaxed state of consciousness; however meditated attention is not actually a term, so choice C can be eliminated. Selective attention refers to the focus of attention on one particular stimulus or task at the exclusion of other stimuli; this is exactly what George must do in order to be productive, so choice D is the best answer.

59. **C is the best answer.** Korsakoff's syndrome is caused by a nutritional deficiency and includes damage to the frontal cortex and thalamus, but not the substania nigra, so choice A is not the best answer. Alzheimer's disease is associated with neurodegeneration in the hippocampus and surrounding areas, so while it is associated with sever motor impairment, it does not fit the characteristic of where the brain damage is. Choice B can be eliminated. Parkinson's disease is both associated with motor impairment and restricted to the substantia nigra so choice C is a strong answer. While it is true that the substantia nigra is located in the midbrain so damage would be in the midbrain and motor impairment would most likely be affected, this is not as specific as Parkinson's disease, so choice C is better than choice D.